THE NATIVE TRIBES OF NORTH AMERICA
A CONCISE ENCYCLOPEDIA

MICHAEL G. JOHNSON

with colour plates by

Richard Hook

MACMILLAN PUBLISHING COMPANY
New York

MAXWELL MACMILLAN CANADA
Toronto

Author's note:
This book is dedicated to Samuel and Julie Cahoon of New Jersey, U.S.A. who made it possible for the author to visit some of the tribal locations, past and present, noted in the text. Thanks are extended to Mr.Timothy O'Sullivan of Stourbridge, U.K., who read the text and added comments for its improvement; to Hilary Hook, and to Ian West, for their generous assistance during the preparation of the text and illustrations.

First United States Edition 1994

Published in Great Britain 1993
by Windrow & Greene Ltd., London

Macmillan Publishing Company
866 Third Avenue
New York, NY 10022

Maxwell Macmillan Canada, Inc.
1200 Eglinton Avenue East, Suite 200
Don Mills, Ontario M3C 3N1

Macmillan Publishing Company is part of the
Maxwell Communication Group of Companies

Printed and bound in Hong Kong

Library of Congress Cataloging-in-Publication Data
Johnson, Michael, 1937 Apr. 22–
The native tribes of North America: a concise encyclopedia / by Michael Johnson.
p. cm.
Includes bibliographical references (p.) and index.
ISBN 0-02-897189-2
1. Indians of North America – Encyclopedias. I. Title
E76.2.J84 1993
970.004'97'003 – dc20 93-23429
CIP

FOREWORD

By Dr. Kate Duncan, Associate Professor of Art History, Arizona State University

As reports on the native peoples encountered on the North American continent made their way to Europe, beginning in the sixteenth century and accelerating as contact between the two worlds increased, a changing, and often composite image of the American Indian developed, based on bits of information filtered through hosts of assumptions. By the nineteenth century the North American Indian had become a figure of imagination and longing in the Euro-American mind. James Fenimore Cooper's *Leatherstocking* tales set in the northeastern woodlands and Karl May's stories of the American west celebrated the image of the Noble Savage – mankind living with strength and nobility of character, yet free and close to nature in a utopian wilderness. Such an image appealed to contemporary cultural values, and honored the sorts of close connections with the earth which were becoming increasingly distant for many due to the industrial revolution and urbanization. Whenever the Indian was pictured, his dress focused the image.

Dress often appealed as exotic. The Mohawk Indian whom Benjamin West placed pensively observing the scene in his large 1771 painting *The Death of General Wolfe* is differentiated by his kneeling position and foreward placement in the tableau, but especially by his muscular seminude body, hair ornament, and elegant fingerwoven bandoleer bag as they contrast with the dress of the British soldiers. The portraits of Charles Bird King from the 1820s and 1830s, which were published by McKinney and Hall soon thereafter, are more documentary but also emphasize dress, now the elaborate acculturated attire of Woodlands chiefs visiting Washington. Images of Plains Indians with commanding feather headdresses and colorful hide garments become important in the 1830s as Karl Bodmer, George Catlin, Paul Kane and others had opportunity to record the peoples of the northern plains. In the early twentieth century the work of such Taos painters as Joseph Henry Sharp and Irving Couse introduced the different but also romantic image of the solemn blanketed Pueblo Indian of the Southwest.

Although it has been the nineteenth century image of the Plains Indian which has particularly captivated the Euro-American mind, the likenesses painted by all of these artists demonstrate the universal human fascination with dress, for both the wearer and the observer; and establish its power, whether portrayed objectively or romantically, to communicate a wealth of information about the wearer.

The detailed illustrations of dress in this encyclopedia also allow us to examine this communication. The requirements and gifts of the environment, and deeply held beliefs regarding reciprocity between humankind and all aspects of the world in which life takes place, are often reflected in the materials used and the cut and ornament of garments so that they may provide both physical and spiritual protection. Dress and ceremonial garments also communicate information about tribal and group membership, social status, rank, age, gender, cultural roles and responsibilities, and individual accomplishment. In addition, nineteenth century dress clothing usually references some of the changes and exchanges which had come with the increasing Euro-American presence. Most examples pictured here incorporate Euro-American-introduced trade goods such as wool and cotton fabrics and glass beads. The dress of the Mandan warrior Flying Eagle (Plate B4), based on an 1833 Bodmer watercolor, provides an example. Flying Eagle's ornamented hide moccasins and leggings, buffalo skin robe with blanket strip, fan and neck ornament incorporate hide, porcupine quills and bear claws and their homeopathic powers, as well as trade cloth and beads which were rare and valuable at the time. All mark him as a man of means and influence.

Michael Johnson has been fascinated with the North American Indians since childhood, with a particular fervor for costume, especially beadwork, and an ongoing interest in the demographics of tribes. This book is a confluence of these passions – and of his conviction, built of answering similar questions again and again about the basic specifics of tribes and aspects of history – that there has been need for a basic, illustrated, single-volume reference encyclopedia on the Indians of North America. The text, which was compiled primarily between 1965 and 1985, combines demographic and linguistic information from earlier sources, especially Swanton (1946, 1952) and Powell (1881), with that from recent tribal reports and those volumes of the new Smithsonian Institution's *Handbook of North American Indians* published through 1990. The regionally organised discussions of each tribe emphasize lifeways in the nineteenth century but also include old and new locations and trace tribes to the present.

The material within these terse sections, each packed with information, makes it clear that American Indian life also remains complex and dynamic today as it continues to adapt and adjust to a changing world.

We have seen that although dress has for centuries been a marker of Indian identity in the Euro-American mind, the image has been largely unbalanced. Information readily available has focused primarily on but a few tribes, neglecting the myriad of tribal and individual differences across the continent. The detailed watercolors which illustrate this book expand this image and allow a glimpse into the breadth and range of clothing which has differentiated Native Americans, especially in the nineteenth century. Along with the wealth of information in the text, they detail and celebrate the diverse richness of culture of the original inhabitants of North America.

Richard Hook's meticulous color illustrations make a compelling contribution to this encyclopedia, much in the tradition of the earlier illustrator, Karl Bodmer. Unable to work from the model as could Bodmer, Hook has turned to photographs, primarily monochrome examples from the turn of the nineteenth century, bringing them to life with the addition of the colors, materials, patterns of ornament and accurate detail of similar objects in museum collections. For example, the Athapaskan woman holding her child in a beaded mossbag (Plate N12) comes from a black and white photograph of a Slavey family group taken at Hay River, NWT in about 1900 by photographer H.W. Jones; the coloring of the beaded design on the mossbag is based on several such bags in Canadian museums. Several of Hook's figures are taken directly from Bodmer watercolors. In addition to dress, illustrations also address the broad range of traditional habitations adapted to the rigor of and the needs dictated by the environment in different parts of the continent; and some of the diverse ceremonies developed by tribes in response to subsistence, spiritual and social needs. Dancers in contemporary powwow dress bring us to the present.

The illustrations and information-rich captions in this encyclopedia engage us and draw us toward the text and its wealth of detailed information. Together they remind us that the image of the North American Indian has actually always been hundreds of images, of diverse peoples living in diverse ways, and remains so today. The encyclopedia provides important help in celebrating and learning about the complexity of Native North American cultures, widening and refocusing the image of the North American Indian.

Kate Duncan
Arizona State University

Contents

INTRODUCTION

In October 1492 Christopher Columbus "discovered" the Americas. The term "discovered" implies that North America was uninhabited: in fact, the whole of the Americas from Alaska to the southernmost tip of South America was populated by a people whose ancestors came from Asia. There is much discussion and disagreement amongst academics as to the age of man in the New World; but migrations from Asia via land, sea and ice bridges near or at the Bering Straits or the Aleutian island chain, which separate Asia from Alaska, may extend back 30,000 years.

These ancient Paleo-Indians somehow filtered down through an ice-free corridor in North America into Central and South America, and in the course of time occupied the whole continent, including the West Indies. Some of the ancestors of the Indians of North America arrived much later, the Eskimo (Inuit) and Athabascan people probably less than 8,000 years ago; the Eskimos have tribes in Asia to this day.

Since Columbus thought he had found the fabled Indies, the native people he encountered in the islands off Florida became known as "Indians". A few years later mariner-explorers "discovered" other natives in Newfoundland with painted red faces – hence the birth of the misnomer "Red Indians". In truth, of course, they are neither. (While recognizing that the term is irritating to a minority of activists, the author has chosen to use "Indians" throughout this text for the sake of brevity, and to avoid anachronism in historical contexts.)

Archaeological and ethnographical speculations, when stripped of spurious theories, reveal that native North Americans have an antiquity and a hunter-gatherer culture of unparalleled historical depth and complexity, which may explain the extraordinary relationship they have maintained with the land and their sense of absolute and eternal belonging with it. These hunters developed beliefs and behaviour patterns which enabled them to exist in an unpredictable physical world where every animate and inanimate object had enormous spirit power which had to be respected and ritually placated. Later a Middle American maize culture developed which spread north into much of the area which now forms the United States.

Europeans were fascinated by the New World natives, and the earliest representations of Indians in European art quickly established a series of visual symbols derived from both North and South American descriptions with which to portray the native American. Indians, shown in suitably dramatic or warlike attitudes and set in scenes of wildly inaccurate geographical and anatomical composition, became visually accepted. Young children today, if asked to draw an image of a "Red Indian", might produce a drawing not too dissimilar from these early representations. The consequent series of simplistic stereotypes of the North American Indian spread far beyond the merely visual; extended by popular writers of "travellers tales" and adventure fiction, they were exploited by the late 19th century "Wild West shows", and subsequently by their 20th century equivalent – the Western film. Until the most recent times gross misinformation or, at best, considerable honest confusion, were widespread both within America and overseas.

Symbols of material culture such as canoes, totem poles, tipis and feather headdresses are shown as characteristic of a commonly shared way of life, rather than of different cultures separated by thousands of miles. The Indian environment is often portrayed as a vast wilderness of mountain and plain, although a considerable proportion of historic North American natives were river, valley, bay and coastal people. The popular media often suggest that the Indian is nearly extinct, although there are probably more North American Indians or people of Indian descent alive today than in 1492. The Indian is presented purely as a hunter, although in fact a large number were gatherers of wild foods, or pursued a farming tradition based on the production of maize (Indian corn). We are told that the Indian never scalped before the white man arrived, although in fact the taking of scalps was known in many parts of North America. We are told that the Indian man never had facial hair: again untrue – people of Asiatic origin have less body hair than Europeans, but they do have it. These misconceptions may seem individually trivial; but they are legion, and they contribute to a cumulative myth which may obscure important truths.

The Indian has been portrayed historically as vain; cruel to captives; a brave fighter, but with no taste for pitched battle; and susceptible to alcohol, with resultant brawls, family disruption and inertia. Alternatively, the Indian has more recently been eulogised as enjoying perfect harmony with Mother Earth or nature; as having a perfectly democratic and egalitarian social organisation; as being eminently spiritual, and considerate of friend, stranger, young and old. In the past few years the Indian has been portrayed as a model conservationist, taking only what he needed from the natural world – notwithstanding the part played by Indians in the promotion of the fur trade. All these images – partial, unbalanced, or at best taken out of context – are highly misleading, and should be taken with a decent amount of scepticism.

It is obvious that the North American Indian could not have resisted successfully the European invasion. Small in numbers (with scarcely the population equivalent to that of a moderately-sized modern American or European city) and scattered over a huge area several times larger than Europe, they had no realistic chance of stemming the tide of white settlement. Intertribal animosities precluded concerted efforts to contain a European invasion until it was much too late. Vast regions were very thinly populated: parts of Kentucky, for instance, Subarctic Canada, and the Plains before the development of the horse-bison culture, were hunting territories with few settlements. Warfare was also endemic in some areas; tribal oral traditions confirm that enmities were often established long before the arrival of whites, and recent archaeological reports from grave sites suggest that intertribal warfare could reach staggering proportions.

The complicated geographical diffusion of tribes with a common ancestral language base suggests continual movement, invasion, migration and conquest long before the white man set foot on the continent. We know of substantial cultures which came and went long before European contact, such as the Hopewell and Adena cultures which were based on Meso-American gardening. The European did not, therefore, disturb a "Garden of Eden", but a continent of tribal groups and cultures that were fully dynamic – and which were able in some instances to adapt to the new technology brought from Europe in their constant struggle with the harsh realities of an unremitting climate and variable resources, particularly in the northeast and far north. The Indians of the High Plains, Boreal Forest and Subarctic were able to modify their native cultures into fairly successful hybrid forms based on the merging of native talents with imported European technology.

Whilst some Indians were able to come to an accommodation with the European, some clearly were not. The coastal peoples of the Atlantic, Gulf of Mexico and California were amongst the first to suffer conquest, subjection, and the effects of European-introduced diseases. Many tribes in these regions disappeared long before the U.S.A. became an independent nation. The reduction in population during these early times was the direct result of the influence of the old European colonial powers: Britain, France and Spain. During the United States period central government policies towards Indians were rarely consistent, often crude and condescending, with resultant tragedies; but no U.S. administration in Washington has ever approved a policy aimed at the deliberate extermination of Indians, despite the charges levelled by some of today's dealers in politicized rhetoric. The actions of frontier mobs, land-hungry settlers, over-zealous local military commanders, gold prospectors, land dealers *et al* cannot always be blamed on a distant government. Californian Indians, particularly, suffered massacres perpetrated by local settlers.

The purpose of this book is not to add to the already existing mass of fable and subjective comment on Native American history, but to give the average interested reader or student some cogent facts about each of the recognised tribes native to North America, north of the Rio Grande River. These include brief historical sketches; intertribal linguistic family relationships; an indication of traditional cultural horizons; locations, and populations both in olden and modern times. The location of the tribes indicated in the text utilizes modern American and Canadian names for states, provinces, counties, rivers, mountains, towns and villages, and for plotting locations the use of a modern Rand McNally road atlas would be a useful tool. Of course, these are not the boundaries recognised by the Indians themselves; their traditional world view and nomenclature were very different.

The colour plates attempt to provide a general overview of the variety of tribal dress and basic artifacts used by widely differing cultural groups across the continent, including the changes introduced by the adoption of Euro-American goods; and also including some of the contemporary ceremonial costume worn by modern Native Americans during the recent period of revitalization of many native communities.

Tribal names are for the most part not the old names the Indians knew themselves. Many names translate simply as the "real men" or "original people". The common, popular, modern names used are derived from various sources. Some are from native terms, either for themselves or those applied by neighbours or enemies, or corruptions of these terms. Some tribal names are anglicised forms of translated native names; others are from French or Spanish sources. We use the tribal names most commonly encountered in history and literature, although it should be noted that some modern Indian groups have successfully reintroduced their own names into modern usage.

We should also recognize that the anthropological and ethnographical reports from which most of our understanding of Native American culture derives have been the work of Euro-American scholars and historians; and that there is considerable resentment over this situation by some modern Native Americans, who suggest that they alone should be the interpreters of their ancient cultures. This again raises the question of the old stereotypes of race and ethnic identity; can modern Native Americans be the only legitimate repository of cultural knowledge, on the basis of racial association?

However, many Indians past and present have written in the language of mass and scholarly communication, e.g. J.N.B.Hewitt (Tuscarora), William Jones (Sac and Fox), J.J.Matthews (Osage) and D.McNickle (Flathead). Many people of Native American heritage are active today in the fields of Indian history and Indian art; and the recently appointed Director of the National Museum of the American Indian, W.Richard West Jr., is a member of the Cheyenne-Arapaho tribes of Oklahoma. A visit by the writer to two excellently run native museums – the Turtle at Niagara Falls, and the Woodland Cultural Centre, Brantford, Ontario – revealed no significant difference in the presentation of material culture and native history from that found elsewhere in American or European institutions; and the curatorial staff have resisted the temptation to insert politicized comment into descriptions of native culture of past times. After all, there are not too many different ways to present a feather headdress or beaded pouch in a glass case. We should also remember that a considerable proportion of Native American decorative material culture was made for white consumption and is distinctively hybrid, in common with the cultures from which it came – which is hardly surprising, following centuries of interaction.

NATIVE AMERICAN POPULATIONS

The accurate number of Native American Indians living north of the Rio Grande River in the U.S.A. and Canada is unknown both for aboriginal times and for today. A conservative estimate suggested by the ethnographer James Mooney gave about 1,250,000 for the late 16th century. This figure has been raised in recent re-examinations, in spite of the paucity of data, to as high as six million, but this is very probably excessive. A rational figure might be two million. The highest concentrations were undoubtedly in the coastal regions: the Atlantic slope in the east, the Gulf of Mexico region in the south and California in the west. Ironically, these areas suffered the greatest reduction in population from contacts and conflicts with, and the effects of diseases introduced by, the Europeans.

During the 20th century Indian population figures vary considerably, due mainly to different criteria applied by the various enumerators regarding just who is or who is not an American Indian. Since the earliest colonial times there has been a continuous and often increasing mixing of Indian and Euro-American peoples which has resulted in the majority of Indians, outside the American southwest at least, being of mixed race. A second problem is that the U.S. Government's Bureau of Indian Affairs, the official bureaucracy controlling some of the remaining Indian lands and Federal services to Indians, have few or no special relations with substantial numbers of Indians in Maine, New York, Virginia, North Carolina and other states. Consequently the figures published by the Bureau of Indian Affairs over the years are usually lower than the figures reported by the U.S. Census, since the former count only Indian people who are enrolled at Indian agencies.

The degree of Indian ancestry required at Indian agencies was often determined by individual Indian councils themselves. The degree of Indian ancestry required for enrolment was usually one quarter Indian descent or more. The U.S. Census enumerators, on the other hand, attempted to include all people whom they considered racially Indian and who were regarded as such in their community of residence; many eastern Indians not on the Bureau rolls were therefore counted in the Census. Until the 1970 U.S. Census, enumerators were the arbiters of who were Indian, whereas that responsibility is now placed on the individual interviewee.

In 1950 the Bureau of Indian Affairs reported 396,000 enrolled Indians at their various Indian agencies and reservations across the U.S.A., of whom 245,000 were resident on the reservations and the rest in adjacent towns and cities, with a growing number moving permanently to larger metropolitan and urban centres. The Census reported 237,000 in 1900; 366,710 in 1940; 532,591 in 1960; 827,108 in 1970; and 1,418,195 in 1980. These U.S. Census figures include Indians inside and outside the Federal Agency system; and a growing number of racially mixed groups in the eastern states who have never been officially recognised as Indians but who have, to a lesser or greater degree, a claim to such ancestry, including groups in Maine, New York, Virginia, and North Carolina. Included also are federally terminated groups; and people who now feel socially acceptable as Indians in a more tolerant society, and who might feel that financial benefits could be obtained by stressing sometimes justifiable claims to tribal ancestry. Today the number of such people in the United States is large enough to make possible an extremely wide range of estimates of the Indian population: in general terms about 1,250,000, of whom 350,000 still live on reservations, and about the same number are full blood Native Americans. The largest U.S. groups are Navajo, Chippewa,

Sioux, Iroquois, Cherokee and Lumbee. The U.S. Bureau of Indian Affairs reported 833,000 "enrolled" Indians in 1985.

In Canada the Indians were forced to make a succession of treaties with the Crown during the 19th and early 20th centuries which established numerous small Indian reserves across the country. These are the Indians reported by the Indian Affairs Branch of the Canadian Department of Citizenship and Immigration. The total population of Treaty Indians was reported as 136,407 in 1949; 179,126 in 1959; and 244,113 in 1969. However, a large body of Canadian people of Indian descent were not enumerated because their ancestors chose to be excluded from the Treaty Band system. Native Indian women married to non-Indians or non-band members and their heirs also lost their status as Indians. These Métis and non-status Indians, now recognized as Canadian native people, probably add another 100,000 to the Indian population. The Métis were initially a mixed French and Indian people living around the Red River area in present day Manitoba, who subsequently fanned out into Alberta and Saskatchewan in the 19th century. Their vocal political campaigns for social and economic rights in recent times have encouraged other mixed and non-status groups to affiliate with them, extending the term Métis far beyond its original limited application. The largest Canadian groups are Cree, Northern Ojibwa, Iroquois, Blackfoot and the extended Métis.

Adding the returns for both the U.S.A. and Canada, the total number of "Indians" with a substantial degree of Indian ancestry would be in excess of 1,600,000 – probably as high as in aboriginal times. The 19th century proposition that the Indian would vanish as an identifiable racial and social entity was in error, and Americans are now aware of another vocal racial minority in their midst. However, the increase in population cannot hide the great tragedies inflicted historically on the Indian by Euro-Americans.

CLASSIFICATION OF INDIAN LANGUAGES

In 1891 John Wesley Powell of the Bureau of American Ethnology, Washington D.C., published the first overall classification of the American Indian languages north of Mexico. Tribes with similar languages may be presumed to have common origins; and the greater the divergence in speech, the longer the period of separation from a common ancestral stock. Some tribes were so weakly organised or so widely scattered geographically that only linguistically can they be called "tribes" in the popular sense. North America had many differing languages, and by the time specialists were making records in the 19th century some dialects were already verging on extinction.

Native American languages consist of a number of distinct families which differ fundamentally from each other in vocabulary and in phonetic and grammatical form. Some of the families, like Algonkian and Athabascan, consist of a large number of distinct languages; others seem to be limited to a small number of languages or dialects or even to a single language. John Wesley Powell's classification of languages north of Mexico recognized no fewer than 55 of these families.

The distribution of these language families is uneven; 37 of them are either entirely or largely found in territory draining into the Pacific Ocean. Only seven linguistic stocks were located on the Atlantic coast line. In the Mississippi valley, Gulf states and adjacent coast ten language families were located. The most widely distributed are:-

1 *Eskimoan*, in Greenland, northern Canada, into Alaska and Siberia.

2 *Algonkian or Algonquian*, several languages on the Atlantic coast, Quebec, Nova Scotia, Canada west to the Rocky Mountains, with groups on the Plains, and the central and southern groups near and south of the Great Lakes.

3 *Iroquoian*, in three area groups:
(1) The region of Lakes Erie, Ontario and the St.Lawrence River.
(2) Eastern Virginia and North Carolina.
(3) The southern Appalachian country (Cherokee).

4 *Muskogian or Muskogee*, including the Natchez, which occupied the Gulf region from the Mississippi delta to Florida and Georgia, and northward to Kentucky.

5 *Siouan*, in three groups:
(1) In the eastern states of North Carolina and Virginia.
(2) A small southern contingent (Biloxi).
(3) The main group on the Plains, and a colony of the Plains group in Wisconsin near Green Bay (Winnebago).

6 *Caddoan*, spoken on the southern Plains, from Nebraska to Texas and Louisiana, and a group in North Dakota.

7 *Shoshonean*, on the American Plateau, in the Great Basin, in Texas and Arizona.

8 *Athabascan or Athapascan*, in three groups:
(1) In the north of Canada from Alaska to Hudson Bay.
(2) On the Pacific coast.
(3) In the Southwest and in northern Mexico.

9 *Salishan*, in British Columbia and northwestern U.S.A. in two sections:
(1) On the coast.
(2) The Interior Salish of the Plateau.

The other 46 families are, in alphabetical order (those marked * are now extinct languages):

Atakapa *	Gulf coast, Louisiana and Texas.
Beothuk *	Newfoundland.
Chimakuan *	Washington.
Chimariko *	Northwestern California.
Chinook	Lower Columbia River.
Chitimacha *	Southern Louisiana.
Chumash *	Southwestern California.
Coahuiltecan *	Lower Rio Grande.
Coos or Kus *	Oregon coast.
Costanoan *	Western California.
Esselen *	Southwestern California.
Haida	Queen Charlotte Islands.
Kalapuya *	Northwestern Oregon.
Karankawa *	Texas coast.
Karok	Northwestern California.
Keres	Rio Grande in New Mexico.
Kiowa	Southern Plains, Kansas, Oklahoma.
Kootenay or Kutenai	British Columbia, Idaho and Montana.
Lutuami	Consisting of the Klamath and Modoc in southern Oregon.
Maidu	Eastern Sacramento Valley, California.
Miwok	Central California.
Piman or Sonoran	Southern Arizona and Mexico.
Pomo	Western California.
Sahaptin or Shahaptian	Middle Columbia River in Oregon, Idaho.
Salinan *	Southwestern California.
Shasta-Achumawi	Northern California and southern Oregon.
Takelma *	Southwest Oregon.
Tanoan	New Mexico on or near Rio Grande.
Tumuqua or Timucua *	Florida.
Tlingit	Southern Alaska.
Tonkawa *	Texas.
Tsimshian	Western British Columbia.
Tunica *	Mississippi River in Louisiana and Mississippi.
Waiilatpuan *	Consisting of Molala and Cayuse, northern Oregon.
Wakashan	Consisting of Nootka and Kwakiutl along the coast of British Columbia.
Washo(e)	Western Nevada and eastern California.
Wintun	North central California.
Wiyot *	Northwestern California.
Yakonan *	Oregon coast.
Yana *	Northern California.
Yokuts	South central California.
Yuchi	Savannah River, Georgia.
Yuki *	Western California.
Yuman	Colorado River in California and Arizona.
Yurok	Northwestern California.
Zuni	New Mexico.

To these later were added:

Siuslaw *	Oregon coast.
Eyak *	Alaska.

This complex classification of native languages is very probably the first approximation to the historic truth. There are many far-reaching resemblances in vocabulary and structure among linguistic families classified by Powell as generically distinct. Scientific comparative work on these diverse languages is still in its infancy; but the following reductions have been made, and may be regarded as either probable or possible, but unverified:

```
WIYOT ).......RITWAN)
YUROK)              )
..............ALGONKIAN).... ALGONKIAN-RITWAN)
....................BEOTHUK)                 )
KOOTENAY..............................KOOTENAY)  ALGONKIAN-WAKASHAN
                                              )
KWAKIUTL).....WAKASHAN)                       )
NOOTKA  )             )                       )
                      )..................MOSAN)
CHIMAKUAN.............)
..........................SALISHAN)

HAIDA.............................................. HAIDA)
TLINGIT       )                                         )  NADENE
ATHABASCAN)........... CONTINENTAL NADENE)
EYAK          )
```

MIWOK-COSTANO)
YOKUTS) .... CALIFORNIAN PENUTIAN)
MAIDU))
WINTUN))
)
TAKELMA..))
KALAPUYA.......................................))
)............ OREGON PENUTIAN)
COOS))) PENUTIAN
SIUSLAW).... OREGON COAST))
YAKONAN) PENUTIAN))
)
CHINOOK...)
TSIMSHIAN...)
)
SAHAPTIN or SHAHAPTIAN))
WAIILATPUAN...........................).............. PLATEAU PENUTIAN)
LUTUAMI ....)

KAROK...)
CHIMARIKO) ....)
SHASTA-ACHUMAWI))...NORTHERN SECTION)
YANA...))
POMO ....))
)
WASHO...)
ESSELEN)..ESSELEN-YUMAN)
YUMAN))........HOKAN)
SALINAN)))
SERI)..SALINAN-SERI))
CHUMASH))) HOKAN-COAHUILTECAN
)) (unverified)
CHONTAL (MEXICO)...))
TONKAWA..........TONKAWA))
COAHUILTECO)))
COTONAME) COAHUILTECO)..............................COAHUILTECAN)
COMECRUDO))
KARANKAWA)

YUKI ....YUKI
KERES ....KERES

IROQUOIAN)....................................IROQUOIS-CADDOAN)
CADDOAN))
....SIOUAN)
TUNICAN-ATAKAPA)..TUNICAN) Distant connections
CHITIMACHA)) suggested but
) remain
YUCHI..)) unverified
NATCHEZ)...MUSKOGIAN).....NATCHEZ-MUSKOGEE)
MUSKOGIAN))
TIMUCUA ....)

PIMAN)
SHOSHONEAN) ....UTO-AZTECAN)
SONORAN-NAHUATL (MEXICO)))
)
KIOWA...).....KIOWA-TANOAN) AZTEC-TANOAN
TANOAN...))
)
ZUNI...ZUNI)

The linguistic classifications shown in this table do not correspond at all closely to the racial or subracial lines that have been drawn for North America, nor to the cultural areas into which the tribes have been grouped by ethnographers. In simple analogy, a language family would approximate the English-German (Germanic) or French-Spanish (Latin) groups of European languages, but the larger groups or stocks would parallel only the designation "Indo-European".

DISTRIBUTION OF CULTURES

Archaeological research has been conducted widely in North America, but the territory is so vast, the tribes so numerous and their movements so many that it has been difficult to associate ancient pre- or protohistoric sites with later historic tribes. There have been attempts: the Fort Ancient site of the Hopewell prehistoric culture north of modern Cincinnati, the largest and one of the best preserved earth-walled sites, c.100 B.C.-500 A.D., has been tenuously linked to the historic Shawnee; the Dismal River site in present day Nebraska has been alternatively suggested as Apachean or more probably Puebloan; Hohokam and Mogollon of Arizona have been linked with the modern Piman, and Anasazi with the Pueblo of New Mexico and northeastern Arizona.

Despite general agreement on the dates when these prehistoric cultural horizons flowered, and on the dating of their extensive remains, close correlation with historic tribes is limited (except for the Pueblos, whose ancestors seem to have been the Mesa Verde and Chaco Canyon peoples). Generally the links are unsubstantiated. Ethnologists have therefore independently divided North America into so-called cultural areas, in which the various tribes during the historic period developed generally similar skills and subsistence levels derived from a generally similar environment. These areas thus tend to coincide with ecological zones, but also to blend together with the cultures of adjacent areas rather than eliminating them. The boundaries between these cultural areas are entirely arbitrary, but they are usually designated as follows:

Northeastern Woodlands: The north Atlantic coast, Great Lakes and adjacent southern Canada.

Southeastern Woodlands: The south Atlantic coast, the Gulf, to the Mississippi and beyond.

Plains and Prairie: Mississippi Valley to the Rocky Mountains.

Plateau: The mountainous area of the northwest U.S.A. and southern British Columbia, Canada.

Great Basin: Most of the present states of Utah and Nevada.

California: Largely, but not entirely, the present state of California.

Southwest: The present states of New Mexico and Arizona plus adjacent parts of Mexico and Texas.

Northwest Coast: Coastal Alaska, British Columbia, Washington and Oregon.

Subarctic: The northern interior of Canada and Alaska.

Arctic: The northern edge of the continent between Alaska and Greenland.

THE TRIBES

The tribal entries which follow are not arranged alphabetically; they are grouped firstly in cultural and geographical areas according to the sequence shown above, and within those areas in groups related by language. The sketch maps provided in each section, while intended only as general guides to distribution both historical and present day, will assist the reader by reference from the text entries.

The names of linguistic families are presented as sideheads in ***bold italic*** type – separately if comprising more than one tribe, and beginning the first line of the tribal entry if not. The names of tribes are presented in **bold** type beginning the first line of each entry; subsidiary groups or bands are discussed in the body of the entry where appropriate, the names of the most significant being presented in *italic* type. The dictates of logic or historical peculiarity modify these general practices in occasional specific cases.

Major linguistic families cross the necessarily arbitrary borders of some of the cultural and geographical areas. Their general characteristics are each summarised in only one area section; cross-references are given in the lists of contents at the beginning of each chapter, where appropriate.

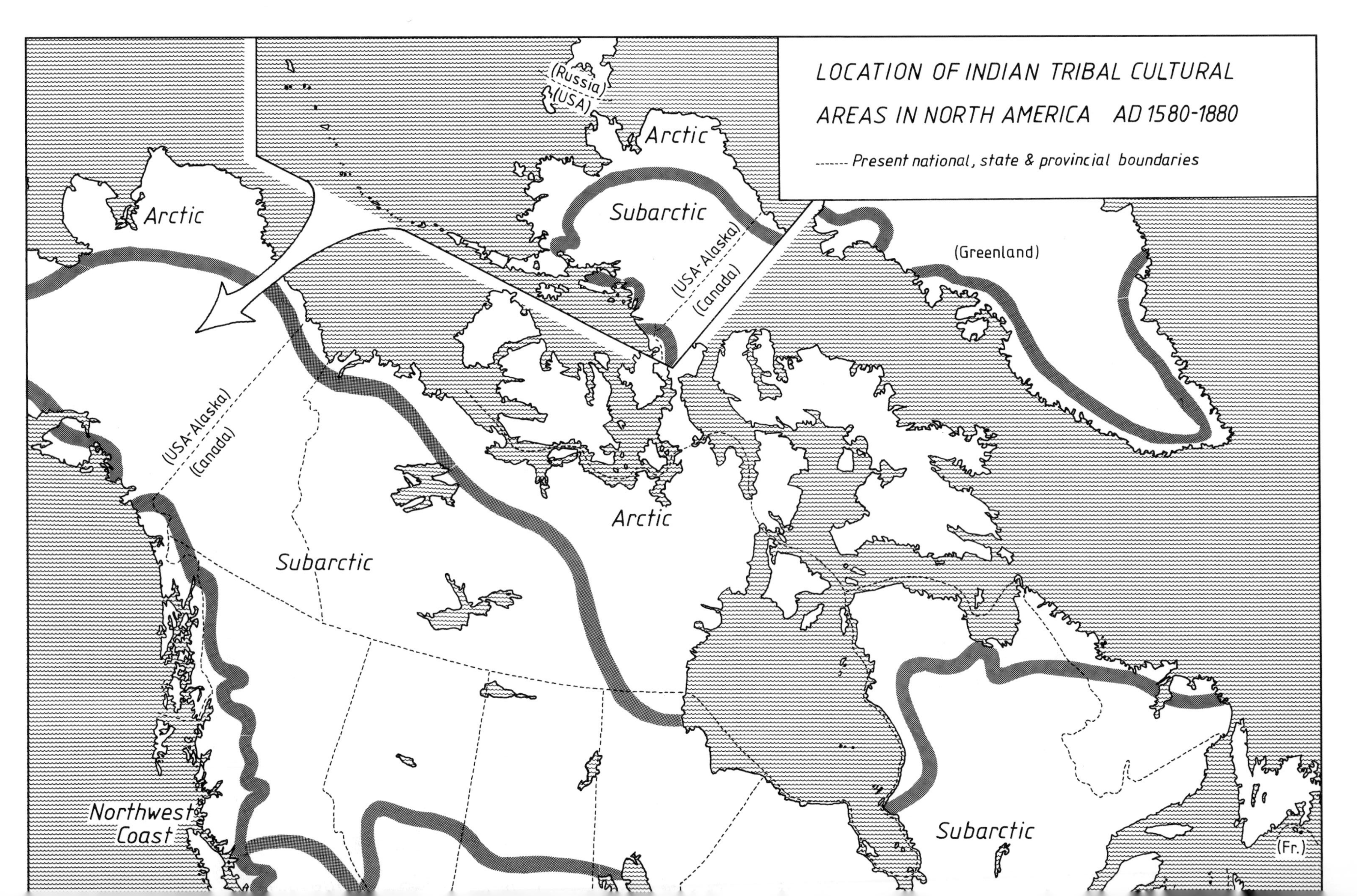
LOCATION OF INDIAN TRIBAL CULTURAL
AREAS IN NORTH AMERICA AD 1580-1880
Present national, state & provincial boundaries
(Russia)
(USA)
Arctic
Subarctic
(USA-Alaska)
(Canada)
(Greenland)
Arctic
(USA-Alaska)
(Canada)
Arctic
Subarctic
Northwest Coast
Subarctic
(Fr.)

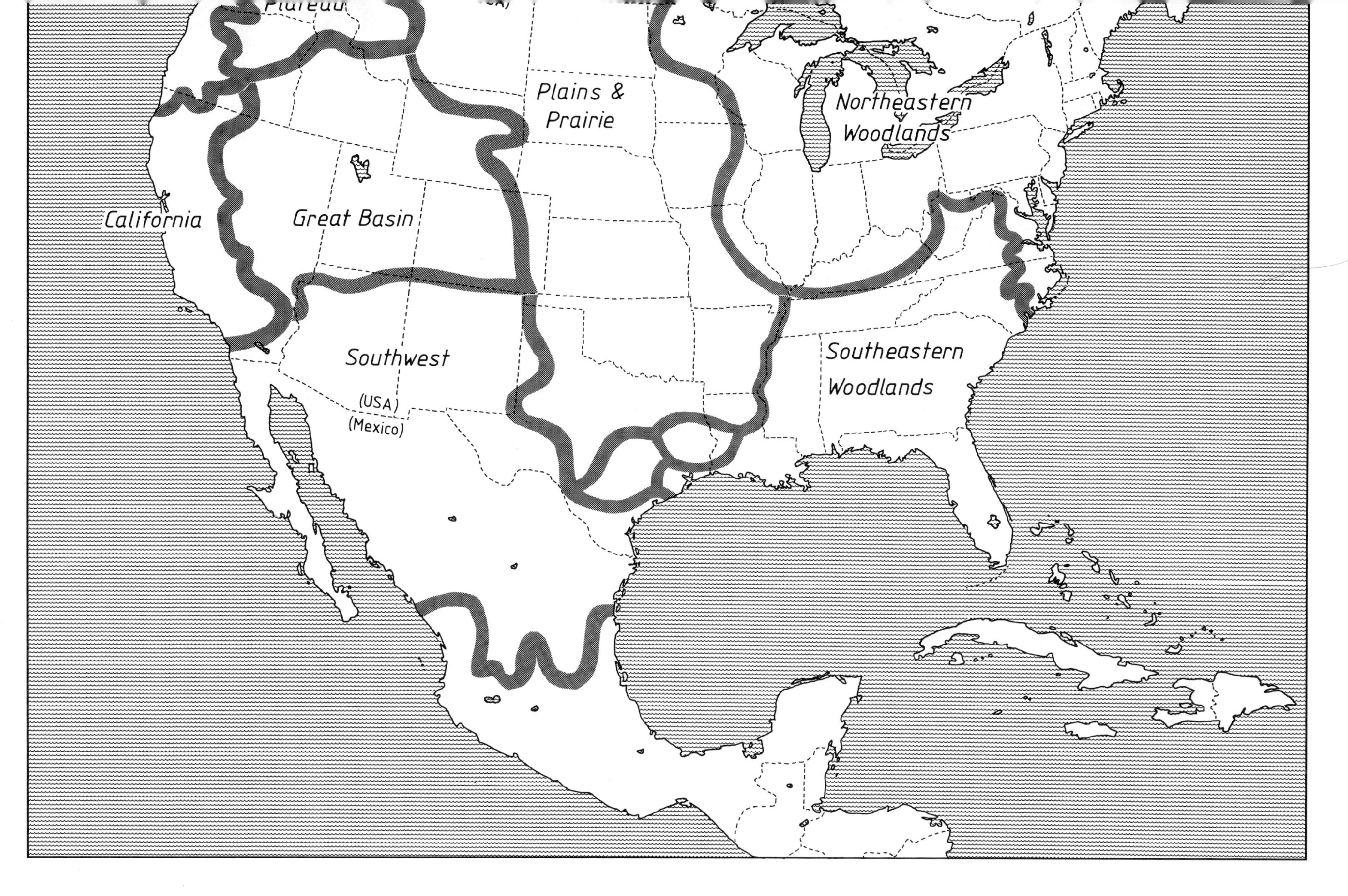

Plains &
Prairie
Northeastern
Woodlands
California
Great Basin
Southwest
(USA)
(Mexico)
Southeastern
Woodlands

NORTHEASTERN WOODLANDS

Language family and tribe	*Meaning*/origin of tribal name, where known
Algonkian (except where noted):	
Micmac	*"allies"*
Malecite	*"broken talkers"*
Passamaquoddy	*"those who pursue the pollock"*
Abenaki	*"easterners"*
Western Abenaki	"
Pennacook	*"downhill"*
Massachusett	*"at the range of hills"*
Nipmuc	*"fresh water fishing place"*
Pocomtuc	-
Wampanoag	*"eastern people"*
Narragansett	*"people of the small point"*
Niantic	*"at a point of land on a river"*
Mohegan	*"wolf"*
Pequot	*"destroyers"*
Lower Connecticut River Tribes	
Paugussett	*"where the narrows open out"*
Wappinger	*"easterners" (possibly)*
Mahican	*"wolf"*
Montauk	place name
Stockbridge	English name
Brotherton	English name
Delaware	English name
Nanticoke	*"tidewater people"*
Conoy	-
Powhatan	*"falls in a current of water"*
North Carolina Algonkians	
Shawnee	*"southerners"*
Miami	*"people of the Peninsula"*
Illini	*"people"*
Potawatomi	*"people of the place of fire"*
Mascouten	*"prairie people"*
Kickapoo	*"he stands about"*
Sauk	*"people of the yellow earth"*
Fox	*"red earth people"*
Menomini	*"wild rice men"*
Winnebago (Siouan)	*"people of the filthy water"*
Ojibwa	*"to roast until puckered up"*
Ottawa	*"to trade"*
Mississauga	*"river with several outlets"*
Algonkin	*"place of spearing fish (or eels)"*
Nipissing	*"at the lake"*
Iroquoian:	
Huron	*"rough"* or *"ruffian"*
Petun	French name (also *"tobacco nation"*)
Neutral	English name
Wenro	*"floating oil"*
Erie	*"raccoon nation"*
Susquehannock	English name
Iroquois (Five Nations)	*"real adders"*
Mohawk	*"man eaters"*
Oneida	*"people of the stone"*
Onondaga	*"people on the hill"*
Cayuga	town name
Seneca	*"people of the mountain"*
Mingo	Delaware term
Tuscarora	*"hemp gatherers"*
Nottoway	*"adders"*

The so-called Woodland cultural area was dominant in the northeastern ecological zone which comprised a central plain between the ocean and the Allegheny-Appalachian mountain ranges, the rich-soiled river bottoms of the Ohio and Mississippi valleys, the Great Lakes and the coastal Maritimes. This is a land of forests, both deciduous and evergreen, which includes from north to south birch, elm, dogwood, oak, hickory, southern pine, mountain ash and eventually, in the southeastern area, mangrove swamp.

The area as a whole is characterized by divergent cultural traditions which developed distinctive processes of skills, art and religion. However, the importance of slash-and-burn agriculture, an influence from Meso-America, was universal except on the northeastern margins.

The first influences from Central America arrived perhaps c.2000 B.C. – crude pottery and polished stone objects have been attributed to this period. Later more sophisticated cultures flourished, such as the Adena of Ohio and Kentucky, 800 B.C.-200 A.D.; this is noted for the flexed position of the dead in, at first, natural mounds and later in man-constructed burial mounds surrounded by earth walls and precincts – the famous Serpent Mound in Ohio is perhaps the most spectacular. This culture produced domesticated plants, squashes, pumpkins, and cord-marked pottery. The Hopewell culture after 100 B.C. saw the culmination of burial ceremonialism and death ritual cults. This culture also produced pottery, stone carving, realistic art forms of birds, animals and human forms in clay, copper, mica and shell.

The last cultural complex was "Mississippian", which re-entered the old Hopewell area at Cahokia and Fort Ancient from c.700 A.D. until the time of the European invasion. This late "Temple Mound" period is characterised by intensive agriculture of a Meso-American type, relatively superior pottery, palisaded and fortified villages, and flat-topped pyramid mounds (Cahokia). During the 15th century a religious cult, known as the Southern Cult, and associated ritual objects were grafted on to the existing temple platform traditions. Although this culture scarcely survived to the time of European contact the earliest white adventurers saw it. De Soto's expedition of 1540 encountered the Mississippian culture as it survived amongst the Creek, Cherokee and Natchez of the southeast, with their class system, distinctive appearance using ear circles and gorget decorations, and the ritual colours of red and white for war and peace. The northern offshoot of this culture was the Woodland pattern which, although divided into various local phases, was the genesis of late Woodland culture.

The Iroquoian Huron were the northern limit of extensive agriculture, albeit crude, and their Feast of the Dead witnessed by French Jesuit missionaries relates to Mississippian traits. The Iroquois epitomised Woodland culture, with their belief in a Creator and *orenda*, the life force, which embodied the health and creativity of all nature, opposed by the spirits of evil and destruction. The Algonkians, too, had a world view characterised by an overwhelming fear of sorcery, and a pantheon of destructive spirits such as the Windigowan, cannibal ice giants, the complete natural world being inhabited by spirit forms. Their supreme spirit was Manito or Midemanido, and they had a great culture hero, Nanabush. Both Iroquois and Algonkian religions were modified over the years by European influences into a curative ambience.

Wood and bark were important materials for the forest Indian, used to fashion canoes of birch or elm bark, and for the construction of toboggans, bows, arrows, clubs, baskets, containers, spoons, bowls, pestles, mortars, cradleboards, drums, lacrosse rackets and ball game sticks. Wigwams were bark or reed mats sewn to a frame of saplings tied with spruce roots.

The Indian peoples of eastern North America experienced a long period of white contact and a gradual Europeanisation of their material culture. The destruction of many eastern coastal tribes by diseases and the subsequent adoption of their remnants and of white captives by interior tribes led to a mixed gene pool and introduced a hybrid quality to surviving material culture and costume decoration. Before the end of the 17th century cloth, beads, silver, trade tomahawks, guns, thread, wool and metal trade goods were known to Indians as far west as the Mississippi River.

Indian dress in the northeast was modified by these European influences, but we can speculate that in pre-contact times hide tunics were worn by men, slit skirts by women, with a wide use of wampum shell for beads and decoration. However, European cloths and trade goods were adopted so quickly that by the 18th century Indians in close association with whites used broadcloth and calico for clothes. The Woodland tribes were expert workers of porcupine quills, fibres, moosehair, paint and later beadwork to decorate symbolically all manner of articles with representations of celestial and mythical phenomena. In the 19th century heavy floralist beadwork became popular for dance costumes, as did cut-and-fold ribbonwork, which still remains popular.

Intertribal warfare seems to have been endemic, and bitter wars during the colonial period seem to have been the continuance of conflicts of ancient times. The treatment of prisoners was reported with horror by those who witnessed their torture. There

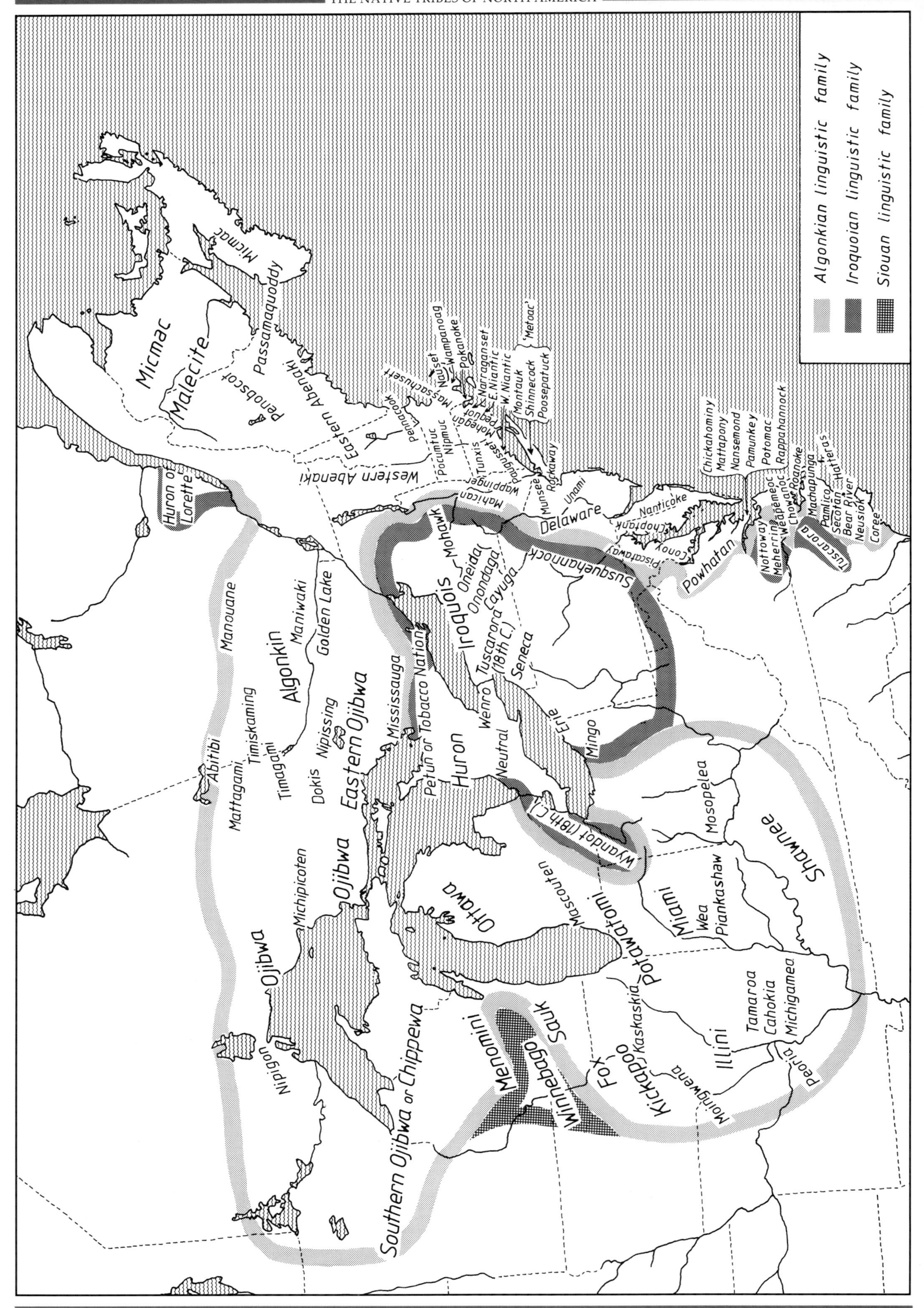
Algonkian linguistic family
Iroquoian linguistic family
Siouan linguistic family
Micmac
Micmac
Malecite
Passamaquoddy
Penobscot
Eastern Abenaki
Western Abenaki
Pennacook
Massachuset
Nauset
Wampanoag
Pokanoket
Narraganset
E. Niantic
W. Niantic
Pocumtuc
Nipmuc
Mohegan
Pequot
Tunxis
Montauk
Shinnecock
Poosepatuck
'Metoac'
Paugusset
Wappinger
Rockaway
Mahican
Munsee
Unami
Delaware
Huron of Lorette
Mohawk
Oneida
Onondaga
Cayuga
Iroquois
Tuscarora (18th C.)
Seneca
Susquehannock
Nanticoke
Choptank
Piscataway
Conoy
Powhatan
Chickahominy
Mattapony
Nansemond
Pamunkey
Potomac
Rappahannock
Nottoway
Meherrin
Weapemeoc
Chowanoc
Roanoke
Machapunga
Pamlico
Secotan
Hatteras
Bear River
Neusiok
Coree
Tuscarora
Manouane
Maniwaki
Golden Lake
Algonkin
Abitibi
Timiskaming
Timagami
Mattagami
Nipissing
Dokis
Eastern Ojibwa
Mississauga
Petun or Tobacco Nation
Huron
Wenro
Neutral
Erie
Mingo
Wyandot (18th C.)
Mosopelea
Shawnee
Ojibwa
Michipicoten
Ojibwa
Ottawa
Mascouten
Potawatomi
Miami
Wea
Piankashaw
Nipigon
Southern Ojibwa or Chippewa
Menomini
Winnebago
Sauk
Fox
Kickapoo
Kaskaskia
Illini
Tamaroa
Cahokia
Michigamea
Moingwena
Peoria

is no doubt that the mutually competitive European colonies exploited and encouraged the Indians in these activities. Conversely, several Indian divines preached against war and the evils brought by whites, and urged the accomodation of the new conditions both materially and psychologically. Such nativistic movements still exist.

Despite centuries of contact and depletion the Woodland people have survived in many areas: a few mixed descent people still claim coastal Algonkian ancestry, the Iroquois still occupy fractions of their old territory, and the Ojibwa are still numerous in the northern fringes of the Great Lakes states and adjacent parts of Canada. The southern Woodland tribes mostly found their way to Oklahoma, and have fully participated in the Pan-Indian cultural revival of recent times. They have also lost a major part of the old traditional culture through mass movement away from family ties on the reservations and into the cities; but such is the force of conservatism amongst some that, for instance, a few Kickapoo retained a semblance of old forest life modified to a Mexican environment, and the Mesquakies purchased their own lands to be free of Government influences. Both groups retained a distinctively Woodland culture until quite recent times.

ALGONKIAN or ALGONQUIAN

One of the most important language families of North America, being spoken aboriginally from the Canadian Maritimes to North Carolina and inland to the Great Plains. The family seems to be divided into three component parts: the divergent Plains branch, Blackfeet, Cheyenne and Arapaho; a Central branch comprising the Cree, Montagnais, Nascapi group, the Ojibwa, Ottawa, Potowatomi group, and the Fox, Menomini, Shawnee, Illinois, Miami group; and finally an Eastern branch. The Eastern branch is not fully classified since several tribes became extinct before linguistic re-cords could be made, but the following divisions may be reasonably accurate: Micmac, Malecite-Passamaquoddy, Abenaki (two dialects), Nipmuck-Pocumtuck, Massachusett, Narragansett, Mohegan-Pequot, Montauk, Unquachog (Long Island), Quiripi (Connecticut), Mahican, Delaware (two dialects), Nanticoke, Powhatan and Carolina. Of all these eastern dialects only Micmac is extensively spoken today. The name of the whole group derives from the Algonkin (Algonquin) proper, a branch of the Northern Ojibwa in Quebec.

TRIBES OF THE NORTHEASTERN WOODLANDS, c. 1585-1780
Linguistic and cultural boundaries are necessarily approximate; this sketch map is intended only as a general guide to distribution. Modern state boundaries are shown as broken lines, for orientation only.

MICMAC An important Algonkian people of Maritime Canada occupying Nova Scotia, Cape Breton Island, Prince Edward Island and in fairly recent times parts of southern Newfoundland. They were amongst the first native people encountered by Europeans on the North American continent when John Cabot took three natives back to England in 1497. Afterwards they were constantly visited by explorers and fishing vessels from France and England, and became intermediaries in a trade between the French on the St. Lawrence River and tribes further south. Consequently they became allies of the French, aiding them in colonial conflicts with the English even after Acadia (roughly, modern Nova Scotia) had been ceded to Great Britain. Since 1779 they have been peaceful, scattered occupants of their former domain, never deported, like many tribes, to the south; but a long association with whites, particularly the French, has seen a gradual loss of traditional culture and traditions and the inevitable mixing of the races. Over the years they have been noted for the fine decoration of birch bark souvenirs with porcupine quillwork and the production of wood split basketry which have been sold to generations of white curio hunters.

Their numbers have usually been reported as about 5,000 in early times, and whilst their present numbers have a large admixture of European descent over 9,800 are found scattered on about 30 reserves and communities, the largest at Restigouche, Quebec (1,400); Eskasoni on Cape Breton Island (1,300); Shubenacadie, Nova Scotia (900); Burnt Church and Big Cove, New Brunswick (1,600). Native language is still spoken by several hundred people, but Catholicism has supplanted most native beliefs for generations.

In ancient times there seem to have been eight subdivisions. They hunted caribou, moose, otter and beaver, and also fished and collected shellfish. Their dwellings were usually conical bark wigwams; transportation was usually by distinctively shaped bark canoes. Hide native dress seems to have been replaced quickly by dark cloth obtained from European traders, which they often decorated with beads and ribbons. They were sometimes also known as *Tarrantine*.

MALECITE or MALISEET A small Algonkian people located along the St.John River in what is now New Brunswick, Canada. They are closely, if not originally, the same people as the Passamaquoddy of Maine and related more distantly to the Penobscot and Abenaki, the four sometimes known as *Wabanaki*. They were also known as "Etchemin", a term also applied to include their relatives. First recorded by the explorer Champlain, they were thence forth under French influence until the British conquest of Canada. Subsequently they lost most of their lands except for a few acres on the St.John and Tobique Rivers, where a number of descendants still remain, with a European admixture from 400 years of white contact. Their native culture was overwhelmed generations ago, the tribe being largely converted to Roman Catholicism. They were noted during the 19th century for excellent beadwork, which survives in several museum collections. Their population was rarely given as more than a few hundred; perhaps 1,800 descendants are still found at their reserves at Woodstock and Tobique in New Brunswick and Viger, Quebec; and a few others in Maine around Presque Isle and Houlton, Aroostook County, with some Micmac.

PASSAMAQUODDY Closely related to the Malecite, this people remained in Maine after the British conquest of Canada in 1759 and have retained a separate identity. They were located on Passamaquoddy Bay, Maine, and along the St.Croix River. Their culture and history is generally the same as other Maritime Algonkian groups. About 1,000 descendants are still reported connected with three state reservations near Princeton and Eastport, Maine. A few have retained their language and a little craftwork, but native traditions, religion and ceremony largely fell into disuse generations ago. In early times they were hunters of moose and caribou but clams, lobsters, porpoise and salmon were also eaten. In recent times they adopted European cultivated garden produce, including potatoes. They, along with their close relatives, once formed a loose confederacy called *Wabanaki*, modelled on the Iroquois form.

ABENAKI The Algonkians of central Maine in the valleys of the Androscoggin, Kennebec, Saco and Penobscot Rivers in several subdivisions, of which the Pigwacket (Pequawket), Norridgewock and *Penobscot* are the largest – the latter often given separate status. The explorer Champlain passed through their territory in 1604, and thenceforth they were under French influence and hostile to the English colonists. They suffered as a result, the Norridgewock and Pequawket divisions being almost wiped out; much reduced in numbers, they withdrew in the late 17th century to French Canada, where they settled ultimately at Bécancour and St. Francis. During the various conflicts between the colonial powers the St.Francis Abenaki retaliated against New England settlements ; they often adopted white captives, such as the Gill family, whose descendants became chiefs and leaders.

In early times their dwellings were bark houses, conical, square or rounded; they hunted deer, moose, muskrat, otter and bear and also ate salmon and eels. Like the other northeastern Algonkians they had a strong belief in supernatural beings, with dances to engage their power, but their adoption of Catholicism led to an abandonment of native religion after their settlement in French Canada. They excelled in the manufacture of bark canoes and containers, the latter often finely decorated with incised curving designs. Hide dress was replaced largely by blankets and clothes obtained in the fur trade.

These old Maine Abenakis have merged with their relatives, the Western Abenaki, at St.Francis, although the old dialect once spoken at Becancour was thought to be true Abenaki (called Wawenock). However, the Penobscot remained in Maine after making peace with the English in 1759, and retained a number of settlements along the Penobscot River, the principal one at Old Town where descendants still remain, with additions from the Passamaquoddy over the years. The Penobscot have a present population of about 850 members including mixed Euro-American and other Indian ancestry. Their language was retained by three speakers in 1970, although some band members spoke Passamaquoddy. The other Abenakis from Maine, sometimes referred to as *Eastern Abenaki*, are now part of the multi-tribal Abenaki of Quebec, returned as numbering 585 at Odanak (St.Francis) and 42 at Bécancour in 1970.

WESTERN ABENAKI The designation Western Abenaki is now that given to the Algonkians who spoke one dialect and once inhabited the upper Connecticut River valley in New Hampshire, Massachusetts and Vermont; they were sometimes referred to in history as *Sokoki*, including perhaps the Pennacook on the Merrimack River and to the north the Missisquoi on Lake Champlain. Their history is much the same as that of their eastern Abenaki relatives: they gradually abandoned New England for French Canada after King Philip's War, 1675-76, and ultimately settled at the St.Francis Mission and Becancour in Quebec, where other Abenakis and New England remnants joined them, and where multi-ethnic descendants remain. There are few reliable estimates for their early population, perhaps 1,500 excluding Pennacook; the St.Francis Indians were given as numbering 342 in 1783, 370 in 1904, with about 200 descendants still living on the reserve in 1973 and several hundreds living elsewhere. Recently a mixed blood group living around

Swanton, Vermont, are also claimants of Abenaki ancestry. During the 19th century many were employed making split-ash baskets which were sold to whites, and which remain in museums. An Abenaki colony once selling these wares lived near Lake George, New York.

PENNACOOK or PAWTUCKET An Algonkian people of the Merrimac River, New Hampshire, and parts of adjacent Maine and Massachusetts, perhaps exceeding 2,000 people. Their history is similar to both the Western Abenaki to the north, with whom they are now usually classified, and the Eastern Abenaki of Maine. They were defeated by Waldron in 1676 at the close of King Philip's War and their remnants withdrew to Canada, uniting with the Abenakis at St.Francis, Quebec. A few people claiming Pennacook ancestry have been reported near Manchester in their old territory until quite recently.

MASSACHUSETT A group of villages about Boston, Massachusetts, between Salem and Brockton along the coast and as far inland as Concord River. They probably spoke the same dialect of Algonkian as the Pawtucket. Probably visited by several voyagers during the 16th century before contact with the English settlement at Plymouth in 1621, they perhaps numbered 3,000 at the time of first European contact, but were reduced rapidly by epidemics of smallpox and other pestilence. They were soon influenced by Puritans who settled their country and who gathered their remnants into small villages of "Praying Indians"(those at Punkapog the only ones to survive in any number), and these remnants intermarried with African-Americans during the 18th century. A few people of mixed descent survived down to the 20th century near Canton and Mansfield in Norfolk County, Massachusetts.

NIPMUC or NIPMUCK A term to cover native villages in central Massachusetts who perhaps spoke an Algonkian dialect connected with the Pocumtuck who lived west of the Connecticut River. They were greatly weakened by the diseases brought by the European settlers, and their remnants settled in villages controlled by whites. Some probably took part in King Philip's War, 1675-76, after which only a few survived. A number of descendants preserve their name to the present day, however; a few acres of land near Grafton, known as the Hassanimisco Reservation, are collectively owned, and a few more people near Dudley and Webster may also have their ancestry. The resurgence of Indian identity in recent times has reactivated the group, who are involved in sponsoring Pan-Indian events. Perhaps 100 people can still justify Nipmuck ancestry today.

POCOMTUC or POCUMTUCK Algonkian villages of central west Massachusetts from Agawam in the south to Deerfield in the north. They may have been connected to the Nipmuc or Wappinger but all are artificial groupings. Their main settlement was Fort Hill, Franklin County, which was destroyed by the Mohawk in 1666. They joined the hostilities in King Philip's War; at its close their remnants fled west to the Hudson and ultimately to the Abenaki at St.Francis, and disappeared as a separate unit.

WAMPANOAG or POKANOKET A convenient grouping of Algonkian people and villages of southern Massachusetts including those on the coast below Marshfield, Cape Cod, Martha's Vineyard Island, Nantucket Island and part of Narragansett Bay, Rhode Island. The *Nauset* of Barnstable County and *Sakonnet* of Rhode Island have been presented separately, but they probably never formed any unified tribal group. We know that their subsistence consisted of deer, bear, squirrel, fish, seafood, gathering and horticulture. Their houses were of varied shape covered with slabs of bark or woven mats. They were known to Europeans at least as far back as 1602, and played an important part in helping the Pilgrim Fathers to establish their settlements after 1620, due mainly to the efforts of their chief Massasoit. However, his son Metacom, sometimes known as King Philip, led a general Indian uprising against the colonists in 1675-76, but was defeated so badly that these Indians were never a force again.

Their remnants settled in various locations, mostly in Bristol and Barnstable Counties, and a number of descendants were still found near Fall River, Herring Pond, Yarmouth, Dartmouth, Mashpee and Gay Head (Martha's Vineyard Island) in the 19th century. The latter two groups survive to the present time and number over 600; although they are racially mixed, the force of modern Pan-Indianism has strongly reinforced their Indian identity and their participation in Indian events.

NARRAGANSETT The Algonkian people who once occupied the whole of the present state of Rhode Island west of Narragansett Bay. They seem to have been closely related to the *Niantic* with whom they ultimately merged. The smaller Coweset, Pawtuxet and Block Island Indians were all more or less the same people. Probably contacted by the explorer Verrazano in 1524, they were known to the Dutch and English from the early 1600s. They had a large population of several thousand which escaped the first pestilence and smallpox of 1617, but many died in 1633. They became friends of the English in 1636 after Roger Williams laid the foundations of the state of Rhode Island by settling amongst them. They remained on good terms with whites until King Philip's War (1675-76), when they joined the hostiles and lost 1,000 men, women and children at the Great Swamp Fight near Kingston. Some fled the country, others joined the Niantic, these together becoming known as Narragansett.

Since that time they have continued to live in the same area, although many left and joined the Brotherton Indians in New York or the Mohegan in Connecticut during the 18th century. Their descendants, numbering about 500 people, are still found in the southern part of Rhode Island around Charlestown and Kenyon, although greatly mixed with other races and having lost all traces of their original Indian culture and language. They have, however, absorbed Pan-Indian influences, hold an annual Powwow, and have revived festivals and church meetings, which gives their descendants a persistent identity.

NIANTIC A small Algonkian people divided into the Eastern branch in Rhode Island and Western branch near New London, Connecticut – separate from their neighbours perhaps only because of their independent sachems (chiefs) – who maintained a nominal pro-English position during King Philip's War (1675-76) under their chief Ninigret. The Narragansett merged with them, and their descendants are no doubt the multi-ethnic group about Charlestown, Rhode Island. The last of the Western Niantic intermarried with Mohegan-Pequot survivors in Connecticut.

MOHEGAN An Algonkian people who occupied the Thames River valley and its branches in Connecticut, confusingly renamed Mohican in popular writings, were closely related and perhaps once the same people as the Pequot. They separated from the Pequot after the destruction of that tribe by white colonists aided by coastal Indians and Mohegans led by Uncas in 1637. They have continued to live in Connecticut, although over the years some joined the Brotherton in New York and the Scaticook. In 1721 they still held 4,000 acres along the Thames River, reduced to 2,300 acres by 1850, by which time many had left their traditional enclave near Uncasville, and in 1861 unoccupied lands reverted to the state. Perhaps some 50 descendants still live near Uncasville, Connecticut. Nearby is the Mohegan Church and the Fort Shantok Point burial grounds. The Tantaquidgeons, Gladys and Harold, the tenth generation descendants of the historical Uncas, still ran a small museum at the rear of their house in 1988, which contained Mohegan material culture. They claimed that 200 descendants of the tribe were scattered throughout the state, all of mixed blood.

The southern New England Algonkians had a subsistence pattern which combined maize horticulture with hunting, and heavy involvement in trade with Long Island Indians for wampum shell money, used also by white settlers, which drew them into the European money exchange at an early date.

PEQUOT An Algonkian tribe, perhaps once one with the Mohegan, together numbering more than 4,000. They occupied eastern Connecticut, particularly around the Mystic River area. Their subsistence foods came from hunting, collecting, maize harvesting, waterfowl and shellfish. The settlement patterns involved villages of several houses of bark-covered saplings, sometimes large enough for a number of families; such dwellings were used by all southern New England Algonkians. The Pequot seem to have been at war with their neighbours at the time of first European settlement, which they strongly resisted under their sachem Sassacus. They were defeated by a combined body of English, Mohegan and Narragansett in 1637, with their principal settlement completely destroyed. Many were sold into slavery in the West Indies, and others fled west; but a few who remained obtained two land grants from the English in New London, Mushantuxet in 1667 and Lantern Hill, 1683, near Ledyard, Connecticut, and both still exist as small state reservations. About 100 people of mixed descent are still connected with these lands; a few families live permanently on the reserves and constitute one of the few surviving Indian groups of southern New England.

LOWER CONNECTICUT RIVER TRIBES A number of small tribes in present day Connecticut, who were in contact with English settlers from 1639 onward: the noted groups were the *Tunxis* near Hartford, *Podunk* near Windsor, *Wangunk* near Wethersfield and *Quinnipiac* near New Haven, centering along the Connecticut River and sometimes collectively called *Mattabesec* by some writers. They have been incorrectly added to the so-called Wappinger group by several historians, but may have shared with the lower Housatonic River groups a separate Algonkian dialect now called Quiripi. They perhaps numbered collectively 2,200 in the early 17th century, but diminished rapidly and sold their lands to English settlers until only a few families remained by the 18th century, and a mere handful of descendants of mixed race by the 19th century.

PAUGUSSETT or LOWER HOUSATONIC RIVER TRIBES A group of four small tribes formerly living on the Housatonic River, Connecticut, when first in contact with English settlers during the early 17th century: the *Paugussett* proper around present day Derby, *Pequannock* near Trumbull, *Potatuck* near Woodbury, and *Weantinock* or *Wawyachtonok* above Danbury in Litchfield County, this last tribe sometimes given as a Mahican group. They diminished in numbers due to epidemics brought by whites and were pressured into land sales. A small mission village, *Schaghticoke* or *Scaticook*, developed from an earlier settlement, was established by Mahwee, a Pequot, early in the 18th century, which became a refuge for a mixed tribal group, mostly Paugussett. Perhaps 50 or so descendants still identify as Scaticook, with four families resident on their small reservation near Bulls Bridge, Kent, Connecticut in 1988; the leading family of the group are surnamed Lamb. A few other Paugussett descendants are also reported from Golden Hill, Bridgeport, and near Colchester, Connecticut.

WAPPINGER and LOWER HUDSON RIVER TRIBES In the restricted sense the Wappinger lived on the east bank of the Hudson River near present day Poughkeepsie, New York, but the term is sometimes extended to include groups below them as far south as the Manhattan Island Indians. Their closest linguistic relatives were the Munsee-Delaware and Mahican with whom they are sometimes classed; but the formation of the Wappinger Confederacy proposed by some writers, which includes the Housatonic and Connecticut River groups, now seems wholly without foundation. The lower Hudson tribes perhaps numbered 3,000 before being wasted by wars with Dutch settlers; the transfer of power in the area to the English brought them under pressure for land, and the last withdrew from Westchester County, New York, in 1756. Some joined the Stockbridge in Massachusetts and the Nanticoke and Delaware in Broome County, New York, and ultimately disappeared as a separate group. Early reports called the northern groups Highland Indians (Hudson Highlands).

MAHICAN An important Algonkian people of the Hudson River Valley in present New York state from the Lake George area south to the Catskill Mountains. The Wappinger (proper), Housatonic River groups and Esopus are sometimes added to the group for convenience. Their culture seems to have been similar to other interior northeastern Algonkian groups, with palisaded villages, bark longhouses and wigwams; they grew maize, fished, gathered and hunted. In August the men returned to their villages for the Green Corn ceremonials and to assist the women in the harvest. They had no pottery, but instead had carved and bark vessels, wooden spoons and dishes. They had canoes, wore skin clothing, and traded wampum to the tribes farther north. Their first contacts with Europeans came in 1609 when Henry Hudson sailed up the Hudson River, and with the establishment of Fort Orange and Albany by the Dutch they were quickly drawn into the fur trade. Despite the ravages of smallpox they were reinforced by defeated New England groups who combined with some Mahicans at Schaghticoke.

From the 1720s on the Mahicans began to move west to the multi-ethnic groups, first on the Susquehanna and then to the Ohio country. The rest resettled first at Stockbridge, Massachusetts, along with the Housatonic in 1736; then after 1756 moved to New York; and finally in 1833 to Wisconsin, where the combined Mahican-Wappinger-Housatonic, now called "Stockbridge", obtained a reservation near Bowler, Shawano County, and several hundred people of mixed Stockbridge and Munsee descent still remain. A few Mahican remained in the Hudson Valley, where a number of rural groups claim their ancestry.

The term Mahican is often confused with another, but separate, tribe of Connecticut, the Mohegan. Both may perhaps claim to have been the inspiration of Fennimore Cooper's *'The Last of the Mohicans'*, but as both peoples still survive his title was in error.

MONTAUK A general term to cover the Algonkians of Long Island, New York, except those at the extreme western end of the island who more properly belong with the Delaware. The same group of tribes are occasionally termed "Metoac". They were famous in history for the production of wampum shell money, which they traded to mainland tribes until the production was taken over by white settlers. They seem to have survived King Philip's War (1675-76) relatively undisturbed, and land grants by the English were given as early as 1666. However, they were subjected to attacks from the Narragansetts, and decreased in numbers due to diseases; after 1775 some joined the Brotherton Indians in New York under Samson Occom, a Mohegan preacher who had formed a new Indian town.

Those that were left on Long Island were the *Shinnecock*, who still retain a reservation near Southampton; the *Poosepatuck*, whose descendants still have a few acres at the mouth of the Mastic River; the Montauk proper, a few people near Montauk Point and East Hampton at the eastern end of Long Island; the *Matinecock* on the north shore in Nassau County; and the *Setauket*, a few descendants of whom were once found in Suffolk County but are now no longer reported. Their original population may have been more than 2,000. In 1900 only 150 Shinnecock and 30 Poosepatuck were reported, much mixed with African-American blood, the Shinnecocks having lost many men in a whaling accident at sea in 1876. The present 200 or 300 descendants hold a Pan-Indian Powwow each summer.

STOCKBRIDGE The name given to a group of missionized Mahican, Wappinger, Housatonic and others originally settled at Schaghticoke, New York (not to be confused with the group of the same name in Connecticut), who subsequently gathered at the town and mission of Stockbridge, Massachusetts, in 1736. They rendered loyal service to the British in the French and Indian War and to the Americans in the War of Independence. Between 1756 and 1785 they joined other groups, at first in Broome and Tioga Counties, New York; and later joined the Oneida along with the Brotherton refugees. The Oneida, Stockbridge and Brotherton all moved to Wisconsin in 1833, the Stockbridge being separately given a reservation southwest of the Menomini near present Bowler, Wisconsin. In 1966, 380 "Stockbridge-Munsee" were still living on the reservation, with an equal number living away. They had lost most of their native traditions before or shortly after their move to Wisconsin, and are now highly acculturated and mostly of mixed white and Indian descent.

BROTHERTON The name of two separate groups of remnant New England Algonkians. The first were a combination of Mahican, Wappinger, Pequot, Mohegan, Narragansett and Montauk who moved to lands given to them by the Oneida in Marshall and Oneida Counties, New York, under a native minister, Samson Occom (1723-1792); they numbered 250 in 1791. The second group were 40 or so Raritan-Delawares from a reservation in New Jersey called Brotherton in Burlington County, who joined the first group in New York in 1802. The combined group moved to Wisconsin in 1833 under the name Brotherton, and a number of descendants are still reported near Appleton.

DELAWARE or **LENI-LENAPE** The most important collection of Algonkian groups of the mid-Atlantic coast, once occupying the Lower Hudson River valley, the western part of Long Island and the whole of the present state of New Jersey south to Delaware Bay. Their dialectic separation from adjacent people is not clear; perhaps even the Wappinger of the Hudson River and the Matinecock of Long Island should really be included in the group. They included the *Esopus* on the west bank of the Hudson; the *Rockaway* and *Canarsee* of Long Island; the *Minisinks* (later called Munsee) on the Delaware River north of the Delaware Water Gap; the *Unami*, a dialect spoken on both sides of the Delaware River in New Jersey and Pennsylvania; the *Raritans* on the Raritan River; a number of minor subtribes occupying Manhattan Island north to present Westchester County, New York; and finally a number of small tribes and villages on the lower Delaware below present Philadelphia who also spoke a variation of Unami and are for our purposes considered as one. In later years they were usually classified in three groups: Munsee, Unami and Unalachtigo but only the former two were true divisions.

They were probably first seen by Europeans in 1524 when Verrazano sheltered in New York harbour, but their history of contact with Europeans began with Hudson's visit in 1609. By the 1630s the Dutch had introduced the fur trade, and the Delaware fought to secure their villages and hunting territories against the encroaching Dutch and northern Indians. The English who succeeded the Dutch induced the River Indians including the Iroquois, Mahican and Delaware into an alliance known as the Covenant Chain. Throughout the 17th century they were swept by smallpox, measles, influenza and plagues, which halved their population. By the 1740s they were being crowded out by whites and began to move west to the Susquehanna and Allegheny Rivers, fighting at times against English settlers, at times for them against the French. They finally made peace at Easton, New Jersey, in 1758 when a reservation was established for some remaining New Jersey bands at Brotherton. By now the Delawares were strung out in settlements from New Jersey to the Ohio country; the western bands actively engaged in frontier warfare until the Treaty of Greenville, 1795, after which some moved west to the White River, Indiana, and later to Cape Girardeau, Missouri. A number of other groups in Pennsylvania and Ohio had been converted by German Moravians and moved to the Thames River, Ontario; still others had joined some Mahican and Nanticoke and sought Iroquois protection, moving with them to Ontario after the Revolution. The Brothertons joined the Stockbridges in New York in 1802, and ultimately moved to Wisconsin with the Oneida in 1833.

During their migration westward the Delawares maintained a way of life transitional between that of the whites and the less acculturated Indians of the interior. Bark longhouses had given way to log cabins; European farming with cattle, horses and swine had replaced native slash-and-burn farming; bowls, dishes, pestles and mortars, fibre bags, tumplines, baskets and mats had been replaced by trade goods. During the 19th century, often in concert with the Shawnee, they moved farther west. By the 1820s they were in southern Missouri and by the 1830s in Kansas, where some settled and became citizens in Ottawa and Franklin Counties. The last major move was in 1867-68 to Oklahoma, where the largest group settled in Cherokee Nation.

Their earlier population may have been 12,000; today they have about 5,000 descendants, all of mixed white or Mahican antecedents. Approximately 350 are on the Six Nations Reserve, Ontario, originally from New York; 500 on the Moravian Reserve near Bothwell, Ontario; 200 Munsee near Munceytown, Ontario, who originally came from Ohio; several hundred are mixed with the Stockbridge and Brotherton in Wisconsin; there are a few citizen Delaware in Kansas; but the largest group are the Registered Delaware of Washington, Nowata, Craig and Delaware Counties in Oklahoma, numbering about 1,100. A hundred or so descendants of Delaware who moved to Oklahoma from Texas with the Caddo and Wichita now live near Anadarko, Oklahoma. There are only a handful of Munsee or Unami speakers today. The Oklahoma Delaware sponsor a Pan-Indian Powwow each summer. A small number never left New Jersey and a few, near Eatontown, claim their ancestry.

The Delawares, occupying a central homeland amongst the Atlantic coast Algonkians, held the priority of political rank; many other tribes claimed to have diverged from them and accorded them the respectful title of "grandfather". The Nanticoke, Conoy, Shawnee and Mahican all claimed a connection with them. Their real name, Leni-Lenape, is equivalent to "real men"; but their common English name is derived from Lord de la Warr, an early governor of the colony at Jamestown, Virginia, although he never set foot amongst the people who have ever since carried his name.

Although the recording of Delaware culture and religion took place long after Christian and other influences may have blurred many cogent facets, they seem to have believed in a great Manito or Creator, whose spiritual agents were present in all living things – trees, flowers, grass, rocks and rivers. Ceremonies were in response to or to control the weather, hunting, harvest, or for the elimination of sickness and catastrophe. The "Big House" Ceremony was still held amongst the Oklahoma Delawares until the 1920s. A wooden building (originally bark) was constructed with twelve faces carved on the interior posts to watch the ceremonials and to carry prayers to the Creator. Their creation myth (shared with other eastern tribes) held that they sprang from a hole in the earth, and that the world was carried on a giant turtle's back. During the 19th century a certain Dr. Brinton produced a series of 183 mnemonic glyphs which he claimed were a record of ancient Delaware history and myths called the *Walam Olum* or "red score". The originals have not survived and some historians believe Brinton's records are questionable.

No tribe was pushed so far from its homelands. A few bands during the 19th century became "mountain men", and many claimed them better military auxiliaries than the Pawnee or Cheyenne. They also mixed their blood lines with several tribes in the west, notably the Flathead and Nez Perce.

NANTICOKE An Algonkian people of the present states of Delaware and Maryland on both sides of Chesapeake Bay and on the north bank of the Potomac River. Although they are frequently delimited to those on the Nanticoke River, a number of other groups can be added as more or less the same people, including the *Nanticoke (proper)*; the *Wicocomoco* on the river of the same name in Maryland; *Choptank* on the Choptank River; *Pocomoke* on the Pocomokee River; *Wicomiss* or *Ozinies* on the Chester River; and *Patuxent* on the Patuxent River, Calvert County. The *Conoy* are usually given separate status; but a number of minor groups on the Northampton Peninsula, Virginia, could also be added, collectively referred to as *Accomac*.

European contact dates from the 1580s, increasing after the establishment of Jamestown in 1607; thereafter a series of disputes with the Maryland colonists led to continual outbreaks of violence. Despite the establishment of reservations at the end of the 17th century, many were forced to leave under Iroquois protection for the Chenango River at Otsiningo – present day Binghamton, New York – along with the Conoy and other remnants. The last of these immigrant Nanticoke were counted amongst the Iroquois at Six Nations, Ontario, or Buffalo Creek, New York, and lost separate identity. Those who remained in parts of their old country intermarried with African-Americans at an early date; although a mixed blood people who identify themselves as "Nanticoke" have remained along Indian River, Millsboro, Sussex County, Delaware, the last native speaker died in 1856. Yet another tri-racial group near Cheswold, Kent County, Delaware, called "Moors", may also have some Nanticoke ancestry. Both the Moors and Nanticoke number several hundred people. A number of baskets and other utility items were collected from them in the early 20th century and appear to have been native in style. Nanticoke descendants now hold a Pan-Indian Powwow each year near Millsboro.

CONOY or **PISCATAWAY** An Algonkian tribe

related to the Nanticoke (with whom they are often classed) who lived on the western shore of Chesapeake Bay and along the Potomac River. They were in conflict with the Maryland colonists after 1634, and were also harassed by the Susquehannocks from the north. Although reservations were established, they were forced to leave for the north with remnant Nanticoke under Iroquois protection, first to Pennsylvania, then to Chenango, Broome County, New York and Owego, when they were last reported as separate in 1793. Some nevertheless seem to have remained in Maryland, presumably intermixing with whites and African-Americans, since a body of tri-racial groups survive around Baltimore and in Charles, Prince George's and Dorchester Counties under names such as Piscataway, Wesort and Portobacco; but their connection with the old Conoy is uncertain.

POWHATAN A large and important collection of Algonkian groups located in the tidewater portion of Virginia from the Potomac River to the north, through the drainages of the Rappahannock, Pamunky, Chickahominy and James Rivers and as far south as the Great Dismal Swamp. From 1607 they were in contact and ultimately in conflict with the English colonists at Jamestown under Powhatan, their paramount chief at that time, from whom the whole group have been named the Powhatan confederacy. They cultivated corn, which was stored on raised platforms after harvesting; hunted, fished and gathered wild plant foods. They wore some buckskin garments frequently fringed, painted and decorated with shells. Their principal subtribes were the *Potomac* below the river that bears their name; *Rappahannock* on the north bank of that river; *Wicocomoco* in present Northumberland County; *Chickahominy* on the upper Mattaponi River, and *Mattaponi* on the lower; *Pamunkey* on the Pamunkey River; *Werowocomoco* in Gloucester County; and *Nansemond* below the James River.

Wars with the colonists in 1622 and 1644 broke them, after which they were restricted to English land grants, exposed to continual harassment by Iroquois and Conestogas, and violated for crimes often committed by these northern Indians. By the end of the 17th century they mainly worked as hunters, scouts and servants for the English, with considerable intermarriage with whites following the famous Pocahontas-Rolfe marriage, and later with African-American slaves. Except on two land grants formal tribal organisation faded; their population of 10,000 at the time of European contact had diminished to a few hundred by the close of the 17th century.

While several hundred people have survived to the present time, only the Pamunkey and Mattaponi can claim unbroken links with their 17th century ancestors, due to their two reservations which continue to the present time: the Pamunkey Reservation, King William County, has some 300 inhabitants,and the Mattaponi Reservation about 200. The remaining groups whose ancestry is less certain, but who claim Indian and tribal descent, are the Upper Chickahominy, Charles City County, Roxbury; Lower Chickahominy, James City County, Boulevard; Rappahannock, Caroline, Essex, King and Queen Counties; Potomac, near Fredericksburg; Wicocomoco, Northumberland County; Werowocomoco, Gloucester County; Nansemond in Norfolk County; plus a few Accomac in Northampton County (old Nanticoke area). All together these groups reported at 3,987 in 1970. Although without ancient tribal traditions, they take part in various Pan-Indian politics and activities designed to strengthen their Indian identity.

NORTH CAROLINA ALGONKIANS These tribes are famous for their connection with the Raleigh colonists who established a settlement in 1585-87 on Roanoke Island at the mouth of Albemarle Sound in present North Carolina. The artist John White, who accompanied the settlers, made a group of watercolour pictures of their villages, dwellings, fishing techniques, and some individual studies which survive in the British Museum, giving us excellent visual evidence of their culture. They show curved roof wigwams, dugout log canoes, fishing nets, costume, body paint and ceremonial dances. The fate of the Roanoke colonists, other than those who returned to England, remains unknown. The 17th century saw the exploration and settlement of the area by the Virginia colonists and a decline in native population, but reformed tribes fought on the side of the English in the Tuscarora Wars. During the 18th and 19th centuries they seem to have merged with African-American populations and only a few of mixed blood survived.

The following were probably the most important tribal groups: the *Weapemeoc* on the north side of Albemarle Sound included the *Poteskeit* and *Paspatank*, and these groups maintained themselves until the Tuscarora War of 1712-13; the *Moratok (Moratuc)*, a settlement 160 miles into Albemarle Sound at the head of the Roanoke River; the *Secotan* on Pamlico Sound, who were superseded in that location by the *Pamlico* and *Bear River* Indians who also existed down to the time of the Tuscarora War; the *Neusiok* on the Neuse River; *Pomeiooc*, a village in an area occupied later by a group called *Machapunga* at Mattsmuskeet Lake, where a reserve with a mixed tribal population survived during the 18th century; *Croatoan*, a village on Cape Hatteras with whom the Raleigh colonists may have taken refuge, were probably the Hatteras Indians who later joined the Machapunga at Mattamuskeet Lake. The *Chowanoc* or *Chawanoke* on the Chowan River, who were probably the largest tribe of the area, submitted to the British in 1675 and were later confined to a reservation on Bennetts Creek; they perhaps ultimately merged with the Tuscarora.

During the 20th century a few mixed descendants were reported on Roanoke Island, near Mattamuskeet Lake and near Hertford, but these now seem to have disappeared. The *Lumbee* of Robeson County, North Carolina, claim the ancestry of the coastal tribes and Raleigh colonists, but this remains unsupported by historical evidence; despite their considerable numbers their tribal origins still remain unclear.

SHAWNEE An Algonkian people whose original home was probably the Cumberland River in Tennessee, but scarcely has any tribe divided so often or moved so much. As far as they can be associated with one area, the Muskingum and Scioto River valleys in the Ohio country were their home during the 18th century, when they were a major frontier tribe actively engaged in warfare against the encroaching white settlers. However, they had also settled in various parts of Pennsylvania during the early part of that century, attracted by the English trade; and one band, *Saluda*, settled for a time amongst the Creek, driving the Yuchi from the middle Savannah region, but subsequently rejoined a main body of the tribe in Pennsylvania. The tribe had five component parts, perhaps originally separate tribes – Chillicothe (Calaka), Kispokotha (Kispoko), Piqua or Pickaway (Pekowi), Sawekela or Hathawekela (Thawikila), and Makostrake (Mekoce) – but their functions seem to have been largely political and ritual. Their subsistence combined hunting with agriculture, but was strongly oriented towards the fur trade since the early 18th century. Their supreme being Creator was female.

They were consistently opposed to white settlement beyond the Appalachian Mountains, switching their alliances between France and Britain to this end. They joined the Pontiac uprising against the British (1763), and fought against the Virginians in Lord Dunmore's War (1774) and later the Americans in the Revolution. They took up arms against the Americans again under the leadership of Tecumseh and Tenskwatawa (The Prophet) at Tippecanoe and in the War of 1812. However, by this time constant warfare had exhausted and split them. Contact with whites over a long period had resulted in a hybrid culture similar to those of other mid-western tribes. By the late 18th century a large body of Shawnee and others had begun to settle in Spanish territory, now Missouri, but the main body of the tribe was still in Indiana and Ohio on the White, Auglaize and Miami Rivers.

By the 1830s most of the Indiana bands, with some Missouri bands (later known as Black Bob's band), had rejoined on a reservation on the Kansas River in northeastern Kansas; but others, wishing to be free of white influence, decamped for Arkansas, Texas and beyond, later being known as "Absentee" Shawnee as they were separate from the main body of the tribe living in Kansas. In 1832 a mixed band of Seneca Iroquois and Shawnee coming direct from Ohio moved to northeastern Indian Territory, now Ottawa County, Oklahoma. In 1870, following the Civil War, the main body of the tribe moved from Kansas to Cherokee Nation, Indian Territory; while the Absentee Shawnee and Black Bob's band obtained lands between the North Canadian and Canadian Rivers in Indian Territory, along with the Potawatomi.

The Ottawa County Shawnee separated from the Seneca in 1867; their descendants, known as the Eastern Shawnee, number about 600. The Cherokee-Shawnee or Loyal-Shawnee of Craig County, Oklahoma, number about 1,100; and the Absentee Shawnee number about 1,000 in Pottawatomie and Cleveland Counties. One community at Little Axe were a relatively conservative group until recently, maintaining traditional Shawnee rituals including the War Dance and Bread Dances. The Loyal and Eastern bands are largely of mixed descent and have been highly acculturated for generations. The census of 1970 gave 2,208.

MIAMI An Algonkian people related to the Illini centered in present Indiana along the Wabash and Eel River drainages during the 18th century, when they were reduced to three small tribes; *Wea*, *Piankashaw* and *Miami proper*. They probably came originally from the Fox River area of Wisconsin. Like other tribes of the area they lived in oval lodges covered with cattail mats, bark or hides, in small villages along river banks, with a mixed farming and hunting economy. Their religion recognized the Master of Life, similar to the Illini. Other ritual activity included the vision quest and the Midewiwin. Their Ohio country became an area of fluctuating colonial intrigue between the French and British in the 18th century, and home to multi-tribal partly acculturated Indian groups seeking refuge from conflicts farther east. Knowing that the loss of their lands would follow American control they fought with the British in the Revolution, and continued resistance against American forces under Harmar in 1790 and St.Clair in 1791, until defeated by Anthony Wayne at Fallen Timbers in 1794.

After the Treaty of Greenville of 1795 they

remained at peace with the Americans but declined rapidly in numbers; and between 1832 and 1840 they moved to reservations in Kansas,.where the Wea and Piankashaw united with the remnant Illini under the name *Peoria*. The Peoria and Miami removed in 1867 to Indian Territory, now Oklahoma, where two highly acculturated mixed descent groups remain in Ottawa County, numbering about 1,090 in 1970. A few escaped removal and maintained themselves in Indiana near Peru, where some 150 mixed descent people are said to survive at the present time.

ILLINI or **ILLINOIS** A group of Algonkian-speaking tribes more or less closely connected, who lived principally along the Mississippi and Illinois Rivers; the *Michigamea* at Big Lake between the St.Francis and Mississippi Rivers, Arkansas; *Cahokia* about Cahokia, Illinois; *Kaskaskia*, originally near present Utica; *Moingwena* at the mouth of the De Moines River, Iowa; *Peoria*, originally on the Mississippi near the junction with the Iowa; and *Tamaroa* near the junction of the Missouri and Illinois Rivers with the Mississippi. Their language was closest to the Miami. As the population of these groups dwindled they often reformed in new locations. They were an agricultural people dependent upon maize;they also gathered wild foods and hunted game, including buffalo.

Their first contacts with the French were with the expedition of Marquette and Jolliet in about 1675; they soon came under French influence, and their decline followed quickly. Visited by smallpox, harassed by Iroquois war parties, demoralised by liquor and poverty and apparently completely missionized, they dwindled from a population of 10,000 to about 400 in 1778. They had gradually moved west of the Mississippi by 1832 when, reduced to a single remnant, they moved to Kansas and united with the Wea and Piankashaw. The final movement was to northeastern Oklahoma under a combined name, Peoria; there a highly acculturated multi-ethnic group has remained, numbering 439 in 1956. They recognised an overall being, the "Master of Life", who was the ultimate source of power and visions. Descriptions of ritual practice centred on warfare, shamanism and the calumet dance.

POTAWATOMI An Algonkian-speaking tribe who probably split from the Ojibwa and Ottawa. The ancient home of the tribe was evidently the lower peninsula of Michigan, but in about 1680 they were driven to the Door Peninsula near Green Bay on the west side of Lake Michigan. During the 18th century they spread south to the present Milwaukee area and the St.Joseph River. By 1790 they had scattered at various times from the Mississippi across the northern tributaries of the Illinois River through southern Michigan to the Detroit area. Their villages were usually established on the edge of the forest adjacent to prairies and lakes. They grew squash, beans and maize, collected plant foods and hunted deer, elk and buffalo. The Potawatomi shared the common Algonkian dual division of clan and social organisation, and their beliefs about the spirit world included the curative Midewiwin, the Grand Medicine Lodge Society similar to the Ojibwa and Menomini.

Historically the Potawatomi first aligned themselves with the French against the English and later against the Americans, until a general peace in about 1815 after which they changed rapidly. Forced out of their homelands, they mainly withdrew across the Mississippi. In 1841 most of the "Potawatomi of the Woods" from southern Michigan and northern Indiana, already partly acculturated, moved to Kansas, although a few bands remained behind (Potawatomi of Huron and Pokagon). The Illinois-Wisconsin Potawatomi moved to a reservation in Iowa and thence to one in Kansas, thus combining the Woods and Prairie bands. The most acculturated tribal members moved to a new reservation in Indian Territory, now Oklahoma, in 1867. A number of other groups, probably multi-tribal and multi-ethnic and small in number, have survived in various locations to the present time.

Their early population was about 9,000 before a decline due to diseases, warfare and absorption into other groups. Their present distribution, by no means all Potawatomi and many no longer living within these communities, is as follows: "Prairie band" near Mayetta, Kansas, about 2,000 plus a number with the Kickapoo near Horton; the "Citizen Potawatomi" of Cleveland and Pottawatomie Counties, Oklahoma, locally 3,000; the Hannahville Community in Upper Michigan, 300; two settlements in Forest County, Wisconsin, 400; two groups in southern Michigan, Potawatomi of Huron and Pokagon, 400; a few are found with the Menomini and Winnebago, 100. In Canada there are substantial numbers with Ojibwa and Ottawa at Walpole Island, Sarnia, Kettle Point and other locations in Ontario. Their total population given in 1970 was 4,626 in the U.S. and 863 in Canada. In 1970 less than 1,000 people still spoke their language.

The most conservative groups were the Forest County Wisconsin and Prairie band Kansas divisions of the tribe; the former were reported to live in appalling poverty as late as 1951. This group retained the Medicine Dance society, War Dance, and the Dream or Drum Dance, a variant of the Plains Grass Dance which spread through the woodlands promoting friendship. The ceremony centres on a large decorated drum symbolizing friendship even with whites, which is treated with great reverence. Both groups have the Peyote cult which spread north during the early reservation period – a part-Christian and part-Indian religion involving the consuming of peyote buttons, a mild narcotic, during night-long rituals, sometimes held in a tipi to aid the sick. Some Kansas Potawatomi are members of the Kenekuk Church founded by a Kickapoo divine in the 19th century; they have sponsored large Pan-Indian Powwows in recent times on their reservation near Mayetta, and participate in similar events each year on the nearby Kickapoo Reservation – the two tribes are now much intermarried. In past years the Potawatomi excelled in ribbonwork and beadwork, their dress costumes being stylistically similar to the Sac, Fox, Kickapoo and other central Algonkians.

MASCOUTEN A tribe of Algonkian-speaking people who probably once dwelt on both sides of the Mississippi near the present Wisconsin-Illinois border. They were very closely related to the Kickapoo, but were in constant warfare with their neighbours, and are first mentioned by French missionaries as inhabiting southern Michigan, where they had been driven by the Ojibwa and Ottawa. In 1712 they united with the Kickapoo and Fox, after being almost exterminated by the French and later by the Potawatomi. The remnant emigrated westward, and they are last mentioned separately in 1779 living with the Piankashaw and Kickapoo on the Wabash River in Indiana. Their name apparently means "Little Prairie People", a title now borne by the Potawatomi Indians resident in Kansas with whom they have sometimes been confused, although these people probably have no Mascouten ancestry.

KICKAPOO An Algonkian-speaking tribe closely related to the Sauk and Fox. The movements of the Kickapoo were so frequent that they cannot be associated with any one specific area, but it is probable that when first known to whites in 1660-1700 their home was in southern Wisconsin, probably around the Milwaukee area. They seem to have been in northern Illinois, Indiana, Ohio and around the Detroit area during the early 18th century, and later in central Illinois and Missouri, extending into country formerly occupied by sections of the Illini. Some worked their way east to the Wabash River, Indiana, becoming known as the Vermillion River Band, whilst those in Illinois became known as the Prairie Band. Their general culture was similar to that of the Sauk and Fox. Hostile to the French, they were later friendly with the English during the Revolution and the War of 1812; and a few joined Black Hawk in 1832. Both bands were in Missouri by the early 19th century and moved thence to northeastern Kansas (1832-1834); but some, wishing to remain free from white restrictions, were already moving to Texas. These ultimately decamped to Mexico where a settlement was established near Nacimiento, Coahuila; a basic forest Algonkian culture was re-established with modifications dictated by their new environment. In 1873 a number (100 or so) from Kansas moved to Indian Territory to a reservation based along the North Canadian River in present Lincoln and Pottawatomi Counties, Oklahoma, while about 250 remained on their Kansas reservation near Horton. These three communities still survive, although economic activities take many far outside their boundaries.

The Oklahoma Kickapoo number about 500, the Kansas group 400 (combined total given as 1,249 in 1970), and the Mexican band 400. Those in Oklahoma and Mexico have long been noted for their conservatism; and the Kansas group are notable for their adherence to the Kenekuk Church – a nativistic movement, part-Christian, based on the reserve and still active, although its members are mostly Potawatomis, with whom they are much mixed. They also have a buffalo herd and a bingo hall, and organise a fine annual Powwow on the reservation.

SAUK or **SAC** An Algonkian people very closely related to the Fox or Mesquakie, formerly living in the vicinity of Green Bay, Wisconsin, towards the end of the 17th century. Their traditional subsistence was identical with that of the Fox, combining hunting with growing maize, beans and squash. Their social organization consisted of about 12 patrilineal clans whose functions were to arrange the various sacred packs ceremonies. Disputes with French traders led to the initial confederation of the Sauks and the Foxes and their migration south from Wisconsin to present Iowa and parts of northern Illinois.

Their treaties with the U.S. Government in the early 19th century , which ceded their lands in Illinois and Wisconsin, were not agreed by all their bands; this led to the Black Hawk War of 1832 when they attempted to re-establish control of an old village site near Rock Island, but, hopelessly outnumbered, Black Hawk was finally driven back into Iowa. In 1837 the combined tribes ceded their Iowa lands and were assigned to a reservation in Kansas; but factional disputes resulted in a band of Fox settling at Tama, Iowa, where they remain separate. The remaining Sauk with a few Fox removed from Kansas to Oklahoma (then Indian Territory) and were assigned lands between the Cimarron River and the north fork of the Canadian River, except for one small group who retained land near the Kansas/Nebraska border. The Sauks' interaction with the U.S. Government in the first half of the 19th century led to a division between the so-called "British" band and a faction friendly to the Government led by Keokuk and his followers.

The present descendants of the Oklahoma Sac and Fox live around allotted lands near Stroud and Cushing, Oklahoma, reported as 996 in 1950, when the small group near White Cloud, Kansas, numbered 129. The Oklahoma bands have an annual Powwow of the Pan-Indian type near the tribal administration complex eight miles south of Stroud, Oklahoma, each summer, which incorporates what little remains of traditional Indian culture and reinforces their tribal unity. The Oklahoma Sauk are officially called the "Sac and Fox tribe of the Missouri".

FOX or **MESQUAKIE** Early reports located the Mesquakie along the Fox River in Wisconsin, living in rectangular bark lodges large enough to accommodate several families, with shelves several feet off the ground on both sides for sleeping and storage of food. They had extensive gardens where squash, beans and corn were grown, usually tended by women. After the harvest was completed the grain and dried squash were cached and the men went on the winter hunts, sometimes making excursions into buffalo country. They also hunted deer and other game to subsidize their horticulture. In recent times the Mesquakie lived usually in wigwams or wickiups of mat-covered bent poles. Their name for themselves is "Red Earth People" which distinguished them from their kinsmen the Sauk, the "Yellow Earth People".

They seem to have been known to French missionaries after about 1640, but were later hostile to the French, who in 1746 drove them from their homes to the Wisconsin River, where they remained until withdrawing to Iowa at the beginning of the 19th century. They united with the Sauk after the Black Hawk War of 1832 in Iowa and in 1842 removed to Kansas; but a number, mostly Mesquakie, established themselves near Tama, Iowa, and have remained there to the present time, their settlement for years a stronghold of traditional Indian beliefs and religious practices. The present population of the Iowa Fox is about 750, although a number live in industrial communities away from the reservation. They have been noted in the past for the production of fine beadwork, ribbonwork and metalwork, and are still producers of fine ceremonial and dance costume. A number also accompanied their kinsmen the Sauk to Kansas and Oklahoma and are officially the "Sac and Fox" tribe because of their combined dealings with the U.S. Government during the 19th century. Their language is still spoken by a number of the tribe at Tama, Iowa. Confusingly, the Tama Mesquakie are officially called the "Sac and Fox of the Mississippi in Iowa".

MENOMINI or **MENOMINEE** An Algonkian tribe located on or near the Menominee River, Wisconsin, who were a typical forest people with a subsistence economy based on hunting, fishing and gathering, although one of their main industries was the harvest of wild rice. Their beliefs included recognition of spirits above the earth, usually considered benevolent, and those of the underworld, such as the underwater panthers, who were dangerous; they shared most of their major ceremonies with the Chippewa, such as the Midewiwin and Dream Dance, and acknowledged the trickster culture hero called (by the Ojibwa) Nanabozho.

They were probably first known to the French (Nicolas Perrot) in 1667; a fort was later built at La Baye on the site of present Green Bay, Wisconsin, which became a French settlement. They were usually firm friends of the French, with whom they often intermarried. They quickly adapted to the fur trade, but in the 19th century the Americans encroached rapidly on Menomini territory; in 1854 they were restricted to a reservation in present Menominee County, Wisconsin, where their descendants remain.

Their history since the establishment of the reservation has witnessed factional disputes between the various religious organisations – Christian (Catholic), native traditionalists, and Peyotists – and social divisions opened between several different economic and ethnic groups. In time the traditionalists came to live principally around one community on the reservation at Zoar, these being partly intermarried Potawatomi. This group kept alive the Dream Dance religion said to be a variant of the Grass Dance of the Plains, along with other old customs. In 1961 the reservation was terminated by the Government on the grounds that they were largely acculturated; but their tribal lumber mill operation became uneconomical, exacerbating various social problems, and a campaign for restoration of reservation status was successful in 1973. They numbered about 3,500 when first known to whites; in 1970 4,307 were reported, all but a handful being of mixed blood. During the 19th century they excelled in beadwork and ribbonwork. They still hold an annual fair and pageant.

WINNEBAGO A Siouan enclave largely surrounded by Algonkians, with whom they shared their major cultural traits, who lived between the Rock and Black Rivers, including the Wisconsin River drainage, in southern Wisconsin. Their closest linguistic relatives were the Chiwere-speaking group: Iowa, Oto and Missouri. The Winnebago had a rich and complex cosmology: a layered universe, Earth Maker (perhaps before Christian influence, the Sun), Midewiwin, and the sacred war bundles, the focus of important ritual and the property of clans. They were noted by the French (Jean Nicolet) as early as 1634, and permanent contacts came after 1665 with the fur trade and the establishment of Prairie du Chien, which drew the Winnebago away from their earlier homes at Lake Winnebago and Green Bay to their location on the Wisconsin River.

They usually aided the French during the colonial wars, and took part in the conflicts with Americans until the treaties of 1829 to 1837. Many had removed to southern Minnesota by 1855, and in 1874 moved again, to a reservation in Nebraska purchased from the Omaha, where their descendants remain. However, not all the Winnebagos left Wisconsin, and others returned from Nebraska to form several small communities around Tomah and Black River Falls, Wisconsin. These two divisions remain today; the population given as 2,832 in 1970 was divided almost equally between the Nebraska and Wisconsin branches. Although most native traditions have fallen into disuse both hold Pan-Indian Powwows. The Wisconsin Winnebago have for years found employment in the tourist centre of Wisconsin Dells. Both groups have a sizable Peyote membership.

OJIBWA or **CHIPPEWA** One of the largest tribes of North America and the principal one of the Algonkian linguistic family. Their original home was Sault Sainte Marie, Ontario, and they were first mentioned by Jean Nicolet in 1640 along with other local groups no doubt related to them. They became deeply involved in the fur trade from about 1670, and in the course of the 18th century spread both east (Mississauga) and northwest (Saulteaux) even to the northern edge of the Plains (Bungi), with a range exceeded only by the Cree, and a descendant population today exceeded only by the Navajo. The Chippewa or Southern Ojibwa are those who spread into the Upper Michigan Peninsula, Wisconsin, Minnesota and the Lake of the Woods area of southwestern Ontario during the early years of the fur trade in the late 17th century in small, widely scattered, autonomous bands. These were not a tribe in a political sense; only in terms of language and some aspects of a commonly shared culture were they one people. Some bands of the Mississaugas and Southern Ojibwa seem to have forged an alliance with the Potawatomi and Ottawa, once designated the "Three Fires", who joined Pontiac's rebellion (1763); but their main energy was directed against the Dakota of central Minnesota, from whom they acquired rich areas of wild rice production.

The land of the Chippewa was a vast network of interlocking waterways, rivers, and lakes with small portages, which allowed relatively swift forest travel in their light birch bark canoes, refined to the most efficient design. Their technology reflected their forest environment producing, bowls, ladles, bows, arrows, snowshoes, lacrosse racquets, musical instruments, cradleboards and fish lures. Birch bark covered their wigwams of various shapes, and was fashioned into containers for carrying, storing and cooking. Buckskin clothing was replaced by cloth obtained from the traders, and its decoration for festive occasions featured the beads, ribbons and silver which they developed to replace quillwork and painting. During the 19th century they developed two distinctive styles of beadwork: one derived from earlier decorative forms using large areas of woven beadwork in geometrical forms, the other floralistic and sewn on black or blue broadcloth, the genesis of this style owed perhaps to the French Canadians with whom they mixed freely or other immigrant Europeans. They also continued the use of porcupine quillwork but this tended to be increasingly restricted to items for the souvenir markets. Their involvement in the fur trade gradually changed native technology: log cabins replaced wigwams, guns, knives, kettles, and steel traps replaced earlier indigenous equivalents.

Social organization was simple, based on family, bands and totemic clans named after an animal or bird, usually exogamous and patrilineal. Their religious beliefs centred on the cosmic force which inhabited trees, rocks, sky, earth and all living things; presiding over all was a paramount spirit, Manito, perhaps personalized as a result of European influences. The Midewiwin or Grand Medicine Lodge was a graded curative society with membership by payment, a feature of which was the shooting of the sacred shell into the candidate's body and subsequent restoration by the Mide priest. In later years they obtained the Dream Dance or Drum religion, an early offshoot of the Plains Grass Dance to which they added religious features.

They began to lose their lands by a succession of treaties after the War of 1812, although they were never transported to areas outside their original domain (except for a small group of Swan Creek and Black River Chippewa, who sold their lands in Michigan in 1836 and moved to join the Munsee in Franklin County, Kansas). They were gradually restricted to reservations in the northern parts of the Great Lakes states where, as the fur trade diminished due to the depletion of game, many gained employment in the logging industry; but these reservations were far from urban centres and the associated opportunities to move to a 20th century wage-earning economy. Consequently the reservations often suffered neglect, social problems, poor housing, poor health and low income. The loss of more reservation land as a result of the Allotment Act in the 1880s also undermined their landbase.

However, in recent times more have moved to urban centres, perhaps 20,000 people of Chippewa descent now living in major cities. Native organisations have now taken over more of the administration and control of their affairs, initiating new social programmes. The population of the Ojibwa (Chippewa) in the U.S.A. was given in 1970 as 41,946, with 50,431 in Canada (including Saulteaux and Mississauga). This figure would be greater, however, if non-treaty Indians were added in Canada. This population is largely of mixed descent, both from their early contacts and affiliation with French trappers and more recent intermarriage with non-Indians. The Chippewa Reservations in the U.S.A. are as follows: *Michigan* – Isabella, Beaver Island, Hog Island, Ontonagon, L'Anse, Bay Mills, plus a number of non-reservation communities; *Wisconsin* – Lac Courte Oreilles, Lac du Flambeau, Mole Lake, Lac Vieux Desert, Bad River, Red Cliff and St.Croix lands; *Minnesota* – Grand Portage, Deer Creek, Leech Lake, Mille Lacs, Vermillion Lake, Nett Lake, Fond du Lac, Red Lake and White Earth. Reserves in *Ontario, Canada* include Pikangikum, Islington, Shoal Lake, The Dalles, English River, Wabauskang, Lac Seul, Eagle Lake, Wabigoon, Rat Portage, Northwest Angle, Big Island, Whitefish Bay, Sabaskong Bay, Big Grassy, Manitou Rapids, Rainy Lake, Sturgeon Falls, Nequagon Lake and Seine River.

A number of reservations hold summer Powwows in which they present Pan-Indian dances; wild rice is still collected in a few places; but the spoken language and Mide religion survive only amongst older people or on remote Canadian reserves. Nevertheless, the Ojibwa/Chippewa are still one of the most important Native American peoples.

OTTAWA A body of Algonkians probably closely related to the Ojibwa, living around Manitoulin Island, Ontario, and the adjacent northern shore of Georgian Bay. Known to the French in the early 17th century, they later moved west and south ahead of Iroquois expansion. Their name seems to signify "trade". Their culture was much the same as that of the Eastern Ojibwa and Hurons, with hunting, fishing and horticulture, until their economy changed due to their involvement in the fur trade. During the late 17th century and in the 18th century they were reported in various locations – Green Bay, Chequamegon Bay, Keweenaw Bay – but gradually Michigan and Manitoulin Island became their main habitat. They ceded most of their Michigan territory during the 1820s and 1830s, and three bands from Ohio were granted a reservation in Franklin County, Kansas, in 1831, from where most moved to Ottawa County, Oklahoma in 1867. Here a highly acculturated group of descendants remain on their old allotted reservation, although many have now left the area.

Of those who remained in their homelands the descendants now occupy a number of reserves on Manitoulin Island and Cockburn Island, Ontario, the largest at Wikwemikong. Much mixed with Ojibwa, they are now usually known as "Odawa", reported as 1,632 in 1970. The Ottawa in the U.S.A. were given as 3,533 in 1970, of which the Ottawa County group in Oklahoma numbered about 500; the remainder live in Mason and Oceana Counties, also in the areas of Traverse City, Cross Village, Mikado, Oscoda and other locations in Michigan. The Ottawa language is still spoken at Wikwemikong, and a large Pan-Indian Powwow is held there each summer. In years past the Ottawa were known for their colourful quilled bark baskets and boxes, which were sold to generations of curio collectors and are often found in museum collections.

MISSISSAUGA or **SOUTHEASTERN OJIBWA** Part of the Ojibwa who remained close to their traditional homelands around Sault Ste. Marie, Ontario, and spread eastwards perhaps as early as the mid-17th century to trade with the French and Indian groups along the St.Lawrence; they filled the gap left after the destruction of the Huron, although resisted by the Iroquois. Some made peace with the Iroquois in 1701, forming a loose alliance (those usually termed Mississauga) on the Ontario peninsula along the east coast of Georgian Bay and around the southern end of Lake Huron. Although missionaries were active during this period traditional religion remained strong; but as the 18th century advanced a generalised Great Lakes Indian culture emerged with a blending of customs, dress and materials which reflected their interaction with Europeans and other tribal groups in the promotion of the fur trade. During the 19th century many bands in southern Ontario adopted farming, log cabins and wooden cottages along with more traditional pursuits, such as the collection of wild rice and maple sap. They hunted deer, and planted corn in a number of southern locations; they excelled in decorative arts – both porcupine quillwork, which they developed eventually for the souvenir markets, and beadwork.

By the end of the 19th century the easternmost groups were highly acculturated, and today many have left their small reserves (of about 50) to live in urban centres. Excluding any within the U.S.A. the following are the major Canadian groups: Walpole Island, Sarnia, Kettle and Stony Point, Rice Lake, Mud Lake, Scugog, Georgina Islands, Rama, Christian Islands, Cape Croker, Saugeen, Moose Deer Point, Parry Island, Shawanaga, Magnetawan, Henvey Inlet, Point Grondin, French River, Dokis, Nipissing, Whitefish River, Mattagami, Matachewan, Wahnapitae, Spanish River, Serpent River, a number of reserve bands on Manitoulin Island mixed with Ottawa (Odawa), Pic-Mobert, Goulais Bay, Garden River, Chapleau, Thessalon, Mississagi River, and others, with an enrolled population of 12,000.

ALGONKIN or **ALGONQUIN** A group of bands of the Ojibwa type who lived on both sides of the Ottawa along the Quebec and Ontario border, Canada. A number of bands were reported by the French, who had contacted them before 1570, but the principal 19th century groups were the *Weskarini* or Algonquin proper on the Gatineau River and other northern tributaries of the Ottawa; the *Abitibi* around the lake bearing their name; and the *Temiskaming* near Lake Temiskaming. Their history is one of firm friendship with the French; Champlain visited an Algonquin village on Morrison's Island in 1613 and established trade relations with them. They represented the northernmost penetration of a marginally agricultural economy in eastern North America, but were largely a hunting people who quickly adapted to the activities of the fur trade, which lasted until recent times. They carried on intermittent warfare with the Iroquois, but in the early 18th century were converted by Catholic missions and in part joined the Mohawk and Onondaga at Oka.

Their present descendants, with a mingling of French Canadian ancestry, number about 3,000, at Barrier Lake, Grand Lake Victoria, Lake Simon, River Desert (Manawaki), Argonaut, Hunters Point, Long Point, Kipawa, Timiskaming and Wolf Point, all in Quebec; plus the band at Golden Lake, Ontario, locally called Algonquin, but who spoke the Ojibwa language. They were once famous for their canoe building.

NIPISSING A branch of the Ojibwa from the Lake Nipissing area, induced by the French to join the Algonquins at the Oka Mission in 1742. They were involved in the French fur trade, and probably participated in attacks on the English settlers in New York. Since that time they have been a part of the Algonquins; but the present bands at Lake Nipissing and Dokis, Ontario, may also be their descendants, and together number about 800.

IROQUOIAN

One of the most important linguistic families of the Eastern woodlands, consisting of a northern branch originally occupying the St.Lawrence valley from Montreal to Ile d'Orleans plus the Huron, Petun and Neutral of present southern Ontario, the Five Nations of New York State and the Susquehannock of Pennsylvania; a southern branch in Virginia and North Carolina comprising the Nottoway, Meherrin and Tuscarora; and finally a divergent southern branch, the Cherokee. The Laurentian groups noted by the earliest 16th century explorers (Jacques Cartier) seem to have disappeared by the 17th century or had perhaps reinforced the others. The Iroquoians were once proposed as distantly related to the Caddoans of the southern Plains, which fitted their assumed southern origins; but both propositions were subsequently discredited, since they seem to have been a northern people as far back as 1,000 B.C.

HURON An Iroquoian people who lived north and west of Lake Simcoe between Nottawassaga and Matchedash Bays, and were first contacted during the early 17th century by the French, who established missions amongst them. The Jesuit missions were able to record much of their culture at that time, and reported a sizable population of 30,000 in over 30 villages, some defended by fortifications but the largest number open and defenceless. They were slash-and-burn agriculturalists and gathered fruits, but were only occasional hunters and fishers. They seem to have been locked in a continuous war with the Seneca, which in 1648-49 became an invasion by the Five Nations in pursuit of expansion and control of the fur trade. Huronia was abandoned; a large number of Hurons were adopted by the Iroquois or fled west, although a few found refuge at Lorette near Quebec City. The Lorette Hurons have modified their culture with strong French Canadian influences over the years, and have constantly intermarried with these Canadians.

Huron (and some Petun) who moved west seem to have gone first to Mackinac and thence to Green Bay, but ultimately to the Detroit area and the Sandusky River region of northern Ohio by the early 18th century. Here they were known to the British as *Wyandot*, and were often involved in the colonial conflicts of the area. For those in the Detroit area a reserve was established in the Anderdon township, Essex County, Ontario, in 1790 but later ceded to the Crown, although a few people of mixed descent survived in the area until the 20th century. By 1817 the Wyandots in Ohio retained only two small reservations, and these were later sold. During the 1840s they removed first to Kansas and after 1853 to northeastern Indian Territory, now Oklahoma.

Throughout their later history they were much mixed with Euro-Americans, often factionalised between Christians and pagans. A number became "citizens" whilst in Kansas and never removed to Oklahoma, these numbering about 300.

By 1961 about 900 Wyandot descendants were recorded at the old Quapaw Agency in Ottawa County, Oklahoma, although only a portion lived on their old lands and just two elderly native speakers were left. A few remained in Wyandot County, Kansas, while 1,041 were reported from Lorette, Quebec, in 1969. The latter group were for many years noted for the production of fine craftwork sold to generations of white curio collectors.

PETUN or **TIONONTATI** An Iroquoian people living close to the Hurons about Nottawasaga Bay in present Ontario, Canada. In 1616 they were visited by Samuel de Champlain, and subsequently came under the influence of Jesuits, who reported two major sub-groups, the Wolves and the Deer. Their culture and beliefs seem to have been identical to those of their Huron relatives. They were also known as *Tobacco Nation* as they cultivated and traded tobacco. In 1649 they were attacked and dispersed by the Iroquois and, although they lost separate identity, a number united with the Hurons and apparently formed an element amongst the later Wyandots.

NEUTRAL An Iroquois people who lived between the Grand and Niagara Rivers in southern Ontario – five days' walk south of the Huron villages, according to early forest travellers. They were so named because they were neutral in the hostilities between the Huron and Five Nations Iroquois. As early as 1626 they were visited by Friar La Roche Dallion, who reported a large population. In 1650-51 they were largely destroyed by the Iroquois, fled west or were absorbed by the Seneca and others, and disappeared from history.

WENRO Part of the Neutral people but on the Niagara River; archaeological sites are attributed to them on the New York side of the international boundary. During the Iroquois expansion in the late 1640s they seem to have united with the Huron and lost separate identity.

ERIE Sometimes called *Nation of the Cat*; an Iroquoian tribe who lived on the southern shore of Lake Erie near present Erie City. A number of archaeological sites in the area south of Buffalo, New York, have also been given Erie status. Apparently they should properly be the *Nation of the Raccoon*, referring to the distinctive robes worn by these people. They became known to Europeans in the 1640s, by which time they were already enmeshed in the complex events of the fur trade, which resulted in Iroquois expansion and their defeat after 1653. The *Black Minqua* or *Honniasont* reported later on the upper branches of the Ohio River in western Pennsylvania and Ohio may have contained Erie descendants, but these too seem ultimately to have been reinforced and absorbed by other Iroquoian groups.

SUSQUEHANNOCK or **CONESTOGA** An Iroquois people of the northern branch of the family known to French Jesuits and Dutch and Swedish colonists. They lived in the valley of the Susquehanna River in present Pennsylvania; constantly harried by the Iroquois during the early 17th century, they also suffered heavily from epidemics. In an effort to contain Iroquois attacks they allied themselves with the Maryland colonists, but by the time of general peacemaking at Albany in 1677 they had been greatly dispersed amongst the Iroquois and Delaware. They continued to decline in numbers, the last of them being murdered by the Paxton Boys in 1765 – an atrocity denounced by Benjamin Franklin.

IROQUOIS or **FIVE NATIONS** A confederacy of five, later six, Iroquoian tribes living in the central northern area of present upper New York State, who, according to legend, were induced to form a league uniting formerly warring nations to preserve the integrity of each but to bind them to a common council with fixed delegates from each tribe. The date of the foundation of the league is probably about 1570 A.D., possibly in response to European contact. The traditionally reported founders of the league were Dekanawida and the historical Hiawatha. In a sense they were a simple democracy where lineage, clan and tribe were represented in policy-making. The league comprised the Mohawk, Oneida, Onondaga, Cayuga and Seneca, living in this order east to west across present central New York State.

They became frequent and bitter enemies of the French, but were friendly to Dutch and English traders working out of Albany; during the 17th century they launched a series of devastating attacks on related tribes who were under French influence, which established their supremacy in the beaver fur trade for a century or more. They were important allies of the British during the French and Indian War (1754-63); but the American Revolution (1775-83) broke them. The Mohawks, Cayugas and some Senecas fought with the British, the Oneida with the Americans. The Americans had laid waste to much of Iroquoia by the end of the war. The Mohawk and Cayuga mainly withdrew to Canada, the Onondaga and Seneca remained in New York, and the Oneida in time moved to Wisconsin.

Culturally the Iroquois seem to have been descendants of the pre-historic Mississippian culture, a complex derived from Meso-American agricultural practices. They raised fields of corn (maize), beans and squash flanking their semi-permanent villages, which supplemented hunting and gathering. The entire process of planting, cultivating, harvesting and preparation of food was in the hands of women, their leaders called Matrons. The ceremonial spirits of maize, beans and squash were called the "Three Sisters". Their religion was dualistic, with the object of pleasing the spirits both friendly and unfriendly. They seem to have had a Creator, at least in later ceremonial practices, and a belief in *orenda*, the natural power of creativity in all things. As the fur trade and ultimately farming became the principal lifestyle of Iroquois communities a curative image predominated in later Iroquois religious life, with important medicine societies such as the False Faces, a mask-wearing society devoted to group wellbeing and healing processes.

At the end of the 18th century, a time of despair for many Iroquois communities, a Seneca divine named Handsome Lake revitalized Iroquois religious life by introducing a strict moral code to a modified ceremonial life, partly influenced by Quakers. This "Longhouse" religion still survives in 12 Iroquois communities at the present time, preserving the remnants of Iroquois culture, language, ritual and drama for a small percentage of their descendants. The term "Longhouse" derives from their ancient bark dwelling which housed several families. From the time of the American Revolution they have gradually modified to a Euro-American culture and have for many generations lived similarly to rural whites, or more recently as wage-earners, a large number living in towns and cities away from their reserves and communities. Their population by 1980 exceeded 50,000 descendants, this total including a large number of persons of mixed European and other tribal ancestry added over four centuries of expansion, conflict and acculturation.

MOHAWK The easternmost tribe of the Iroquois League, who once lived mainly in the valley of the Mohawk River in present east-central New York State. After the formation of the League of Five Nations they were the "keepers of the eastern door" of the confederacy. With the encouragement of the Dutch traders at Albany they became perhaps one of the most aggressive peoples of the area, and were, no doubt, responsible for the depletion of some of the tribes on their borders. During the 17th century they were firm friends of the Dutch and British. The French explorer-soldier Samuel de Champlain had attacked their settlements and henceforth they were enemies of the French until, between 1667 and 1720, during breaks in the conflicts between France and Britain, more than a third of the Mohawks withdrew to French Canada under Jesuit missionary influence.

The Mohawks remaining in New York continued to support the British during the French and Indian War, and gave considerable assistance during the American War of Independence under Joseph Brant (Thayendanegea), an Anglicized Mohawk leader. At the end of the war the Mohawks in the British cause took refuge in Canada with a large party of Loyalists, and obtained a tract of land on the Grand River along with groups of other Iroquois until all six Iroquois tribes were represented (the Tuscarora having joined as a sixth nation). In 1784 another group established a settlement near Kingston, Ontario, known as the Tyendinaga Band. A few subsequently left for the west as fur trappers and finally settled in Alberta; a few others went to Gibson and Watha near Georgina Bay, Ontario.

The history of the French Mohawks developed quite separately. During the latter part of the 17th century they went first to La Prairie, where they were joined by some Onondagas and Algonkians. Subsequently they formed settlements at Oka (Lake of Two Mountains); later Caughnawaga (Kahawake) and St.Regis (Akwesasne) were founded. They usually assisted the French in colonial conflicts. All these groups have survived until today as reserve bands, and the Mohawk population consists of the following groups: Oka, on the north side of the St.Lawrence, Quebec – 1907 population 507, in 1970, 777; Caughnawaga, on the south side of the St.Lawrence – 3,198 reported in 1949 and 4,515 in 1970; St. Regis, on the U.S. border partly in Quebec, Ontario and New York 1,800 reported in 1945 on the American side, 1,100 in Quebec and 600 in Ontario in 1949. In 1970 2,963 were on the Canadian side. At Tyendinaga at Bay of Quinte, Ontario, 2,111 were reported in 1970, and in the same year at Six Nations Reserve on the Grand River, Ontario, 3,974 were reported as Mohawk by descent. A few are at Gibson and Watha on Parry Sound, Georgina Bay, Ontario, given as 206 in 1970; and a few (called Michel's band) in Alberta, descendants of fur traders, numbered 125 of mixed descent in 1949.

These figures give a present population in excess of 15,000, although largely of mixed ancestry. They are noted for having accepted the various forms of Christianity, although a Longhouse is now thriving on the St.Regis-Akwesasne Reservation amongst a largely Catholic population. Their men have also been noted in recent times for working as steel erectors on high rise structures and bridges throughout the U.S. and Canada. Recently several families from Akwesasne have established another community at Ganienkeh near the northern end of Lake Champlain.

ONEIDA "People of the stone", in allusion to the Oneida stone, a granite boulder near their former village: a tribe of Iroquoian stock forming one of the Six Nations of the Iroquois League. They lived about Oneida Lake and in the region southwards to the Susquehanna River. They were not loyal to the league's policy of friendliness towards the British and were inclined towards the French, being practically the only tribe to fight for the Americans in the War of Independence. They were attacked by Joseph Brant's Mohawks during that war, and were forced to take refuge in the American settlements until the war ended. Factionalism and a reduction in their land base in New York State persuaded a large body of Oneida to remove to new homes in Wisconsin, where the Menomini relinquished land for their use in 1838. Another group purchased 5,200 acres near London, Ontario in the 1840s, independently from the Oneidas already at Six Nations. A few remained in New York State at a small settlement near their old homes or on the Onondaga Reserve.

In 1926 some 3,238 Oneidas remained in the U.S.A., 2,976 on or near their Green Bay Reservation, Wisconsin, and 262 in New York State. In 1972 the Oneida of the Thames near London, Ontario, included 1,964 members, of whom 1,200 were residing on the reserve lands; and 802 Oneidas by lineage were reported from Six Nation Reserve, Brantford, Ontario, in 1973. A few hundred were mixed together with several Iroquois groups in New York, chiefly at the Onondaga Reservation or near the Oneida settlement. The Wisconsin Oneida had over 6,000 members but only 2,000 residents on or near tribal lands near Green Bay in 1972. The majority of Oneida became Christians before leaving New York, although a Longhouse minority survives at the Thames Band Reserve near London, Ontario.

ONONDAGA An important tribe of the Iroquois Confederation, formerly living on the mountain, lake and creek bearing their name in present Onondaga County, New York State, extending northwards to Lake Ontario and southwards perhaps to the head waters of the Susquehanna River. In the Iroquois Councils they are known as "they are the bearers". Their principal village, also the capital of the Confederation, was called Onondaga, later Onondaga Castle; it was situated from before 1654 to 1681 on Indian Hill in the present town of Pompey, and in 1677 it contained 140 cabins (500 population). It was removed to Butternut Creek, where the fort was burned in 1696. In 1720 it was again moved to Onondaga Creek, and their present reservation in New York State is but a few miles away.

Until the present century the Onondaga of the Grand River or Six Nations Reservation, Ontario, Canada had nine clans: Wolf, Turtle, Bear, Deer, Eel, Beaver, Ball, Plover (Snipe) and Pigeonhawk. The Wolf, Bear, Plover, Ball and Pigeonhawk clans each have only one federal chieftainship; the Beaver, Turtle and Eel clans have two federal chieftainships, while the Deer clan has three. The marked difference in the quota of chieftainships may be due to the adoption of other clans and chieftainships which have long been extinct. In the Iroquois ceremonial and social assemblies which exist to the present time, the Onondaga tribe itself constitutes a tribal phratry, while the Mohawk and the Seneca together form a second, and the Oneida and Cayuga (originally) and later the Tuscarora formed the third tribal phratry. The functions of the Onondaga phratry are in many respects similar to those of a judge holding court with a jury.

In the middle of the 17th century their population was 1,700, but during the 18th century the tribe divided; part stayed loyal to the League's historical friendship with the British while others, under the direct influence of the French Catholic missions on the St.Lawrence River, Canada, migrated there to form small Iroquois colonies – by 1751 about 800 Onondaga were said to be living in Canada. On the outbreak of the American Revolution nearly all the New York Onondaga, together with the majority of the other Iroquois tribes, joined the British; and at the close of the war the British granted them a tract of land on the Grand River, Ontario, Canada, where a portion of them still live mixed with other Iroquois groups. The rest are still in New York State, the greatest number being on the Onondaga Reservation and the others with the Seneca and Tuscarora on several reservations.

In 1906 those in New York were returned at numbering 553; in 1920 510 were returned from the Onondaga Reservation alone. On the Six Nations Reserve, Ontario, about 400 of a total Iroquois population of 5,400 were reported as Onondaga in 1955. In 1956 894 Iroquois were returned from the Onondaga Reservation, the greater proportion of these of Onondaga descent, although most tribal members have some white ancestors and an admixture from other Iroquoian tribes. In 1973 560 Onondaga were reported amongst the Six Nations at Grand River. The Onondaga in New York and Ontario continue to practise the Longhouse ceremonials including the Midwinter and Harvest rites. The New York Onondaga Reservation remains the theoretical centre of traditional Iroquois political and legislative life.

CAYUGA A tribe of the Iroquoian family and of the Iroquois Confederation, formerly occupying the shores of Cayuga Lake in present New York State. Their local council was composed of four clan-phratries, and according to tradition this form became the pattern of that of the confederation of the Five (later Six) Nations, in which the Cayuga had ten delegates. In 1660 they were estimated to number 1,500 and in 1778 about 1,100. At the beginning of the American Revolution a large part of the tribe removed to Canada and never returned, while the rest were scattered among other tribes of the Iroquois League. After the Revolution they sold their lands in New York; some joined the Seneca of Sandusky in Ohio, and some the Oneida who later moved to Wisconsin. The mixed Seneca-Cayuga ultimately found their way to Oklahoma.

The Cayuga of the present time are much mixed with the other Iroquois people, as well as having an admixture of white blood; the largest element of them in New York State are on the Cattaraugus Reservation, where some of their descendants have mixed with the Seneca. The largest number, however, live on the Six Nations Reserve on the Grand River, Ontario, Canada, where 1,450 were reported in 1955 amongst the general Iroquois population; the same group were reported to number 2,525 in 1973. On the Grand River today two Cayuga Longhouse congregations still number several hundred, and continue the traditional ceremonials organised by the Seneca revivalist Handsome Lake at the close of the 18th century. Another Longhouse group survives amongst the Seneca-Cayuga of Oklahoma – a group of many Iroquoian elements.

SENECA A tribe of Iroquoian lineage and of the Iroquois Confederation. They called themselves "people of the mountain", and were once the most populous tribe of the Iroquois Confederation, with a range in western New York State between the Genesse River and Seneca Lake. They became the most important tribe of the confederation, and on the defeat of the Erie and Neutral tribes they occupied the country near Lake Erie and south along the Allegheny Mountains. Consistently friendly towards the British, the Seneca fought for them in the French and Indian War and later in the American War of Independence, although some remained neutral. General John Sullivan destroyed Seneca villages and crops in 1779, and many fled to British protection. The last time the Seneca took up the hatchet was in 1812 during the American invasion of British Canada.

Instead of receding before the Europeans as their rapidly increasing population pressed upon their remaining lands in New York, they tenaciously maintained their ground, and when forced to make territorial concessions to the whites they managed to preserve a few tracts for their own use, which they continue to occupy. The present Seneca descendants are on three reservations in western New York at Allegany and Cattaraugus (the Seneca Republic), plus Tonawanda near Akron. The small Cornplanter tract in Pennsylvania was flooded by the Kinzua Dam in the 1960s. In 1890 these groups numbered about 3,000; in 1906, 2,742; in 1956, 3,528; and in 1970, 4,644. There are also several hundred Senecas amongst the descendants of the mixed Seneca-Cayuga of Oklahoma, and 345 Seneca were reported from Six Nations, Ontario, in 1973. Each Seneca Reservation has a Longhouse congregation, and the Allegany Senecas run the Seneca-Iroquois National Museum at Salamanca, New York.

MINGO In the 18th century detached branches of various Iroquois groups occupied parts of northern Ohio; these were usually known as Mingo – the name appears as early as 1750 – and they were constantly reinforced by kinsmen from New York. They were known collectively as "Seneca" by the early 19th century, when they had ceded most of their lands to the U.S. and settled on two reservations in Ohio: one at Lewistown on the Great Miami River (mixed with Shawnees), and the other on the Sandusky River near Fremont. By this time a number of Cayugas had also joined them, bringing total numbers to perhaps 500. They were subsequently forced to cede these reservations in 1831-32 for new lands in Kansas and, now called "Seneca of Sandusky", they were ultimately united with more relatives from New York on the Neosho Reservation. In 1869, after the Civil War, they and other eastern relocated groups of the area were reassigned lands in the southern portion of the Neosho Reservation within Indian TerrItory, present Ottawa County, Oklahoma. During the past century they have been known as the *Seneca-Cayuga* and, although their ancestry is mixed with a dozen other tribes and with whites, over 1,000 people are still members of the group (though only 11 fluent native speakers remained in 1962). A Longhouse with an annual Green Corn Dance is held each August near Turkey Ford, Oklahoma. However, most members of the group no longer live permanently in the area.

TUSCARORA An Iroquoian tribe originally of present North Carolina who divided from their northern kinsmen perhaps 600 years ago; they lived along the Pamlico, Neuse and Trent Rivers in north-eastern North Carolina in the piedmont and coastal plain. Their final defeat by white settlers in 1711-1713, following years of persecution and usurpation of their lands in the Carolinas, resulted in their move north to join the Iroquois League of New York State

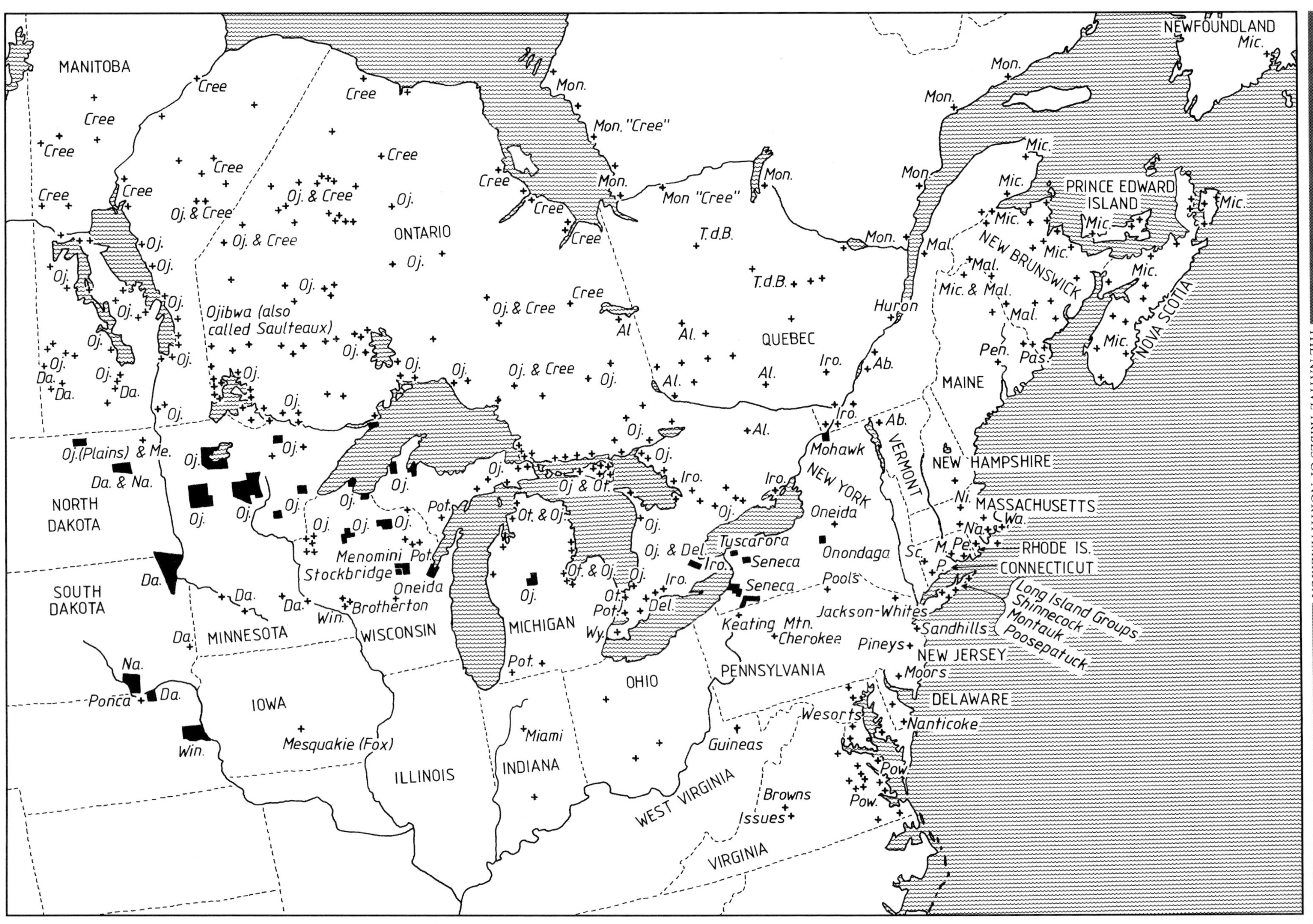
MANITOBA
Cree
ONTARIO
Oj. & Cree
Ojibwa (also called Saulteaux)
Mon. "Cree"
Mon "Cree"
Mon.
T.d.B.
QUEBEC
Al.
Iro.
Ab.
Huron
NEWFOUNDLAND
Mic.
PRINCE EDWARD ISLAND
NEW BRUNSWICK
NOVA SCOTIA
Mal.
Mic. & Mal.
Pen.
Pas.
MAINE
VERMONT
NEW HAMPSHIRE
Ni.
MASSACHUSETTS
Wa.
Na.
M.
Pe.
Sc.
P.
RHODE IS.
CONNECTICUT
Long Island Groups
Shinnecock
Montauk
Poosepatuck
NEW YORK
Mohawk
Oneida
Onondaga
Tuscarora
Seneca
Pools
Jackson-Whites
Sandhills
Pineys
NEW JERSEY
Moors
DELAWARE
Nanticoke
Keating Mtn.
Cherokee
PENNSYLVANIA
Wesorts
Pow.
Guineas
Browns
Issues
WEST VIRGINIA
VIRGINIA
OHIO
Oj. & Del.
Del.
Ot.
Pot.
Wy.
Ot. & Oj.
Oj & Ot.
MICHIGAN
INDIANA
Miami
ILLINOIS
WISCONSIN
Menomini
Stockbridge
Oneida
Brotherton
Win.
MINNESOTA
Da.
IOWA
Mesquakie (Fox)
Oj.(Plains) & Me.
Da. & Na.
NORTH DAKOTA
SOUTH DAKOTA
Na.
Ponca

as a sixth nation. They were formally adopted in 1722; nevertheless, there was a Tuscarora Indian band in Bertie County, North Carolina later during the 18th century, and the last of them did not move north until 1803. During the American Revolution part of them moved to British Canada, where their descendants are amongst the Iroquois of the Six Nations Reserve on the Grand River near Brantford; others remained in New York State on a reservation which bears their name near Niagara Falls. In the War of 1812 some Tuscaroras performed meritorious service to the Americans and protected the life of Gen. Peter B. Porter, and as a result Tuscarora women from their reserve were permitted to sell their craftwork on the Porter family property next to Niagara Falls for many years.

The tribe has been one of the most acculturated of the New York Iroquois groups; the lack of the diagnostic northern Iroquoian mask-making complex and the revised Longhouse religion that are associated with other Iroquois groups reflects the abandonment of native culture in favour of Christianity (Baptist) and rural farming. However, apparently not all of Tuscarora blood moved north; a number, perhaps mixed with Pamlico, Mattamuskeet and Machapunga, may have added a strain to the modern Person County Indians and Lumbees of North Carolina. In their North Carolina days they perhaps numbered 5,000. In 1890, 400 Tuscaroras were on their New York Reservation, and about 700 in 1970; those at Grand River were given as 789 in 1973. For the most part they are now a highly acculturated people.

EASTERN WOODLANDS TRIBES, 20th CENTURY

Key to abbreviations:

Ab	=	Abenaki
Al	=	Algonkin
"Cree"	=	Locally called Cree
Da	=	Dakota (E. Sioux)
Del	=	Delaware
Iro	=	Iroquois, Six Nations: Mohawk, Oneida, Onondaga, Cayuga, Seneca, Tuscarora
M	=	Mohegan
Mal	=	Malecite
Me	=	Métis
Mic	=	Micmac
Mon	=	Montagnais
Na	=	(in east) Narragansett; (in west) Nakota/M. Sioux, Yankton & Yanktonai
Ni	=	Nipmuc
Ot	=	Ottawa
Oj	=	Ojibwa (called in USA 'Chippewa')
P	=	Paugussett
Pas	=	Passamaquoddy
Pe	=	Pequot
Pen	=	Penobscot
Pow	=	Powhatan groups, incl. Pamunkey, Upper & Lower Chickahominy, Mattaponi, Rappahannock
Pot	=	Potawatomi
Sc	=	Scaticook
TdB	=	Tête de Boule
Wa	=	Wampanoag
Win	=	Winnebago
Wy	=	Wyandot

NOTTOWAY A small tribe of Iroquoian lineage who lived around the middle course of the Nottaway River in the southern area of Virginia in present Southampton County. A second tribe on the Meherrin River below them, the *Meherrin*, also of Iroquoian stock, were closely related. They are part of the same branch of the family as the Tuscarora. They seem to have acquired elements of Euro-American culture before the close of the 17th century, and the Nottoways finally settled on lands near Sebreel and Courtland, perhaps largely merging with African-Americans. In 1825 they numbered 47, but only nine were reported in 1859. Bill Lamb, who died in 1960, claimed to be three-quarters Nottoway and the last of his people.

Two other small ethnic groups may have completed this section of the Iroquoian family: the *Coree* and *Neusiok* or Neuse River Indians, who lived southeast of the main Tuscarora area, but almost nothing is known of them. Some Meherrins apparently left Virginia and crossed to North Carolina and reportedly had a reservation between 1705 and 1729, of which parts were still being sold by an Indian named Sallie M. Lewis (1838-1904) in the 19th century; a few people around the towns of Ahoskie and Winton in North Carolina still claim their descent. The last we hear of the Coree is a remnant who joined the Indians at Mattamuskeet Lake in Hyde County, North Carolina, after the Tuscarora Wars; a few descendants of these "Machapunga" survived until the 20th century.

SOUTHEASTERN WOODLANDS

Language family and tribe	*Meaning*/origin of tribal name, where known
Muskogean (except where noted):	
Apalachee	*"people on the other side"*
Chatot	-
Hitchiti	*"to look upstream"*
Alabama	*"to camp"* or *"weed gatherer"*
Koasati	*"white cane"*
Tuskegee	*"warrior"*
Biloxi (Siouan)	*"first people"*
Pascagoula	*"bread people"*
Ofo (Siouan)	*"dog people"*
Pensacola	*"hair people"*
Mobile	*"to paddle"*
Napochi	*"those who see"*
Chakchiuma	*"red crawfish people"*
Houma	*"red crawfish"*
Acolapissa	*"those who listen and see"*
Bayogoula	*"bayou people"*
Taensa (Natchez)	-
Natchez (Natchez)	*"warriors of the high bluff"*
Chickasaw	*"to leave"*
Choctaw	*"red"* or *"flat"*
Muskogee	*"swampy ground"*
Seminole	*"separate","runaway","wild"*
Yamasee	*"gentle"*
Cusabo	*"Coosawhatchie River people"*
Calusa (affiliation unknown)	*"fierce people"*
Timucua (")	*"earth"*
Yuchi (Yuchi)	*"those far away","yonder"*
Tunica	*"those who are the people"*
Chitimacha	*"those who have pots"*
Atakapa	*"man eaters"*
Caddoan*:	
Adia	-
Natchitoches	*"paw paw"*
Hasinai	*"our own folk"*
Kadohadacho	*"real chiefs"*
Iroquoian**:	
Cherokee	*"people of a different speech"*
Siouan***:	
Manahoac	*"they are very merry"*
Monacan	*"digging stick"*
Tutelo	-
Saponi	*"shallow water"*
Nahyssan	-
Occaneechi	-
Cheraw	-
Moneton	*"big water people"*
Keyauwee	-
Sissipahaw	-
Eno-Shakori	*"mean"*
Cape Fear Indians	-
Waccamaw	-
Pedee	*"something good"*
Wateree and others	-
Catawba	*"separated or strong people"*

* see p.82
** see p.35
*** see p.74

The agricultural basis which provided the northern woodland peoples with their subsistence economy provided an even stronger basis for the Indians of the southeastern area of the U.S.A. within the present states of Alabama, Georgia, Mississippi, South Carolina, Tennessee and neighbouring states to the north. The Circum-Caribbean and Meso-American influences on the prehistoric cultural horizons of the Ohio valley, such as Adena and Hopewell, called "Mound Builder" cultures, left a strong legacy with the later Mississippians whose descendants became known to the European. Whilst the Mississippian culture left agricultural practices, ritual and religious traits, social and class systems of honoured men and common people, Caribbean type material such as feather mantles, litters, wooden stools, platform beds, cane weaving, fish poisoning and blowguns, linking the Gulf tribes to the Carib of the West Indies, were equally strong.

The largest linguistic family of the southeastern area were the Muskogian people or smaller groups who may have been in lesser degrees distantly related to them, except for the Iroquoian and Siouan representatives and a few independents. The land occupied by these tribes was almost unbroken forest which once stretched from the Atlantic to the Mississippi, providing a varied supply of nuts, berries, roots, fish and game to add to the agriculture of the interior tribes. Villages were clusters of reed or bark covered dwellings, usually ranged along the rivers and creeks, with open central plazas or squares where the chiefs and nobles lived close to the council and ritual houses.

The most important religious festival projected to modern times has been the Green Corn celebration, or *busk* as it is called by conservative Creeks in Oklahoma; this is a maize festival, and part of a complex which extended from the Seminole of Florida to the Iroquois in the north. The celebration was an occasion of amnesty, forgiveness and absolution from crime; it lasted four to eight days and was performed in the town square, the "square grounds" of the present Oklahoma Creeks. The ceremonial involved the taking of emetic drinks which produced vomiting to ceremonially cleanse the body, around the lighting of the new fire constructed of logs pointed at cardinal points – a world renewal complex of doubtless Mississippian origins. The persistent and symbolic use of the colours red for war and white for peace, plus regard for the Sun, sanctification, priesthood, animal spirits, theory of disease and certain medical practices also echo back to Mississippian origins; but there were few animal medicine-societies such as we see in Iroquoian culture.

The southeastern tribes had regular trails running through the present Gulf states, allowing travel over long distances for war and trade. Canoes, usually the dugout type, facilitated some water travel. War parties were highly organised, made solemn and binding by pipe, calumet and war bundle ceremonials.

The French and Spanish explorers of the 16th and early 17th centuries saw these southern cultures in their pristine condition; however, by the 18th century many of the coastal tribes had been ruined by diseases and wars with the Europeans, who had also turned tribe against tribe in colonial conflicts. For a time the larger interior tribes maintained themselves effectively enough by wholesale adoption of European material culture and frontier life reflected in log cabin dwellings, clothing, domesticated farm animals, and the adoption of Christianity – the Cherokee even had their own newspaper and kept African slaves. This did not save them from removal to Indian Territory, now Oklahoma, where a substantial number of Cherokee, Creek, Choctaw, Chickasaw and Seminole survive, much mixed with white and African-American ancestry; although a group of Cherokee remained in North Carolina, Choctaw in Mississippi, Seminole in Florida and a few Creeks in Alabama.

MUSKOGEAN

This family constituted one of the largest of the continent and the one dominant in the southeastern area. They seem to fall into several dialectic divisions and a large number of so-called tribes. The extent of these are the subjects of considerable debate, since their movements were so numerous between initial contact with the Spanish in the 16th century and the more extensive contacts with the French and British in the 18th century. The dialectic groups were perhaps: (A) the Apalachee and their associates in Northern Florida; (B) Hitchiti, mostly in central Georgia, later becoming Lower Creeks, (C) Alabama in Alabama State, later becoming Upper Creeks; (D) Choctaw and Chickasaw in Mississippi; (E) Tuskegee Upper Creeks; (F) Yamasee-Cusabo; (G) Muskogee of Alabama and Georgia; then more diversely, (H) the Natchez of Mississippi, and (I) Calusa of Florida. The Muskogean linguistic family has in turn been distantly linked to the Tumucua, Yuchi and Tunican families, and more improbably to the Iroquois and Caddoans. The true Muskogeans had crystalized into the Creek, Seminole, Choctaw and Chickasaw by the early 19th century, when they removed to Indian Territory, now Oklahoma.

APALACHEE Once a large and powerful Muskogean tribe of Northern Florida, numbering 7,000 people, between the Aucilla and Ochlocknee

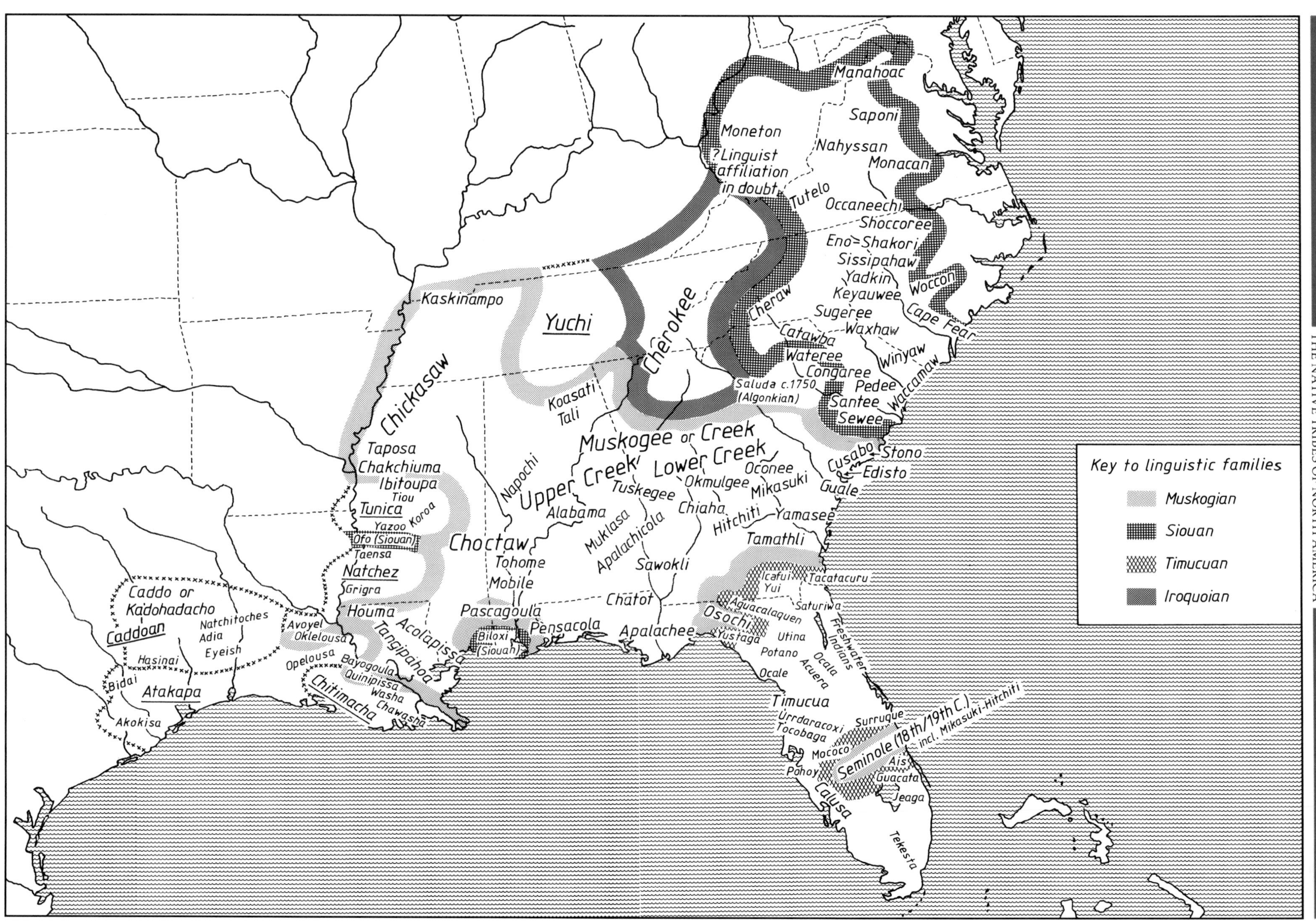

Key to linguistic families
Muskogian
Siouan
Timucuan
Iroquoian
Manahoac
Saponi
Moneton
Nahyssan
Monacan
?Linguist affiliation in doubt
Tutelo
Occaneechi
Shoccoree
Eno=Shakori
Sissipahaw
Yadkin
Woccon
Keyauwee
Cheraw
Sugeree
Cape Fear
Catawba
Waxhaw
Wateree
Winyaw
Congaree
Saluda c.1750 (Algonkian)
Pedee
Waccamaw
Santee
Sewee
Kaskinampo
Yuchi
Cherokee
Chickasaw
Koasati
Tali
Muskogee or Creek
Upper Creek
Lower Creek
Taposa
Chakchiuma
Ibitoupa
Tiou
Tunica
Koroa
Yazoo
Ofo (Siouan)
Taensa
Natchez
Grigra
Houma
Napochi
Alabama
Tuskegee
Okmulgee
Oconee
Mikasuki
Cusabo
Stono
Edisto
Guale
Chiaha
Hitchiti
Yamasee
Muklasa
Apalachicola
Tamathli
Choctaw
Tohome
Mobile
Sawokli
Pascagoula
Chatot
Icafui
Yui
Tacatacuru
Saturiwa
Aguacalaquen
Osochi
Yustaga
Freshwater Indians
Utina
Potano
Ocala
Acuera
Ocale
Caddo or Kadohadacho
Caddoan
Natchitoches
Adia
Eyeish
Hasinai
Bidai
Atakapa
Akokisa
Avoyel
Okelousa
Opelousa
Acolapissa
Tangipahoa
Bayogoula
Quinipissa
Washa
Chawasha
Chitimacha
Biloxi (Siouan)
Pensacola
Apalachee
Timucua
Urrdaracoxi
Tocobaga
Surruque
Seminole (18th/19th C.) incl. Mikasuki-Hitchiti
Mococo
Pohoy
Ais
Guacata
Jeaga
Calusa
Tekesta

Rivers around St.Marks. The Spanish gathered them into collective and defenceless mission towns, which were gradually destroyed by the Creeks and Yuchi (under British influence) from South Carolina, with a final invasion in 1702-1704. The remnant seem to have moved first to Mobile Bay and then to Louisiana or Oklahoma, where a few remained in the 19th century, but are now extinct.

CHATOT First contacted by the Spanish in 1539 west of the Apalachee on the lower reaches of the Apalachicola and Chipola Rivers of Northern Florida. They suffered the same fate as the Apalachee and moved to Louisiana in the 18th century, where a few remained later on the Sabine River, but nothing more is known of them. They perhaps numbered 1,000 in Spanish colonial days. Although geographically closest to the Apalachee, their linguistic relatives may have been the Yamasee and their associates.

HITCHITI A substantial group of Muskogean-speaking tribes forming a dialectic division of the family, divided originally into several tribes occupying the area about the Chattahoochee and Flint Rivers in Georgia, also at various times the Apalachicola River in Northern Florida. During the 18th century they became associated with and part of the Lower Creeks, and ultimately shared their fortunes and fate. The original tribes were the Hitchiti proper, *Apalachicola, Sawokli, Okmulgee, Oconee, Tamali (Tamathli), Chiaha, Mikasuki* and probably the *Osochi*. After forming the "Lower Creeks" during the 18th century some Oconee and Tamathli, joined later by Mikasuki, moved to Florida, and have become one of the two Seminole groups still associated with southern Florida. After the removal of the Creeks to Oklahoma a few Hitchiti, Apalachicola and Chiaha remained separate but are now counted as part of Creek Nation.

ALABAMA A Muskogean tribe on the Alabama River close to its junction with the Coosa and Tallapoosa Rivers in Alabama. They formed with the Koasati a separate dialectic division of the family, and came to be regarded as part of the Upper Creeks, although some retained their separate identity. They probably absorbed two smaller tribes who may have been closely related: the *Tawasa*, once on the Chattahoochee River, and the *Pawokti* of the Choctawhatchee River. After 1763 they began a movement westward which ultimately led in 1854 to the establishment of a reservation in Polk County, Texas, where they combined with the Koasati. Some moved with the general Creek emigration to Indian Territory, where descendants retain their identity near Weleetka, Okfuskee County. In 1700 they numbered perhaps 2,000; in 1944, 152 were returned as separate in Oklahoma, and 415 Alabama-Koasati were reported from Polk County, Texas, but largely of Alabama descent.

TRIBES OF THE SOUTHEASTERN WOODLANDS, c. 1600-1730
Linguistic and cultural boundaries are necessarily approximate; this sketch map is intended only as a general guide to distribution. Modern state boundaries are shown as broken lines, for orientation only. Note that the Caddoan family are included by some in the Plains cultural area; and that the linguistic affiliation of the Timucuan tribes is in doubt. Underlined names indicate small linguistic groups distinct from the larger groupings indicated by the shading key.

KOASATI or **COUSHATTA** A Muskogean tribe closely related to the Alabama, whose later history is associated with the area at the junction of the Coosa and Tallapoosa Rivers, Alabama. The *Muklasa*, another group of that area (Montgomery County), may have been an associated tribe. During the 18th century they became politically part of the Upper Creeks, and ultimately removed as part of the Creeks to Oklahoma in the 19th century; their descendants are found in Okfuskee and Hughes Counties. However, before this move a number had already settled on the Red, Sabine, Neches and Trinity Rivers in Louisiana and Texas; a number later joined with the Polk County Alabama in Texas; and others settled in the Kinder-Elton area in Allen, Jefferson-Davis, Washington and St. Landry Parishes, Louisiana. The Oklahoma Koasati numbered about 150 in 1950; the Alabama-Koasati of Texas, about 500 in 1970; and the Louisiana Koasati about 500 of mixed descent. There is good reason to believe that the *Kaskinampo*, an ancient tribe reported by the explorers De Soto, later Marquette and Joliet, on the Tennessee River in northern Alabama, were connected with the Koasati, and probably ultimately united with them or the Chickasaw.

TUSKEGEE A Muskogean people, probably related to the Alabama group. They were known at various times in several locations, mostly in Alabama, including the Tennessee River in the northern part of the state, on the Chattahoochee near Columbus, and near Fort Toulouse (Alabama Fort) on the junction of the Coosa and Tallapoosa Rivers, when they established themselves as an Upper Creek faction. With removal to Oklahoma they finally settled around Beggs, where their descendants are counted as Creeks.

(continued on p. 55)

PHOTOGRAPH CAPTIONS

Pages 47 to 54

(Unless specifically credited to another source all photographs are from the author's collection.)

(1) Eastern Sioux brave, c.1860s, probably photographed in Minnesota by J.E.Whitney. Note gunstock-shaped wooden club, and pipe with twisted stem and catlinite bowl, typical of western Woodland groups.

(2) The Crane, probably a Winnebago warrior, possibly photographed in Sioux City, Iowa, by Gurnsey and Illingworth, c.1860s. The buckskin shirt and leggings are intrusive, but the roach and turban are typical of western Woodland groups.

(3) Iroquois couple pounding corn with pestle and mortar, probably photographed on the Six Nations Reserve, Ontario, c.1890. The split log house is typical of the adaption to white rural life; one of the baskets appears to be of the native splint ash type. (Cambridge University Museum of Archaeology & Anthropology)

(4) Ojibwa (Chippewa) men on Red Lake Reservation, northern Minnesota, c.1900. Several wear heavily beaded bandolier pouches; the floralistic patterns are thought to have developed through a combination of European folk art with native curvilinear decorative traditions. (Courtesy St.Michael Mission, Fort Totten, North Dakota)

(5) Eastern Ojibwa (Chippewa) woman photographed at Muncey Town, Thames River, Ontario, 1907. Three small groups of Chippewa, Muncey-Delaware and Oneida-Iroquois have reserves south of London, Ontario. Although this lady is probably Chippewa she wears a characteristically Iroquoian cloth dress, cape, skirt and pouch. The same pouch also figures in a contemporary photograph of the Oneida Chief John Danford.

(6) Ojibwa (Chippewa) or Potawatomi baby, Wisconsin, c.1905, showing the protective wooden hoop characteristic of Woodland cradle boards; and the decorative cloth securing bands, unlike the laced bag used on cradles by the Northern Ojibwa and Cree of Canada. (Photograph W.H.Wessa)

(7) Seminole group, Florida, c.1895. A few of the Seminole people escaped removal to Indian Territory by surviving in the dense southern Florida swamplands. Before the 20th century development of their distinctive patchwork quilting they had adopted European-type clothes fashioned in unique styles, with these horizontal bands of contrasting coloured cloth stitched to coats and skirts.

(8) The Seminole Chief Billy Bowlegs, from a daguerrotype, c.1852. A leader during the Third Seminole War (1856-58), he wears a silver headband with traded ostrich feathers, and bandoliers of braided wool and beadwork. (Cambridge University Museum of Archaeology & Anthropology)

(9) Meraparpa or Lance-Mandan, probably photographed during a Mandan and Arikara delegation to Washington D.C., 1874. His buckskin shirt is decorated with quillwork strips; his hair is wrapped in fur, and the three upright, decorated eagle feathers perhaps signify warrior status.

(10) Blackfoot Brave Dog Society members, c.1910. (Harry Pollard Collection, Provincial Museum & Archives of Alberta, Edmonton)

(11) The Plains Cree Chief Poundmaker, photographed c.1880 by G.Moodie, Maple Creek, Saskatchewan. This important Cree leader, an adopted son of the Blackfoot Chief Crowfoot, was a guide for the Marquis of Lorne, Governor General of Canada, during a visit to the West; he was later imprisoned for his part in the Northwest Rebellion, 1885, and died the following year. He gave his name to a band and reserve of his people, still extant in Saskatchewan.

(12) Two Guns White Calf, a Blackfoot, photographed c.1910 with a youth, probably by Walter McClintock. He wears a fine buckskin shirt and leggings beaded in typical Blackfoot designs of the period.

(13) Blackfoot women, c.1910, probably by McClintock. Left, buckskin dress with elk tooth and beadwork decoration; right, trade cloth dress with basket bead and thimble decoration.

(14) Bird Rattler (1859-1939), photographed in 1927: after an adventurous youth this Blackfoot man eventually became a successful Montana farmer, a tribal judge, and keeper of the Piegan sacred Circle Dance Medecine Pipe Bundle until his death. (Photograph Glacier Studio, Browning, Montana; courtesy Ian West)

(15) Eagle Child: this superb portrait illustrates the facial characteristics of the Blackfoot Indian; and the flaring eagle feather bonnet, with white discs and horsehair trim at each feather tip, beaded browband and ermine drops, which replaced in popularity the "straight up" style during the late 19th century. (Glacier Studio, courtesy Ian West)

(16) Little Wound of the Oglala subtribe of the Western or Teton-Sioux (who today prefer the term Lakota), photographed by Heyn of Omaha, probably during the I898 Trans-Mississippi Exposition at Omaha. He wears typical ceremonial clothing of his nation, with the then-popular "war bonnet" with eagle feather trailer.

(17) Delegation of Brulé Sioux (Lakota) to Washington D.C., June 1870; left to right: Fast Bear (Mato Ohanco), a senior warrior of the Wazhazha band; Spotted Tail (Sinte Galeska), head chief of the Brulé subtribe; Swift Bear (Mato Luza), chief of the Corn Owners band; Yellow Hair, another senior warrior of the Wazhazha. Right rear is Capt.D.C.Poole, to whose Carlisle Indian School in Pennsylvania children were often forcibly sent for insensitive indoctrination in white ways.

(18) Joe Iron Pipe, of the South Piegan division of the Blackfoot nation, with his wife and son, c.1910. The lady wears a cloth dress with beaded belt. He wears typical Blackfoot full dress, with the traditional "straight up" bonnet, and holds a beaded guncase. (Provincial Museum & Archives of Alberta)

1

2

3

4

5

6

7

8

9

10

11

12

13

14

15

16

17

18

(continued from p. 45)

BILOXI A small Siouan enclave amongst the Muskogeans, located on the lower Pascagoula River and near Biloxi, Mississippi; they were noted by the French explorers Iberville and Bienville in 1699, but they may have come from the north not long before. The *Moctobi* and *Capinans* were possibly subgroups. Under French influence they moved to the Pearl River area until 1763, transferring later to the Red River country of Louisiana, and Angelina County, Texas. A few ultimately joined the Choctaw in Oklahoma and Louisiana. A number of their descendants are merged with the Louisiana Choctaw at Jena, LaSalle Parish, Lecompte Rapides Parish, and amongst the mixed Tunica-Avoyel-Ofo-Choctaw remnants in Avoyelles Parish – perhaps 100 or so of mixed descent. They never numbered more than a few hundred.

PASCAGOULA A tribe closely associated with the Biloxi but perhaps of Muskogean connection, on the Pascagoula River in Jackson, George and Perry Counties, Mississippi. Visited by Bienville in 1699, they later moved to Louisiana with the Biloxi and merged with local Choctaw in the 19th century.

OFO A small tribe of probably Siouan extraction who are believed to have descended the Mississippi River by 1673 from somewhere in southwestern Ohio, where they were known at one time to the French as *Mosopelea*. By 1686 some of them were with the Taensa, and as late as 1784 had a separate village above Point Coupée, Louisiana. A remnant is supposed to be merged into a mixed group of Indian descendants near Marksville, Louisiana.

PENSACOLA A small Muskogean tribe apparently of the Choctaw dialectic division, who occupied Pensacola Bay in northwest Florida when first known to the Spanish in the 16th century. However, by the time the Spanish post at Pensacola was established in 1698 they had moved inland and presumably westward. Their remnants merged with other groups, perhaps the Choctaw. They probably never numbered more than a few hundred.

MOBILE The largest of a group of Muskogean tribes who occupied an area around Mobile Bay, Alabama, when first known to the Spanish, who inflicting heavy losses in a battle with these people in 1540. Later they were farther north in Wilcox County, returning closer to Mobile post (the present city of Mobile) during the French occupation. They must have numbered several thousand in the 16th century, but perhaps only 1,000 by the mid- 18th century, combined with others. Their ultimate fate is unknown, but they perhaps merged with the Choctaw. The *Tohome* on the west bank of the Tombigbee River, Washington County, Alabama, and the *Naniaba*, were probably subdivisions or closely related. They gave their name to "Mobilian", a trade jargon used in the Gulf region.

NAPOCHI A tribe reported living somewhere around the junction of the Tombigbee and Black Warrior Rivers in Hale County, Alabama, by early Spanish expeditions. They may have become the Acolapissa, Quinipissa and Napissa of the 17th and 18th centuries, living in Mississippi and Louisiana.

CHAKCHIUMA A Muskogean people of the Choctaw group, known to Spanish explorers (1540-41) and later to French settlers in Louisiana. They seem to have lived around Leflore County in Mississippi at the junction of the Yazoo and Yalobusha Rivers. During the 18th century they were at war with the Choctaw and Chickasaw, with whom their remnants probably united (or they may possibly have joined the group known as Houma). Two other groups of the same area were the *Taposa*, mentioned by Iberville (1699) living close to the Chakchiuma, and the *Ibitoupa* on the Yazoo River in present Holmes County, Mississippi; these probably merged with the Choctaw.

HOUMA A Muskogean tribe possibly descended from the Chakchiuma; when known first to the French in the 17th century they lived on the east side of the Mississippi River in Wilkinson County, Mississippi. Later they established themselves near New Orleans, where they remained throughout most of the 18th century around Ascension Parish, Louisiana. During the 19th century they seem to have moved into the more inaccessible areas of Terrebonne and Lafourche Parishes, where as many as 4,000 of their descendants, virtually all French-speaking Creoles, are still reported around the Grand Caillou, Dulac and Golden Meadow areas. Claude Medford (1972) reported one lady who knew some of their words and phrases. He also suggests that the Biloxi, Atakapa and Chitimacha have combined with the Houma to form these descendants. In earlier times they may also have absorbed the Acolapissa tribes and the *Okelousa*, a tribe reported in the 18th century as having lived in Pointe Coupée Parish on the west side of the Mississippi in Louisiana, who may have been in turn descended from an ancient people of De Soto's time. These are not the Okelousa of Atakapan connection.

ACOLAPISSA A Muskogean tribe reported by Bienville in 1699 located on the Pearl River, Louisiana, but they may have been descended from the Napochi of the 16th century. In 1702 they moved to Lake Pontchartrain. Another people, the

Tangipahoa, on the river of that name in Louisiana, were probably an associate tribe. During the 18th century they seem to have moved to the Mississippi above New Orleans and merged with the Bayogoula and Houma. At the beginning of the 20th century a small Indian group were reported near Bayou Lacombe, St.Tammany Parish, Louisiana, who may have been of Acolapissa and/or Choctaw ancestry, but nothing has been heard of them recently.

BAYOGOULA A people of Bayou Goula, Iberville Parish, Louisiana, visited by Iberville in 1699. They seem to have been connected with the *Mugulasha* and *Quinipissa*, perhaps with the Acolapissa, as divisions of a single tribe numbering perhaps 1,500 in 1650. During the 18th century they seem to have merged with the Houma.

TAENSA A Muskogean tribe, related to the Natchez, who lived near present St.Joseph in Tensas County, Louisiana, and who were reported by La Salle in 1682. They moved several times during the 18th century, ultimately merging with the Chitimacha. Another group known as Little Taensa or *Avoyel*, apparently closely related, were mentioned by Iberville in 1699 in the neighbourhood of Marksville, Avoyelles Parish, Louisiana. A small mixed blood Indian remnant combined with Tunica, Ofo, Biloxi and Choctaw still survived in the area in 1980.

NATCHEZ This was the largest of a group of three tribes, including the Taensa and Avoyel, who spoke a divergent language of the Muskogean family, living close to the present site of the city of Natchez, Mississippi. After a bloody war with the French in 1729-1730 they were defeated, and their remnants ultimately settled amongst the Upper Creeks and Cherokee. A number accompanied the Cherokee and Creek to Oklahoma, where a few descendants survive near Braggs and Concharty, Muskogee County; a few other descendants are said to be amongst the multi-ethnic so-called Summerville Indians of South Carolina. They were generally similar in culture to the Muskogeans; they developed a sun worship with a perpetual fire in a temple, and a caste system of suns, nobles, honoured men, and commoners or "stinkards". They perhaps numbered 3,500 before 1700.

CHICKASAW An important Muskogean tribe of northern Mississippi and adjacent Tennessee and Arkansas, and at one time along the Tennessee River in Northern Alabama. They were located by De Soto in 1541; in the 18th century they were first in contact, then in conflict with French explorers and settlers during the colonial wars between France and Britain, when they remained consistent allies of the British. They fiercely repelled all invasions of their territory by other Indians and whites at least up to the time of the American Revolution.

In the early 19th century they gradually ceded their lands to American settlers and between 1836 and 1847 removed to Indian Territory, forming one of the so-called "Five Civilized Tribes", setting up a quasi self-governing nation with a capital at Tishomingo until the Civil War. During this period they seem to have completely modified to Euro-American rural culture, native culture, dress and ancient institutions falling into disuse. Their descendants live in several southern Oklahoma counties, particularly Pontotoc, Johnston and Love, and adjacent towns and cities. They are today largely of mixed Indian, white and African-American descent, numbering 4,204 in 1910 and 5,616 in 1970. Their closest relatives were the Choctaw.

CHOCTAW The largest Muskogean tribe, living in present south-central Mississippi when contacted by Hernando De Soto in 1540. Over a century passed before they were again contacted by whites, the French explorers Pierre le Moyne and Sieur d'Iberville. Like the Creeks, they grew corn as a staple crop as well as beans, pumpkins, melons and sunflowers; they had over 100 villages. Following French settlement in Louisiana in 1699, they formed a close association with the colony in their struggles with the Chickasaw and the British. During the American Revolution their warriors served on the side of the Americans; and in the War of 1812 they fought with Andrew Jackson against the Creeks. In 1805 they began a series of treaties with the United States; finally, in 1830 at the Treaty of Dancing Rabbit Creek, they ceded most of their remaining lands in Mississippi for new lands in Indian Territory, now Oklahoma.

Before removal west they had partly modified to a Euro-American culture, adopting garden vegetables, poultry, hogs, cattle, horses and European clothing. By 1838 some 18,000 Choctaws were in Indian Territory, forming one of the so-called "Five Civilized Tribes", having a separate form of government based at Tuskahoma until adopted into the state of Oklahoma. The acculturation process begun in Mississippi continued during the 19th century, so that little native culture remained. However, not all Choctaws moved to Oklahoma; a substantial number maintained themselves in several communities in Mississippi at Pearl River, Tucker and Bogue Chitto, Neshoba County, Red Water and Standing Pine, Leake County, Conehatta, Newton County, and Bogue Homo in Jones County. A few are also found near Jena and other places in Louisiana. The present Oklahoma Choctaw are

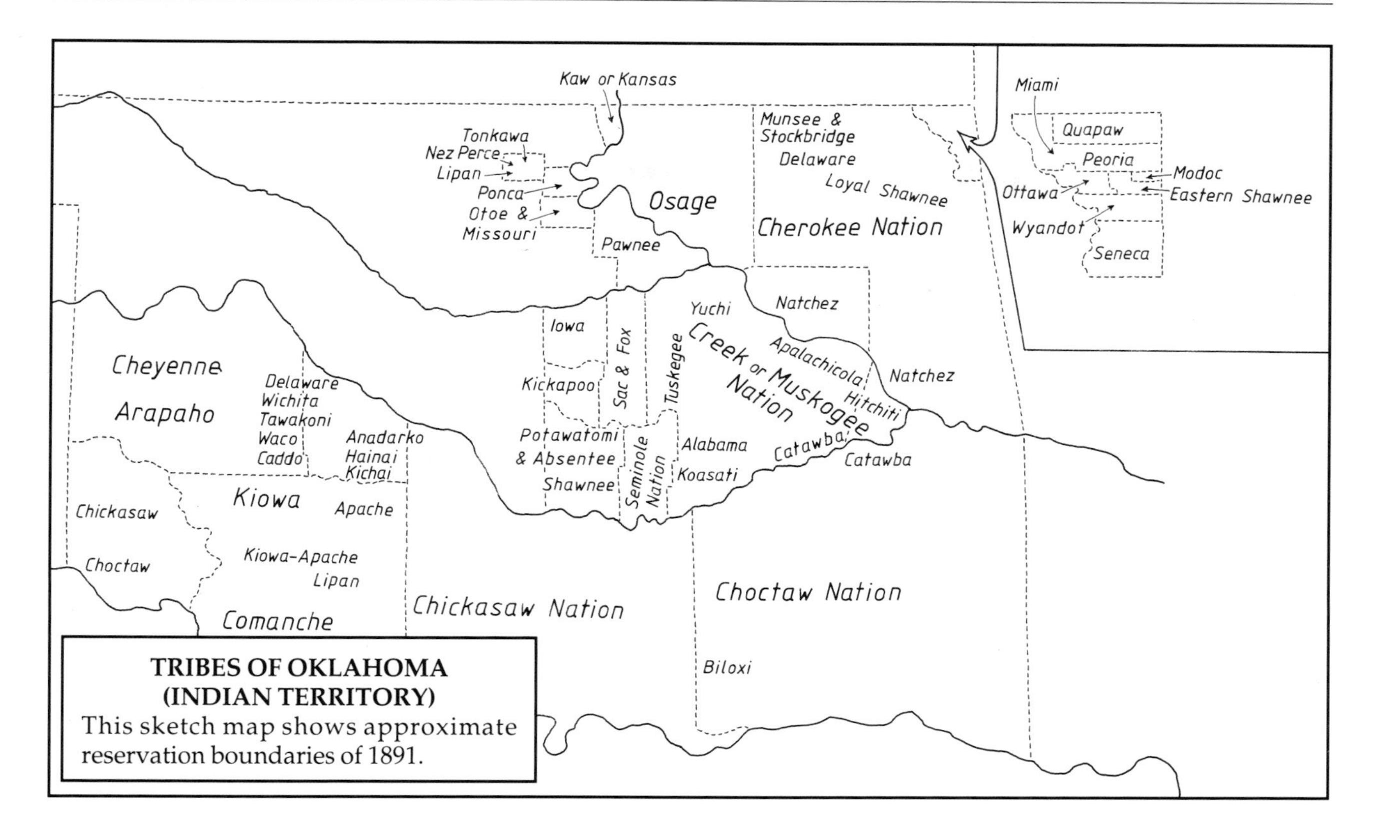

TRIBES OF OKLAHOMA (INDIAN TERRITORY)
This sketch map shows approximate reservation boundaries of 1891.

found principally in McCurtain, Pittsburg, Le Flore, Pushmataha and Choctaw Counties and in many towns and cities of southeastern Oklahoma; they were reported to number 19,000 in 1944. The Mississippi Choctaw were reported as numbering about 3,000 in 1950. A combined census of 23,562 in 1970 included Oklahoma, Mississippi and Louisiana Choctaw. The Oklahoma Choctaw are largely of mixed descent, with some white and African-American ancestry.

MUSKOGEE or **CREEK** One of the largest and most important groups of the Muskogean family, comprising a loose confederacy of tribes closely related by language in Georgia and Alabama, called "Creeks" by the British in allusion to their villages being located close to rivers and creeks. They were generally divided into two branches. The "Upper Creeks" of Alabama were centered along the Alabama, Coosa and Tallapoosa Rivers, comprising the *Coosa* and *Tulsa* in Tallapoosa County; *Abihka* in Talladega County; *Atasi*, Macon County; *Pakana* and *Tukabahchee*, Elmore County; *Hilibi*, Tallapoosa County; *Holiwahali* (who probably included the *Kolomi*, *Fus-Hatchee*, and *Kanhatki*) in Elmore and Montgomery Counties; and the *Okchai* and *Wakokai* in Coosa County. The "Lower Creeks" resided chiefly east of the Chattahoochee River in Georgia, and comprised the *Kasihta* close to the present site of Columbus, Georgia; *Coweta* on the Ocmulgee River, later moved near Columbus; and *Eufaula* in Clay County, Georgia and Talladega County, Alabama (some also emigrated to Florida and became Seminoles). During the 18th century both these Upper and Lower groups were reinforced by other local Muskogean groups – the Alabama and Koasati affiliated with the Upper Creeks, whilst the Hitchiti groups joined the Lower Creeks, and non-Muskogean Yuchi and Shawnee also joined the confederacy at various times.

The Creeks and Muskogeans generally were heirs of Mississippian horticulture, involving the planting of maize, beans, cane, millet, tobacco and sunflowers. They gathered nuts and wild fruits, hunted deer and bison in the west, and stored nut oil and bear fat. Their settlements were formed of a main town with small villages surrounding it; the towns contained a "square" where public and religious gatherings were held. Most tribes were divided into matrilineal totemic clans. Houses were of logs and poles with mud or thatched roofs, sometimes palisaded villages; later log cabins of the white frontier type were adopted, along with a considerable amount of Euro-American material culture, from the early 18th century onward. The Green Corn festival or *busk* was a major religious rite, a form of which still survives amongst a number of conservative Oklahoma Creek communities. Each town or small tribe elected a chief or *micco*. Certain towns were consecrated to peace and were designated "white towns", while others, set apart for war ceremonials, were designated as "red towns". From a method of time-keeping with sticks to record the days a war party might be on the trail, the term "Red Stick Creeks" was sometimes used by whites.

Their history in contact with whites begins with De Soto's expedition in 1540, and further Spanish contacts were made in 1559 and 1567. Later they became at first enemies but eventually allies of the British colonies of South Carolina and Georgia, and aided the British against the Apalachee (1703-1708) and Spanish Florida. After the Revolution constant hostilities with Americans climaxed in the Creek War of 1813-14, with the defeat and submission of Weatherford, their principal leader, followed by the cession of a greater part of their lands to the United States. In 1832 they finally agreed to move to new lands in the west – Indian Territory, now Oklahoma – and in 1836 the majority of Creeks made the journey, by land and river, in appalling conditions and at great cost in lives.

With remarkable fortitude they adjusted to their new rich soil lands along the Arkansas River, and organised a quasi-government at Okmulgee with a legislature composed of two houses – the House of Kings and the House of Warriors. The mixed bloods, descended from early European traders, claimed the largest tracts of good farming lands, while the poorer full bloods sought the rural back country. The Civil War disrupted the Creek, now one of the so-called "Five Civilized Tribes"; as slave-holders they were mostly drawn in on the Southern side, and subsequently lost many possessions as whites pillaged their country. After the Dawes Act in the 1880s allowed tribal lands to be allotted with spare domain opened to white settlement, a substantial proportion of their lands passed to whites.

The present descendants of the Creeks and their associates are in McIntosh, Hughes, Okmulgee, Creek and Muskogee Counties, Oklahoma, formerly Creek Nation; also in the cities of Tulsa and Sapulpa, and throughout Oklahoma and the United States. Their population prior to their removal from Georgia and Alabama was about 22,500; in 1857 they were reported to number 14,888. Later figures have been confused by the division into full bloods, Creeks by "blood", African-American freedmen and intermarried whites. In 1930, 8,760 were returned from Oklahoma; in 1950, 9,752; and in 1970, 17,004 including Alabama and Koasati. A few descendants of those who remained in the east live near Atmore, Southern Alabama.

SEMINOLE The later Muskogean tribe of Florida consisted initially of immigrant Lower Creeks from the Chattahoochee and Flint Rivers, Georgia – mostly Oconee and Mikasuki of the Hitchiti group, who occupied the area of Northern Florida following the destruction of the Apalachee people. They seem to have been known as Seminole from about 1775. More Creeks and African slaves fled into Spanish territory from hostilities in the Alabama and Georgia areas as the newly independent U.S.A. pressured the Creeks for land. These later immigrants, mostly true Creeks (Muskogee speakers) from the Upper Creek villages, tripled the Seminole population following the "Red Stick War" of 1813-14.

The Americans invaded Florida in 1817-1818 and destroyed African-American and Seminole towns in present Jefferson County. By 1819 Florida passed to the U.S.A. by treaty, and in 1823 the Seminoles agreed to move south to a tract of land in the centre of Florida. In 1832 a number of chiefs agreed to move west to Indian Territory, now Oklahoma, and subsequently the majority were induced to follow or captured and sent west; but a number continued stubborn irregular warfare, although continually driven south (the Second Seminole War, 1836-1842). Their leader, Osceola, seized while under a flag of truce, was taken to Fort Moultrie, Charleston, South Carolina, where he died in 1838. Although the majority of Seminoles had left Florida a few hundred were allowed to remain in the southern swamps, where a number remain today.

Those who were forced to move to Indian Territory formed one of the so-called "Five Civilized Tribes" in present Seminole County, Oklahoma, and their subsequent history is much the same as that of the neighbouring Creeks. Two "square grounds" are still used for old Green Corn festivals and ball games; but most Seminoles are Baptist or Presbyterian, and fully integrated into the economic life of the wider society of Seminole County. They number about 8,000 (1980 figures). The Florida Seminole remained largely independent from white influence until the early 20th century; they still occupy the Brighton, Immokalee and Big Cypress Federal and State reservations, plus land along the Tamiami Trail. Divided between Muskogee and Mikasuki (Miccosukee) speakers, they numbered over 1,000 in 1980. The Florida Seminoles still perform the sacred Green Corn Dance; and have also developed colourful quilted costumes which have become popular with tourists.

YAMASEE The most important Muskogean tribe of eastern Georgia, dialectically probably connected with the coastal tribes, though the Yamasee were always located inland on the Ocmulgee River above its junction with the Oconee. They are probably the "Altamaha" mentioned in 1540 and were in contact with Spanish missions in Florida in the 17th century, when some moved down to St.Augustine. They later appear in South Carolina in 1715 when a tragic war broke out between them and the English colonists, which largely destroyed them. A few ultimately joined the Creeks and Seminoles; a mixed blood group has survived in Burke County, Georgia, until recent times, although their connection with the old Yamasee is still unverified. This group is sometimes reported as "Altamaha-Cherokee" and numbers 100 or so.

CUSABO A Muskogean people of the coast of South Carolina between Charleston and Savannah, Georgia, and along the Ashley, Edisto, and Coosawhatchie Rivers. The *Guale* on the Georgia coast, the lower Savannah River and St.Catherines Island, in contact with the Huguenot colony at Port Royal from 1562, seem also to be connected with them. The Spanish from St.Augustine, Florida, made several attempts to missionize them until the arrival of English settlers in 1670. A number of Cusabo assisted Barnwell in his expeditions against the Tuscarora in 1711-12 and against the St.Augustine mission in 1720. They seem ultimately to have joined Catawba, Creek or Florida Indians, although a large multi-ethnic group known as the "Summerville Indians", who live in and around Dorchester County, South Carolina, may contain a portion of their ancestry, particularly from the Edisto River group. Spanish missionary influence on the Guale towns alternated with periods of warfare, thereby reducing them to submission until their virtual extinction in the 18th century.

CALUSA An Indian people of southern Florida, including all the groups south of Tampa Bay to the Florida Keys and Indians in the interior around Lake Okeechobee. They were visited by the Spanish as early as 1513, but missionary attempts do not seem to have been successful and were finally abandoned in 1569. Thereafter no permanent settlement was ever made by the Spanish in that area. They were nomadic hunters and fishers moving from place to place with nature's cycle. Despite their isolation they must have diminished rapidly in population from perhaps 3,000. A few remained until the Seminole came into Florida and some, no doubt, incorporated with them or finally crossed to Cuba; they are now extinct. They are presumed to have been of Muskogean connection, perhaps closest to the Choctaw, or alternatively to the Timucua. The following tribes were probably connected with them: *Ais, Guacata, Jeaga*, and *Tekeska*.

TIMUCUA or **UTINA** A collective term for the Indians of northern Florida, probably of the Muskogean family or a divergent branch, possibly a separate family. They lived in large houses grouped in permanent towns with extensive cornfields surrounding their villages. They probably numbered 13,000 when De Soto passed through their country in 1539, followed by French settlers who were supplanted in turn by Spanish in 1565. They were gradually conquered by the latter, and missionized by Franciscans. They rebelled in 1656; and suffered from pestilences which raged in the missions at various times. The remaining Timucua were concentrated into missions about St.Augustine, Florida, but continued to be harassed by northern Indians and the English. The last of them were in Volusia County, Florida, in 1736, probably ultimately becoming incorporated into the Seminole. The following tribes were perhaps associated with them: *Acuera, Fresh Water Indians, Icafiu, Mocoçco, Ocale, Pohoy, Potano, Saturiwa, Surruque, Tacatacuru, Tocobaga*, and *Yustaga*.

YUCHI An important southeastern tribe of Georgia who apparently lived in a number of locations including present-day Tennessee, but usually associated with Georgia and South Carolina, particularly the Savannah River country and even northern Florida. At various times they lived with the Creeks on the Ocmulgee, Chattahoochee and Tallapoosa Rivers during the 18th century. Their language is classified as a separate linguistic family or a very divergent Muskogean branch. In general culture they were similar to the Creeks. The Yuchi moved to Indian Territory in two main groups: one identified with the Lower Creeks (McIntosh party), which arrived at Fort Gibson in 1829, and a larger party with the Upper Creeks from Alabama in 1836. During the Civil War they divided in sentiment between Union and Confederacy, basically echoing the old Lower and Upper Creek alliances. There were four Yuchi settlements in Indian Territory, near Depew, Kelleyville, Bristow and Mounds. In recent times they have been concentrated around Sapulpa and Mounds, and were reported to number 1,216 in 1949, although often counted amongst the general Creek population. The Yuchi still have two square-grounds where they hold annual Green Corn Dances in summer, one near Bixby, the other near Kelleyville.

TUNICA The Tunican linguistic family consisted of a small group of tribes that occupied the valley of the Mississippi close to where the present states of Louisiana, Arkansas and Mississippi adjoin. They comprised the *Koroa* on the lower Yazoo, but often reported in other locations; *Yazoo*, also on that river; *Tiou* on the upper Yazoo, but ultimately united with the Natchez after having been driven from their homes; *Grigra* on St.Catherines Creek, Mississippi, also adopted by the Natchez; and the *Tunica proper*, a few miles north of the junction of the Yazoo River with the Mississippi.

They were probably visited by early Spanish and French explorers, and missionary priests were in contact with them from 1699. They were usually firm friends of the French, and suffered at the hands of the Natchez as a consequence. After 1731 they gradually decreased in numbers, some remaining in their old haunts, others combining with other tribes, until some time between 1784 and 1803 when their combined remnants moved to an area near Marksville in Louisiana near the Red River. Here a small tribally and racially mixed group has survived until recent times. The whole group probably numbered about 2,500 before suffering the effects of European diseases, and by the early 18th century perhaps a few hundred were left. The census of 1910 gave 48 "Tunica"; and by 1970 about 200 Indian people of mixed descent are reported from Avoyelles Parish, Louisiana, including a few occupants of the old Marksville Reservation. They are, however, of Ofo, Avoyel, Biloxi, and Choctaw as well as Tunican ancestry. The extension of the language family to include the tribes other than the Tunica proper is largely circumstantial, although some authorities have suggested a connection with the Chitimacha and more distantly with the Atakapan tribes.

CHITIMACHA A group of three tribes forming a linguistic family who lived on the shores of Grande Lake, plus parts of the coast and delta regions of the Mississippi River in Louisiana: the *Chitimacha proper* of Grande Lake, *Chawasha* on Bayou La Fourche, and *Washa* in Assumption Parish. They went to war with the French in 1706 after the killing of St.Cosme, a missionary to the Natchez, in response to treachery against them. The war lasted 12 years, after which the eastern groups, Washa and Chawasha, settled near Plaquemine and gradually diminished. The Chitimacha at Grande Lake, however, retained a small reservation near Charenton, Louisiana, where a mixed blood remnant has continued to live.

The population of the whole group may have exceeded 3,000 in 1650. The census of 1910 returned 69, and that of 1930, 51. The Bureau of Indian Affairs reported 89 resident on the Chitimacha Reservation, St.Marys Parish, in 1950, although a total count including all descendants would be 300-400. They are famous for their basketry and a few women have continued the craft until recent times. In pre-French times, and in common with others along the lower Mississippi, their houses were of palmetto leaves over a framework of poles. They hunted deer with bow and arrow or blowguns with cane darts, collected vegetable foods, and planted maize and sweet potatoes. Linguists have linked them with the Tunica and Atakapa families into the Tunican stock, but this is largely speculative.

ATAKAPA A group of tribes who occupied the Gulf coast of Louisiana and eastern Texas from Vermillion Bay to Galveston Bay, including the *Akokisa* on the Trinity River, Texas; the *Atakapa* proper on the Neches, Sabine and Calcasien Rivers; an *Eastern Atakapan* group on the Mermenton River; and Vermillion Bayou *Opelousa* near present Opelouses, Louisiana. Later the *Bidai*, *Deadose* and *Patiri* – small groups on the middle course of the Trinity River, Texas – were added.

They were first noticed by Spanish and French explorers, including Bernard de la Harpe, who carried off some of them to New Orleans in 1721. In 1779 the Eastern Atakapas helped Spanish expeditions against the British. However, they had sold most of their lands to the French Creoles by the early 19th century, and ultimately disappeared. The Atakapa in the Calcasien Parish area near Lake Charles, Louisiana, held together longer, and the ethnologists Gatshet (1885) and Swanton (1907-8) visited the few remaining members of the tribe and recorded their language. A few Creoles and "Sabines" of the area claim their ancestry. Of the Texas branches nothing is known after about 1805. They are perhaps distantly related to the Tunica and Chitimacha.

ADIA A Caddoan tribe formerly located near present Robeline, Natchitoches Parish, Louisiana. Iberville found them in 1699; missions were later established amongst them, but destroyed by the French in 1719. By 1805 they were at Lake Macdon near the Red River; and in about 1830 the last of them joined other southern Caddoans and merged into a composite group "Caddo",losing separate identity. Another small tribe, the *Eyeish*, probably connected to them linguistically, lived on Ayish Creek, a tributary of the Sabine in northeastern Texas; they were visited by the Spanish in 1542, but by the early 19th century they were extinct or had joined other related groups. The Adia, Eyeish, Natchitoches, Hasinai and Kadohadacho constituted the southern branch of the Caddoan family.

NATCHITOCHES A small confederacy of Caddoan tribes in northwestern Louisiana, principally along the Red River from the present city of Natchitoches to Shreveport. The *Yatasi* were the largest subtribe of the group. In 1700 Bienville reported 400-450 members. Later they descended the Red River closer to French settlements, and probably united with French Creoles, or joined their relatives the Hasinai in Texas. They are no longer a separate group.

HASINAI A Caddoan confederacy of small tribes of northeastern Texas, including the *Anadarko* and *Hainai*, living on upper Neches, Trinity and Angelino Rivers in Nacogdoches, Rusk and Cherokee Counties. Encountered by the Spanish in the 16th century and by survivors of the la Salle expedition in 1687, they were missionized by the Spanish after 1690. They later moved west to the San Antonio area, to a reservation on the Brazos River in 1855. By 1859 their remnants were united with the Kadohadacho as a composite group called "Caddo" in southern Oklahoma, where their descendants remain. They perhaps numbered 3,000 in 1700, but are now not reported separately from Caddo.

KADOHADACHO or **CADDO** The largest of the southern Caddoan confederacies who lived in northeastern Texas and adjacent Arkansas and Oklahoma, particularly around the Great Bend of the Red River near present Texarkana. They were probably known to the Spanish and French before the establishment of La Harpe's trading post in about 1719, which cemented permanent white contact with them. They provided a bulwark against the northern Indians, and suffered as a consequence, withdrawing to the vicinity north of Shreveport, Louisiana. In 1835 the Caddo ceded their lands to the U.S.A. and moved to Texas, joining the Hasinai, Cherokee or Chickasaw. Those with the Hasinai on the Brazos River removed in 1859 to Indian Territory, where their descendants still live in the vicinity of Binger, Caddo County, now Oklahoma. They perhaps numbered 2,400 in 1700. In 1872 the composite "Caddo" including Natchitoches and Hasinai numbered 392; in 1944 1,165 Caddo were reported, and 1,207 in 1970, although now mostly of mixed descent through intermarriage with Euro-Americans and Wichitas.

They were originally a sedentary people, cultivating their fields and raising corn, beans and pumpkins like other tribes of the Southeastern Woodlands. They did take to horses, however, and raised livestock. Although now rural Americans, they still hold tribal dances near Binger and join the inter-tribal American Indian Exposition held annually at Anadarko, Oklahoma.

CHEROKEE A large and important tribe who once occupied the southern Appalachian Mountains, the Great Smoky Mountains and valleys of the upper Kanawha, Savannah, Hiwassee, Tuckasegee, Coosa and Tennessee Rivers in present eastern Tennessee, western North Carolina and northern Georgia and Alabama, comprising an area of 40,000 square miles. Echota, a settlement on the south bank of the Little Tennessee River, seems to have been considered the capital of the Nation. They were first known to Europeans following De Soto's expedition in 1540, and later held a great mountain area between the English settlements on the Atlantic coast and the French and Spanish garrisons along the Ohio and Mississippi. However, unlike their distant relatives the Iroquois, they lacked the political cohesion to assert a balance of power, and were often factionalised and divided amongst themselves. There seem to have been a number of minor dialects spoken within the group, but their distant linguistic connection with the Iroquoian family has been firmly established, although their separation from the parent stock may have taken place over 2,000 years ago.

They had over 60 villages, which were connected to the outside world by seven main groups of trails; by this means the Cherokees could visit the Iroquois, Chickasaw, Catawba and the Gulf tribes. Early Cherokee dwellings were built of poles covered inside and out with interwoven twigs or mixed clay and grass; some structures housed several families. However, by the 18th century Cherokees had largely adopted the log cabin styles of white frontier settlers, along with other European material, social and religious influences. At the centre of each village was a circular council house where religious, political and social gatherings took place. They were a farming people, growing maize, beans, squash, pumpkins and tobacco, these activities being largely controlled by the women. They also were gatherers, hunters and skilful fishers. They used bows and arrows and reed blowguns before the introduction of firearms. Pottery and basketry were expertly made, as were elaborately carved pipes, some of which have been preserved in museum collections. Europeans introduced horses, pigs and other farm animals, and the Cherokee became accomplished husbandmen.

The religious and political activities of the people were organised by the White Peace Organization, the rituals of war by the Red War Organization. Each had a complex round of ceremonials, including six great festivals held in the council house: Planting Corn, First Green Corn and Ripe Green Corn, Feasts of the New Moon and of Reconciliation, the New Fire Rite and Bounding Bush Feast. The Red War Organization arranged war parties and victory dances. They also held the ball game indigenous to eastern North America, a rough team game still played by Eastern Cherokees.

The Cherokee were mostly on the side of the French in the French and Indian War and on the side of the British in the Revolutionary War; they became the object of hatred for land-hungry settlers, and peace was not restored until 1794. From this time until their removal to Indian Territory they suffered a period of increasing political pressure and cessions of lands, which resulted in groups moving to Arkansas and Texas. Finally, following the Treaty of New Echota in 1835, a large portion of the tribe, including most of the mixed bloods under John Ross, were forcibly removed to Indian Territory; this journey involved intense suffering and the loss of a quarter of their numbers – an episode known ever since as "The Trail of Tears". A number of Cherokee escaped removal; and in 1889 a reservation was formally established around a number of conservative communities near the Great Smoky Mountains, North Carolina. This is known as the Qualla Reservation of the Eastern Cherokees.

The Western Cherokee of Indian Territory, now Oklahoma, contained the highest proportion of the most acculturated members of the tribe, operating schools, newspapers, and churches and owning African-American slaves. They also included a number of conservatives who had moved west ahead of the main body in 1838. The Western Cherokees had a quasi National Government and were known as one of the "Five Civilized Tribes" of Oklahoma. As supporters of the Confederacy during the Civil War they suffered war casualties, and retribution under the Reconstruction Treaty of 1866; but they have maintained a substantial population within their old area in northeastern Oklahoma. In 1920, 36,432 were reported in Oklahoma and in 1930, 45,238; in 1970 they were returned as 66,150, which included the Eastern band, separately returned as 1,963 in 1930. The present Oklahoma Cherokee are largely of mixed descent and live predominantly in Cherokee, Adair and Delaware Counties, particularly around Tahlequah, their 19th century capital; however, members of the tribes live throughout the state and widely across the country, and have for the most part become one of the most successfully integrated Indian people in American society. The use of Sequoyah's alphabet in their schools during the 19th century was a major reason why the Cherokee rapidly became a literate people.

The Eastern Cherokee were a more conservative portion of the tribe until recent times. The present population is about 4,000, with a number of relatively full blood communities. They have retained the Ball Game (played by each man with two sticks to catch the ball, the object being to get the ball through a goal); old games, dances and basketry are seen at their annual Cherokee Indian Fair; and they operate a reconstructed "Oconaluftee Indian Village" and Museum. However, a now more dominant mixed blood element in the main Cherokee village have exploited the local tourist trade with the provision of "fake" Indian attractions in recent years. Both groups also operate outdoor dramas, "Unto These Hills", in an attempt to show their own version of Cherokee history. Besides the two main bodies of the tribe substantial numbers of rural people, in Tennessee particularly, also claim their ancestry.

EASTERN SIOUANS

A number of ancient tribes in the central eastern states of the U.S.A. are now included into an eastern branch of the Siouan linguistic family, largely on circumstantial evidence based on old historical associations. The linguistic position of the Catawba is well known as a divergent Siouan branch; however, a vocabulary collected from Tutelo descendants amongst the Grand River Iroquois in the 19th century, thought to be of Siouan extraction and much closer to the Plains languages, suggests an extensive distribution of old tribes of the Piedmont region of Virginia and the Carolinas who may have been Siouan in speech. The Tutelo and their Saponi kinsmen incorporated a number of remnant splinter groups before seeking refuge amongst the Iroquois. The formation and limits of the grouping are by no means fully accepted, however. The total population of the whole group exclusive of Catawba was perhaps no more than 6,000 in the 17th century. The ethnologist James Mooney suggested that the later Robeson County Indians (now called Lumbee) of North Carolina were probably of mixed Eastern Siouan ancestry.

MANAHOAC A small tribe, possibly of Siouan extraction, who lived about the upper Rappahannock River in northern Virginia, numbering perhaps 1,000. They apparently joined the combined Saponi, Occaneechi and Tutelo, but nothing else seems to be known of them after 1728.

MONACAN A group of small tribes who held the upper valley of the James River in Virginia; first contacted by colonists in 1607, they were still noted separately as late as 1702. A few people of Amherst County, Virginia, still claim their ancestry. They may have been of Siouan stock.

TUTELO A name given to several combined tribes of Virginia but specifically to those people around Salem, Virginia. Their remnants along with others were settled at Fort Christanna on the Meherrin River in 1714, and ultimately journeyed north to be formally adopted by the Cayuga in New York in 1753. Later their descendants moved to the Six Nations reserve in Ontario, where the last full blood Tutelo died in 1871, and the last speaker, John Key, in 1898 – though not before their language had been recorded.

SAPONI A tribe originally from near Lychburgh, Virginia, thought to be of the Siouan family due to their association with the Tutelo, with whom some merged at Fort Christanna before they finally united with the Iroquoian Cayuga in New York State in 1753. However, two considerable groups of mixed descent people survive not far from their old territory across in North Carolina in Person, Warren and Halifax Counties; called *Haliwa*, these claim Saponi ancestry. It is also possible that they have left an element amongst the modern Lumbee.

NAHYSSAN A small tribe whom John Lederer found in 1670 on the Staunton River, Virginia. Their subsequent history was probably essentially similar to that of the Saponi and Tutelo.

OCCANEECHI A small tribe who lived near present Clarksville in Mecklenburg County, southern Virginia. They seem ultimately to have joined the Saponi and Tutelo in the 18th century, and nothing further is known of them. They are thought to have been of Siouan stock by their association with the Tutelo.

CHERAW or **SARA** A tribe originally located close to Chattooga Ridge, in the northwestern corner of what is now South Carolina, when first contacted by Spanish explorers. In 1670 John Lederer reports them on the Yadkin River, North Carolina, and later they moved near the southern boundary of Virginia. The last of them seem to have joined the Catawba, and a number may possibly have merged with the Indians of the Lumber River. They are thought to have been of Siouan connection, and numbered 510 in 1715. The *Yadkin* reported on the river of the same name in 1674 may have been the same or a closely related people.

MONETON An ancient tribe west of the Blue Ridge in Virginia and the Kanawha River, West Virginia. They seem to have met Europeans in 1671 and 1674, but subsequently to have disappeared or merged with other tribes. On circumstantial evidence they have been grouped with the Eastern Siouan tribes.

KEYAUWEE A tribe found by Lawson in 1701 near present High Point, Guildford County, North Carolina. Despite reported plans to join the Saponi and Tutelo closer to the settlements about Albemarle Sound, the last heard of them is in 1761 when their town was located close to the boundary of the two Carolinas. For convenience they are classified as Eastern Siouans.

SISSIPAHAW A group who lived on the Haw River, Alamanee County, North Carolina. Lawson and Barnwell noted them, and later connected them with the Shakori. They apparently united with other tribes during the Yamasee War of 1715 against the English, after which nothing is known of them.

ENO-SHAKORI Probably two separate tribes: the Eno on the Eno River in Orange and Durham Counties, North Carolina, and the Shakori in Vance, Warren and Franklin Counties, who may have been identical to the Sissipahaw. They apparently combined in one village called *Adhusheer* in about 1700. Although they were encouraged to join other groups closer to the Virginia settlements for protection, the last heard of them is in South Carolina, when they probably united with the Catawba.

CAPE FEAR INDIANS Name given to the Indians on the Cape Fear River, North Carolina, who were probably known to early voyagers and friendly to early European settlements in the area. In 1711-12 their warriors accompanied Barnwell against the Tuscarora, and later aided the whites against the Yamasee in 1715. They probably numbered several hundred in 1600, and about 200 in 1715; and a few of the modern so-called Summerville Indians of South Carolina claim their ancestry.

WACCAMAW A small group of Indians, probably of the Siouan family, who lived on the Pee Dee River, South Carolina, near the border with North Carolina, about 100 miles northeast of Charleston. The *Woccon* may have been a division of the same people. It is possible that a number of their descendants are included in the Lumbee of Robeson County, North Carolina; and about 300 people of mixed descent perpetuate the name "Waccamaw" about 37 miles from Wilmington, North Carolina, near Lake Waccamaw in Columbus and Bladen Counties. The *Winyaw* were very probably connected with them in ancient times.

PEDEE A small tribe of supposed Siouan connections who lived on the Great Pee Dee River, South Carolina, and most probably closely related to the Cape Fear and Waccamaw. A few mixed descent people survived until the end of the 18th century.

WATEREE Probably the most powerful tribe of central South Carolina as far back as the time of the Spanish settlements at St.Helena, they lived on the Wateree River below present Camden. Although they aided Barnwell against the Tuscarora, their involvement in the Yamasee War of 1715 caused their ultimate decline; but they remained as a separate tribe until 1744, when they sold their remaining lands to a white trader and disappeared from history. Other small tribes who survived up to the Yamasee War period and who are assumed to be connected together in the Eastern Siouan linguistic group in South Carolina were the *Santee* of the Santee River; *Sewee* about Moncks Corner, Berkeley County; *Congaree* on the Congaree River near

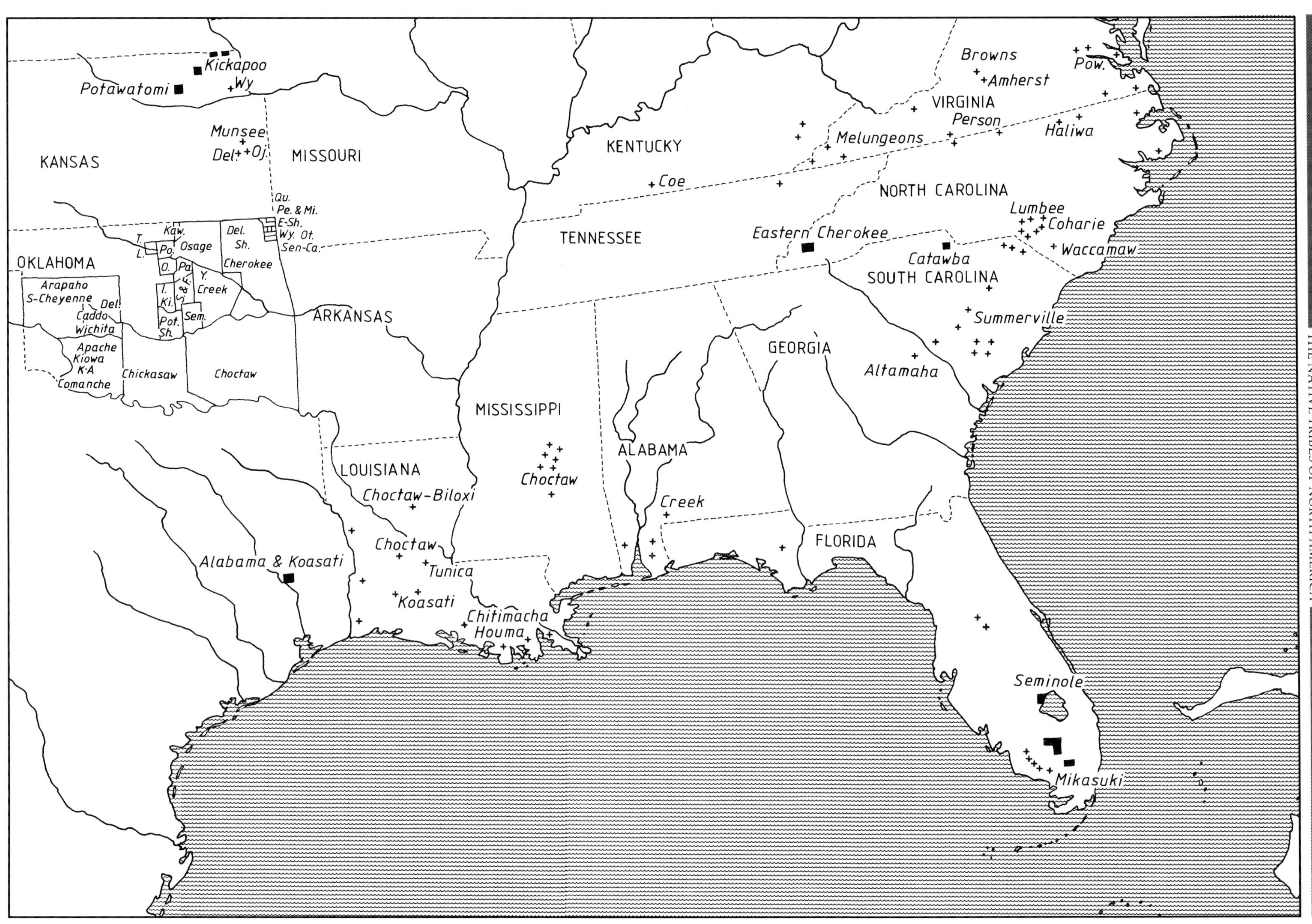

Kickapoo
Potawatomi
Wy
Munsee
Del+ +Oj
KANSAS
MISSOURI
KENTUCKY
Coe
Melungeons
VIRGINIA
Browns
Amherst
Person
Haliwa
Pow.
NORTH CAROLINA
Lumbee
Coharie
Waccamaw
Eastern Cherokee
Catawba
SOUTH CAROLINA
Summerville
TENNESSEE
Qu.
Pe. & Mi.
E-Sh.
Wy. Ot.
Sen-Ca.
Kaw
Osage
Del.
Sh.
Cherokee
OKLAHOMA
T.
L.
Po.
O.
Pa
Y.
Creek
Ki.
Pot.
Sh.
Sem.
Arapaho
S-Cheyenne
Del.
Caddo
Wichita
Apache
Kiowa
K-A
Comanche
Chickasaw
Choctaw
ARKANSAS
GEORGIA
Altamaha
MISSISSIPPI
Choctaw
ALABAMA
Creek
FLORIDA
LOUISIANA
Choctaw-Biloxi
Choctaw
Tunica
Koasati
Chitimacha
Houma
Alabama & Koasati
Seminole
Mikasuki

Columbia; *Sugeree* in York County; and *Waxhaw* in Lancaster County. They all suffered in consequence of the Yamasee War, some being sold into slavery; others emigrated to Florida or united with the Catawba, to whom most of them may have been related. A body of mixed blood people called *Summerville Indians* – descended from Winyaw, Edisto (Yamasee) and others – survive in Dorchester County and probably contain their ancestry.

SOUTHEASTERN TRIBES, 20th CENTURY

Compare Oklahoma section with p.57 sketch map of Indian Territory. This map includes communities today claiming Indian descent which are discussed briefly in our final chapter 'The Indian Today', e.g. Melungeons, Person, Lumbee, Summerville, etc.

Key to abbreviations:

Del	=	Delaware
E.Sh	=	Eastern Shawnee
I	=	Iowa
K-A	=	Kiowa-Apache
Kaw	=	Kaw or Kansas
Ki	=	Kickapoo
L	=	Lipan
O	=	Otoe & Missouri
Ot	=	Ottawa
Pa	=	Pawnee
Pe&Mi	=	Peoria & Miami
Po	=	Ponca
Pot	=	Potawatomi
Qu	=	Quapaw
Sem	=	Seminole
Sen-Ca	=	Seneca-Cayuga
S&F	=	Sac & Fox
Sh	=	Shawnee
T	=	Tonkawa
Wy	=	Wyandot
Y	=	Yuchi

CATAWBA or **KATAPU** The largest of the Siouan tribes of the east, and the only representative of the whole group to survive to the 20th century under their old name. Their language seems to have formed a divergent Siouan branch which possibly extended to include other tribes such as the Santee, Congaree, Sewee and Sugeree – small tribes whose remnants seem to have merged with the Catawba during the 18th century. They were probably contacted by the Spanish in 1566-67; and in 1701 John Lawson found them on the Catawba River near the present state boundary between North and South Carolina. Subsequently at constant war with the Iroquois and Shawnee, they were nevertheless usually friendly with the English colonists of South Carolina, aiding them against the Tuscarora in 1711-13 and later against the French and northern Indians. Smallpox reduced them in 1738 and 1759 and they never played a prominent role in history thereafter, although they served as scouts for the Americans in the Revolution. They continued to decline in numbers but obtained a reservation in York County near Rock Hill, South Carolina, a portion of which they have continued to occupy until the present time. During the 19th century a few Catawba people journeyed west and a few settled near Scullyville, Oklahoma, a number in Arkansas and a few with the Mormons in Colorado.

The York County Catawba numbered 490 in 1780; 450 in 1822; 120 in 1881; 166 in 1930; and 300 by 1970. They are of mixed blood; the last full blood Catawba, Robert Lee Harris, died in 1954, and the last fluent speaker of their language, Chief Sam Blue, in 1952. They are in dispute with the State of South Carolina for compensation for lands lost in the 18th century. In 1690 the Catawba probably numbered 4,000. They were skilful in making pottery and weaving baskets, and a few have continued these crafts until recent times.

PLAINS AND PRAIRIE

Language family and tribe	*Meaning*/origin of tribal name, where known	Language family and tribe	*Meaning*/origin of tribal name, where known
Algonkian* (except where noted):		Arikara or Ree (Caddoan)	*"horns"* or *"elk"*
Plains Cree	-	Omaha	*"those going against the wind or current"*
Plains Ojibwa	-	Ponca	*"sacred head"*
Sarsi (Athabascan)	*"not good"*	Iowa	*"sleepy ones"*
Blackfoot or Blackfeet	English, *"black moccasins"*	Oto or Otoe	*"lechers"*
Gros Ventre or Atsina	*"gut people"*	Missouri	*"people with dugout canoes"*
Assiniboine or Stoney (Siouan)	*"one who cooks with hot stones"*	Kansas	*"wind people"*
Cheyenne	*"red talkers"*	Osage	*"one who carries a message"*
Arapaho	*"trader"*	Quapaw	*"downstream people"*
		Caddoan:	
Siouan (except where noted):		Pawnee	*"a horn"*
Sioux or Dakota	*"allies"*	Wichita	*"big arbour"*
Mdewakanton -Sioux	*"spirit lake dwellers"*	Tawakoni	*"neck of land in the water"*
Wahpekute-Sioux	*"leaf shooters"*	Waco	English name
Wahpeton-Sioux	*"village in the leaves"*	Kichai	*"going in wet sand"* or *"red shield"*
Sisseton-Sioux	*"swamp villagers"*	Shuman (affiliation unknown)	-
Yankton-Sioux	*"dwellers at the end"*		
Yanktonai-Sioux	*"little dwellers at the end"*	**Kiowa**	*"principal people"*
Teton-Sioux	*"dwellers on the Prairie"*	**Uto-Aztecan****:	
Crow	*"bird people"*	Comanche	Spanish term
Mandan	Dakota name	Padouca	-
Hidatsa or Minitaree	*"willows"*	*see p.21	**see p.137

Of all North American Indians the former native inhabitants of the Prairies and Plains are the most popularly and widely known. Their area ranged from the Mississippi valley in the east to the Rocky Mountains of the west and from the Saskatchewan River in the north to the Rio Grande in the south. The western High Plains are very arid and are marked off by their short grass vegetation. The east, with a higher precipitation, is the Prairie, characterized by its dark soil and tall grass. The whole area was once home to teeming game, bison, pronghorn antelopes, wolves, coyotes, deer and bears. The main river systems run west to east to link to the Missouri and the Mississippi, along which forested patches were to be found.

The cultural traits which came to characterize the High Plains peoples were dependence on the bison (buffalo), limited use of roots and berries, limited fishing, absence of agriculture in the High Plains, use of the tipi, skilful use of bison and deerskins, rawhide, geometric art, and the travois; social characteristics included camp circle organisation, division into bands, and men's societies; and religious traits included the Sun Dance, sweat lodge and vision quest observances, and scalp dances. However, this culture was relatively late and was dependent upon the introduction of the horse, and to a lesser extent upon changes in tribal locations farther east pressing tribes into the eastern plains, together with the introduction of the gun, the fur trade and trade goods, causing continuous change from the 17th century onward. The tribes which are firmly associated with this way of life were the Blackfoot, Gros Ventre (or Atsina), Assiniboine, Crow, Sioux, Cheyenne, and Arapaho, all of whom entered the plains from the east; the Kiowa, who came from the north; and the Comanche, who split from the Shoshone.

The Prairie culture is much older and is characterized by semi-sedentary village tribes along the Missouri, Republican and Platte Rivers, whose subsistence was based on maize agriculture supplemented with seasonal hunting. Such tribes were the Pawnee, Arikara, Hidatsa, Mandan, Omaha, Ponca, Oto, Missouri and Osage. They had been influenced by the highly developed Mississippian culture which in turn developed from prehistoric Mexican impulses. Several elements contributed to the ultimate mix in Plains culture from this source: earth lodge dwellings, steatite sculptures for pipes, ceremonial and religious organisations, small effigy altar platforms, perhaps the medicine bundle complex and the calumet or peace-pipe complex. A third influence came from the Rocky Mountain tribes – the Shoshone, Salish and Shahaptian groups – whose mythology concentrated around the Trickster and culture hero Coyote, and seems to have been integrated into Plains Indian folklore. Marginal groups were the Caddoan tribes in the southeastern regions, partly modified eastern groups such as the Cree and Ojibwa in the north, and Apachean groups in the southwest. For three hundred years these three cultures intermingled increasingly.

The old Prairie tribes belonged to two language families: the Siouan, a word derived from the Sioux (Dakota), and the Caddoan. The Winnebago, a woodland people, were a remnant of the Siouans left in the east as they gradually moved west, then north and south to occupy the river bottoms and raise beans, squash, tobacco and corn. The Caddoans spread out from America's agricultural heartland; the Arikara followed the Siouan Mandan north; the Pawnee occupied the central Republican, Platte and Missouri areas; while the southern Caddoans were found in Kansas, Texas, Oklahoma and Arkansas – the Wichita erected their grass thatched lodges as far north as the Great Bend of the Arkansas. The three Blackfoot tribes were the vanguard of Algonkian movement in the north. The most important movement, however, was the appearance in the northern plains area of the Dakota from the prairies and woods of Minnesota. The Western Dakota turned into nomadic Plains Indians, plundered the Missouri village tribes and dislocated ethnic groups who were on their way west, such as the Arapaho, Gros Ventre and Cheyenne; the latter were a semi-sedentary group in the Prairie region until this period.

The final impetus in forming the Plains culture was given when horses were introduced from the Spanish colonies in the southwest. The horse was soon integrated into the existing culture patterns; it supplanted the dog travois, added the horse cult complex, and allowed these now mounted peoples to spread over the western plains. Two routes for the spread of horses have been suggested from the minimal documentation. One traces them from the Spanish and Pueblos in the Santa Fé area to the Utes of the Basin by 1640, thence to the Shoshone, thence to the Plateau and the Crow, and finally to the Blackfoot by about 1730. The alternative route combines horses from two sources, Santa Fé and San Antonio, thence to the Kiowa and Comanche, and thence north to the Dakota. From both probable routes horses were traded for corn and robes at the Mandan villages, and from them to the Assiniboine, Cree and Plains Ojibwa in exchange for European trade goods.

The religious patterns of the equestrian Plains tribes were partly a reformulation of the religion of the Prairie people adapted to the nomadic way of life in amalgamation of older features of different groups. The Prairie tribes reflected a half-sedentary way of life combining seasonal cultivation of the soil with seasonal hunting of buffalo; the corresponding religious patterns were a mixture of hunting beliefs and rituals connected with the agrarian calendar and social functions, notably the Calumet ritual, peace and war pipes, and ceremonies for the promotion of the growth of corn. The Pawnee developed a high god concept, star and cosmological mythology, medicine bundles, and even human sacrifices to the Morning Star.

The world view of the Plains and Prairie tribes conceived the everyday world of the Indian as a mysterious part of the great cosmic structure. Over this world the sky elevates its dome, the seat of the great powers – a Supreme Being, star gods, supernatural beings held by great supernatural power known to the Sioux as Wakan. Two great ceremonial stand out above all others: the Sun Dance, and the Okeepa of the Missouri village tribes, the Mandan.

The Sun Dance

The Sun Dance was the most important of all Plains Indian ceremonies, although missing among the Pawnee, Kiowa-Apache and Comanche (who held one Dance in 1874). The term Sun Dance is a misnomer, although male dancers gaze towards the

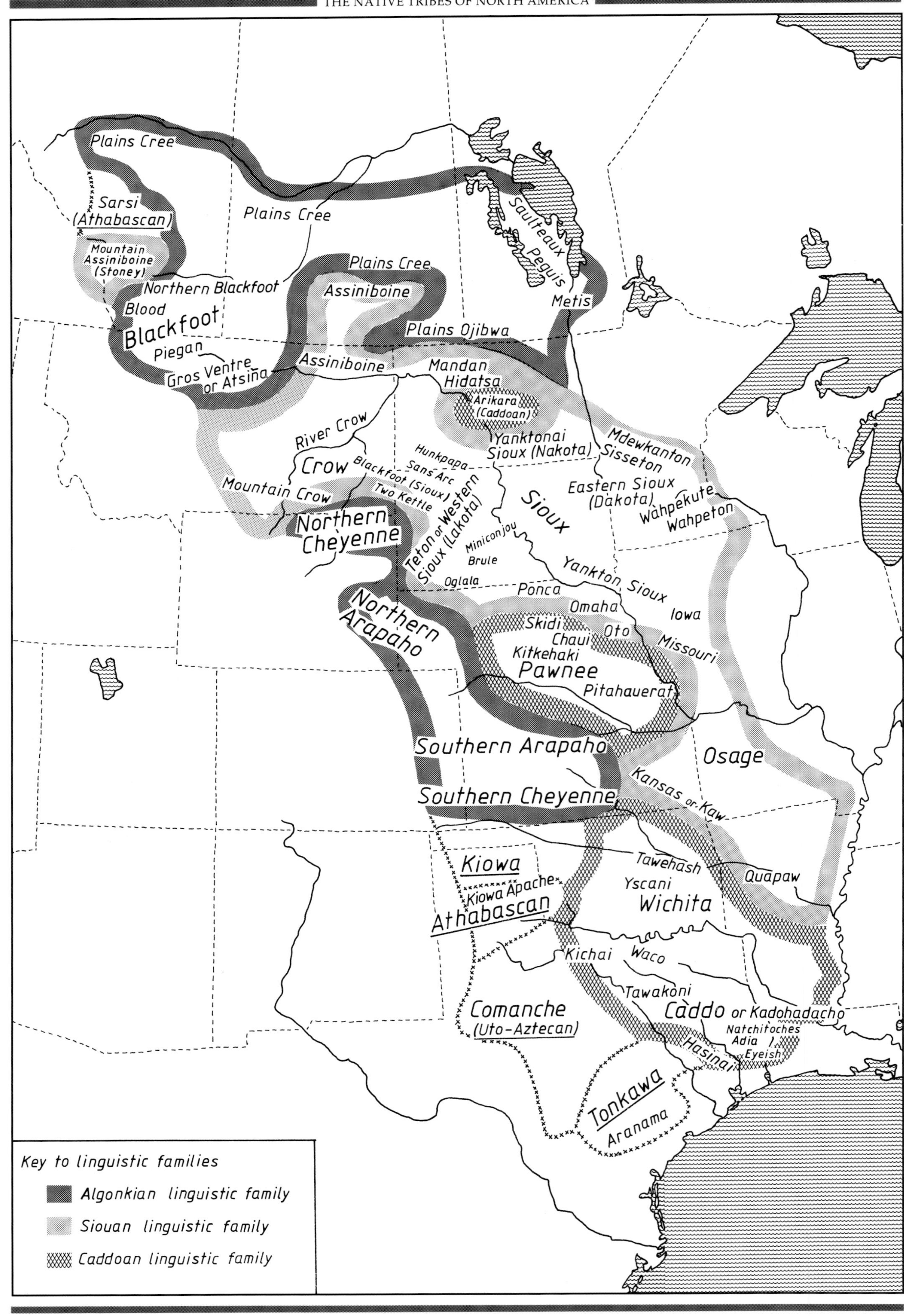
Plains Cree
Sarsi (Athabascan)
Mountain Assiniboine (Stoney)
Plains Cree
Plains Cree
Saulteaux
Peguis
Metis
Northern Blackfoot
Blood
Blackfoot
Piegan
Gros Ventre or Atsiña
Assiniboine
Plains Ojibwa
Assiniboine
Mandan
Hidatsa
Arikara (Caddoan)
Yanktonai Sioux (Nakota)
Mdewkanton
Sisseton
Eastern Sioux (Dakota)
Wahpekute
Wahpeton
River Crow
Crow
Mountain Crow
Hunkpapa
Sans Arc
Blackfoot (Sioux)
Two Kettle
Northern Cheyenne
Teton or Western Sioux (Lakota)
Miniconjou
Brule
Oglala
Sioux
Yankton Sioux
Iowa
Ponca
Omaha
Skidi
Chaui
Oto
Missouri
Kitkehaki
Pawnee
Pitahauerat
Northern Arapaho
Southern Arapaho
Osage
Southern Cheyenne
Kansas or Kaw
Kiowa
Kiowa Apache
Athabascan
Tawehash
Yscani
Wichita
Quapaw
Kichai
Waco
Tawakoni
Comanche (Uto-Aztecan)
Caddo or Kadohadacho
Natchitoches
Adia
Eyeish
Hasinai
Tonkawa
Aranama
Key to linguistic families
Algonkian linguistic family
Siouan linguistic family
Caddoan linguistic family

rising morning sun or centre pole during the public phase of the ceremony. The purpose of the ceremony is very diverse; basically, however, it is a re-creation ceremony or world renewal rite. The Plains Cree in the north considered it a thank-offering for the re-awakening of all nature after the silence of winter. They call it the "Thirsting Dance" because the participants did not drink during its performance. Formerly it was mostly held in June, the springtime of the northern plains; however, recent modified nativistic and part-Christian versions of the rite are usually celebrated in July and August.

Of all Plains tribes the Cheyenne had the most concisely and consciously preserved meaning of the Sun Dance. They called the Sun Dance shelter New Life Lodge or Lodge of New Birth, where the ceremony re-creates, re-forms, re-animates the earth, vegetation, animal life, etc., while offering thanks to a Supreme Being. There is no doubt that the Sun Dance has attracted ritual and cultural traits that have little to do with its original meaning, such as the Crow tribe's vow for revenge, and overemphasized elements, such as the self-torture of the Lakota (Sioux) rite.

The basic pattern of the Sun Dance is highly uniform and was usually initiated during the winter months by a man or woman who had made a vow to do so in thanks, or who had a visionary command to do so. In the pre-reservation days scattered bands would gather, often approaching the rendezvous in a ceremonial manner, making four stops en route. Secret preliminaries began in a tipi between the pledger and shamans (priests), usually old men with esoteric knowledge of the ritual. These preliminaries were to purify the participants, and to learn the sacred songs and ritual paint designs. At the same time a distinguished warrior or group of warriors killed a buffalo bull with one shot; similarly, scouts located a suitable forked tree which would be "killed" by a virtuous woman or captive and cut down; both would be transported to the Sun Dance site. In the meantime a larger number of men would erect a circle of ten to 20 posts, up to 20 yards in diameter with an entrance to the east. The centre pole would be erected with a bundle of brush near the top (the Thunderbird nest); the head or skin of the killed buffalo bull, and other objects such as a Sun Dance doll (Blackfoot) or offering of cloth might be affixed. Rafters would join the posts to the centre pole.

The public second phase of the ceremonials would begin with the formal procession of barefoot, kilt-clad, white-painted dancers into the lodge, taking their places on both sides of the altar. Gazing constantly at the centre pole or the sun they would raise and lower their heels, bending their knees, blowing their eagle-humerus whistles at every beat of the drum. They continued dancing for several days and nights, hoping in this way to obtain a vision or at least to arouse the pity of a supernatural being. In both the preliminary and public phases of the rite, lesser ceremonies would interwork: male and female initiation into societies, the curing of the sick, exhibitions of supernatural power, the recounting of warrior deeds, and distribution of wealth. Finally, among several tribes, those participants who had vowed to do so would have themselves pierced through the pectoral muscles with skewers by means of which they would be tethered to the centre pole. They would dance back and forth attempting to tear themselves free, gaining supernatural aid through their ecstasy of pain. The public ceremony usually lasted four days.

The history of the Sun Dance remains obscure; superficially it resembles the Okeepa ceremony of the Mandan of North Dakota, suggesting a Siouan origin for the rite. Others believe that the impressive resemblances between the Sun Dance and the Spirit Dance of the Plateau may indicate a common origin – a belief reinforced by the easy adoption of the ceremony, albeit Christianized, by 20th century Plateau-Basin groups such as the Shoshone, Bannock and Ute as a nativistic revitalization movement. Still others look to a recent origin of the Sun Dance, with rapid diffusion from a possible Cheyenne or Arapaho genesis. The following tribes share significant resemblances: (1) Arapaho, Northern and Southern Cheyenne; (2) Blackfoot and Sarsi; (3) Ponca and Western Sioux; (4) Assiniboine, Plains Cree, Plains Ojibwa; (5) Santee Sioux; (6) Shoshone, Ute, Kiowa and Kutenai.

The Sun Dance was probably related to the Okeepa ceremony vividly described by the artist explorer George Catlin in the 1830s. It centered on "Lone Man" who restored the earth after a great flood by use of the "Big Canoe" or ark of wooden planks symbolically representing a protective wall. The ritual was a cosmic new year ceremony to ensure abundance of bison and a new beginning,

TRIBES OF THE PLAINS AND PRAIRIE, c.1750s-1850

Linguistic and cultural boundaries are necessarily approximate; this sketch map is intended only as a general guide to distribution. Modern state boundaries are shown as broken lines, for orientation only. Note that the southern Caddoan peoples near to the Gulf coast are included by some in the Southeast Woodlands cultural area. Underlined names indicate linguistic groups distinct from larger groupings indicated by the shading key.

involving collective (as opposed to individual) vision quests, and spiritual instruction and initiation for youths. Both rituals communicated an idea of a unified religious Universe.

Besides the great collective festivals, warriors and individuals sought the help of animal spirits through visions induced by fasting and dreaming. High Plains warriors developed a range of age-graded military societies, each having its chiefs. Other organisations, mystical in character, were dream societies deriving power from dreamed animals, buffalo or elk, which provided sexual power. In a time of despair following the loss of much of their culture in the 19th century there appeared several nativistic movements, such as the Ghost Dance of the 1880s-1890s and the Peyote cult – a mixture of Mexican Indian, Christian and Plains Indian symbolism. Recently Pan-Indianism has taken on some features of tribal rejuvenation; the old Prairie Grass Dance has provided its ritual features.

Among the characteristic features of material culture, the hide tipi probably originated in the far north, and some buckskin apparel and large combat shields perhaps came from the Plateau, linked to the Plains via trade routes. Plains warriors developed militaristic and religious art with geometric painting and pictographs. Male society costume contained animal and bird elements associated with game tracking and battlefield scavengers. The Plains peoples were superb quillworkers and later beadworkers, and decorated male and female dress with geometric designs, perhaps influenced heavily in the late 19th century by imported Middle Eastern rugs. Elements of material culture which may have come from the eastern forests were rawhide box trunks, but now shaped as rawhide envelopes; and certain forms of pictographic art which seem related to the art of the forest people, particularly memory aids etched on bark. The 19th century saw the influx of European trade goods – cloth, beads, metals and guns – together with the spread of material culture from the Cree, Ojibwa and Métis from Canada, which added to the cultural mix of the whole region.

PLAINS CREE The general term given to cover the Cree bands living partly or wholly on the prairies of Saskatchewan and Alberta from the mid-18th century onwards. On cultural grounds they have been considered distinct from their Woodland Cree cousins, because of their adoption of Assiniboine traits which are essentially "Plains" in format – notably, ceremonials, and the development of a dependence on the buffalo (bison), in common with the Blackfeet, Assiniboine and Gros Ventre, whom the Plains Cree displaced from the Saskatchewan River. In the late 18th century they were reinforced by bands of Swampy Cree who partially modified to the Plains culture, but were to remain largely marginal. The marginal bands between the Swampy and Plains Cree were sometimes referred to as "Bush Cree"; however, we consider here the true Plains Cree and the "Bush Cree" together and independent from the Swampy and Woods Cree, in fact a distinct tribe. The Plains Cree bands were:

(1) Calling River Assiniboine and Qu'Appelle valleys, mostly now under the File Hills and Crooked Lake Agencies. The Calling River Cree or Qu'Appelle Cree were a marginal division of the "Bush Cree" and have mixed their blood considerably with the Plains Ojibwa.

(2) Cree-Assiniboine An extension of the Calling River band in association with the Assiniboine and probably a mixture of the two tribes, located near the Wood and Moose Maintains (Saskatchewan), now mostly under the File Hills-Qu'Appelle Agency (Piapot's band) and Crooked Lake Agency (White Bear). Mr.N.J. McLeod, Superintendent of the File Hills-Qu'Appelle Agency, in a well-documented description of the Cree and Saulteaux of his agency (personal correspondence, Dec. 16th, 1955), claims: "Piapot's Band are of the Plains Cree tribe of Indians and are somewhat different from other Cree tribes in that they are descendants of Indians who lived by hunting the buffalo, whereas some of the Cree tribes lived in and along the fringes of the bush areas and are known as Willow or Bush Crees"; therefore claiming that the Calling River people were "Bush" or marginal, in sharp contrast to Piapot's band.

(3) Touchwood Hills Between Long Lake and Touchwood Hills, now largely on the Poormans, Day Star and Gordons reserves.

(4) Rabbitskins Roaming the Assiniboine River between the Calling River and Touchwood Hills bands, with whom they are now mixed under the File Hills-Qu'Appelle and Touchwood Agencies. The Rabbitskins were a "Bush" group tethered to the trading posts during the 19th century, at which time they were closely associated with groups of Bungi or Plains Ojibwa.

(5) House People Living near the junction of the North and South Saskatchewan Rivers, mostly above the north branch. The House People were partly "Bush Cree" and partly true Plains Cree, and are now principally on the Mistawasis and Sandy Lake (Ahtahkakoops) reserves under the Shellbrook Agency.

(6) Parklands People A "Bush" or Willow Cree group on the South Saskatchewan near its junction with the north branch. They are now under the Duck Lake Agency at Beardy's and Fort-a-la-Corné reserves.

These were a late extension of the Swampy Cree under fur trader influence.

(7) River People On and below the north branch of the Saskatchewan River and the Battle River. These are true Plains people and were one of the largest Plains Cree groups. Their descendants are mostly on the Poundmaker, Sweet Grass, Red Pheasant and Little Pine reserves of the Battleford Agency. These people were closely related to the Alberta or Beaver Hills Cree.

(8) Beaver Hills People The largest Plains Cree grouping and the most important division of the Prairie Cree. These Plains Cree inhabited the Saskatchewan beyond Onion Lake, Neutral Hills, and Beaver Hills to the headwaters of that river. They are now mostly at the following reserves: Onion Lake (Saskatchewan), Saddle Lake, Alexander, Ermineskin, Samson, Montana, Sunchild, and John O'Chiese, under the Saddle Lake, Edmonton, Hobbema and Stoney-Sarcee Agencies. On many reservations they have mixed with their old allies, the Assiniboine (Stoney), particularly at Wabamun, Stoney-Plains and Morley; and with the Blackfeet and Sarsi, their former enemies, near Calgary.

(9) Rocky Boy and United States Cree After the development of the American fur trade on the Missouri during the early 1800s, Plains, Swampy and Métis Cree in small groups wandered through Montana and North Dakota. After the second Métis rebellion in Saskatchewan in 1885 some hundreds of Plains Cree removed to Montana to escape the Canadian authorities for their part in the Riel uprising. A reservation called Rocky Boy near Havre (Montana) was established for landless Plains Cree and Plains Ojibwa in 1916, but many more remained as landless refugees on several Montana reservations.

The total number of Plains Cree in the early 19th century may have been 15,000 before smallpox took its toll. Cree conquest of the western forest seems to have been complete by the late 18th century, when Alexander Henry met them on Lake Winnepeg in 1775; and by Daniel Harmon's day, about 1820, they were linked to the Assiniboine and venturing out on the Prairies. Finally, by 1876, most of the Plains Cree had submitted to Canadian authority, although they participated in the uprising against the Government in 1885 alongside the Métis.

Plains Cree culture included procuring buffalo for meat and hides. The acquisition of the horse, probably as early as 1750, facilitated bison hunting and regulated tribal movements. Their material culture also resembled High Plains forms in the use of the skin (later canvas) tipi, buckskin clothes for male and female, some tattooing, and decorated ceremonial costume with fine quillwork and beadwork in geometrical and later floralistic designs. Warrior and rank societies existed for men, such as Buffalo Dancers, Kit Fox and Prairie Chicken Societies. The concept of a single all-powerful creator and supernatural power in all phenomena was endemic. They had the Sun Dance (some reserves still hold them) or Thirsting Dance, the vision quest, smoking tipi rite, medicine bundles, and other Plains ceremonial complexes. The present population of Plains Cree descendants exceeds 20,000.

PLAINS OJIBWA or **BUNGI** In parallel with the Plains Cree, groups of Woodland Ojibwa first established themselves on the edges of the Plains (the Parklands) by about 1790, and later some bands became true High Plains Indians. They left their homelands in Minnesota and Ontario and finally occupied an area of southwestern Manitoba, northern North Dakota and southeastern Saskatchewan. The great expansion of the Ojibwa began in the 18th century after they secured firearms from the French and English. Those who lived on the northern edges of the Prairies are often called Saulteaux (pronounced "sotoe"), but those who successfully adapted their culture to life on the Plains are Plains Ojibwa or Bungi, although no sharp division actually existed. They now employed the hide tipi, the horse, and the Red River cart obtained from the Red River Métis; and exploited the bison and pronghorn antelope, which replaced deer, moose and beaver as the chief sources of sustenance in their new environment. Clothing styles were also modified, including shirts and leggings for men and single-piece dresses for women. Both geometrical and later floralistic decoration for their ceremonial clothes were common. They also adopted the Sun Dance, although the Midewiwin (Great Medicine Society) survived amongst a few bands; and they had a warrior-police society, "Okitsita", similar to other Plains tribes. During the later 19th century they adopted the Grass Dance, a variant of the Omaha Dance, the Drum Religion and later the Peyote cult.

Today many Plains Ojibwa reserves hold secular Powwows sharing features with other northern Plains Indian groups. In most areas they are heavily mixed with Métis, perhaps most of their present 32,000 population being of mixed descent. Their present descendants are at Turtle Mountain, North Dakota; Rocky Boy Reservation, Montana (merged with Cree); Gamblers, Keeseekoowenin, Long Plain, Peguis, Rolling River, Roseau River, Sandy Bay, Swan Lake and Waywayseecappo, all in Manitoba; and Cote, Fishing Lake, Kahkewistahaw, Keeseekoose, Kristino, Muscowequan, Muscowpetung, Nut Lake, Ochapowace, Pasqua,

Sakimay, Shesheep, Saulteaux and White Bear in Saskatchewan. A number are descendants of marginal Plains bands and some are also of Cree origin.

SARSI or **SARCEE** A small Athabascan-speaking tribe who once lived along the upper waters of the Saskatchewan River in present Alberta, Canada. They were probably at one time part of the Beaver Indians but joined the Blackfoot for protection against their enemies, the Crees and Assiniboines, perhaps some time in the late 18th century. Their customs thenceforth were greatly modified by their long residence amongst the Blackfoot. They seem always to have been a small tribe, perhaps numbering 750 people before smallpox decimated them in 1836 and scarlet fever in 1856. In 1877, along with other southern Alberta Indians, they ceded their lands for a small reservation near Calgary where a small group, much mixed with other Indian groups, has continued to live. In 1881 they numbered 396; in 1924, only 160; in 1949, 201; and in 1970, 467. Their language is now used by only a few older people, and they have lost their Sacred Peace Pipe and Beaver bundles. They do, however, sponsor an annual Powwow and run a cultural centre on the reserve. Their close proximity to Calgary has resulted in largely complete acculturation.

BLACKFOOT or **BLACKFEET** The historic Blackfoot, an Algonkian people, were a loose confederacy of three closely related tribes: the Blackfoot or *North Blackfoot* (Siksika), the *Blood* (Kainah), and *Piegan* – also spelt Peigan in Canada – (Pikuni), with a close alliance with the Atsina and Sarsi. They once held an immense territory stretching from the North Saskatchewan River, Canada, to the headwater of the Missouri River in Montana, including the foothills of the Rocky Mountains. They seem to have moved from the east and were the vanguard of Algonkian relocation in the west. David Thompson, an explorer for the Hudson's Bay Company, made the first extensive record of Blackfoot culture when he wintered with them in 1787-1788; he found that horses, guns, and metal objects of European manufacture had preceded him by at least 50 years. They seem to have been in conflict with the Snake Indians, usually assumed as Shoshone, whom they ultimately appear to have expelled from the area. Despite the ravages of smallpox, particularly among the Piegans, the pre-reservation Blackfoot became the most powerful tribe of the northern Plains.

They were a typical Plains tribe, as exemplified by a dependence on the buffalo for food, for tipis, bedding, shields, clothing, and containers; by the development of bands from common ties of kinship, and by functional age-graded men's societies and warrior societies, including formalised religious organizations. The band functioned as a group, with a dependence upon the generosity of the able and wealthy few among the young and old. Religion included the wide use of "bundles" containing symbols (usually remnants of birds, animals and objects) of the power of dreamed or vision experience. These personalized sources of power were opened at times, with accompanying rituals for group benefit, for health, hunting and prestige. Each of the three tribes held an annual Sun Dance, the Plains world renewal complex enacted in a specially constructed "Medicine Lodge" which, in spite of Government pressures, has been held periodically until recent times. As late as 1958 the Bloods still held the Medicine Pipe Dance by the Horn Society, the strongest native religious group still extant. Their principal deities were the Sun and a supernatural being, Napi, or "Old Man". Their dead were deposited in trees, sometimes in tipis erected for the purpose on hills.

During the 19th century they diminished in number, from some 15,000 to about 6,750 in 1862. Many died of starvation with the final disappearance of the buffalo. After 1877 the Canadian Blackfoot settled in three reservations: the North Blackfoot near Gleichen, the North Piegan near Brocket and the Blood at Cardston. The South Piegan were finally restricted to a reservation on the eastern side of the Glacier National Park, Montana, with the administrative agency at Browning. These Blackfoot had established relations with the American fur companies on the Missouri and had suffered the worst in smallpox outbreaks. The years after 1884, following the collapse of their hunting economy, were largely dominated by the effort of adjustment to white rural life, farming, stock-raising, and more recently to an industrial wage economy.

In contrast to pre-reservation days, Blackfoot culture has become no longer monolithic. In common with most other Plains Indian resident reservation communities they are socially divided by religion, by social achievement and by blood. However, in the recent past a renewed awareness of "Indian culture" has led to an increased participation even by the mixed bloods in Pan-Indian Powwows, which are often performed several times a year. The South Piegans promote the annual North American Indian Days at Browning and similar events are held by the Bloods, North Piegans and North Blackfoot; but the sacred bundles have mostly fallen into disuse. They still have colourfully painted canvas tipis which are erected at major social gatherings, including the Calgary Stampede. The Blackfoot historically made beautiful costumes – elaborately decorated men's warrior costumes of shirts and leggings with eagle feather headdresses, and full length buckskin women's dresses, adorned with beadwork. This ceremonial dress, modified over the years, is still worn at the modern Powwows, together with an ever-changing array of dancers' costumes having little reference to older Indian dress. The Blackfoot population in 1970 was 18,000, of whom 9,900 were Montana Blackfeet, largely of mixed antecedents, and only half now resident on the Blackfeet Reservation. In 1970 the Bloods numbered 4,262, the North Piegan 1,413, and the North Blackfoot 2,355, all in Alberta, Canada.

GROS VENTRE or **ATSINA** An Algonkian tribe of the northern Plains, considered once part of the Arapaho but for much of the 19th century allies of the more powerful Blackfoot. Their French name apparently derives from the movement of the hands over the abdomen to indicate hunger in the Plains Indian sign language used by Indians of differing speech to communicate. This sign also signifies abdominal tattooing, and thus confuses these people with the Hidatsa (Gros Ventre of the Missouri), who are a completely separate Siouan tribe. Their culture and history parallel those of the Blackfoot, their powerful neighbours to the west. Their home for most of the 19th century was between the South Saskatchewan River in Canada and the Missouri River in Montana, particularly around the Milk River. They share the Fort Belknap Reservation, Montana, with part of the Assiniboine; and numbered 1,045 in 1954, and 1,519 in 1970. During the years a considerable amount of craftwork was carried on by the women of the reservation. Pan-Indian Powwows include social dances such as the Grass Dance, Tea and Owl Dances danced by couples and derived from white two-steps, and the Fool or Clown Dance, associated with the Gros Ventre, Assiniboine and Blackfoot of Montana and Alberta.

ASSINIBOINE or **STONEY** Formerly a large Siouan tribe whose language confirms a close link with the Yanktonai Sioux, from whom they probably separated not long before the appearance of white traders in their vicinity. They occupied an area between Lake Superior and James Bay, adjoining territory then dominated by the Crees and their association with the Hudson's Bay traders. Early reports distinguish between Assiniboine of the meadows and woods during the 18th century. They appear to have been in a slow migration westward during the early 19th century, when they seem to have formed a northern division from Moose Mountain along the South Saskatchewan and Qu'Appelle Rivers, and a southern division who ranged south to the Missouri River and west to the Cypress Hills. They suffered a drastic reduction in population due to the ravages of smallpox during the 19th century which persuaded a number of the Saskatchewan Assiniboine to move to the foothills of the Rocky Mountains; this group became known as "Stoney", apparently an allusion to their method of cooking with hot stones. Their culture was much the same as that of the Blackfoot during the 19th century but, like the Crees, they have a long association with white traders.

Those who remained in Canada were located on several reservations. The Mosquito, Grizzly Bear's Head and Lean Man's bands settled near Battleford, Saskatchewan; Pheasant Rump's and Ocean Man's bands settled near Moose Mountain (later moved to the White Bear Reserve); Carry the Kettle settled at Fort Qu'Appelle; Joseph's and Paul's bands near Edmonton and Chiniquay, Wesley and Bearspaw near Morley – the largest group. The Canadian Assiniboine numbered 1,371 in 1904; and those settled on two reservations in Montana – Fort Peck and Fort Belknap – totalled 1,234, a huge reduction from an aboriginal population of perhaps 10,000. In 1970, Mosquito-Grizzly Bear's Head numbered 387, a few were at White Bear, and Carry the Kettle numbered 734 – all in Saskatchewan; Alexis recorded 490, Paul's 575, and Chinquay, Wesley and Bearspaw (Stoney) 1,610, all in Alberta; while 2,219 were divided almost equally between Fort Peck, where they are mixed with Yanktonai, and Fort Belknap, where they are mixed with Gros Ventre. As a rural and now an urban minority ethnic people their 20th century condition is much the same as that of other western Indian groups. The Morley Stoney participated for years in the "Banff Indian Days" celebration, a colourful show of tipis and Indian costume. The Assiniboine are one of those upper Missouri River tribes who were immortalized by the artists Catlin and Bodmer, who recorded Plains Indian life in its near pristine grandeur during the 1830s.

CHEYENNE An important Algonkian tribe of the High Plains, whose earliest known home was present Minnesota between the Mississippi and Minnesota Rivers. They seem to have been in contact with La Salle's Fort on the Illinois River in 1680. At this time they lived in fixed villages, practised agriculture and made pottery, but lost these arts after being driven out onto the Plains to become nomadic bison hunters. They became one of the focal points of the Plains culture, characterized by tipi dwelling, development of age-graded male societies, geometrical art, and the development of a ceremonial world renewal complex, the Sun Dance. They were constantly pressed further into the Plains by the Sioux, who later became their firm allies, finally establishing themselves on the upper branches of the Platte River. Later, in consequence of the building of Bent's Fort on the upper Arkansas River in Colorado in 1832, a large part of the tribe moved south to the Arkansas while the rest remained on the North Platte, Powder and Yellowstone Rivers. Thus came into being the geographical division of the tribe into the Northern and Southern Cheyenne. Their population before the cholera epidemic of 1849 was about 3,000.

From 1860 to 1878 they were prominent in warfare against the whites, acting with the Sioux in the north and with the Kiowa and Comanche in the south, and probably losing more than the other tribes in proportion to their number during these conflicts. In 1864 the tribe suffered a severe blow in the notorious Chivington massacre in Colorado, and again in 1868 at the hands of Custer on the Washita; on both occasions Cheyenne camps were attacked. The Northern Cheyenne joined the Sioux as active participants against Custer's final campaign in Montana in 1876 after the Government's failure to protect hunting grounds, as specified in the 1868 Fort Laramie Treaty, from gold prospectors and railroad surveyors. Despite the tribes' success in the battle of the Little Big Horn that June, Mackenzie secured their surrender; and in 1877 a portion of the Northern Cheyenne was brought to Oklahoma to be colonized with the Southern Cheyenne, who had agreed to move to a reservation located in western Indian Territory by the terms of the Medicine Lodge Treaty of 1867.

Reservation conditions were harsh and became intolerable, causing Little Wolf and Dull Knife to make a heroic return to the north country. Despite internment at Fort Robinson, Nebraska, and a second break for liberty, about 60 rejoined those who had remained in the north and in 1884 were assigned a reservation on the Tongue River, Montana, where their descendants remain. In this comparatively rugged, isolated country Cheyenne descendants have struggled with problems of poverty and readjustment to rural and recently urban American culture.

In 1954 the Northern Cheyenne numbered 2,120, but there has been an increase in the numbers of those of mixed Cheyenne and white blood in recent years; however, traditional beliefs surrounding the Sacred Buffalo Hat and the Sun Dance persist. The Southern Cheyenne are found in Custer, Roger Mills, Canadian, Kingfisher, Blaine and Dewey Counties, Oklahoma, parts of the allotted Cheyenne and Arapaho Reservation opened to white settlement in 1892; in 1950 there were 2,110 Southern Cheyenne. They, too, have retained traditional symbols of ethnic unity, the Sacred Medicine Arrows; although they are nominally Christian, Peyotism has a strong following in the south. Both groups sponsor Pan-Indian Powwows at various times when other tribes attend. In 1970 the Cheyenne numbered in total 6,872. In ancient times the Cheyenne had a subordinate tribe, the *Sutaio*, who were absorbed finally in about 1830.

ARAPAHO An Algonkian-speaking tribe of the Plains, being originally one people with the Atsina. The origins of the tribe are not known, but tradition has it that they came from the headwaters of the Mississippi River or even Canada. They formed the most aberrant group of the whole Algonkian family, which points to a long separation from their parent group. The Arapaho were often noted for their religious and contemplative disposition, less warlike than the Cheyenne. They were a nomadic equestrian people, hunting bison, developing military and age-graded organizations, and observing the annual Sun Dance. After crossing the Missouri River they pressed on to the headwaters of the Platte River, to the edge of the Rockies in present eastern Wyoming by 1820; and by 1835 a portion of the tribe had moved south to the upper Arkansas River in eastern Colorado, thus forming the Northern and Southern branches of the tribe. At this time they were in constant alliance with the Cheyenne, but were often at war with the Shoshone, Ute and Pawnee, and also raided with the Kiowa and Comanche with whom they had friendly relations.

The history of the Southern Arapaho is similar to that of the Southern Cheyenne. They entered into treaties with the U.S.A. in 1861 and at Medicine Lodge River in southern Kansas in 1867, which assigned them to lands in western Indian Territory, now Oklahoma, where descendants remain. The Northern Arapaho were assigned to the Wind River Reservation, Wyoming, after making peace with the Wind River Shoshone with whom they share the reservation. Wind River is well watered, with rich natural resources, and supports Indian-owned cattle; but the Arapaho have had serious social and economic problems over the years. The Southern Arapaho are found mostly in rural Blaine and Washita Counties, Oklahoma, much mixed with the Cheyenne. In pre-reservation days the Arapaho probably numbered 3,000; in 1923 the Southern Arapaho numbered 833 and the Northern branch 921; in 1950, the Southern branch 1,189; and in 1960, the Northern Arapaho 2,279. In 1970 the combined population was given as 2,993. They were strong adherents to the Ghost Dance movement of 1890.

SIOUAN

An important language family of American Indians whose ancestors probably originated in the Mississippi valley, where the most highly developed

North American civilizations existed. Tribal traditions seem to indicate movement from this general area along the Missouri, ultimately to dominate the central Plains. However, a divergent branch, the Catawba, and their associates are found in the Carolinas; and late 19th century texts collected on the Iroquois Grand River Reservation in Ontario from adopted Tutelo descendants strongly suggest a close relationship to the western division of the family; and subsequently a number of absorbed or extinct tribes of Virginia, the Tutelos' ancient home, have been added to the family on purely circumstantial evidence. The Western Siouans are the Dakota-Assiniboine group, comprising the Dakota, Nakota and Lakota (including the seven great Sioux tribes in three linguistic sections) and the Assiniboine; the Dhegiha, comprising the Omaha, Ponca, Kansa, Osage and Quapaw; the Chiwere, comprising Iowa and Oto-Missouri; the Winnebago, Mandan, and finally the Hidatsa-Crow.

SIOUX or **DAKOTA** Collective terms used by the United States and Canadian Governments to designate the largest section of the Siouan linguistic family – seven tribes, all very closely related. When first mentioned by the early white explorers in the mid-17th century all seven tribes lived within what is now the southern half of the state of Minnesota; and several of the tribes have a tradition of residence at Mille Lacs, Minnesota, which seems still to have been a home for several bands when Hennepin and DuLuth visited them 250 years ago. Culturally they seem to have been a Woodland and Prairie people, living in bark lodges and practising slash-and-burn horticulture, fishing and hunting. Their name seems to be of French-Ojibwa extraction, meaning "adders". Pressure during the 18th century from the Ojibwa, who were supplied with firearms by the French, began a western movement, with several tribes crossing the Missouri River and developing a strong horse culture dependent upon the bison, tipi dwelling and a truly nomadic way of life. In time they became known for their stubborn resistance to white encroachment.

Their own name, Dakota, means "allies", and they were once known as the Seven Council Fires before their westward dispersal. *Dakota* is the name of the whole nation in the eastern dialect, *Nakota* in the middle dialect, and *Lakota* in the western dialect. The seven tribes were:

(1) Mdewakanton or Mdewakantonwan, sometimes Bdewakanton, meaning "Spirit Lake village" referring to Mille Lacs Lake in Minnesota.

(2) Wahpekute – "leaf shooters".

(3) Wahpeton or Wahpetonwan – "village in the leaves".

(4) Sisseton or Sisitownan – "swamp villagers".

These four tribes formed the true Dakota or Santee (Isanti) section.

(5) Yankton or Ihanktonwan – "dwellers at the end village"

(6) Yanktonai or Ihanktonwanna – "little dwellers at the end."

These two tribes formed the Nakota or middle section of the nation.

(7) Teton or Titonwan – "dwellers on the Prairie".

This single tribe were the Lakota or western branch of the nation.

MDEWAKANTON-SIOUX A Sioux tribe of the Eastern or Santee division of the nation who formerly lived at Mille Lacs at the head of the Rum River, Minnesota, but are later associated with the region of the west bank of the Mississippi River from Winona to Red Wing in southeast Minnesota. The economy of the Santee rested on hunting, fishing, gathering (wild rice) and a horticulture complex of respectable antiquity. They lived in bark gable-roofed houses, also wigwams. Bison hunts were organized by appointed hunt chiefs, and band chiefs were usually hereditary, with an appointed *akicita* (police) from the warrior societies. Dress was modified during the 18th and early 19th centuries by the adoption of cloth, sashes and coats from traders; but they retained shirts, leggings, and soft-soled moccasins, and Santee women wore the two-piece Central Algonquian style dress consisting of a wrap-around skirt and loose blouse. The Santee were expert at ribbonwork and beadwork, including floralistic, zoomorphic and geometrical designs applied to ceremonial dress. Their chief ceremonies were the Medicine Dance which resembled the Algonkian Midewiwin, the Thunder Dance, and some bands adopted the Sun Dance.

In 1851 they sold their lands to the Government and moved to the upper Minnesota River area. They were the principal participants in the 1862 uprising against the whites in Minnesota, which resulted in their capture and dispersion. Some fled to Canada under their chief Little Crow, while those who survived the ordeal were placed principally on the Santee Reservation, Knox County, Nebraska (mixed with Wahpekute); Upper Sioux Reservation near Granite Falls, Lower Sioux Reservation near Morton, Prairie Island near Red Wing, Prior Lake near Shakopee (all in Minnesota), and the Flandreau settlement on the Big Sioux River, South Dakota, all mixed with other Santee. Before 1851 there were seven bands of Mdewakanton, including the Kiyuksa (a name used by bands of other Sioux tribes) and Kapoza. The Santee of the Niobrara Reservation, Nebraska, numbered 1,075 in 1904 and

1,400 in 1955, but many had left the area. A few are in Canada at Sioux Valley (Oak River) and Birdtail near Birtle, Manitoba, but not separately reported.

WAHPEKUTE-SIOUX A branch of the Santee or Dakota division of the Sioux group on the Cannon and Blue Earth Rivers in southern Minnesota, particularly around the old Faribault's Trading Post. Lewis and Clark found them on the Minnesota River below the Redwood River junction. After the sale of their lands in 1851 some joined the Mdewakanton, with whom they are sometimes referred to as the "Lower Council Sioux" in distinction from the Sisseton-Wahpeton, the "Upper Council Sioux". Following their participation in the affair at Spirit Lake, Iowa, in 1857 and the Minnesota outbreak of 1862, the Wahpekute fled mostly to Canada and to the Missouri. Those on the Missouri combined with the Mdewakanton on the Santee Reservation on the Niobrara River, Knox County, Nebraska, where a portion of their descendants, about 400 strong, remained in 1955. In Canada, where some descendants of Chief Inkpaduta's band remain, they are found at Sioux Valley Reserve (Oak River) near Griswold, Manitoba, mixed with the three other Santee tribes, numbering 899 in 1970. A few others were incorporated amongst other Santee at Oak Lake near Pipestone, Manitoba, and Sioux Wahpeton Reserve (Round Plain) near Prince Albert in Saskatchewan. A handful no doubt merged with the few Mdewakanton in the small remaining Minnesota communities, and a few more are said to have accompanied the Yanktonai to Fort Peck, Montana.

Most of the Eastern Sioux groups have over the years assumed the rural culture of the European immigrant farmer but at a lower economic level. The Wahpekute Sioux today do not exist as a separate tribal group, having mixed with other communities as a direct result of the 1862-63 campaign during which General Henry H. Sibley and his troops scattered the Santees, many fleeing to Canada.

WAHPETON-SIOUX The traditional home of the Wahpetons was about Little Rapids, some 45 miles from the mouth of the Minnesota River's junction with the Mississippi, but after 1851 they removed to Lac-Qui-Parle and Big Stone Lake in the western part of Minnesota. They are sometimes grouped with the Sisseton into the "Upper Council Sioux". They were involved in the outbreak of hostilities between the Eastern Sioux and whites in 1862, as a result of which they were scattered over a wide area. Most were ultimately gathered on the Sisseton or Lake Traverse Reservation in South Dakota, where in 1909 the combined Sisseton-Wahpeton numbered 1,936. A few Wahpeton were included with Sisseton and Yanktonai at Devil's Lake (Fort Totten) Agency, North Dakota, where the three together numbered 1,013 in 1904. In 1956 the enrolled population at Sisseton was 3,672 and at Devil's Lake (Fort Totten) 1,500. A number also fled to Canada, their descendants in Manitoba at the Birdtail Reserve near Birtle numbering 187 in 1970, and those at Long Plain Sioux Reserve near Portage La Prairie 224 in the same year. These are mostly Wahpeton descendants, as are a few mixed with other Santee at Oak River, Oak Lake, Manitoba, and Standing Buffalo and Round Plain, Saskatchewan. The Eastern Sioux in Minnesota have traditionally been the only persons who possessed the right to work the pipestone quarries of southern Minnesota where ceremonial pipes were made, and more recently novelty souvenirs.

SISSETON-SIOUX The largest of the four Eastern Sioux or Dakota tribes, who claim an origin around the headwaters of the Rum River, Minnesota, in the area of Mille Lacs when first met by whites in the 17th century. Later they seem to have been located about the junction of the Minnesota and Blue Earth Rivers in Minnesota and at Traverse des Sioux. By the 1840s some had moved to the Lake Traverse and the James River country. The majority were located on the Sisseton Reservation in South Dakota and combined with the Wahpeton. A few joined other Santee at Oak River (Sioux Valley), Manitoba, and larger numbers of their descendants are at Standing Buffalo Reserve near Fort Qu'Appelle and Moose Woods or White Cap Reserve near Dundurn, both in Saskatchewan. In 1956 the Sisseton-Wahpeton at Lake Traverse (Sisseton Reservation) numbered 3,672; in 1970 Standing Buffalo numbered 514 and Moose Woods 148. Before their dispersal following the war of 1862 there were about six bands including those of Sleepy Eyes, Red Iron and Grey Thunder, all prominent chiefs. The band called "Dryers on the Shoulder" lived near Lake Traverse and were great buffalo hunters; they apparently formed the principal group of the Standing Buffalo Reserve in Canada.

YANKTON-SIOUX One of the seven divisions of the Sioux and one of the two which form the Nakota or geographically the Middle Sioux. They were probably in the vicinity of Mille Lacs with their relatives during the 17th century. In 1708 they were on the east bank of the Missouri River about the site of Sioux City, Iowa; they were not separately noted again until Lewis and Clark found them in the region of the James, Big Sioux and Des Moines Rivers in southeastern South Dakota neighbouring Iowa and Minnesota; in 1842 they were noted on the

Vermillon River in South Dakota. They seem to have been well known to traders along the Missouri, and through the efforts of Chief Palaneapape they were restrained from joining the Santee in the Minnesota outbreak of 1862.

In 1858 they ceded all their lands to the U.S.A. except for a reservation on the north bank of the Missouri near Wagner, South Dakota, where their descendants have lived ever since. They were generally indistinguishable from their close relatives the Yanktonai. Lewis and Clark estimated their numbers at 4,300 with the Yanktonai; in 1867 there were 2,530 Yankton alone; in 1909 they were reported as numbering 1,739; in 1945, 1,927; and in 1956, 2,391. A few incorporated with other Sioux on various reservations and are no longer reported separately, and many have intermarried with non-Indians over the years; perhaps fewer than half of the present inhabitants of reservations in eastern South Dakota are full blood members of their respective tribes. The Yankton are said to have had eight bands, the Cankute or "Shooters-at-the-Tree" being the most noted.

YANKTONAI-SIOUX The more dominant of the two Nakota branches of the Sioux nation, speaking the same dialect as the Yankton. Their homeland included the drainages of the James and Big Sioux Rivers and the Coteau du Missouri. The economy of these Middle Sioux, like the Missouri River groups they had displaced, rested on a base of hunting, fishing, gathering and river bottom horticulture. Great tribal bison hunts took place twice a year, taking them far west of the Missouri. They used the skin tipi, and skin-covered wikiups resembling those of bark found amongst the Santee; they also made or used abandoned earth lodges. They also employed the "bull boat", a round hide river craft probably adopted from the Mandan, Hidatsa and Arikara. The Sun Dance was their most important religious ceremony. The Yanktonai divided into two divisions: the Upper Yanktonai in six bands of which the Kiyuksa ("Breakers of the Rule") and Pabaksa ("Cutheads") were the most prominent, and the Lower Yanktonai or Hunkpatina. In the 17th century the Assiniboine are said to have divided from the Yaktonai and moved to Canada; they still refer to themselves as *Nakoda*, but are now considered as a separate people.

The Yanktonai took part in the War of 1812 on the side of Great Britain. They took no part in the Minnesota War of 1862, and made treaties of peace with the U.S.A. in 1865, being divided between reservations on the Missouri. The Upper Yanktonai descendants are on the Standing Rock Reservation on the North-South Dakota border, and on the Devil's Lake (Fort Totten) Reservation, North Dakota (mostly Pabaksa). The Lower Yanktonai are found on Crow Creek Reservation, Fort Thompson, South Dakota, and on the Fort Peck Reservation, Wolf Point, Montana. In 1956 the combined Sisseton-Wahpeton-Upper Yanktonai of Fort Totten numbered 1,500; the combined Teton and Upper Yanktonai of Standing Rock 4,324; the Lower Yanktonai and Teton of Crow Creek 1,132; and the Lower Yanktonai (locally called Yankton) and Assiniboine of Fort Peck were reported to number 3,881.

TETON-SIOUX The largest and most powerful of all the original seven branches of the Dakota or Sioux Indians, in fact outnumbering the other six tribes together. They became the Western Sioux, or in their own dialect *Lakota*, following their migration onto the High Plains in the late 18th and early 19th centuries. They were divided into seven bands: Hunkpapa, Minneconjou, Sihasapa (or Blackfoot – no connection with the Algonkian Blackfoot), Oohenonpa (Two Kettle), Sicangu (or Brulé), Itazipco (Sansarcs) and Oglala. Leaving their original home in Minnesota, they were around Lake Traverse by 1700 and on the Missouri by 1750; by about 1820 they claimed the whole of western South Dakota centering on the Black Hills. They transformed completely to a bison-hunting economy supplemented by deer and antelope, lived in conical skin tipis, and secured vast herds of horses.

The Western Sioux had an elaborate system of warrior societies, including the *akicita* or soldiers, Kit Foxes, Crow Owners (referring to a special type of dance bustle), Strong Hearts (famous for their unique ermine skin horned headdresses worn in battle). These societies often fought as a unit whenever possible. Another type of organisation, completely mystical in character, were the dream societies such as Buffalo and Elk Dreamers. Although details of organization differed from band to band, the council and chiefs emerged as the principal governing body. The supreme councillors amongst the Oglala were "Shirt-Wearers". Their dress consisted of skin shirts and leggings for men decorated with porcupine quills or later beads; women wore skin dresses, often heavily beaded; much decoration was in characteristic geometric designs. The Sun Dance was the great focal point of summer camps. They also had Yuwipi, a night cult, probably Woodland in origin, and the "shaking tipi rite". Burial was invariably of the scaffold type; "winter counts" were pictographic calendar histories on buffalo robes. Warfare and hunting were important male activities, the elaborate age-graded warrior societies each having their own customs.

As a result of the California Gold Rush of 1849 and the discoveries of gold in Colorado and

Montana in the 1860s, white men in greater numbers began crossing Lakota-Sioux lands and killing buffalo. The Sioux became resentful, attacking wagon trains and prospectors and outfighting soldiers. Finally, at the treaty of Fort Laramie in 1868, Chief Red Cloud demanded that white men should be kept out of their country – that the Great Sioux Reservation, the whole of present South Dakota west of the Missouri, be reserved exclusively for Sioux use. For a few years the treaty held, until in 1874 gold was discovered in the Black Hills, traditionally a sacred area. This, together with the U.S. Government's inability to keep white prospectors, immigrants and hunters out of the area, led to a series of bitter conflicts which climaxed in the defeat of Custer's command in June 1876 on the Little Big Horn River, Montana, and the ultimate surrender of Crazy Horse in 1877 and Sitting Bull in 1881. The Great Sioux Reservation was divided into smaller reservations – Pine Ridge, Rosebud, Lower Brulé, Cheyenne River and Standing Rock – followed by further losses of land during the allotment and subsequent sale of unoccupied areas. Thus began years of squalid reservation life, restrictions on religious ceremonies, poor housing, the boarding school system which took children away from their families, and lack of employment opportunity in areas remote from economic activity.

Today there is a wide racial and cultural range on the Sioux reservations and, despite some recent improvements, they are beset by social problems. The distribution of the modern Western or Lakota Sioux is as follows: the Hunkpapa are mostly at Standing Rock Reservation and a few at Wood Mountain Reserve, Saskatchewan; the Minneconjou are at Cheyenne River Reservation; the Sansarc, Sihasapa and Two Kettle are also at Cheyenne River; the Upper Brulé are at Rosebud Reservation; the Lower Brulé at the Lower Brulé Reservation; and the Oglala at Pine Ridge Reservation – although there has been some mixing. It was at Pine Ridge that the Wounded Knee massacre of Indian people took place in 1890 during the Ghost Dance movement; this has become a tragic symbol of Indian subjection by whites, and was the last significant "military" engagement between whites and Indians.

Despite poor surroundings the Sioux have a tremendous esprit de corps and some still possess a hauteur and openness of character; much of the belated understanding and reverence for "Indian culture" found today stems from the activities of modern Sioux people. During the 1860s the Grass Dance (so called because of sweetgrass braids worn by the participants) or Omaha Dance (because it came from the Omahas) was adopted by the warrior societies, whose own rites were falling into disuse. The lively songs and male dances, called "war dances" by whites, became a main social activity at Indian gatherings on the reservations, and quickly spread to most northern Plains tribes, the Assiniboine, Blackfoot, and Gros Ventre each adding their own rites, usually of a social nature, to the performance. For years only men participated, but in recent times women and children take part as well. The Omaha Dance became the basis for the modern Powwow complex in the central and northern Plains (where it is still called Grass Dance), an outward manifestation of Pan-Indianism which parallels and even merges with a similar movement which spread from Oklahoma. Today, as in the past, Powwows are held on all reservations.

In 1904 the Lakota were distributed as follows: Cheyenne River, 2,477; Lower Brule, 470; Pine Ridge, 6,690; and Rosebud, 4,977 – when added to the Middle and Eastern branches they totalled 26,175, including Assiniboine, within the U.S.A. In 1956 there were 4,983 enrolled at Cheyenne River; 705 at Lower Brule; 9,875 at Pine Ridge; and 8,189 at Rosebud. In 1970 there were 47,825 Sioux (Western, Middle and Eastern) in the U.S.A. and 5,155 in Canada (the only Teton representatives in Canada are 70 people at Wood Mountain). Today a large number of Sioux people live in Denver.

CROW An important Siouan tribe of the northwestern Plains who split from the Hidatsa, an agricultural village people who lived in earth-covered lodges on the Missouri River, perhaps 350 years ago. In time the Crow were divided into two main bands: the River Crows lived along the Missouri and Yellowstone Rivers, and the Mountain Crows in the mountain valleys of southern Montana and northern Wyoming; a third, smaller band was known as "Kicked in the Bellies". Prior to the Lewis and Clark expedition of 1804-1806 few white men had seen the Absarokee or Crow Indians, although the Verendryes brothers had visited them in 1743 and called them "Beaux Hommes". After Lewis and Clark came various fur traders, and trading posts such as Forts Liza and Cass forged permanent white contacts with the Crow. The artist Catlin portrayed them as one of the most colourful native tribes on the northern Plains in the 1830s. By 1864 the Bozeman Trail led right through Crow country, and this was followed by the building of military forts – Reno, Phil Kearny and C.F.Smith – to protect the immigrants (despite their abandonment during the Sioux wars). On the whole relations with whites, though often strained, remained largely peaceful. They signed treaties with the U.S.A. in 1825, and recognised their boundaries as defined by the Fort Laramie Treaty of 1851; this was followed by a second Laramie Treaty in 1868 which established the Crow Reservation, although this was subsequently reduced in area. The present Crow Reservation is south of Billings, Montana in Bighorn County. The administrative centre is Crow Agency.

Except for the cultivation of tobacco the Crow abandoned agriculture after their separation from the Hidatsa and became a true, nomadic Plains people, heavily dependent on the horse for bison-hunting, though they also gathered roots and berries for food. They also developed their own styles of ceremonial costumes, with dyed porcupine quillwork and later beadwork decoration of unique composition. The Crows have fared better than most Indians in their adaption to American culture, although they are still distinctively Indian, and hold the colourful "Crow Indian Fair" each August. They originally numbered perhaps 8,000 before smallpox reduced them. In 1944 there were 2,467; in 1954, 3,416; and in 1970, 3,779.

MANDAN The largest and most important of the three Upper Missouri River horticultural tribes, who lived in dome-shaped earth-covered lodges stockaded into villages; planted maize, beans, and pumpkins; but also hunted bison. They no doubt once resided somewhere near the Mississippi valley and the heartland of gardening North America; the Winnebago were perhaps their closest relatives, but their speech shows a long separation from their parent Siouan family, and they entered their historic region several generations before the Hidatsa. Prior to the 1782 smallpox epidemic they outnumbered the three Hidatsa villages, with perhaps 3,800 people. Their first recorded contact with whites was in 1738 when Verendrye visited them, at which time they had nine villages near the Heart River. These had been reduced to only two at the time of Lewis and Clark in 1804: Metutehanke and Puptari, below the mouth of the Knife River on the west bank of the Missouri River. During the 1830s the artists Bodmer and Catlin captured in paint some of the most outstanding scenes of native America ever recorded, including chiefs, villages, and important religious ceremonies such as the Okeepa.

In 1837 they were destroyed by smallpox, only 137 people being said to survive. These joined the Hidatsa and were settled on the Fort Berthold Reservation in North Dakota, where a few descendants perpetuate their name. In 1906 they numbered 264, and in 1937 345, but they are now largely merged with the Hidatsa. Together with the Arikara they form the "Three Affiliated Tribes of the Fort Berthold Reservation". Among the ceremonies observed by the three tribes the Okeepa warrants special attention because of its complexity and great antiquity. It is a four day spectacle involving self-torture, the drama of "Lone Man" who saved the tribe from disaster, and other origin myths. The Mandan villages were an important trade centre for nomadic tribes and the northern tribes; from them material culture diffused over a wide area. Reconstructions of Mandan villages can be seen at Knife River near Stanton and Fort Abraham Lincoln State Park, Mandan, North Dakota.

HIDATSA or **MINITAREE** A Siouan tribe on the upper Missouri River in North Dakota who, according to tradition, came from somewhere to the northeast but met and allied themselves to the Mandan and shared with them the agricultural pursuits for which they have become famous. They were in reality a group of three closely related village tribes – Hidatsa, Awatixa and Awaxawi – who were visited by the explorer-trader Thompson in 1797 on the west side of the Missouri near the mouth of the Knife River in present Oliver County, North Dakota, with a population then estimated at about 1,330. Before this time, but after their arrival on the Missouri, the people later called Crow had split from the Hidatsa after a dispute. The Hidatsa movement to the Missouri has been put as early as c.1550. Despite a low rainfall the Hidatsa, Mandan and Arikara were successful as horticultural, earth lodge-dwelling peoples, and became known to a succession of traders and explorers during the 18th century, their villages being a focal point of trade between the nomadic Plains people and the Indians to the north who were in closer contact with the fur trade. They were visited by Lewis and Clark in 1804 and by the artists Catlin and Bodmer in the early 1830s.

In 1837 a terrible smallpox epidemic reduced them to a few hundred survivors consolidated in one village, which was moved in 1845 to Fort Berthold, where they have resided ever since. In 1907 they numbered 468; in 1970, 1,705, including a number who are part Mandan. They were also once known as "Gros Ventre of the Missouri", but have no connection with the Atsina, also known as Gros Ventre.

ARIKARA or **REE** The third of the upper Missouri River horticultural tribes, a Caddoan people and a relatively late off- shoot of the Skidi Pawnee. In the 1780s French traders reported them below the Cheyenne River in present South Dakota. In 1804 Lewis and Clark found them between the Grand and Cannonball Rivers close to the present boundary between North and South Dakota, and already weakened in numbers due to smallpox. They were also often on unfriendly terms with the Mandan, Hidatsa and surrounding Sioux. For a time they apparently rejoined the Skidi on the Loup River, Nebraska, but subsequently returned north and by 1851 were on the Heart River. In 1862 they finally joined the Hidatsa and Mandan on the Fort Berthold Reservation, North Dakota, where their descendants have since remained. Despite their early hostility to Americans some Arikara served as scouts for the U.S. Army during the Indian Wars. Over the years their lands were allotted, and the Missouri bottom lands lost during the Garrison Dam development in the 1950s.

In 1804 they numbered 2,600; the census of 1930 gave 420; in 1945 the reported figure was 780; and in 1970, 928. The "Three Affiliated Tribes of the Fort Berthold Reservation" now run a museum which exhibits buckskin clothing and historical items. There are usually at least four Powwows held each year on the reserve: the White Shield, Mandaree, Little Shell and Twin Buttes Powwows, which are combinations of the northern Plains and Pan-Lakota intertribal forms.

OMAHA A Siouan tribe of the Dhegiha dialectic group who are thought to have moved west from the Mississippi valley, perhaps even from the Ohio valley; and unverified connections have been made to link these Siouans with the ancient people who built the great earthworks of southern Ohio. The Dhegiha, according to tradition, moved along the Missouri River, except for the Quapaw who crossed the Mississippi into present Arkansas. The Omaha continued along the Missouri for about 800 miles above its confluence with the Mississippi, where the explorers Lewis and Clark found them in 1804, in what is now northeastern Nebraska between the Platte and the Niobrara Rivers. In common with other tribes of the region the Omaha lived in earth-covered lodges in permanent villages but also used the conical skin tipi during hunting trips in pursuit of buffalo. In 1820 the Omahas had a permanent village in present Dakota County, Nebraska; they planted maize, beans, pumpkins and watermelons and were also employed in obtaining furs for white traders. They were visited in 1833 and 1847 respectively by the artists Bodmer and Kurz who made important records of their material culture.

In 1854 they ceded their lands to the U.S.A. in return for a reservation in Thurston County, Nebraska, a portion of which was ceded to the Winnebago in 1865. They were reported to number 2,800 in 1780, but were reduced by wars with the Sioux and by smallpox in 1802 to a few hundred. In 1906 they numbered 1,228; and in 1954 about 1,700, of whom fully half were no longer on the reservation, a large proportion of which was occupied by non-Indians. The Omaha descendants hold an annual Powwow near Macy, Nebraska, each summer on the Omaha Reservation, which serves as a unifying tribal event. Many of the customs, beliefs and ceremonies of the tribe were recorded in the 19th century with the help of Francis La Flesche, a prominent mixed blood member of the tribe.

PONCA A branch of the Omaha Indians who separated from their parent tribe at the mouth of the White River, South Dakota, and finally associated themselves with the region around the junction of the Niobrara River with the Missouri in present Knox County, Nebraska. Ponca villages were usually located on a river or creek terrace where gardens could be cultivated on nearby bottom lands. They also hunted bison, deer and antelope. Their dwellings were both earth lodges and skin tipis. They were usually at war with the Sioux, from whom they seem to have adopted the Sun Dance. By treaty in 1858 they ceded their lands to the U.S.A. for a reservation at the mouth of the Niobrara River, which the Poncas were forced to leave in 1876-77 for Indian Territory, where they were finally given lands on the Salt Fork of the Arkansas River which became the Ponca Reservation until allotment. A few Ponca under Standing Bear made a dramatic return home to Nebraska and were allowed to stay after nationwide publicity had been given to their plight. The "Northern" Ponca retained lands near Niobrara, but quickly assumed white culture, and finally were federally terminated in 1962, most tribal members having left the old reserve.

The Southern Ponca still live partly on their old reservation lands near White Eagle in Kay and Noble Counties, Oklahoma; and have been one of the principal groups contributing to the Oklahoma Pan-Indian complex during the 20th century. Their Powwows have been developed from the remains of Prairie tribal warrior society rituals, the Hethuska or Inlonska dances. These secularized forms, with rather baroque "feather" costumes, have become popular with many tribal groups, and their modern Powwows are a focus of ethnic unity. The Southern or Oklahoma Ponca numbered 784 in 1907; 950 in 1950; and about 1,200 in 1970. The Northern Ponca numbered 263 in 1906, and 397 in 1937, but are now so scattered as to make enumeration difficult.

IOWA A small Siouan tribe who lived on the Blue Earth River, Minnesota, when first reported by the French explorer Le Sueur in 1701. Later they were located near the Platte River in Nebraska, Iowa and northern Missouri, where Lewis and Clark met them in 1804. In 1824 they agreed to a move from their homeland to Great Nemaha Reservation in northeastern Kansas along with some of the Sauks and Foxes, where they settled in 1836. During the allotment of the Nemaha reservation a number of Iowa moved to seek homes in Indian Territory; and in response to a plea to Government officials were assigned a reservation in present Payne and Lincoln

Counties, Oklahoma, to the west of the Sauk and Fox of Oklahoma. The Iowa spoke a dialect of the Chiwere branch of the Siouan family, being closely related to the Oto and Missouri and more distantly to the Winnebago. Culturally they were close to the Sauk and Fox; but by the time of Lewis and Clark they were involved with traders from St.Louis and lived in a single village of 800 souls, raising corn and maize but hunting buffalo seasonally.

The Kansas Iowa are still connected with their allotted reservation on the Nebraska-Kansas border north of Hiawatha, Kansas; they numbered 246 in 1907, and 540 in 1945. The Oklahoma Iowa numbered 78 in 1920 and 114 in 1945, mostly near Perkins in Lincoln and Payne Counties. The total number of Iowa, Oto and Missouri was 2,366 in 1970. Today their descendants are much mixed by intermarriage with whites and other Indian tribes.

OTO or **OTOE** A Siouan tribe of the Chiwere group with a tradition of a separation from the Winnebago and a later separation from the Missouri Indians near the mouth of the Iowa River. They gradually removed west, first to the Des Moines River, then to the Missouri River, thence to an area on the south side of the Platte River in present southeastern Nebraska. They were always a small tribal group who maintained themselves amongst enemy tribes. They were rejoined by the remnants of the Missouri at the time of the establishment of a reservation on the Big Blue River near the present Nebraska-Kansas state border line; and were finally removed to Indian Territory in 1882. The Oto were never prominent in history; they lived in permanent villages of earth lodges similar to the Omaha and Kansas, but when visited by Lewis and Clark in 1804 they were already in poor condition. In Oklahoma their reservation in Noble County was allotted against considerable opposition, but the Oto-Missouri descendants still live partially around their old agency and near Red Rock, Oklahoma. Each July the Otoe-Missouri (current spelling) host a typical Oklahoma Pan-Indian Powwow near the old agency lands which representatives of many tribes attend for colourful dances. On tribal lands today they, like many other groups, run a successful bingo hall; disparities in gambling laws make this a useful commercial opportunity.

MISSOURI A small Chiwere Siouan tribe, at one time the same people as the Oto, with a tradition of a separation from the Winnebago. Later the Missouri and Oto divided, the former living for a time on the Grand River, a branch of the Missouri in present northern Missouri state, while the Oto moved to the Des Moines River in Iowa. Wasted by wars with the Sauk, Fox, Osage and Kansa as far back as 1748, they reunited several times with the Oto. Finally about 90 Missouris joined the Oto on the Big Blue River and accompanied them to Oklahoma, where the two tribes became officially the "Otoe-Missouri tribe of Oklahoma", the Missouri having since disappeared as a separate people.

KANSAS, KANSA or **KAW** An important Siouan tribe of the Dhegiha group very closely related to the Osage; their name signified "Wind People". They lived, as their name suggests, on the Kansas, Republican and Big Blue Rivers in northern Kansas and adjacent Nebraska. The explorer Marquette heard of them living in this region as far back as 1673, apparently succeeding some Caddoan tribes on the Prairies of the Kansas River, but their western advance was checked by the Cheyenne. They had semi-permanent earth lodge villages, grew crops, hunted bison, and were often considered warlike by surrounding tribes. In 1815 the Kansa were said to have 130 earth lodges and a population of 1,500; the agent O'Fallon estimated 1,850 in 1822; but they were drastically reduced by smallpox over the next few years. They first agreed with the U.S. authorities to move to a reservation at Council Grove on the Neosho River in 1846, where the Kaw Indian Mission still stands. However, these lands were directly on the Santa Fé Trail; and in a succession of agreements they finally moved to Indian Territory in 1873. There were only 209 left in 1905.

The Kaw Reservation in Oklahoma was located in Kay County, where approximately one third of 600 descendants still live, being mostly of mixed blood. Some old French-Kaw families are still extant, having been well educated over the years, their Indian traditions largely disappearing within the first generation of their move to Indian Territory.

OSAGE The largest and most important Dhegiha Siouan tribe, part of a Siouan movement which divided into the Omaha, Ponca and Kansas, who ascended the Missouri River, the Quapaw going south to the Arkansas while the Osage remained on the Osage River in central-western Missouri state. The tribe was divided into the Great Osage, centering in Vernon County, and the Little Osage on the west side of the Little Osage River. They were in part an agricultural people, raising small crops of corn and squash near their permanent villages, but they depended upon the bison for much food and clothing. Their hunting territory extended to the west, which brought them into contact – and continuous enmity – with the Kiowa and Comanche of the High Plains. Although tribal life and religion existed until the late 19th century, they had a long association with various Spanish and French traders with whom there were some quite early intermarriages, resulting in a reputation for haughty Latin manners. The first European notice of them was by Marquette in 1673, and they had already established relations with the French traders before 1719. After 1802 the Osage also traded at the "Three Forks" near present Okay, Oklahoma, at the junction of the Arkansas with the Neosho and Verdigris Rivers, having separated from the Missouri bands.

The Osage made several treaties with the U.S.A. during the early 19th century by which they ceded their lands in Missouri and Oklahoma for part of southeast Kansas centering in present Neosho County. After the opening of these lands following the Civil War they faced intolerable conditions; however, the sale of remaining lands allowed the purchase of a reservation in Indian Territory, now Osage County, Oklahoma. Having recovered from the many difficulties suffered in Kansas they fell heirs to oil and mineral deposits during the late 1890s and early 1900s which brought great wealth to some Osage families. The present Osage population is widely dispersed over the U.S.A. About one third of their membership lives in three towns on the old Osage Reservation at Gray Horse, Hominy and Pawhuska.

By 1980 the language was known fluently to only about 25 old people, and almost all tribal members were of mixed white and other Indian tribal descent. They are, however, presenters of three annual Powwows at each village, in which they promote their Inlonska dances, derived originally from the Kansa and Ponca to the west of them in about 1880. Their male dancers are widely known as "straight" dancers, lacking the baroque feather "fancy" costumes associated with other Pan-Indian Oklahoma Powwows. The Osage once numbered 6,500 before being reduced by smallpox to 1,582 in 1886; in 1950 there were 4,972 enrolled members of the tribe, of whom only about 480 were full Osage. Over the years their association with French settlers and missionaries has resulted in most present day Osages being nominally Roman Catholic. The Osage are noted producers of fine ribbonwork decoration on their dance clothing, and presently run a tribally owned museum at Pawhuska.

QUAPAW or **ARKANSEA** A member of the Dhegiha Siouan group; their name apparently signified "Downstream People" and they were the most southern of the group. According to tribal traditions they continued down the Mississippi into present Arkansas state, whilst others turned up the Missouri River. Although De Soto's expedition may have met them in 1541, the first recorded contact was by Père Marquette, who during his memorable journey down the Mississippi in 1673 rested at the Quapaw village on the Arkansas River not far above its junction with the Mississippi. He describes their dome-shaped bark-covered cabins, their corn kept in baskets, wooden dishes and pottery. They were also visited by La Salle in 1682 and Tonti in 1686. They were an important people of the area, with remarkable pottery, and living in palisaded villages; but their early contacts with the French on the Mississippi brought diseases, and intertribal conflicts in promotion of the fur trade, hence most Quapaw left the Mississippi valley for the south side of the Arkansas River. By 1761 they had merged with ruined tribes, notably the Illini, whilst the Quapaw remained the nucleus of a diminishing people.

In 1818 the Quapaw ceded all their lands to the U.S.A. except for a strip between Little Rock and Arkansas Post below Gillett, Arkansas. This was ceded in 1835 for lands in southern Kansas and northern Indian Territory, which in turn were ceded except for a section in the northeastern corner of Indian Territory, now Ottawa County, Oklahoma. This became the Quapaw Reservation, but was allotted in 1895. Over the years their population dropped from perhaps 6,000 in the 16th/17th centuries to a meagre 305 in 1909, these mostly of mixed French and other Indian ancestry from groups who had merged with the Quapaw. In 1945 they numbered 610, and by 1970 about 750. Despite their acculturation the Quapaw descendants sponsor a large annual Powwow of a Pan-Indian type near Devil's Promenade, Miami, Oklahoma, including Straight Dances, Stomp Dances and other activities.

CADDOAN

An important language family who probably once lived in the Lower Mississippi valley region, according to tribal traditions. Their agricultural background suggests links with Mississippian culture. The family consisted of many small tribes grouped into confederacies. Commencing in the south, these were the Kadohadacho or Caddo, Hasinai, Natchitoches with the Adia and Eyeish, of Louisiana, eastern Texas and Arkansas; the descendants of the three first tribes became the later "Caddo". In Oklahoma and adjacent Texas were the Wichita, Tawakoni, Waco and Kichai, who ultimately became the "Wichita"; on the Platte River, Nebraska, were the four Pawnee tribes; and finally there were the Arikara, who seem to have split from the Pawnee two and a half centuries ago and migrated along the Missouri into what is now North Dakota.

PAWNEE The largest and most important tribe of the Caddoan linguistic family, probably the last to migrate in a northeasterly direction, reaching the valley of the Platte River in Nebraska. They were essentially an agricultural people, cultivating corn, beans, squash and pumpkins; they also hunted buffalo and other game abundant in Pawnee territory in early times. Whilst in Nebraska they lived in four groups of earth lodge villages, each with its own chief, council and medicine bundles: the Skidi or Wolf Pawnee, Pitahauerat or Tapage Pawnee, Kitkehahki or Republican Pawnee, and the Chaui or Grand Pawnee. Through their sacred bundles, shrines, priests and religious ceremonials they were connected with the supernatural heavenly and cosmic forces to heal diseases, call game and ensure harvests. They believed that all these were created by one deity, "Tirawa".

The Pawnees' first contact with Europeans was probably with the Coronado expedition in 1541; a guide in his party is thought to have been a Pawnee. They obtained horses either directly or indirectly from the Spanish settlements, and French traders were established amongst them by 1750. After the Louisiana Purchase St.Louis became an American trading centre, and subsequent contact with immigrants through their territory brought decimation from cholera and smallpox, which reduced their population from perhaps 10,000 in 1838 to about 1,300 in 1880. In a succession of treaties with the U.S.A. they ceded all their lands except for a reservation in present Nance County, Nebraska; but in 1874-76 all four bands moved to Indian Territory, where an agency and reservation was established below the Arkansas River adjoining the Osage. However, their surplus lands – after the infamous allotments were completed – were opened to white settlement in 1893. Pawnee rural descendants still live in and around Pawnee and Skedee, Pawnee County, Oklahoma. They numbered about 1,260 in 1950, and 1,928 in 1970, with a considerable admixture of white and other Indian ancestry.

They still sponsor the Pawnee Homecoming Powwow each summer, to which other tribes are invited and to which Pawnee men serving with the U.S. Army often return (a military tradition which goes back to the 19th century). This Powwow is of the popular Pan-Indian type established in Oklahoma during the early 20th century, which has been derived from the blending of the culture of a number of tribes forced to Oklahoma during the second half of the 19th century. The songs and dances are based on old Ponca, Kaw and Osage forms, in turn influenced by warrior society rituals of the Omaha, Sauk and Fox, which are known as Hethuska or Inlonska. Subsequently modified in form, dance and dress, the Oklahoma Powwow has become a highly successful social function which has spread far beyond the tribes who developed it.

WICHITA The largest known historic tribe of the southern Caddoan-speaking group, who lived along the Canadian River in present Oklahoma and were presumably the people the explorer Coronado found in 1541 in the area called "Quivira". In 1719 the French commandant Bernard de la Harpe found them on the Arkansas River, Oklahoma, one of several related tribes of the area known collectively as "Pani Pique". American Government relations began in 1834 when Colonel Dodge from Fort Gibson, Indian Territory, held a council with the Wichita and other tribes on the North Fork of the Red River. In 1859 they agreed to settle on a reservation south of the Canadian River, where they were joined by most of their relatives and by the Caddo with their associates from the Brazos Reserve in Texas. They were disrupted by the Civil War and, generally in an impoverished condition, were subsequently allotted lands in severalty by 1901. In early times the Wichita probably numbered 1,600, with their related tribes perhaps more than 3,200; in 1910 there were 318 "Wichita"; 385 in 1937; and 485 in 1970. Most Wichitas now live around Gracemont north of the Washita River in Caddo County, Oklahoma; they are the descendants of true Wichita, Tawakoni, Waco, Kichai and others. The *Tawehash* of early reports were probably at least part of the Wichita.

TAWAKONI A tribe of Caddoan speech and of the Wichita group who lived on the Arkansas River in present Muskogee County, Oklahoma when visited by La Harpe in 1719, but who subsequently drifted south into Texas after the close of the French and Indian War in 1763. They were with the Wacos on the Brazos River near present Waco, Texas, in 1779; and were among the tribes on the Brazos in 1859 when persuaded to move, along with the Caddo, to a reserve on the Washita River in Indian Territory. They ultimately affiliated with the Wichita people and are no longer reported separately, but no doubt have descendants amongst the present day Wichita-Caddo of Oklahoma. Like their relatives they were buffalo-hunters and good horsemen, but they also raised crops of corn and later wheat and vegetables, and owned livestock before leaving Texas.

WACO These Caddoan people were no doubt part of the tribes visited by La Harpe in 1719, and may have been the *Yscani* of early reports. However, they were in northern Texas by 1779 under this name; and part of the people moved in 1859 from the Brazos River to the Washita River, Indian Territory, where they combined with the Wichita and are no longer reported separately. Their descendants are counted as "Wichita" and are in Caddo County, Oklahoma. Villages of the Wichita tribes were distinguished by dome-shaped houses covered with grass thatch.

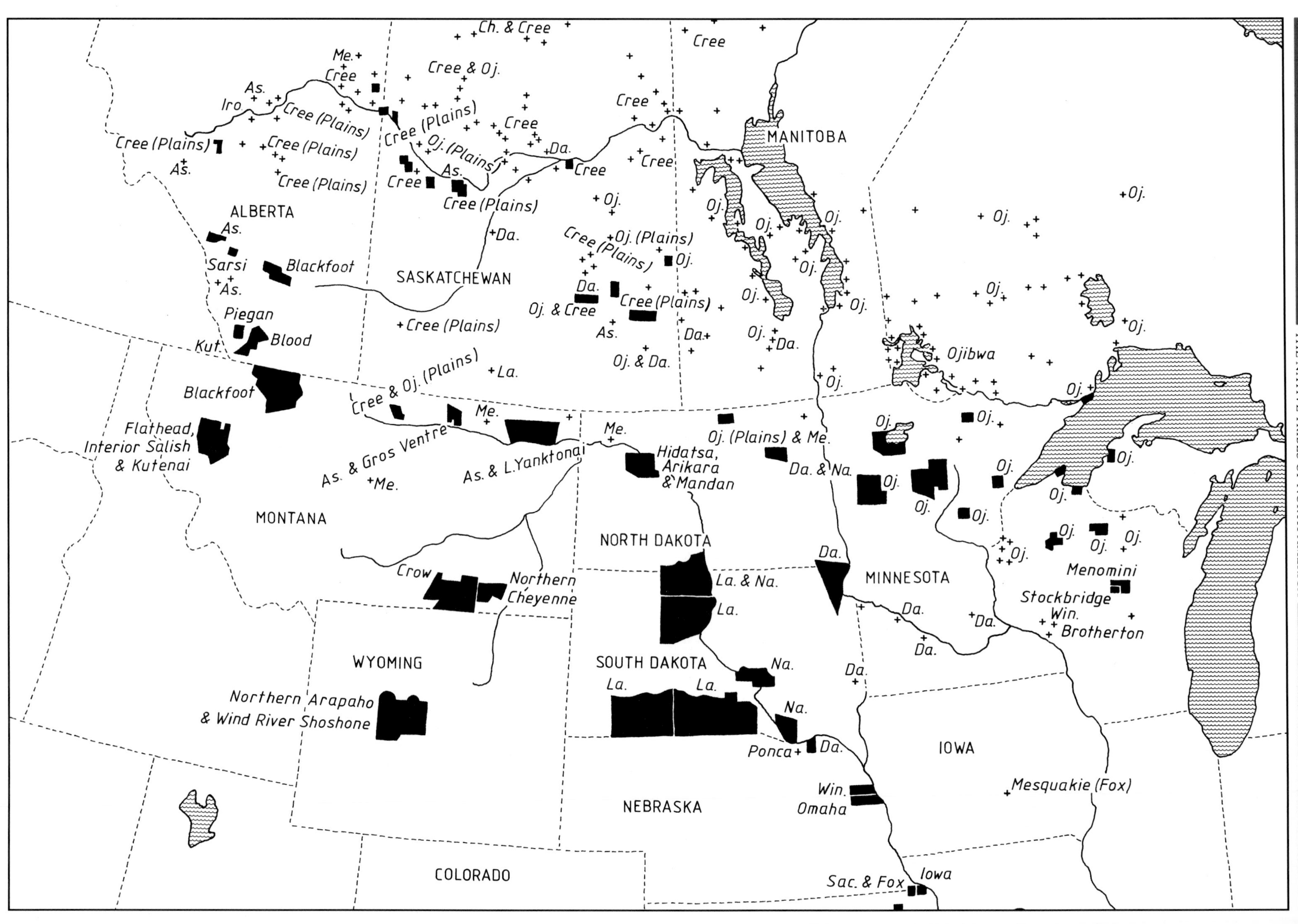
MANITOBA
SASKATCHEWAN
ALBERTA
MONTANA
WYOMING
COLORADO
NEBRASKA
SOUTH DAKOTA
NORTH DAKOTA
MINNESOTA
IOWA
Ojibwa
Menomini
Stockbridge
Win.
Brotherton
Mesquakie (Fox)
Iowa
Sac. & Fox
Win.
Omaha
Ponca
Hidatsa, Arikara & Mandan
Oj. (Plains) & Me.
Da. & Na.
La. & Na.
Northern Cheyenne
Crow
As. & L.Yanktonai
Cree & Oj. (Plains)
As. & Gros Ventre
Blackfoot
Blood
Piegan
Sarsi
Kut.
Flathead, Interior Salish & Kutenai
Northern Arapaho & Wind River Shoshone
Cree (Plains)
Oj. (Plains)
Ch. & Cree
Cree & Oj.
Oj. & Cree
Oj. & Da.
Iro

KICHAI A Caddoan tribe who were living on the upper Trinity River in Texas in 1701, probably intermediate between the tribes which became collectively either Caddo or Wichita. Some were part of the Indians who moved to the Wichita Agency, Indian Territory, from the Brazos Reservation in Texas in 1859. Their descendants are counted as "Wichita" today and live in rural Caddo County, Oklahoma.

SHUMAN or **JUMANO** A people who from early Spanish reports were associated with various places in Texas and adjacent states, once thought to have been Caddoan, Apache or Uto-Aztecan. They were reported on the Rio Grande in 1535, and trading in eastern Texas in 1685. They are not clearly reported after 1740; if they were indeed Caddoan then some no doubt merged with the Wichita; more probably the last of them joined the Hispanicized groups around El Paso, Texas, and in Mexico, where a descendant was still living at Senecú in 1897.

KIOWA According to their own tradition the Kiowas' earliest known home was in Montana, and they were in possession of the Black Hills of western South Dakota during the 18th century. They were probably expelled from this region by the Dakotas arriving from the east, and began a movement south to the Arkansas and the headwaters of the Cimarron River and northern Texas. By 1790 they had established friendly relations with the Comanche. At some time, perhaps in the late 17th or early 18th centuries, a small Athabascan tribe, the Kiowa-Apache, joined them, and remained as a subtribe until reservation days. The Kiowa developed into a formidable and typical Plains tribe; their language forms an independent family, but is distantly related to the Tanoan family of Pueblo Indians. Despite ravaging the southern Plains and even northern Mexico with their Comanche allies, they developed a lucrative trade relationship with the Pueblos.

They became known to the Americans in the early 19th century and were reported on the prairies of the Arkansas and Red Rivers in 1820. A treaty at Fort Atkinson in 1853 attempted to establish peace on the Sante Fé Trail which ran through Kiowa territory, but with little success. The Kiowa suffered from the cholera epidemic of 1849 and smallpox in 1861; but despite their reduced numbers and agreement (1865 and 1867) to relinquish their tribal lands for a reservation in present southwestern Indian Territory, now Oklahoma, they continued to raid Texas. These raids climaxed in the fight at Adobe Wells in 1874, after which the Kiowa Chief Satanta was arrested and later committed suicide. Some Kiowa warriors were even imprisoned and sent for three years to Florida. Much of Kiowa history was contained in a pictographic form known as "calendar histories", recorded by the ethnologist James Mooney.

By the late 1870s the Kiowa and Comanche were finally restricted to their reservation in southwestern Oklahoma, suffering further tragedies from epidemics and starvation after the disappearance of the buffalo in 1879; their transition from tribal to reservation life was attended by much misery. Their population before the epidemics of the early 19th century may have been more than 2,000, but was barely a thousand by the time of their final surrender at Fort Sill in 1875. In 1924 they were reported to number 1,699, and in 1970 4,357, with a considerable number of mixed tribe and race including Mexican and other Indian ancestry, particularly Comanche. The present population live principally in Caddo County, Oklahoma, with the largest community near Carnegie. After several decades of dormancy a Kiowa warrior society has been revitalized representing a distinctively Kiowa contribution to Oklahoma Pan-Indianism, the "Gourd Dance". It has now been formally organised in four separate factional divisions which promote Kiowa ethnic identity among both rural and urban tribal members. Gourd Dance clan members are often invited to attend Powwows throughout Oklahoma; they sing and dance holding distinctive rattles and fans.

COMANCHE The Comanche spoke a Shoshonean language, and perhaps split from the Shoshone after obtaining horses during the late 17th century, to become the most skilled horsemen of the southern Plains and truly nomadic. They were then associated with the area around the North Platte River; later moving south, they ranged at the headwaters of the Cimarron, Brazos, Red and Canadian Rivers. They harried the Spaniards all the way into Mexico, replenishing their herds of horses by trade or by attacks on settlements. They were at first enemies, later close friends of the Kiowa, and together they often closed the Santa Fé Trail. They often adopted white women captured on their raids.

One of their first official dealings with Americans

PLAINS TRIBES, 20th CENTURY

Key to abbreviations:

As	=	Assiniboine
Da	=	Dakota (E. Sioux)
Kut	=	Kutenai
La	=	Lakota (W.Sioux)
Me	=	Métis
Na	=	Nakota (M. Sioux), Yankton & Yanktonai
Shos	=	Shoshone
Win	=	Winnebago

came in 1834 when Colonel Henry Dodge met several Comanche representatives at a Wichita village on the Red River. They remained periodically hostile to Texans and Americans until the famous Medicine Lodge Council of 1867, held in Kansas just north of the Oklahoma state border – one of the most memorable and colourful gatherings of southern Plains Indians. As a result of this treaty, and of military action against the Cheyenne on the Washita in 1868, the Comanche settled on a reservation in southwestern Indian Territory, now Oklahoma. Early reservation life was marked by much suffering and starvation resulting in hostile outbreaks and military reaction. The last of the Comanches to accept reservation life were the Kwahadi band under Quanah Parker, who surrendered in 1875. Parker, son of a white captive, became an influential leader during early reservation life.

The Comanche had several subtribes, the best known being the Kwahadi or "Antelope" band, the Yamparika or "Yap Eaters", the Nokoni, Tanima, Kutsveka, and Penateka or "Wasps", the most southern band and vanguard of the Comanche southward migration. The Comanche lacked the extensive ceremonialism of other Plains tribes, the Sun Dance not being an important aspect of their culture; their bands were more self-managing. Their buckskin clothing was emphasized by heavy fringing rather than by beadwork or other decoration. Their tipis were built on a four-pole basis like those of their Shoshone relatives and unlike the three-pole form used by their neighbours. Their population has often been overstated; it was perhaps 4,000 in the early 19th century, and 2,538 in 1869; reduced to 1,476 in 1910, it recovered to 4,250 in 1970, including a considerable admixture of Spanish, Mexican-Indian, Anglo and recently other Oklahoma Indian ancestry.

Most modern Comanches live in the rural and urban parts of present Caddo, Kiowa, Comanche and Cotton Counties, Oklahoma. The changes brought by acculturation to white American life have resulted in tribal schisms between liberals and conservatives, Christians and Peyotists, and full bloods and mixed bloods. The Comanche, together with the Kiowa, were the principal conduit of the Peyote cult to other Oklahoma tribes. The religion, derived from Mexican Indians by way of Lipan and Mescalero Apaches, was adopted by the Comanche in the 1880s; it involved the sacramental eating of peyote, a mild narcotic, and compounded elements of native and Christian beliefs, but developed in Oklahoma into its present two divergent rites. The Comanche have also been keenly involved with the Oklahoma Pan-Indian Powwow complex of the 20th century.

PADOUCA Early in the 18th century the Padouca are recorded as a people of western Kansas, usually considered as Comanche; however, several historians have suggested that they may have been Apachean, even the first great tribe to have attempted to form settlements and grow crops in the heart of the High Plains country – although archaeological evidence now suggests that the agriculturalists at least were Puebloan. If they were Apachean, perhaps the Lipans and Kiowa-Apache were all that were left of them by the 19th century. Recently the Comanche theory seems more acceptable to historians. A tribe reported as *Gatakas* seem to have been close allies of the Kiowa, and this was probably an early term for the Kiowa-Apache; or alternatively part of a composite "Padouca" who moved south through the Great Plains before the Kiowa-Comanche but who subsequently disappeared from history, at least under that name.

PLATEAU

Language family and tribe	*Meaning*/origin of tribal name, where known	**Language family** and tribe	*Meaning*/origin of tribal name, where known
Shahaptian:		**Salishan:**	
Nez Perce	French – *"pierced noses"*	Flathead or Salish	*"people"*
Palouse	-	Kalispel	*"camas"* (plant)
Wallawalla	*"little river"*	Coeur d'Alene	French – *"awl heart"*
Umatilla	-	Spokan	*"sun people"*
Yakima	*"runaway"*	Colville	English name
Klickitat	*"beyond"*	Senijextee	*"lake people"*
Tenino	-	Okanagan	place name
		Sanpoil & Nespelem	-
Waiilatpuan:		Sinkiuse	band name
Cayuse	-	Wenatchee	place name
Molala	place name	Chelan	-
		Methow	-
		Thompson	English name
Lutuamian:		Shuswap	-
Klamath	*"people"*	Lillooet	*"wild onion"*
Modoc	*"southerners"*	**Kutenai**	division name

The Indians living in the present states of Idaho, Washington, eastern Oregon, parts of adjacent states and Canada constituted a culture area known as the Plateau. Generally the area consists of barren uplands, mountains with patches of forest and lakes; it is cut by two great river systems, the Columbia and its tributary the Snake. The inhabitant tribes subsisted on wild plants and vegetables, camas, bitterroot, berries and seeds; salmon, other fish, deer, elk and mountain sheep. The Indians lived in conical or gable pole structures covered with brush or cattail mats; later Plains type tipis became common. The people were non- agricultural and lacked formal organization, but had a complex theology involving personal spirits and a belief which portrayed illness as the temporary loss of one's soul.

The horse reached the Umatilla in Oregon as early as 1739, moving north among the Indians of the Continental Divide. The mobility provided by the horse allowed yearly hunting and raiding to the plains of Montana. The Nez Perce had strong trade relations with the Crow and Flathead. In later days skin tunics for men and dresses for women superficially resembled Plains costumes, and there were similarities in decoration of ceremonial dress. Many tribes produced fine basketry. Following the explorers Lewis and Clark, missionaries and traders had modified native life in the area by the 1840s; and a number of conflicts occurred between white intruders and the Cayuse, Yakima, Nez Perce and Palouse. Although most of the larger Inland Salish and Shahaptian tribes survived the invasion smaller western groups suffered greatly, particularly the Cayuse, Molala and groups close to the Columbia River.

SHAHAPTIAN or SAHAPTIAN

A linguistic family of the American Plateau region occupying the valleys of the Columbia and Snake Rivers in Washington, Oregon and Idaho. They have been linked with the Cayuse, Molala, Modoc and Klamath into the larger so-called Shapwailutan stock. The Shahaptians as a whole were noted for their superficial adoption of cultural traits from the Plains Indians during the 19th century.

NEZ PERCE The most important tribe of the Shahaptian family occupied lands between the Bitteroot Mountains in the east and to the junction of the Snake and Columbia Rivers in the west. They made their homes along the Clearwater and Snake Rivers and in the Wallowa valley in what is now Idaho. They had strong trading links with the northern Plains Indians, particularly with the Crow, and made seasonal bison-hunting visits to the Montana Plains. In 1805 the explorers Lewis and Clark passed through their territory. They concluded treaties with the United States Government in 1855 and 1863 (which only a portion of the tribe recognised), and agreed to the reservation set aside near Lapwai, Idaho. In a desperate attempt to reach Canada in June-October 1877 some Nez Perce under their famous leader Joseph made a masterly 2,000-mile retreat through Idaho and Montana, but were forced to surrender to Generals Miles and Howard only a few miles from the border. As a result some of Joseph's band were sent to Indian Territory, but returned later, either to the Lapwai Reservation or Colville Reservation, Washington. They numbered 6,000 in the early 19th century; in 1895 1,457 were on the reservation at Lapwai; in 1906, 1,534, and 83 on the Colville Reservation. In 1985 they numbered 2,015, perhaps 400 of these being full blood, mostly on or around their Idaho reservation. They continue to hold root festivals and Powwows which show a continuing Indian tradition.

PALOUSE A group of Shahaptians occupying the Columbia River valley above its junction with the Snake, centering on the Palouse River valley. They included the Chimnapum, Wanyukma, and Wanapum or Sokulks; and the confusing term "Wanapam" has been added, but this is probably the same as Wanapum, the people who lived around Priest Rapids on the Columbia. Although included in the Yakima Treaty of 1855, only a few moved to various reservations, most choosing to remain in their homelands. As a result few Palouse or Wanapum remain today. The Shahaptians were a village people with few political tribal organisations. On the whole Plateau life involved wintertime occupancy of river villages and summertime camping at fishing and root-digging grounds. The Winter Guardian Spirit Dance was the major religious ceremony of the Plateau tribes. Smohalla, an Indian religious leader of the 19th century, was a Wanapum.

WALLAWALLA or **WALULA** A group Of Shahaptians on the Wallawalla River on the south side of the Snake near its junction with the Columbia. Closely related to the Nez Perce, they were met by Lewis and Clark in 1805, and subsequently traders and trappers soon filtered into their domain. They moved to the Umatilla Reservation, Oregon, following the Wallawalla Treaty in 1855. Perhaps numbering over 1,000 in pre-reservation days, they were returned as 397 in 1910 and 623 in 1945. They have now largely merged with the Cayuse and Umatilla and are known as the "Confederated Tribes of the Umatilla Reservation".

UMATILLA The Umatillas lived on the lower Umatilla River near its junction with the Columbia in present Umatilla County, Oregon. Reported to number 1,500 in 1780, they had dwindled to a few hundred by the time of the Wallawalla Treaty of 1855 when they were assigned to the Umatilla Reservation along with the Wallawalla and Cayuse. They numbered 272 in 1910 and 161 in 1950; but are a large element in the confederated "Umatilla" including the other groups, given as 1,234 in 1956 and 1,578 in 1985. They still hold root feasts, and participate in the Powwows at the Pendleton Roundup each September.

YAKIMA This important group of Shahaptians occupied the valley of the Yakima River, a northern tributary of the Columbia on the east side of the Cascades Mountains in present Yakima County, Washington. Several small groups are usually given Yakima status: the Kittitas or Upper Yakima, Pshwanwapam and Mical lived north of the main body; the Taitnapam, who may have been closer to the Klickitat, were in Skamania County; the Topinish, Atanum, Pisko and others formed minor groups. Lewis and Clark estimated the population of true Yakimas as 1,200 in 1806. In 1855 the United States made a treaty with the Yakima and 13 other smaller tribes and bands by which they ceded their lands, and the Yakima Reservation was established, upon which all the participating bands were to be confederated under the name Yakima under a distinguished leader, Kamaiakan. Provisions of the treaty were not ratified until after the Yakima War, 1855-56, and a number of groups, particularly the Palouse, never moved to the reservation.

The collective name "Yakima" has for many years been used to designate all the confederate groups on the agency built around the true Yakima, which also includes some Wishram and Wasco of Chinookian origin. This collective group numbered 2,933 in 1937, and 6,853 on or adjacent to the reservation in 1984. Powwows, rodeos, Salmon Feasts and Fairs, expressions of continuing Yakima Indian life, are regularly held.

KLICKITAT This group lived along the Klickitat and White Salmon Rivers, Klickitat County,

Washington state. They were related closely to the Yakima groups but also intermarried with the Cowlitz to the west, and possibly numbered 600 in 1780. They were included in the Yakima treaty of 1855 and moved to the Yakima Reservation, where they have merged over the years into the "Yakima" population. In 1910, 405 were reported separately; in 1970, only 21.

TENINO A group of Shahaptian bands and villages principally along the Deschutes and John Day Rivers, mainly on the south side of the Columbia River in Oregon, including the Tyigh, Tilkuni, Tukspush (or John Day Indians) and Waiim (or Wyam), to which can be added for convenience the Tapanash and Skinpah on the north side. Although a few seem to have gone to the Yakima Reservation the majority, following the Wasco Treaty of 1855, moved to the Warm Springs Reservation, Oregon, where a merged Wasco-Tenino-Paiute population remains. In 1945, 544 Tenino were reported plus a few John Days. In 1985 over 2,000 "Warm Springs" were enrolled. A few Waiams continued to occupy old fishing sites along the Columbia until recent times. Root feasts and Powwows are still popular on the Warm Springs Reservation.

WAIILATPUAN

A small linguistic family, now thought to be close enough to both Shahaptian and Lutuamian to constitute one stock, "Shapwailutan". Only two tribes form the family, the Cayuse and Molala.

CAYUSE A tribe of the upper Wallawalla, Umatilla and Grande Ronde Rivers in northeastern Oregon, although they originally came from the Deschutes River area. They are particularly famous for their horses. They were involved in the so-called "Whitman mission massacre" of 1847, largely caused by squabbles over land ownership and fears about measles epidemics. Settled on the Umatilla Reservation, they numbered 404 in 1904, and 370 in 1937; but have largely merged into the "Confederated Umatilla", a composite of Umatilla, Wallawalla and Cayuse.

MOLALA This second branch of the Waiilatpuan family lived on the eastern slopes of the Cascades Mountains of central Oregon, and later on the Santiam and Molala Rivers on the west side. The last of these people were said to be on the Grande Ronde Reservation, and a few may still be in the Lincoln County area of Oregon. The census of 1910 gave 31, but they are no longer separately reported.

LUTUAMIAN

A small linguistic group formed by two tribes of southern Oregon, the Klamath and Modoc. The group is connected with the Shahaptian and Waiilatpuan into the larger Shapwailutan stock.

KLAMATH The Klamath lived in the area of rivers and marshes around upper Klamath Lake, Oregon. They ceded their lands to the United States in 1864 and were provided with a reservation, which they shared with the Modocs and some Paiutes. Over the years they became very mixed with Euro-Americans and lost much of their Indian culture, which led to the termination by the Bureau of Indian Affairs of the reservation's status and of all government programmes and assistance. However, the tribe's descendants are pressing for renewed government recognition. In 1958 a total of 2,133 were enrolled, being all the people of Klamath, Modoc and Yahooskin Paiute descent living on and off their former reservation.

MODOC The southern branch of the Lutuamian family, they lived around lower Klamath Lake, Tule Lake and Clear Lake in northern California. The Modocs are remembered for their stubborn resistance to American troops in the Lava Beds of northern California in 1872 under their leader, Captain Jack. As a result a number were sent into exile in Indian Territory, although some returned; a few descendants remain in Oklahoma today. The majority of Modocs, however, were incorporated amongst the Klamath on the Klamath Reservation, and have 300-500 descendants, some around the town of Chiloquin, Oregon; but few, if any, are full blood Modoc.

SALISHAN

The Salishan tribes of the mountains, valleys and rivers of the Canadian Cordillera and the American Plateau regions, while linguistically connected to their kindred of the coast, were much different in culture. Their house types were the conical mat lodge, sometimes extended to communal lodges, and winter semi-underground dwellings. In common with other Plateau Indians they were well developed in the skills of fishing, making baskets and woven bags and dressing skins. In later years they obtained a veneer of Plains culture and adopted the tipi of the popular type, particularly the eastern groups such as the Flathead.

FLATHEAD or **SALISH PROPER** The easternmost Salishan tribe living in western Montana in the valleys between the Rocky Mountains and the Bitterroot Range. They apparently obtained their name because, in contrast to tribes farther west, they did not deform the heads of children by compression with a board in the cradle. During the first half of the 19th century the Flatheads were involved in the fur trade, and generally relations with whites were friendly; they were missionized by the Roman Catholics in the 1840s. They signed a treaty with the U.S.A. in 1855 and were assigned a reservation around Flathead Lake, Montana, where they were ultimately combined with part of the Spokan, some Lower Kalispel, most of the Upper Kalispel or Pend d'Oreilles, and some Kutenai. The true Flathead were usually reported to number around 600; in 1909, 598. The population of the whole "Confederated Salish-Kutenai" of the Flathead reservation was given as 3,085 in 1937; 3,630 in 1945; and 5,937 in 1980, of which only half resided on the reserve. Flathead culture was superficially much like that of the Plains tribes, although they never held the Sun Dance. The Arlee Powwow is held in July, and other cultural events are expressions of their continuing cohesion as an Indian people.

KALISPEL This Salish tribe were also known as Pend d'Oreilles in reference to the large shell earrings which some of them wore. They were divided into the Upper Kalispel of western Montana, around Thompson Falls on the Clark Fork of the Pend d'Oreille River, and the Lower Kalispel extending into present northern Idaho up to Priest Lake, almost to the Canadian border. Like the Flathead they participated marginally in the horse-bison culture, but Plains traits were superficial. They were dominated by the fur trade and Catholic missionaries from the 1840s. Most of the Upper Kalispel and a few of the Lower Kalispel joined the Flatheads on the Flathead Reservation, numbering 640 and 197 respectively in 1905. The Lower Kalispel are also found on the Kalispel Reservation at Usk, Washington, established in 1914, and a few on the Colville Reservation. The Kalispel element of the combined confederated "Salish-Kutenai" are no longer reported separately, but the Usk Lower Kalispel numbered 259 in 1985.

COEUR d'ALENE or **SKITSWISH** The country occupied by this Salish tribe was almost wholly within the present state of Idaho on the headwaters of the Spokane River, Coeur d'Alene Lake, below Lake Pend d'Oreille. Missionary work began amongst them in the 1840s. The Coeur d'Alene Reservation in Benewah County, Idaho, was established in 1873, and for the majority of their descendants has been home since that time. They numbered 494 in 1905; 608 in 1937; and 440 in 1970. They sponsor an annual Powwow at Worley.

SPOKAN A Salishan tribe on the Spokane and Little Spokane Rivers in eastern Washington, closely related to their eastern neighbours. They became associated with white traders after the establishment of Spokane House in 1810; and were assigned to several reservations in the late 19th century, but principally the Spokane Reservation, Wellpinit, Washington, and some with the Flathead in Montana, reported as 454 and 135 respectively. In 1937 they were reported to total 847, and in 1985, 1,961. Summer dances, games and exhibits are still held at Wellpinit.

COLVILLE Originally a small Salishan tribe around Kettle Falls on the Columbia River below the Canadian border. They became associated with the Hudson's Bay post at Fort Colville after its establishment in 1825. In 1872 the Colville Reservation was established on the western and northern sides of the Columbia adjacent to the original Colville domain, and the Colville have been there ever since, although now incorporated with many other tribes to form the modern "Confederated Tribes of the Colville Reservation". These tribes include the Sinkiuse or Columbia, Wenatchee, Chelan, Sanpoil, Nespelem, Okanagan, Lake or Senijextee, and a few Nez Perce and Spokan. True Colville numbered 334 in 1907, and 322 in 1937, but the whole "Confederated Colville" 3,799 in 1985. Rodeos and Powwows are still regularly held in summer at Omak, Washington.

SENIJEXTEE or **LAKES** This Salishan tribe lived on the Columbia River north of Kettle Falls, and on the Kettle River into Canada to Lower Arrow Lake. Those on the south side of the international border joined the various tribes of the Colville Reservation, being reported as 542 in 1909. Any north of the border seem to have merged with the Okanagan.

OKANAGAN or **SINKAIETK** This interior Salish tribe lived along the Okanagan River, Washington, north across into Canada on the Similkameen River and Lake Okanagan. They were estimated to number 2,500 in around 1790. The Canadian bands were settled on reserves around Lake Okanagan, at Okanagan, Westbank, Penticton, Upper and Lower Similkameen and Osoyoos, numbering over 1,500 in 1970. A few southern Okanagan were enrolled at the Colville agency, numbering 187 in 1906, and now part of the "Confederated Colville".

SANPOIL & NESPELEM Two closely related Salishan groups on the Sanpoil and Nespelem rivers in north central Washington state. They made no treaty with the Government, although ultimately most appear to have moved to the Colville Reservation. The Sanpoils numbered 202 in 1915 and

(continued on p. 123)

COLOUR PLATE CAPTIONS

The purpose of these plates, which naturally cannot be considered as remotely comprehensive, is to present a visual introduction to some of the basic material cultural traits of a selection of the Native American peoples. Central to our choice of subjects – all of which are illustrated from primary reference sources – is the wish to dramatize the enormously wide and varied range of cultures native to the North American continent.

Plate A: Costume

(A1) Arctic: Baffin Island Eskimo man, c.1577
Sketches made during Frobisher's expedition show both men and women wearing sealskin parkas with a long rear tail; this later disappeared from men's costume, perhaps in imitation of European jackets, but was retained by women.

(A2) Arctic: Alaskan Eskimo woman, c.1895
Women's caribou parkas of northern Alaska and the Mackenzie delta region of Canada had deep side scallops, and hood ruffs. Parka styles varied considerably across the Arctic. Sealskin was important in the east. Men's parkas sometimes had ears and attachments in zoomorphic reference to prey animals as an aid to hunting; women's sometimes had circular or diagonal inserts projecting a uterine reference, symbolizing the maternal role; hoods were often large enough to carry babies. Leggings and boots were combined. In winter two layers of clothing were often worn, the inner layer with fur inside, the outer with fur outside.

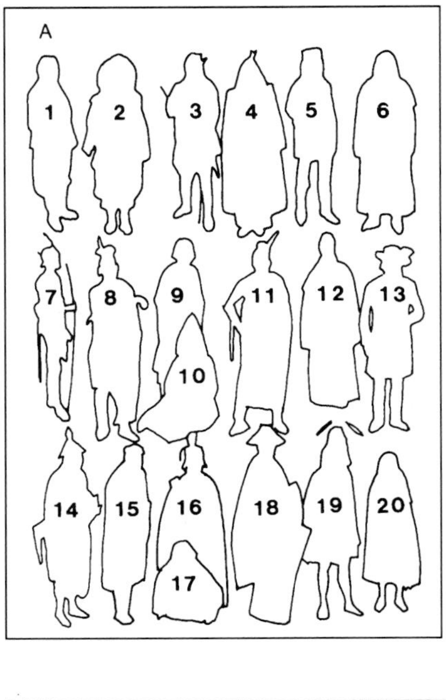

(A3) Subarctic: Kutchin man, c.1862
Northern Athabascan men's summer dress of Western tribes was characterized by a long-sleeved pullover shirt with a distinctive pointed lower edge, combined moccasin-trousers, and mittens. Usually of caribou hide, garments were decorated with dentalium shells and porcupine quillwork, the seams often highlighted with red ochre. After about 1850 Subarctic clothing began to be greatly modified in cut and materials by European influences.

(A4) Subarctic: Swampy Cree woman, c.1780
A few painted garments with dot, circle and linear designs have survived in museums, attributed to Eastern and Swampy Cree of the Hudson Bay area before European styles and materials became influential. The rare side-fold dress, cape, hood, moccasins and pouch display quilled and beaded ornamentation.

(A5) Subarctic: Nascapi man, c.1880
Caribou hide clothing, perhaps partly fitted, seems to have been characteristic of circumpolar costume in aboriginal times, probably being modified by European contact into more complex tailoring. The Nascapi, Montagnais and Eastern Cree have a tradition of magnificent painted garments, paint being applied in lines scored on the skin surface. Designs, apparently once predominantly linear, were no doubt symbolic hunting aids, and often used the flattened form of double curve typical of Northeast Algonkians. Note the cap, rounded bullet pouch, mittens, and moccasins without front seams but gathered around a large vamp.

(A6) Subarctic: Slavey or Chipewyan woman, c.1885
Northern Athabascans of the Mackenzie drainage have a tradition of relatively tailored clothing, although this dress is also heavily influenced by European materials. The cape and cuffs are black velvet decorated with floralistic beadwork; the moccasins are the common Subarctic form with a centre seam and U-shaped instep vamp.

(A7) Northeastern Woodlands: Carolina Algonkian warrior, c.1585
Watercolour sketches made by John White, one of Raleigh's colonists, near the settlement at Roanoke Island in 1585-87 are preserved in the British Museum. He reported that warriors from around present-day Albemarle Sound, NC, decorated their bodies with paint and pearls (probably shells or Roanoke wampum). This warrior, derived from White's drawings, has a skin apron, and a bow probably of maple or hazel.

(A8) Northeastern Woodlands: Iroquois warrior, c.1776
He holds a ball-headed maple war club (these often being carved and incised); and wears a silver gorget traded from his white allies, a sash with interspaced beads, buckskin leggings and moccasins decorated with porcupine quillwork.

(A9) Northeastern Woodlands: Saulteaux woman, c.1820
One of the earliest recorded women's dresses in the Northeast was the skin (later, trade cloth) slip supported over the shoulders with two straps to which a separate cape or sleeves were added in cold weather. This very loose garment required a belt tied behind.

(A10) Northeast Woodlands: Micmac woman, c.1830
Early 19th century Micmac clothing used European materials but retained the beauty of traditional design. Women wore curious peaked hoods with old double-curved designs in beadwork, and skirts had rich parallel-lined silk ribbon appliqué. Moccasins were now made with large vamps over the instep, covered with bead- or ribbonwork.

(A11) Northeastern Woodlands: Fox (Mesquakie) warrior, c.1830
Based on the paintings of Karl Bodmer and George Catlin, this warrior from the period of the so-called Black Hawk War wears a roach with an eagle feather, a bear claw necklace, and a blanket; a quirt hangs from his wrist and he holds a metal trade tomahawk.

(A12) Northeastern Woodlands: Kansas Potawatomi woman, c.1870
Silver brooches decorate clothing made entirely of cloth, which had replaced leather amongst the Woodland peoples by the mid-19th century. She wears the wraparound skirt, an old pattern, but now decorated with the cut-and-fold ribbonwork which had wide distribution from the Canadian Maritimes to the eastern Plains; it developed into its most colourful forms among Southern Woodland peoples, some now removed to reservations in Kansas and Indian Territory. The art was also adopted by Missouri valley tribes such as the Omaha, Osage and Kaw, whose women produced superb examples of silk ribbonwork on ceremonial clothes. Both real silver traded from whites, and later "German silver" made by their own smiths, were used for ornamentation.

(A13) Northeastern Woodlands: Huron of Lorette chief, c.1840
The remnant Huron group which settled near Quebec city gradually adopted French cultural traits, but retained a number of indigenous crafts. Moosehair embroidery and quillwork, used to decorate souvenir trade items, also appeared on the cuffs, shoulders and collars of men's dress clothes. He wears a French Canadian-made assumption sash, probably derived from and replacing the native-made finger-woven sash of fibre or traded woollen yarn.

(A14) Northwest Coast: Nootka man, c.1778
A sketch made at Nootka Sound, Vancouver Island during James Cook's third voyage is the basis for this man, wearing a woven hat with a whaling scene, and a fur cloak. He has ear pendants and facial painting; and carries arrows with barbed bone points in a fur quiver, and a bow of the type used for hunting land game and sea otter, and warfare.

(A15) Northwest Coast: Haida shaman, c.1880
Masked shaman with bird down decoration in his hair and around his neck. The blanket of commercial wool is worn over a tunic-kilt of native textiles, shredded cedar bark and twisted mountain goat wool, with brilliant blue-green designs, woven like the so-called Chilkat blankets imported from the Tlingit of southern Alaska; the bottom edge is fringed with puffin beaks.

(A16) Northwest Coast: Kwakiutl woman
Chief's wife holding a broken "copper" (see under A18), inviting a rival chief to at least match its value or acknowledge his social inferiority. Her tunic-dress of trade cloth is covered with cut-out totemic figures in contrasting colours; the "button blanket" cloak is covered with designs outlined in white shell-like traded buttons.

(A17) Northwest Coast: Haida woman
She is wrapped in a trade blanket and wears a silver nose ring and a large labret through the lower lip, a symbol of high rank.

(A18) Northwest Coast: Haida chief, c.1888
The ceremonial basketry hat is painted in red, white and black designs showing the crest of the wearer. His Chilkat blanket is woven by women, with cedar bark and goat wool motifs designed by men to represent their clan or lineage crests. Shield-shaped plaques of sheet copper, brought in by Europeans, were highly prized as wealth symbols, representing the value of wealth distributed at Potlatch ceremonies to validate the social status of the sponsor.

(A19) Northwest Coast: Cowichan/Halkomelem spirit dancer
An early representation of the Spirit Dance headdress originally of hair, sometimes later of wool, and topped with feathers. Dancers used twirling movements hinting at the identity of the spirit power, usually an encounter with an animal in human form as a guardian spirit. The complex, still active among modern Coast Salish, with initiation and dramatic ritual usually held in winter, is used as therapy for illness and alcohol or drug abuse.

(A20) Northwest Coast: Nootka woman, c.1900
This young woman wears her hair in woollen bands with strings of beads, tipped with traded thimble "jinglers", signifying puberty. The comb pinned to her cedar bark cloak enables her to touch her head without violating menstrual restrictions.

Plate B: Costume

(B1) Plains: Cree man, c.1780
The Cree had penetrated the northeastern Plains of present Saskatchewan and Manitoba by the late 18th century. Surviving evidence of male dress suggests that these marginal Plains people retained partly fitted hide tunics and quilled and painted decoration reminiscent of Subarctic Algonkian prototypes. The placement of diminished discs and strips appears intermediate between Subarctic garments, and the loose-fitting hide shirts with larger strips characteristic of early 19th century northern Plains warriors.

(B2) Plains: Cree woman, c.1790
A dress of this type collected in the Upper Missouri region by Lewis and Clark in 1804-05 is no doubt of Cree origin. It is constructed with one fold – one seam on the side and along the top. The painted decoration is clearly related to early Subarctic garments where red and black bands predominate; the beaded discs perhaps derive from central Subarctic sun symbols, as present on fitted coats with multicoloured designs attributed to late 18th/early 19th century Cree, Ojibwa and Métis.

(B3) Plateau: Spokan man, c.1846
The Canadian artist Paul Kane travelled west across the interior, reaching Fort Vancouver in December 1846. Near Fort Colville he painted an Indian with combined bowcase and quiver as well as a second bow, and wearing this pierced buckskin shirt imbued with protective power.

(B4) Plains: Mandan warrior, c.1833
From a Bodmer painting, winter 1833-34; the warrior, Flying Eagle, has a bear claw necklace and eagle wing fan indicating high rank; wolves' tails attached to his heels indicate warrior status. His robe is decorated with a quilled band with rosettes, his leggings with "pony" beadwork, and his moccasins with both beads and quills. Blue beads (transported by traders using pack ponies) were the first European-manufactured beads to be widely used in this region.

(B5) Plains: Assiniboine warrior, c.1833
Inspired by a Bodmer painting of a visitor to Fort Union on the Missouri in June 1833, he wears a loose-fitting hide shirt and a robe, and holds a rawhide combat shield with protective designs and "medicine"; the bow-lance, reported from a number of tribes, was probably dual-functional.

(B6) Plains: Comanche warrior, c.1840
The principle defence of the Plains warrior was the rawhide shield, usually made from the bison's thickest breast hide, and protected when not in use with a soft buckskin case. Shields were painted with symbols and had small "medicine" attachments. This warrior's eagle feather bonnet is taken from a

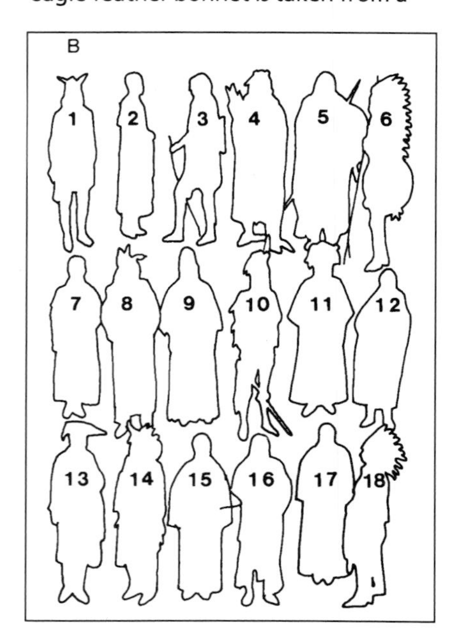

known example collected before 1850, the browband with pony beads and triangular designs recalling Plateau/Basin Shoshone work; the Comanche had previously separated from the Shoshone.

(B7) Plateau: Nez Perce woman, c.1900
Cloth replaced hide late in the 19th century. The dress's square-cut yoke gave a "bat wing" effect, and sleeves terminated above the elbow; it was worn over a blouse. The yoke was often decorated with cowrie shells, and elk's teth or carved bone imitations; the primary source for this example seems to show brass tacks, an unusual addition. The Nez Perce are famed for their large twined storage bags of cornhusk with designs in native fibres or traded wool; the designs probably influenced the rather massive quality of late Plateau beadwork. Nez Perce moccasins were usually of side seam construction; floralistic beaded designs appeared quite early during the fur trade era in the Plateau region.

(B8) Plateau: Salish man, c.1880
The Hudson's Bay Company were the primary European influence in much of the Canadian interior and western U.S.A. until the early 19th century. Among the trade goods they introduced were the English woollen "point" blankets, so named from lines marked on the edge denoting the weight and thus the value in trade for furs. Traders, Métis and Indians made them into winter *capote* coats. These were popular among northern Plains tribes and marginal Salish (Flathead), whose western Montana location was a crossroads for styles of native dress and ornamentation. The fur cap is embellished with peacock and eagle feathers. Note loop necklace, and pipe bag.

(B9) Plateau: Yakima woman, c.1885
The older, classic dress of the Plateau and northwestern Plains was constructed of two elk skins forming the front and back, sewn together; to straighten the shoulder line the tail ends were folded over and stitched down. Plateau women decorated the upper part with bands of large pony beads strung loosely and sewn to the skin. Her basket hat of native fibre has a deep triangular design in bear grass false embroidery.

(B10) Plains: Blackfoot man, c.1890
Pierced skin decoration was recorded in the East among the Ojibwa and Eastern Sioux, and in the West among the Blackfoot, Flathead and Plateau tribes. Members of the Brave Dog Society of the Blackfoot wore shirts of this type when in dress representing the grizzly bear. Blackfoot moccasins were originally of side seam construction or later separate sole forms, but usually soft- soled. This youth also wears a loop bead necklace, porcupine head roach and topknot hairstyle; and carries a sabre, probably as society insignia but also a useful weapon.

(B11) Plains: Blackfoot woman, c.1895
Blackfoot dresses were originally made of two large elk skins joined at the shoulders with a fold-over, although a small separate yoke became more common; later a deeper yoke, shaped and curved around an imaginary deer tail relating to the original shape of the hides, was sewn or laced to the two hides forming the skirt. In 1885-1905 square-cut dresses of red or dark blue stroud cloth became popular; later still separate cloth yokes or capes reinforced with sacking, over cloth or sateen dresses, were in vogue. Blackfoot women usually covered the upper part of dresses and capes with horizontal bands of wide lazy stitch beadwork in seed or pony beads fringed with tubular "basket" beads and traded thimbles. Triangular cloth patches on the front of the skirt – possibly a uterine or bison symbol – were a Blackfoot feature. The feathered headdress signifies an officer of a women's society.

(B12) Plains: Osage woman, c.1900
The Osage and Kaw of the southern Prairies came into proximity with resettled southern Woodland tribes after their removal to Oklahoma, and probably adopted from them the techniques of ribbon appliqué. Besides cut-and-fold geometrical patterns the Osage are noted for horse and hand motifs, sometimes found on so-called "friendship blankets"; the hand was an old, possibly Mississippian symbol of esoteric significance. This young woman also wears "German" (nickel) silver brooches.

(B13) Plains: Omaha man, c.1868
His costume is characteristic of the Missouri valley tribes. The otter fur turban, with the tail folded and protruding at the side, is decorated with ribbonwork and beaded at the front with the hand motif common amongst the Omaha, Osage and Pawnee. Grizzly bear claw necklaces were characteristic of the southern Woodlands and Prairies, although never numerous because of the difficulty of obtaining them (particularly from the now-extinct Plains grizzly). Highly valued, the claws were considered to be imbued with the strength and valour of the bear; the hunter might offer a speech of apology after killing one. The necklace sometimes had an otter skin pendant down the back. He wears buckskin leggings, probably untailored, with bottom tabs and frontal beadwork in realistic animal designs, also noted among the Pawnee. The Omaha, in common with the Winnebago, also made moccasins with the ankle flap extending around the front over the instep.

(B14) Plains: Crow man, c.1880
Crow men were among the most impressively dressed of all Plains people. The earliest known surviving warrior shirts have porcupine quill strips on the arms and over the shoulders, in techniques known as quill-wrapped horsehair and diagonal weave. In the late 19th century, linked by trade to other, notably Plateau peoples, the Crow developed geometrical beaded designs in characteristic flat mosaic surfaces of greens, blues, yellows and pinks. Men's shirts were heavily fringed with ermine tails, and trade cloth leggings often had contrasting coloured "boxes" at the front with beaded lanes. Northern Plains tribes also favoured the loop bead necklace.

(B15) Plains: Cheyenne woman, c.1880
A bucksin dress of classic southern Plains three-hide type: front and back forming the skirt, with the yoke a large, folded rectangle sewn to the skirt tube in a straight seam. Two bands of beadwork are sewn half way between head aperture and seam, and one band along the shoulder fold. Along the bottom are zig-zag motifs, and corner extensions simulating the legs of the original animal shape. Sioux women also wore a three-hide dress, although the yoke hide was less deep, and was sometimes separate and covered with seed beadwork. All Plains women substituted cloth for hide in the early reservation years.

(B16) Plains: Arapaho man, c.1880
Wholesale use of white trade goods had considerably modified central Plains dress by the third quarter of the 19th century; this man wears a set of horizontally strung "hairpipes" and a nickel silver cross. His pipe has a red catlinite bowl; his pipe bag, and moccasins, show geometrical patterns also favoured by the Sioux and Cheyenne (although details differed), executed in seed beeds in sinew-sewn ridged lanes – "lazy stitch". Central Plains moccasins by now had hard soles sewn to separate uppers, a style thought to be white-influenced.

(B17) Plains: Western Sioux woman, c.1900
Lakota woman wearing a blue trade cloth dress heavily decorated with dentalium shells – slender, cone-shaped shells open at each end, brought to the central Plains by white traders from c.1860. Tubular ornaments in conch shell, later in silver and brass, for hair decoration (hence "hairpipes") were used by Eastern tribes, and by the 19th century shell pipes were being drilled by white manufacturers in New Jersey for the Western Indian trade; after 1880 these were made from polished cattle bone. Women usually strung them vertically, men horizontally into breastplates.

(B18) Plains: Western Sioux man, c.1895
Lakota ceremonial dress gradually lost its religious symbolism as warrior societies fell into disuse and ceremonials tended toward a merely social character. War bonnets and war shirts were worn by some older men irrespective of the spiritual, obligatory or status requirements of pre-reservation days. However, the reservation Sioux developed distinctive beadwork in increasingly complex geometrical designs, including matching strips for buckskin shirts and leggings. Leggings of buckskin or cloth were sometimes made with outstanding flaps, a style originally brought to the New World by the Spanish.

Plate C: Costume

(C1) Southeastern Woodlands: Timucua man, c.1562
From paintings by Jacques Le Moyne, cartographer and artist to the French Huguenot colony on the St.John River, of the Timucua peoples in the fortified towns of northern Florida, 1562-64. Their men had distinctive hairstyles, wore feather crowns and ear plugs, were heavily tattooed, and seem to have used metal ornaments.

(C2) Southeastern Woodlands: Choctaw warrior, c.1735
Two French artists recorded lower Mississippi valley tribes in the early 18th century: Antoine du Pratz the Natchez and Chitimacha, 1718-34; and A. de Batz the Choctaw, Natchez, Tunica and others, 1732-35. This Choctaw, with warrior face paint, holds Chickasaw scalps on a pole.

(C3) Southeastern Woodlands: Choctaw ball game player, c.1830
Catlin recorded the face paint, broad decorated belt and horsetail ornaments in c.1830. Known in both Northeastern and Southeastern Woodlands, this team game – often played violently as a substitute for war – was named "lacrosse" by the French from the racket's resemblance to a bishop's crozier. In recent times the Iroquois used one racket, the Choctaw and Cherokee two.

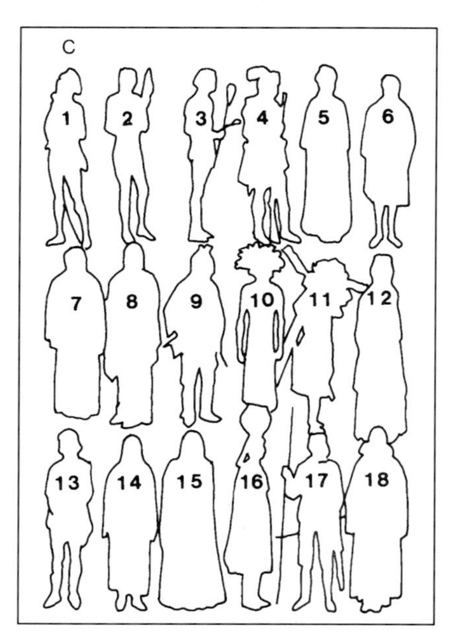

(C4) Southeastern Woodlands: Cherokee chief, c.1825
The ceremonial dress of Southeastern leaders at the time of removal to Indian Territory mixed European materials with native styles. Moccasins remained the eastern centre seam type; cloth or occasionally buckskin leggings with front seams may have been native derived; this European style coat has an open front and large collar; the cloth turban features a silver band and imported feathers. Some Cherokee, Creek and Seminole triangular flap bandolier pouches survive, decorated in unique curving symmetrical beadwork designs of an almost African quality; one example has gold-plated beads.

(C5) Southeastern Woodlands: Florida Seminole woman, c.1920
The isolated Seminole developed distinctive costume; from c.1895, with the use of sewing machines, seamstresses produced cut and sewn patchwork quilting for women's dresses in narrowing bands of increasingly complex designs, as on this skirt and blouse; note also multi-strand bead necklace.

(C6) Southeastern Woodlands: Florida Seminole man, c.1925
The "Big Shirt", with horizontal patchwork quilting bands, was developed from earlier coats. The original "Long Shirt" seen in early 19th century paintings of Creek, Cherokee and Seminole men had a full length front opening and a collar or cape; worn over a plain shirt, it may have been inspired by 18th century European style. Quilting first appeared on it, replacing horizontal bands of contrasting colour cloth, in c.1910; the "Big Shirt", opening to the waist only, appeared c.1915; and the modern Seminole shirt seems to be a variation of this, without the skirt.

(C7) Great Basin: Ute woman, c.1885
Late 19th century costume showed characteristics of the neighbouring Shoshone, Jicarilla and Plains tribes; eastern Ute bands adopted lazy stitch beadwork superficially resembling Cheyenne and Arapaho work. Note facial and hair paint; the ankle length dress is made of two skins (probably deer), tails up, with a fully beaded yoke (sometimes separate) forming the upper part; the silver conch belt is a traded Navajo item.

(C8) Great Basin: Ute man, c.1885
Men's shirts had long triangular neck flaps, probably an exaggeration of the original hide shape (or representing knife sheaths worn from the neck by Eastern tribes). Shirts and leggings were usually heavily fringed, with beaded strips in stepped and large triangular elements.

(C9) Great Basin: Southern Paiute man, c.1872
At this date John W.Powell, later of the Smithsonian Institution, and photographer John K.Hillers recorded Southern Paiute men and women wearing buckskin clothing which resembled that of the Ute and Shoshone. It has not been confirmed as of Paiute make; but the buckskin cap and sandals are more typically Paiute.

(C10) California: Diegueño (Tipai) dancer, c.1880
For ceremonials men wore feather headdresses and elaborate face and body paint. During the Whirling Dance a leading dancer wore a kilt of eagle feathers.

(C11) California: Pomo man in Bole-Maru dress, c.1925
The Kuksu religious system of secret men's societies performed rituals to restore perpetual harmony with ghosts, ensure fertility and the first fruits, and aid curing. Performers impersonated spirits, human and animal ghosts and divinities, wearing elaborate costumes including large feathered headdresses ("Big Heads"). The Kuksu fell into disuse from the 1870s; but revitalization cults later infiltrated north central California, and one echoed the remnant of Kuksu, though limited to human ghosts evoked by male or female dreamer priests (Maru). The Bole-Maru cult also included end-of-the-world and ultimately Christian concepts; it still has a few Pomo reservation adherents.

(C12) California: Tolowa woman, c.1890
Classic two-piece skirt of the Klamath River area: a narrow buckskin apron panel with clam and abalone shells covers a fibre and beaded skirt fringed with abalone "tinklers". Note strings of shell beads, and basket hat.

(C13) Southwest: Yuma (Quechan) man, c.1860
Though Yuma men frequently went naked, in cooler weather both men and women wore rabbitskin robes, or blankets traded from the Hopi. Men rolled their long hair with mesquite sap or mud and daubed pigment over the entire body for warfare. Yumas sometimes wore moccasin-boots with separate rawhide soles.

(C14) Southwest: Western Apache woman, ceremonial dress, c.1930
For the girls' puberty ceremony Western, Chiricahua and Mescalero Apache women wore the two-piece buckskin dress, a large cape extending to the waist over a separate skirt, heavily fringed, painted and decorated with single lanes of beadwork and tin cone "jingles". Yellow-coloured

moccasin-boots, with hard soles turned up at the toe, were sometimes beaded with mountain spirit motifs. Her necklace is of loomed beadwork.

(C15) Southwest:
Mohave woman, c.1880
Women originally wore only skirts of willow bark or later of cloth or yarn; some photographs show a large shawl, however. Hair was worn loose, and complex facial tattoos were common. Elaborate netted beaded collars were characteristic; a simpler necklace is worn here, with a jew's harp hanging from it.

(C16) Southwest:
Zuni Pueblo woman, c.1970
Women's dress changed more slowly than men's, and traditional styles are retained for fiesta occasions. They are based on the old-style manta, a fine wool rectangle in black or brown woven in a diagonal twill, held together at the sides with ornate silver pins, and worn over sateen blouses and lace petticoats. Pueblo women wear white buckskin moccasins with a wide strip wound round the legs up to the knee. The ceremonial bowl is of characteristic Zuni design.

(C17) Southwest: Navajo hunter, c.1895
Navajo silverwork, copying Mexican techniques, perhaps dates only from the return from imprisonment at Fort Sumner; at first Mexican coins were worked with simple metal tools, but by 1930 commercial blowtorches and solder were being used alongside files, saws and punches. This hunter (note fur and skin quiver/bowcase slung over right shoulder) wears a "squash blossom" necklace, and a sand-cast naja pendant of supposed Islamic inspiration; the shoulder strap of a pouch for tobacco and small items bears plain silver buttons; his belt conches have embossed centres stamped from large dies, the sparse decoration hammered with chisels. Later turquoise and more elaborate designs were introduced, spreading to the Zuni and Hopi, and increasingly designed for sale to whites; but good Navajo work retains its massive quality. Navajo moccasin-boots have rawhide soles and buckskin uppers varying only in their extent.

(C18) Southwest:
Jicarilla Apache woman, c.1895
From the most Plains-like Apache tribe apart from the Kiowa-Apache, she wears a separate yoke cape similar in construction to Sioux, Cheyenne and Southern Ute capes, beaded in the curving parallel lanes and solid blocks of lazy stitch beadwork popular among Rocky Mountain tribes. Wide leather belts with silver button decoration were characteristic of Jicarilla women. Small bags of horse mint were sometimes tied to garments, for perfume and as love charms.

Plate D: Ceremonies

(D1) Arctic:
Alaskan Inuit Wolf Dancer, c.1915
He wears a wolf head mask, and sealskin dance mittens with rattling puffin beaks.

(D2) Northeastern Woodlands:
Penobscot Clown Dancer, 19th century
The only Eastern Abenaki group to remain in Maine were one of the few pockets of eastern seaboard peoples who retained elements of traditional culture late enough to be recorded by ethnographers. The Clown or Trading Dance was a popular gaming ceremony performed at night; the clown wears a deer mask, mooseskin coat, and buckskin moccasins with large U-shaped instep vamps.

(D3, D4) Northwest Coast: Kwakiutl winter ceremony dancers, c.1900
These expressed, in long, dramatic public ceremonial, the characteristics of sinister supernatural beings, to reclaim for humanity tribal members believed to have fallen victim to their influence during winter visitations. (D3) The briefly seen bee or wasp dancer; the arm slats clack when in motion. (D4) Hamatsa bird monster masks had clacking, string-operated lower beaks; shredded cedar bark fringes covered the shoulders under a full-length bark cape. Dancers became members of the secret societies they had represented in the dramas.

(D5) California:
Yurok Jumping Dancer, c.1896
Performed, often by visiting Hupas, at Weitchpec in NW California, where Northwest Coast cultural traits were influential, this dance was held semi-annually, alternately with the White Deerskin Dance. Headdresses were of redheaded woodpecker feathers, worn with buckskin aprons and dentalium shell currency necklaces, the latter also carried in the elkhorn purse.

(D6, D7) Northeastern Woodlands:
Iroquois ceremonialists, c.1840
Two male societies performed at several of the annual festivals in the agricultural calendar. The Corn Husk Faces (D7) heralded the Maize, Bean and Squash deities – the life-supporting "three sisters". Misshapen wooden masks characterized the False Faces, exorcising illness and evil during the midwinter festival.

(D8) Plateau: Flathead singers, c.1907
With the increasing social function of Plains/Plateau ceremonialism early this century, specialist "singing" groups (never called "drummers") provided accompanying songs for Owl, Grass, Tea and Rabbit Dances. Western bass drums, more reliable in sound, often replaced native drums; each "singer" used a single drumstick, and for certain dances performers knelt around the drum.

(D9) Plains: Arikara Bear Dancer, c.1900
The Bear Society was one of nine making up the prestigious Medicine Fraternity. Annual medicine bundle ceremonies began with the first thunder of early spring and continued through the summer in public, secret and conjuring performances. The ceremonies coincided with various stages in the growth of maize and squash crops.

(D10) Plains:
Cheyenne Sun Dancer, c.1890
This most important Plains festival is described in the introduction to the Plains and Prairie section of the text. Details of this world renewal rite varied between tribes. Cheyenne dancers were painted symbolically: the lower body white, the upper body black (clouds) with white dots (hail), the blue central rectangle representing the morning star and the blue facial circle, the sun. Wreaths of willow were usually worn around head, limbs and body.

(D11) Plains: Mandan White Buffalo Cow Dancer, c.1833
The women's White Buffalo Cow Society of the Mandans was seen dancing at Fort Clark by Karl Bodmer at Christmas 1833. These aged women wore face paint, and on their heads a broad piece of the skin of the white buffalo cow with a tuft of feathers.

(D12) Plains: Mandan Buffalo Bull Dancer, c.1833
After Bodmer: a member of the Buffalo Bull Society, who imitated the motions and sounds of the animal when dancing. He wears a bison's head mask, carries a shield, and holds a lance perhaps of a ceremonial type, similar to bow-lances and society staffs of other tribes.

(D13) Plains:
Lakota Grass Dancer, c.1890
The Grass or Omaha Dance was adopted by the Sioux from Missouri valley tribes in the 1860s-70s, presum-

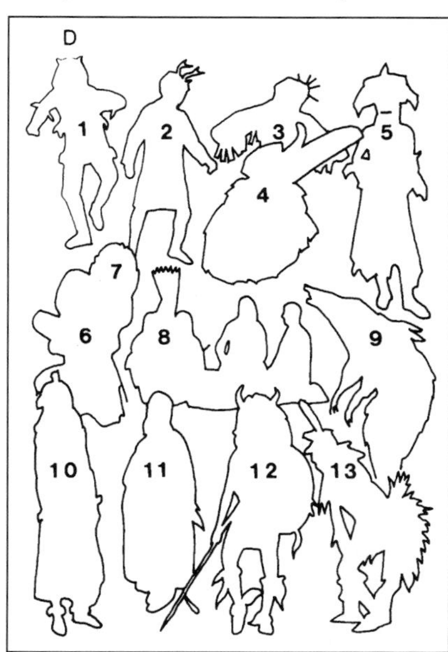

ably to replace redundant rituals of their own warrior societies; they added their own (usually social) rites to the performances. The symbolism of the traditional dress was retained: the roach, braids of sweet grass in the belt, two upright feathers, and a back bustle – a collection of feathers from birds which scavenged the battlefield; these elements were often worn over dyed sets of trade underclothes.

Plate E: Ceremonies

(E1) Southwest:
Navajo sandpainting, c.1950
Dry "paintings" using pulverised materials serve as temporary altars during the various "ways" or healing rites, depicting supernatural beings in human or anthropomorphic forms, often in pairs or larger multiples. Yeibichai masked dancer spirit representations are often depicted during night-long curing rites and – unlike fixed sand paintings for commercial sale – are always destroyed before dawn. Another ceremonial, the Blessing Way, is performed for general wellbeing and to restore harmony with a universe which the Navajo recognize as an orderly, all-inclusive system of complimentary good and evil spiritual components.

(E2) Plains and Northeastern Woodlands: ceremonial pipes, c.1820
(Top to bottom) Crow, Woodlands, Yankton Sioux, Potawatomi. The use of sacred pipes seems to have developed from the Woodlands calumet ceremony, and ancient Mississippian cultures in which decorated wands of feathers with complete bird heads were used in rituals of war, peace and alliance (hence "peace pipe"). Smoking tobacco lifted the thoughts via the smoke to the sky, linking the earth with the supernatural; offering the mouthpiece to the four cardinal points was also considered sacred. Bowls were usually of steatite, carved stems of ash, oak or hickory, often decorated with porcupine or bird quill wrapping.

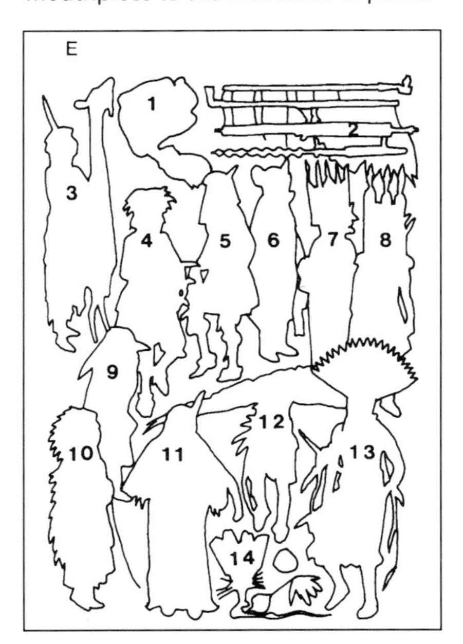

(E3) California:
Hupa White Deerskin Dancer, c.1896
The Hupa, Yurok and Karok had two major world renewal rituals, correlating with seasonal availability of major food resources: the Jumping Dance (see D5) for the spring salmon run, and the Deerskin Dance for the fall acorn harvest and second salmon run. Performers held albino or other oddly coloured deerskins aloft on poles, or carried obsidian blades covered with buckskin.
Some, as here, wore wolfskin headbands and kilts of civet pelts.

(E4) Southwest:
Hopi Snake Dancer, c.1900
Rain brings rattlesnakes to the surface; they are thus associated with this rain dance for the benefit of crops. The ceremony is still performed in Hopi villages by the Snake-Antelope societies in alternate years with the Flute societies. Continual brushing of the snakes' backs with an eagle feather wand prevents them from coiling and striking; during the dance a gatherer or guard controls them in conjunction with the carrier. Note dyed feather headdress, black and white face and body paint, kilt embellished with the sign of the serpent, and numerous silver and turquoise necklaces.

(E5) Southwest:
Zuni Rain Dancer, c.1890
The Zuni have probably the most complex of all Southwest native religions, with six esoteric cults plus an ancestor cult. This dancer has a half-mask of painted leather with a horsehair beard, pink clay body pigment, a kilt traded from the Hopi, and spruce garlands.

(E6) Southwest:
Hopi Heu-Mish Kachina-Mana, c.1950
For approximately the first half of each year the Kachina spirits who link humans with gods are believed to live among the Hopis; for the rest of the year they remain underground in the San Francisco Mountains. During the former period most are impersonated by masked, costumed men in rain, crop, fertility and blessing rituals; each of the 300 impersonations has a unique costume, and miniature Kachina dolls are made to instruct the young. The Kachina-mana ("maids", though actually costumed men – note imitation of butterfly-whorl hairstyle) provide musical rhythms for the season's final Ninian ceremonial in July.

(E7) Southwest: Hopi Butterfly Dancer, c.1970
The second half of the Hopi religious year sees the unmasked plaza dances of the Snake-Antelope, Flute, Butterfly, Maraw and other societes on dates set by the solar or lunar calendar. Hopi lady Butterfly dancers wear black mantas, woven belts in red, black and green, false hair fringes, and carved tablita headdresses with painted butterfly and other designs.

(E8) Southwest:
Hopi She-Eu-Mish Kachina, c.1950
One of the most dramatic Kachinas, this black-painted singer/dancer in the Ninian ritual wears a kilt, sash, and a masked headdress bearing complex symbolism of sprouting cornflowers, the rainbow, sun and rain clouds; he carries a gourd rattle and a feather.

(E9) Plains:
Assiniboine Clown Dancer, c.1910
Like the Plains Cree Windigo, Dakota Heyoka and other male Plains "contrary" societies, the Clown Society was probably originally mystical and curative; membership came usually through dreams of the Thunderbirds, the Cree Windigokan ice giants, etc. Members wore ragged clothes and buckskin or canvas masks with long noses; in dances they assumed outlandish postures, often dancing backwards, and they sometimes used "backwards" speech. They also seem to have been an adjunct to the formal Sun Dance proceedings.

(E10) Plains:
Kiowa woman in warrior dress, c.1875
Derived from a Kiowa pictograph showing a woman honouring her returning warrior husband by dancing while wearing his bonnet and holding his bow. She wears a red sleeved cloth dress with a blue body and red side gussets, the bodice decorated with elk teeth. This is a known surviving dress, which tends to confirm the accuracy of native pictographic art.

(E11) Plains:
Pawnee woman Ghost Dancer, c.1890
Born of the wretchedness of early reservation life, the Ghost Dance cult gave hope that the whites would disappear, that the dead would rise, and that game and the traditional life would return. It was the most famous of a series of dreamer cults; the son of a leader of the preceding movement of 1870, Wovoka (Jack Wilson), a Paiute of the Walker River Reservation in Nevada, experienced visions which precipitated a movement eventually embraced by over 30 tribes. Wovoka gave directions for ritual dances, and advised adherents to live peacefully in a prescribed manner. The movement spread to the Sioux at Pine Ridge Agency, South Dakota, where the agent's overreaction to a minor incident led to the Wounded Knee massacre of December 1890. Special clothing was worn for ceremonies among the cult's Plains adherents, with various painted symbols: magpies, crows (messengers from the spirit world), hands, stars, pipes and bison.

(E12) Southwest:
Tesuque Pueblo Eagle Dancer, c.1930
The Rio Grande Pueblos have several animal dances involving impersonation and mimicry; the Eagle Dance, dramatizing the relationship between humans and the sky powers, has become a popular exhibition, performed by groups even as far afield as the northern Plains. The dancer wears a headpiece, gourd beak and wing feathers.

(E13) Southwest:
Apache Mountain Spirit Dancer, c.1930
Also called Gahn Dancers, they impersonate the sacred spirits who drive away sickness and evil and bring good fortune. Over black buckskin hoods with false eyes of abalone or turquoise they wear towering wooden headdresses painted with symbols of strength, and challenge the forces of evil by charging at each other in the dark beside a fire. Several Apache groups retain the ceremony, usually combined with the girls' puberty rite. He wears a buckskin kilt, and characteristic Apache boots with rawhide upturns at the toe.

(E14) Plains:
Peyote cult accoutrements, c.1930
The Peyote cult or Native American Church, the most widespread Pan-Indian religious movement of this century, combines elements of Mexican, Plains Indian and Christian religions. Of ancient Mexican origin, the ceremonial use of the narcotic peyote seems to have reached the Oklahoma Indians via the Lipan or Mescalero Apache. It developed into two rituals: the more strongly Christian influenced Big Moon Way, and the Half Moon Way, the terms describing the shape of sacred altars. Ceremonials take place by night in a canvas tipi; the ceremonial leader or Roadman uses a hawk feather fan, gourd rattle, and staff, all appropriately decorated, and the peyote is usually consumed in "button" form – as illustrated here, with an Arapaho fan and an Osage rattle.

Plate F: Habitation

(F1) Plateau: Umatilla mat lodge, c.1860
Before adoption of Plains type canvas tipis in the late 19th century, Plateau peoples used pole lodges covered with either cat-tail (bullrush) or tule (reed) mats, usually sewn but sometimes twined. The conical shape was only one of several ground plans, including rectangular, and parallel-sided with one or both ends rounded; the Yakima had a structure with vertical walls and gable roof resembling West Coast house shapes.

(F2) Great Basin: Northern Paiute mat lodge, c.1860
This group, with the Eastern Mono, Washo, Monache and some Yokuts, used three main dwelling types. Those used in winter (and in large versions as men's assembly or sweat lodges) had a frame of beams on four forked posts (or a ridge beam on two) over a circular floor excavated to about two feet; outer rafters leaning in against the beams gave an oval shape; a thatched grass and earth covering left a central smoke hole.
A conical type (illustrated) lacked the beams and posts, outer rafters set inside the excavated depression being brought together, tied to a hoop at the apex, and covered with rush mats, again with a smoke hole. Thirdly, many types of temporary, unexcavated travelling dwellings used cone-, dome-, or gable-shaped bough frames usually covered with brush.

(F3-F6) Northeastern Woodlands and Subarctic: Wigwams
The term applies to several Woodland forms; the four main types were domed, peaked and tipi shapes, and the bark house. The domed wigwam, of ironwood saplings driven into the ground and bent over to form arches, was covered with birch or elm bark or reed mats. The peaked roof lodge had a series of pointed arches connected by a ridge pole, also covered with bark or mats. The tipi shape had a conical frame of poles covered with bark. The bark house was a rectangular structure of poles with bark sheet outer covering. Most of these single-family homes had central smoke holes. Ceremonial lodges were similar to the domed type, but longer and open-ended. Canvas was also sometimes used as a covering. Wigwams were in use in isolated areas until c.1900; a few are still made for special occasions. We show (F3) Ojibwa wigwam; (F4) Cree domed wigwam; (F5) Winnebago rush mat domed wigwam; (F6) Potawatomi elm bark domed wigwam.

(F7) Arctic:
Polar Inuit summer tent, c.1915
In summer all Inuit moved into skin tents; this *tupik* varied in construction and size, the simplest a seal or caribou skin cover lashed to a wooden frame, with thin-scraped hide over the doorway to admit light. More substantial interseasonal *qarmaq* dwellings had covers which could be raised over collapsed igloos or supported on whale rib arches and poles, insulated with moss and secured to the ground with boulders.

(F8) Southwest: Apache wickiup, c.1880
Light poles were set in a rough circle of shallow holes, bent inwards, tied together, and covered with thatched grass or brush tied on with yucca fibre in regular overlapping courses; the structure, five to seven feet high and six to ten feet in diameter, was partially covered with earth in winter.

(F9) California:
Western Mono bark house, c.1860
The Monache used conical thatched, oval earth, and conical bark houses, sharing the first two forms with the Yokut, Eastern Mono and Northern Paiute; the third was primarily Monache as suitable bark was only available at their higher elevations on the western slopes of the Sierra Nevada. The bark house was unexcavated, with a centre post (or two with a ridge beam) supporting a few large poles covered with cedar bark slabs.

(F10) Northwest Coast:
Salish temporary house, c.1870
The coast Salish people around Puget Sound built cedar plank houses of monopitch, double pitch and hip end forms, though lacking the carved and painted facades of more northerly tribes. Temporary summer camp dwellings, as illustrated, were constructed of poles covered with cedar bark or skilfully woven cat-tail mats.

(F11) Southeast and Plains:
Southern Caddoan grass house
Early French and Spanish reports indicate long use of this type by the ancestors of the Wichita and Caddo of Arkansas, Oklahoma, Texas and Louisiana, in semi-permanent villages of up to 80 houses. A circle of heavy cedar beams supported a secondary circle of lighter poles leaning in against them, then drawn and tied together at the apex; horizontal ribs secured the construction, with long grass thatch tied to the ribs in overlapping layers. Communal lodges may have been as tall as 25 feet, family lodges smaller. They have not been in use since c.1900, but there are a few reconstructions at "Indian City", Anadarko, Oklahoma.

(F12) Southeast:
Choctaw house, Louisiana, c.1825
Moving west in the early 19th century, some Choctaw adopted pole frame

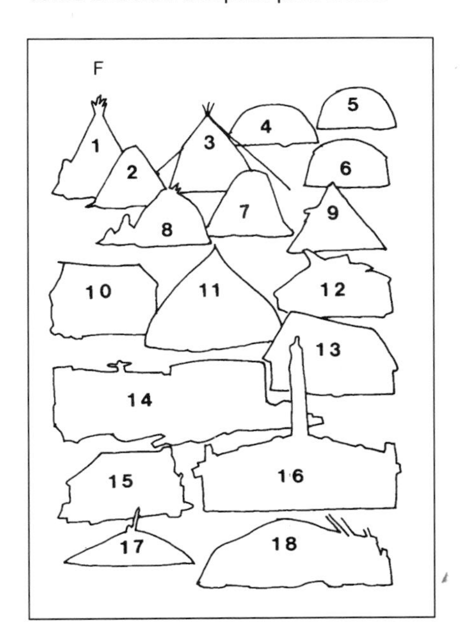

and palmetto leaf houses as once used by the Lower Mississippi tribes. The original Choctaw dwellings were probably similar to those decribed in the early 18th century for the Cherokee and Natchez – low, square, with rounded tops, covered with corn stalks or mixed clay and straw.

(F13) Southeast: Seminole chickee
This probably evolved after the Seminoles' forced retreat into the Florida swamplands, and can still be seen in use. Frame and rafters were poles cut from small trees, effectively roofed with overlapping palmetto fronds; living quarters were raised internal platforms, and kitchens were separate. Similar dwellings were probably once common throughout the Gulf Coast territories of extinct peoples such as the Calusa.

(F14) Northwest Coast:
Kwakiutl village, c.1885
Part of a village on Gilford Island, between the mainland and Vancouver Island. The cedar plank houses show white influence (jack roofs, windows); but the painted sea monster and carved double-headed serpent (*sisiutl*) on the gables indicate the house of an important leader. Villages usually faced the water – note beached canoes.

(F15) Southeast:
Cherokee log cabin, c.1840
18th century association with Carolina settlers led to the gradual replacement of houses built of vertically set interwoven poles, covered inside and out with clay mixed with grass, by the log cabins typical of white frontiersmen. A few Eastern Cherokee in North Carolina still used stone-chimneyed log houses until recent times.

(F16) Northwest Coast:
Haida house, c.1880
North West Coast peoples used varying construction forms for houses of thick cedar planks on massive beams and columns with portal-framed gable ends, the roof beams supporting overlapping plank roofs. The Haida often used six roof beams, supported on corner columns and via portals at each gable positioned either side of facade posts carved with the crests of the owner and his wife; the original entrance was at the base of the post. Many families could live in such a house (some of which were up to 50 feet long), each with their own apartment on platforms separated by mats or partitions.

(F17) Plateau:
Thompson pit house, c.1850
Tribes of the Southern Cordillera of British Columbia and the Plateau area used differing types of semi-subterranean house, up to 30 feet wide and four to six feet in depth, entered by a roof ladder. Exclusive to the Okanagan, Thompson, Lillooet, Shuswap and Chilcotin was the pyramidal roof with a circular pit obtained by hip rafters on internal posts, and use of four or six logs to form the hatchway.

(F18) Plains:
Pawnee earth lodge, c.1865
The floor was excavated to about a foot deep; the framework was a skeleton stockade of heavy posts on which rafters were laid upwards to central posts supporting the smoke hole and outwards to an outer bank of earth. Willow purlins laid horizontally on the rafters supported the earth and sod covering. The entrance was a long covered way built of poles with earth covering; this faced east, and its length varied between the Missouri valley tribes. The west side of the lodge, where corn was stored, was considered sacred. Several related families usually occupied the lodge, which was about 40 feet in diameter and 15 feet high.

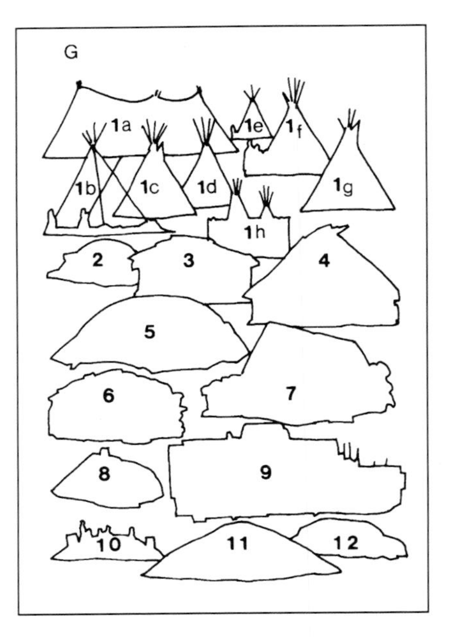

Plate G: Habitation

(G1) Plains: Tipis
The conical tipi probably evolved from Subarctic prototypes; early forms were relatively small, before the coming of the horse allowed transportation of larger covers and longer poles. Basic construction was fairly constant throughout the Plains: a tilted cone of straight, slim, peeled poles (usually lodge pole pine, cedar or spruce) slotted into a foundation frame of three or four poles. Three-pole foundations were used by the Cheyenne, Arapaho, Sioux, Assiniboine, Kiowa, Gros Ventre, Plains Cree, Mandan, Arikara, Pawnee, Ponca, Oto and Wichita; four, by the Crow, Blackfoot, Sarsi, Shoshone, Omaha, Comanche, Hidatsa, Kutenai, Flathead and Nez Perce. Foundation poles were usually tied together over the spread ground cover, then hoisted, the remaining poles being slotted into the crotches which they formed. In three-pole foundations one pole faced east and formed a door pole on the south side; four-pole foundations formed a rectangle, the rear two remaining low at the back and appearing as a "swallow-tail" in the completed lodge. The tipi usually faced east towards the rising sun; being an imperfect cone it had a back steeper than the front, which tended to brace it against the prevailing winds.

Covers were usually of dressed buffalo cow hides before the destruction of the herds in the 1880s, and thereafter of traded canvas duck, usually white. Most 19th century tipis were about 12 to 18 feet high, requiring some 12 skins sewn together and cut to a half-circle plan. The cover was hoisted onto the frame with a single lifting pole and spread around the sides; the edges pinned together at the front; and the bottom edge staked down. The cover included two "ear" extensions at the top of the sides, forming smoke flaps held out by external poles; adjusted to the prevailing wind, these helped drag smoke through the gap left at the top. A liner five or six feet in height ran around the inside of the poles, fastened to them and to the floor. A fireplace of stones was made centrally somewhat towards the rear; family beds were usually on the south side, those of guests on the north; at the rear were placed backrests of slender rods, weapons and medecine bundles.

Some covers and liners were painted with naturalistic or geometrical symbolic patterns, usually peculiar to the owner, and associated with the intense esoteric spiritual nature of the lodge. We illustrate (G1b) women erecting a Blackfoot tipi; and two others with typical Blackfoot designs: (G1c) a Rainbow Lodge with human figure, and (G1d) a Yellow Painted Otter Lodge. Blackfoot lodges usually have the bottom section painted black, or red with white spots representing the puffballs seen on the Prairies; the upper edge may be flat, representing the prairie, or in semi-circles or points, for hills and mountains. The central area, between earth and sky, is occupied by natural elements, usually dream animals with major organs highlighted, males on the south side, females on the north. The top section was usually black for the night sky, with white discs on the smoke flaps representing the Pleiades and Great Bear constellations with a maltese cross, a moth or a morning star – connected with sleep and dreams.

(continued on p. 115)

Plate A

Plate B

Plate C

Plate D

Plate E

Plate F

Plate G

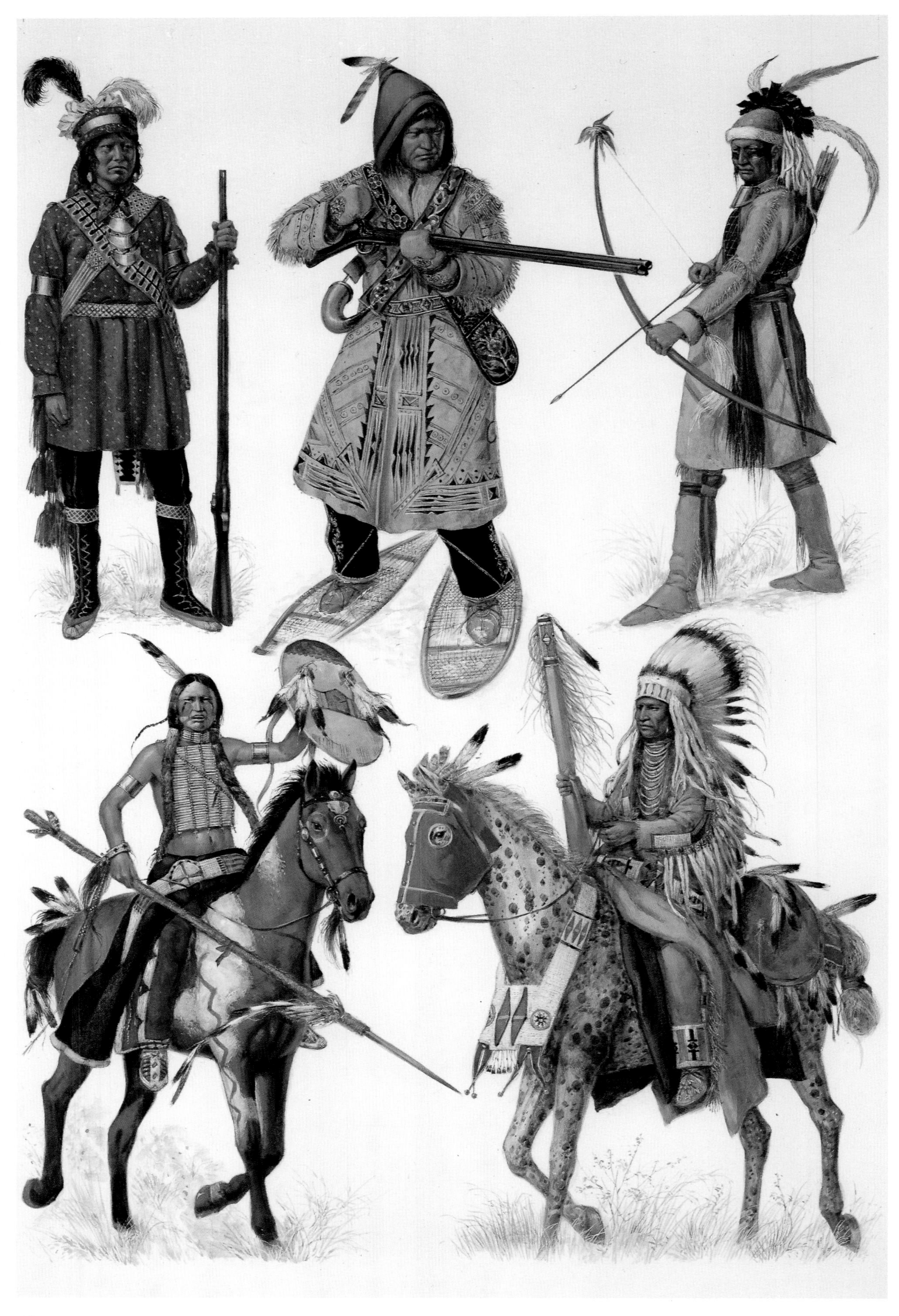

Plate H

Plate I

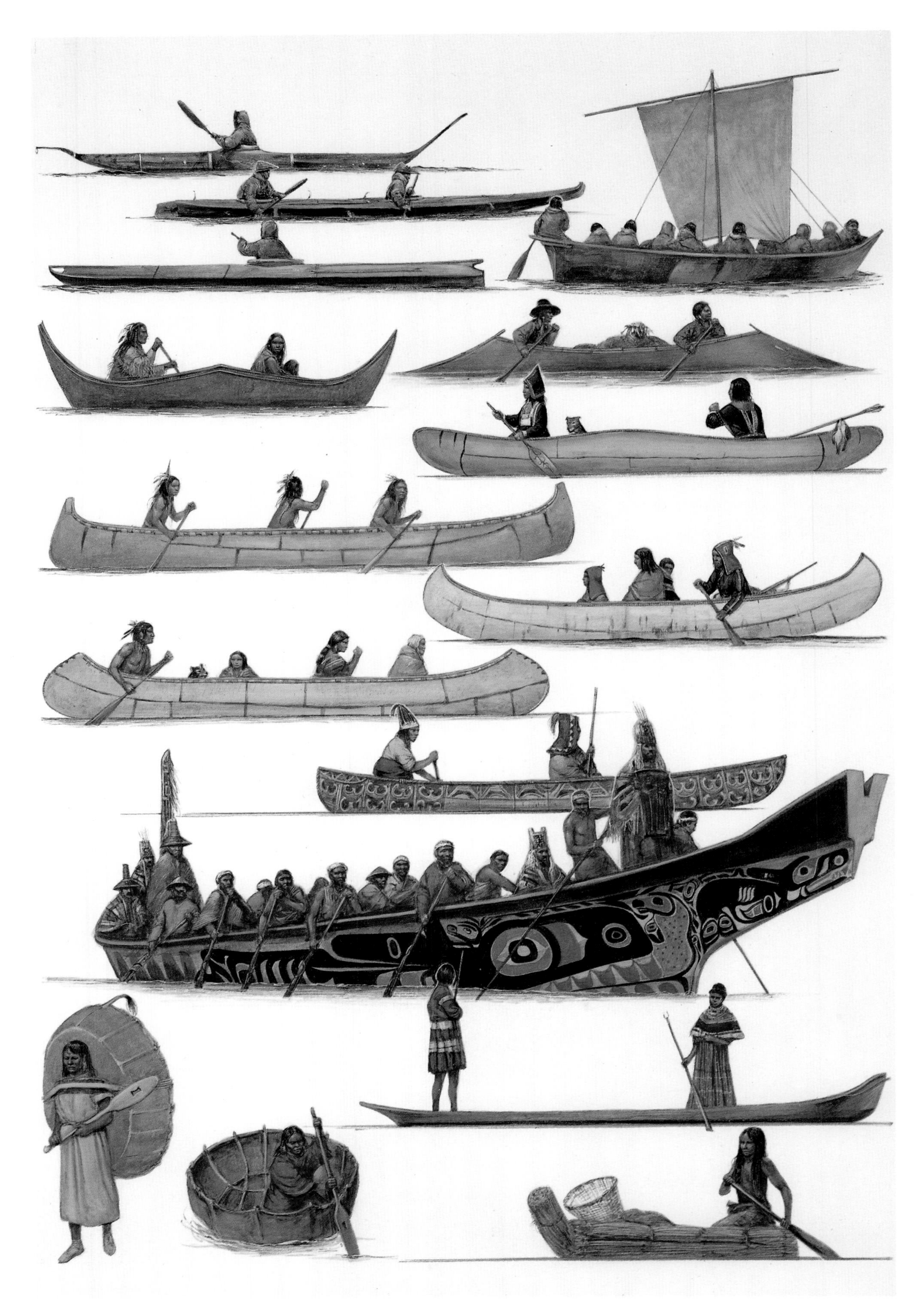

Plate J

Plate K

Plate L

Plate M

Plate N

Plate O

Plate P

(continued from p. 98)

Modern Crow people prefer their tipis unpainted for the annual "Crow Fair", with long poles protruding at the top (G1e). The Kiowa of the southern Plains also have a tradition of painted lodges; (G1g) is the Black Striped lodge of the holy man Beaver Cap.
(G1f) is a Wind River Shoshone skin lodge owned by Chief Washakie.
(G1h) shows the use by the Cheyenne of windbreaks to ward off dust during Oklahoma summers. The tipi was adopted by Plateau tribes during the 19th century; (G1a) is an Umatilla extended lodge using canvas instead of cat-tail mats over a peaked construction.

(G2) Arctic: Central Inuit igloo, c.1950
Although popularly synonymous with the Inuit peoples the igloo or iglu was actually used only by the central tribes – the Iglulik, Netsilik and Copper Eskimo. It was made in a domed shape of skilfully angled blocks of frozen snow excavated from the floor by a cutter working inside; daylight was admitted by a translucent piece of ice fitted above the entry tunnel. Communal and multi-chambered examples are reported, but the average diameter was about 12 feet. Still made today, they afford protection against winter weather for short periods, or as temporary hunting bases.

(G3) California/Northwest Coast: Hupa plank house, c.1870
Tribal groups in northwest California made permanent family houses of split redwood cedar planks supported on eaves beams and roof poles; the three-pitched roof and circular entrance were characteristic of the Hupa, Yurok and Karok. Interiors were excavated, leaving a "shelf" between exterior walls and pit, the pit sides revetted with horizontal planks.

(G4) Northeastern Woodlands: Sauk elm bark house, c.1880
Shorter, but of similar construction to Iroquois longhouses, Sauk and Fox bark lodges formed villages of up to e.g. 90 houses in the mid-18th century. A few were still being built in the 1880s after removal to Indian Territory.

(G5) Southwest: Pima earth lodge, c.1900
Basic construction of the Pima and Papago house was around beams set on four forked posts forming an eight-foot square; willow poles set in the ground round the perimeter were bent inwards and lashed to the beams, extending across to form a flattish dome roof; the exterior was thatched, then covered with a thick layer of earth. Smoke escaped through the single low doorway, usually facing east.

(G6) Southwest: Navajo log hogan, c.1950
The more recent form, still in use in remote areas, is hexagonal and of horizontally laid logs. From the eaves upwards (five or six feet above the ground) the log courses are drawn in progressively to form a dome, which is covered with earth. The interior is excavated to about two feet, leaving a low "shelf" running round inside the walls, with a central fire pit.

(G7) Northeastern Woodlands: Iroquois longhouse, c.1650
Used by all northern Iroquoian peoples including the Six Nations and Huron, this community dwelling ranged from 30 to 200 feet in length and 15 to 25 feet in width. The frame of forked upright posts and horizontal beams had flexible horizontal tie poles and triangular or rounded roof supports. The sheathing of elm, hemlock, basswood or cedar bark formed overlapping shingles, secured by outer poles tied through to the interior poles. The longhouse had two doors and several smoke holes, but no windows; inside was a central hallway between curtained-off family booths. Logs replaced bark due to 18th century white contacts. The 12 remaining longhouses on various reservations – synonymous with the survival of Iroquois traditions, and used for meetings and ceremonials – have two stoves, a central bench for ritualists and side seats for various clans, although externally they are conventionally boarded rural buildings.

(G8) Southwest: Navajo conical hogan, c.1900
This older form than (G6) was built around three forked logs locked in a tripod; two logs were added four feet apart on the east side to support a door frame. Poles, brush and sometimes cedar bark were piled around the framework, the whole being thickly covered with earth, leaving a smoke hole at the apex. Doorways sometimes projected like dormers, and were usually closed with a blanket.

(G9) Southwest: Pueblo
Most northern Rio Grande community dwellings are of sun-dried mud or adobe and straw bricks, forming honeycombs of rooms, sometimes terraced; the walls, thickly plastered with mud inside and out, are often whitewashed. (Acoma, however, is of rubble and clay; Zuni of both stone and adobe bricks; and Hopi towns have walls of dressed stone laid in adobe. These are almost the only pre-contact towns, though many others are close to ancient sites.) Most towns have plazas for public dances and subterranean Kivas for secret rituals. Traditionally each clan of a tribe occupies one section of the building; nowadays most rooms have doors and windows, but historically access was to upper floors only, by ladders. Taos is perhaps the most impressive of these towns, in part six storeys high. Note Spanish/Moorish derived domed ovens in foreground.

(G10) California: Wintu pit house
The peoples of the upper Sacramento River area spent part of the year in substantial circular earth-covered family lodges, about 12 to a village; larger versions served as men's assembly and "Big Head" dance houses. They had one or more centre posts; a ring of posts supported beams and rafters covered with brush, bark and earth. Access was by ladder via the roof smoke hole.

(G11) California: Konkow-Maidu earth lodge, c.1870
Semi-subterranean earth-covered multi-family dwelling or men's assembly house, usually constructed in spring for winter use. It was circular, 20 to 40 feet in diameter, and excavated to a depth of about four feet.

(G12) Arctic: Polar Inuit winter house, c.1900
Northern Greenland winter house, similar to those of the ancestral Thule people, constructed of flat stones, whale ribs, driftwood and sod. Here the central entrance is flanked by two side doorways to storerooms; and surmounted by a window – these were sometimes covered with translucent gut skin.

Plate H: Warriors

(H1) Southeast: Seminole, c.1835
Warrior chief of the Second Seminole War, 1835-42, by which date Seminole costume was a unique blend of native and European materials. The belt, garters, and perhaps the sash echo aboriginal prototypes seen on figures engraved on shell objects from Spiro Mound, Oklahoma, though by this date made of trade wool and beads. The buckskin moccasins are a form of the classic Eastern one-piece centre

seam type. The bandolier and pouch (usually with a triangular flap) are probably syncretistic in origin, derived from both aboriginal and European models. The native breechclout and leggings were made in both buckskin and cloth at this date. The cut of the cloth smock-coat is thought to be of European inspiration, though early reports suggest that buckskin prototypes existed in the Southeast. Crescentic gorgets of silver or other metals were traded or made from coins: the uniform insignia of the 18th-early 19th century European military officer, the gorget was widely popular among the Eastern peoples.

(H2) Subarctic: Cree, c.1815
Warrior/hunter from the James and Hudson Bays area, clothed against the harsh climate. Native in origin, the hood, coat, leggings and mittens already show European influence in the tailored cut and decorative refinements; yet more baroque, Europeanised forms would develop as time passed. Woollen leggings, powder horn strap and bullet pouch are heavily beaded in floralistic designs, probably of European inspiration; but the painted designs on the coat and porcupine quilled belt and shoulder decoration are old native techniques. Most Eastern Cree moccasins are of moose or caribou hide with a heavy puckered seam round the instep vamp; Western Woods Cree moccasins have a centre seam from vamp to toe.

(H3) Northeastern Woodlands: Iroquois, c.1812
European trade tomahawks, guns, cloth and silver had already been used among Northeastern Woodlands peoples for more than a century. Use of the bow was by now rare in many areas, restricted to some hunting or circumstances when firearms were in short supply; Woodland bows, often of hickory or hazel with braided sinew strings, could exceed six feet in length; arrows were sometimes of elder, quivers of bark or rush. The buckskin cap is decorated with traded feathers, cut feather clusters and ermine skins.

(H4) Plains: Arapaho, c.1870
The Arapaho, Cheyenne and Western Sioux of the central Plains resembled one another in dress, ornamentation, and use of trade goods, the latter including blanket cloth, bone hairpipes, silver, German silver and beads. These partly replaced hide robes, shell beads and native forms of decoration, notably porcupine quillwork, by the mid-century. The development of seed beadwork after the 1850s is characterized by hourglass, triangle, diamond and stripe designs perhaps derived from earlier quilled or painted parfleche and rawhide designs. The warrior holds a rawhide shield and a typical Plains lance; a quirt hangs from his wrist, and a blanket with beaded strip ornamentation lies across his lap. His horse is painted and decorated with eagle feathers, its bridle with German silver.

(H5) Plateau: Nez Perce, c.1877
Material culture and dress show similarities born of friendly trade relations with the Crow of Montana: horse collars, gun cases, bandolier bags and blanket strips bore similar beaded designs, e.g. hourglass shapes, isosceles triangles and crosses, and similarly sophisticated use of colours such as pink and blue, stitched down on hide or cloth in a flat mosaic form. Nez Perce warriors wore both upright and flared bonnets; a style intermediate between the two is illustrated. The Nez Perce were famous for these Appaloosa horses.

Plate I: Warriors

(I1) Plains: Cheyenne, c.1870
The Dog-Men (to whites, "Dog Soldiers") were the largest of several age-graded military societies, numbering perhaps half the Cheyenne males of 15 and older and including a chief, seven assistants, and four warriors selected for bravery to protect the society from enemy raids. These four, as illustrated, wore special skin or cloth scarves decorated with eagle feathers, over their heads or one shoulder and trailing to the ground; the supreme demonstration of bravery was to stake this to the earth with a red peg, symbolizing willingness to fight to the death on the spot. Their headdress was of erect magpie, owl, hawk or crow feathers surmounted by eagle tail feathers. Ceremonial regalia included eagle bone whistles, dew claw rattles and skunk skin belts, and they held a bow and arrow during ritual dances.

(I2) Northwest Coast: Tlingit, c.1860
Armour of heavy hide and wooden slats is worn with a heavy wooden helmet with totemic crest mounted on a wooden collar with vision and ventilation slits. The knife and club had blades of whale bone, trade iron or copper, and crest images. Early hide clothing probably approximated that of the interior Athabascans; moccasins resembled the Subarctic form with vamp, front toe seam, or sometimes blunt squared toe seam. Inter-clan wars to avenge injury or insult were sometimes settled by mock battles.

(I3) California: Karok, pre-1870
In northwest California family or village feuds usually resulted in little more than retaliatory activity, and might be settled by payment, with the parties acting out a formalized war dance. Male dress was limited to a buckskin breechclout or apron, with moccasins for long journeys; warriors might add wooden slat armour. The principal weapon was the yew bow with sinew backing and string; syringa wood arrows were carried in shell-decorated fur quivers.

(I4) Southwest: Western Apache, c.1860
Perhaps the hardiest of all Native American warriors, a few hundred Apaches defied other tribes, Mexicans and the U.S.Army until the 1880s. Although popularly shown wearing much Euro-American clothing they had their own distinctive dress. Buckskin shirts with cut or applied fringing were decorated with yellow ochre and lines of beadwork and silver buttons. Warrior and ceremonial buckskin caps bore eagle, turkey, ibis or owl feathers. Calf-length moccasins with rawhide soles extended at the toe were often painted and beaded in lines. Rawhide shields were invested with great protective and concealing powers by painted black, yellow, green and white designs of stars, crescent moons, sun, birds, bats and spirit forms, often split into cardinal sections or groups of four elements.

(I5) Plains: Kiowa, c.1875
The Kiowa of the southern Plains, often allied with the Comanche, were known for elegantly painted and fringed hide garments. Some shirts and leggings were painted yellow or blue-green, with twisted fringing, but at this period only minimal edge and seam beadwork. Moccasins often had heel and instep fringes and double tongues. Here an otter fur turban with trailer is decorated with ribboned and beaded rosettes. He has an otter skin bowcase and quiver, with strike-a-light and whetstone cases hanging from the latter; and carries a painted rawhide shield. Although known throughout the Plains, in later years the use of lances seems to have been largely ritualistic, as firearms became more widely available.

Plate J: Transport

(J1) Arctic: Caribou Eskimo kayak
About 20 feet long and usually narrow, this decked, one-man hunting canoe was more widely employed than the *umiak*. The flat-bottomed or V-shaped frame of (usually driftwood) fir, pine, spruce or willow is rigid without its (usually seal) skin covering – unlike bark canoes, which collapse on removal of the bark. The Inuit or "Caribou Eskimo" on the northwest side of Hudson Bay favoured an extended prow and upraised stern, tilted cockpit, and double-bladed paddles.

(J2) Arctic: Aleut baidarka
About 25 feet long, these have two, occasionally three cockpits, and sharp sterns; the term has also come to be used in Alaska to designate Aleut or Inuit kayaks with forked bows. Provision was often made to hold a harpoon catch or trade goods on the deck, sometimes in a wooden frame.

(J3) Arctic: Western Alaskan kayak
About 15 feet long, these typically had sharp vertical ends, a handling hole in the bow, and a flat-rimmed cockpit; they were noted for their speed. Single-bladed paddles were sometimes used.

(J4) Arctic: Inuit umiak
Known in various forms, up to 40 feet long, from Kodiak Island to Greenland, this open-topped cargo boat was sometimes used for walrus hunting and whaling. Its wooden frame was covered with sea, whale or walrus hide; up to a dozen crew could paddle, though sails (or recently, outboard motors) might be installed.

(J5) Subarctic: Beothuk canoe
Only models have survived; of almost V-shaped section, they appear to have had a flared and upswept profile, and were reported to need ballast to maintain stability.

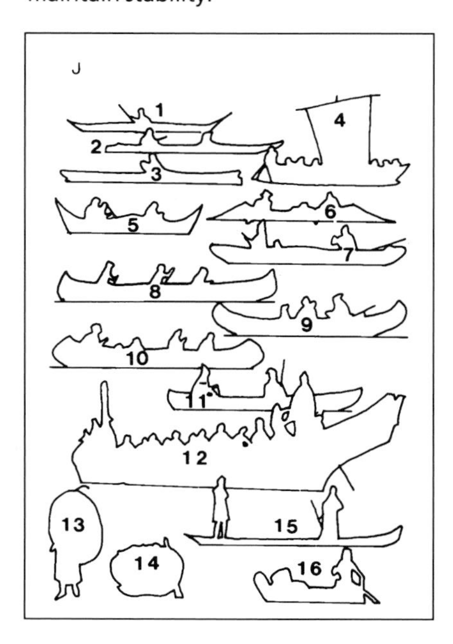

(J6) Plateau: Kutenai canoe
"Sturgeon nose" canoes were characteristic of the Kutenai and Shuswap of southern British Columbia.

(J7) Northeastern Woodlands: Micmac canoe
Birch bark canoes, distributed over the whole Subarctic and Northeastern Woodlands as far south as northern Minnesota, Wisconsin, Michigan, New Hampshire and Maine, were efficient for forest travel, being light enough to be propelled by a single-bladed paddle and carried overland by portage between waterways.
Major tribal distinctions in prow and stern shape and sheer of gunwales can be identified; the Micmac canoe had this curved prow and stern, and some were large enough to carry a sail for ocean use. The curved stem pieces, thwarts, headboards, ribs, floor sheathing and gunwales were usually of white cedar, heated into shape; the bark was usually sewn with black spruce roots.

(J8) Subarctic and NE Woodlands: Eastern Ojibwa canoe
This high-ended shape is also found among the Algonkians; they perhaps belong to the same generic form, although some hybrids with the Abenaki construction are reported. This construction and silhouette probably inspired the much larger fur trade canoe used by many tribes, Métis and whites across the interior of Canada in the 18th and 19th centuries.

(J9) Subarctic: Eastern Cree canoe
The Cree and Montagnais of Quebec province developed this "crooked" shape, thought to aid turning. In the far north the frame was sometimes spruce or larch, and spruce bark was occasionally used; in later years canvas, nails, tacks and twine replaced native materials.

(J10) Northeastern Woodlands: Ojibwa/Chippewa canoe
This graceful, rounded, "long nose" shape was characteristic of the western Ojibwa (Chippewa) of Wisconsin, Minnesota and western Ontario. Bark seams were sealed with spruce resin gum.

(J11) Northeastern Woodlands: Abenaki canoe
In the southern Maritimes some Abenaki and Malecite canoes were painted or scraped with symbolic protective or personal designs. As metal tools became available the French Canadians and Indians developed larger canoes for the fur trade, carrying "brigades" of 12 or more men. A number of hybrid tribal forms also evolved.

(J12) Northwest Coast: Tlingit and Haida canoe
The southern Tlingit made canoes of red cedar, but all Tlingit preferred the great Haida canoes, up to 60 feet long with masts and sails, which could carry several tons of freight. Such "war canoes" purchased by Tlingit chiefs bore their carved and painted crests at bow and stern.

(J13, J14) Plains: Hidatsa bullboat
Made from two buffalo hides stretched over a willow bough frame, these were light enough to be carried on the back but large enough to hold several people or a considerable load. They were used by the Missouri River tribes, Mandan, Hidatsa and Arikara, and occasionally by neighbouring Sioux.

(J15) Southeastern Woodlands: Seminole dugout canoe
In the absence of birch bark of suitable quality, Florida and Gulf Coast peoples used simple hollowed treetrunk canoes with rounded or pointed ends. Until recently the Seminole made slender boats from single cypress logs, with stern platforms for poling through the swamps.

(J16) California: Pomo balsas
Canoe-shaped raft of tied reed (tule) used by fishermen on Clear Lake and its swampy environs, but unsuitable for ocean mammal hunting.

Plate K: Transport

(K1) Northwest Coast: Muckleshoot tumpline basket, 19th century
For collecting and storing fruit, vegetables and shellfish women of the Coast Salish tribes used baskets, large ones being supported by a tumpline across the forehead. Baskets in the Cascades region were mainly coiled: stiff coils of cedar or spruce roots decorated by covering with strips of coloured bear grass or cherry bark – a technique known as imbrication. Twined basketry was favoured north and south of this region. This young Muckleshoot woman wears a rain-repellent cape and skirt of shredded cedar bark.

(K2) Subarctic: Ahtna tumpline, c.1870
Ahtna woman using the tumpline to carry camp equipment. This tribe of the Copper and Chitina Rivers, Alaska, belonged to an ancient trade network involving other Athabscan tribes, Inuit, Eyak, Tlingit, and possibly the Siberian Chukchi. Travel was mostly on foot; in winter snowshoes and hand-drawn load-bearing toboggans were used.

(K3) Basin: Southern Paiute baskets, c.1880
Woman with twined conical burden basket on chest tumpline, and close-coiled tray used to sift mesquite meal.

(K4) Southeastern Woodlands: Choctaw tumpline basket, c.1880
Louisiana Choctaw woman with large burden basket on a chest tumpline. Almost all Eastern basketry used the simple plaiting technique and available materials. The Choctaw and Creek made fine river cane baskets of this

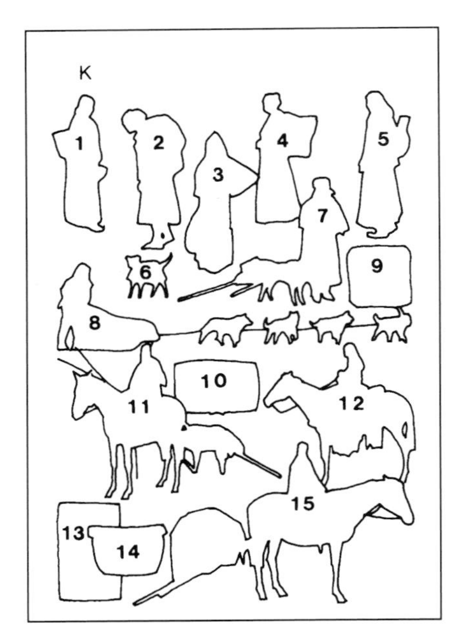

"cow nose" shape; the Chitimacha, colourful baskets of narrow cane splints; the Cherokee and Catawba mainly used oak splints, the Northeastern tribes ash.

(K5) Southwest:
Western Apache water basket, c.1900
Young woman carrying water in a *tus*, a twined basket of coarse splints caulked with juniper leaf paste and sealed with pine pitch.

(K6) Subarctic: Tanana dog, c.1880
The only domesticated animal in the North in aboriginal times was the small dog, and only among the Chipewyan were they used to carry burdens. Not until larger varieties were introduced by whites did most native peoples use them as pack and sledge animals.

(K7) Plains: Blood dog travois, c.1870
The dog travois of the thinly populated High Plains in pre-horse nomad times seems to have been a uniquely Native American device, and was the only alternative to back-carrying for lodges and other burdens. It was carried forward into the 19th century horse culture as the "big dog travois". Spanish 16th century explorers met villages of pedestrian hunters in the South with dog travois – perhaps Athabascan/Apachean groups; northerly explorers reported the Snakes, at least partly of Shoshonean origin, using them while retreating west on foot before the Blackfoot; and among the latter the dog travois was occasionally used until reservatuion days.

(K8) Subarctic:
Northern Athabascan dog team, c.1910
The dog team and its accoutrements were added to the aboriginal flat-bottomed, hand-drawn toboggan by Europeans and Métis during the fur trade era, using European breeds stouter than the lightly built aboriginal dogs. For deep snow and narrow trails a toboggan was preferred to a runnered sledge, with a team of four to eight dogs in a tandem hitch. A fully caparisoned team had belts, tasselled and beaded blankets, and standing irons adorned with pompoms. Sledges with raised runners and cariole sleighs of white manufacture were also used later in some areas.

(K9) Subarctic: Northern Athabascan dog blanket, c.1910
These strapped-on "tapies" were part of the embellishment added for show on arrival at a settlement. Of dark cloth or velvet backed with canvas, they had wool fringes, sleigh bells, and beadwork in tight floralistic forms – popularised in the Northwest during the fur trade era through Cree and Métis influence.

(K10) Plains:
Blackfoot parfleche, c.1870
Parfleches were folded envelopes of rawhide – untanned buffalo or other skin – which can be moulded when fresh and wet, and dries hard, waterproof but semi-flexible. Usually folded from a single sheet, with flaps secured by thongs through burnt holes, they were used for carrying dried food and clothing; the Blackfoot made additional holes allowing attachment to saddle or travois frame. They were painted, usually only on the end flaps, with bold designs in pigments mixed with buffalo hoof glue. Characteristically smaller than most, Blackfoot parfleches tended to curved designs and triangles in solid colours.

(K11) Plains: Blackfoot travois, c.1870
These were usually considered the property of women. The shafts of lodge pole pine were crossed and tied above the horse's neck and also tied to the saddle. The flared, dragging poles were secured as a frame by two notched main cross struts; secondary struts and willow tipi backrests formed the load platform.

(K12) Southwest:
Western Apache woman, c.1890
For moving camp, or a food-gathering expedition, the horse bears rawhide saddlebags decorated with rawhide cut-outs and red cloth; a *tus* (water container); and a buckskin-fringed burden basket. The best construction technique for pack baskets was twining: a set of vertical warps with two or more horizontal wefts which were twined around each other.

(K13) Plains:
Cheyenne parfleche, c.1870
These were noted for delicate designs on their nearly square flaps: double outline borders enclose an uncoloured space divided longitudinally by a decorated area enclosing small brown figures. Green, blue, yellow, red and brown were commonly combined.

(K14) Plains:
Lakota storage bag, c.1870
Buckskin "tipi bags" were used for clothing and household articles. This bag has typical Teton-Sioux ridged lazy stitch beadwork of the second half of the century, in geometrical designs developed through the trade availability of small seed beads.

(K15) Plains:
Cheyenne improvized travois, c.1870
These were widely seen among the Plains peoples: a temporary load platform was tied between dragging lodge poles. Children could be confined and protected by a cage of bent willow covered with hide.

The Plains Indian pony
The pony was not a beautiful animal; but it was sturdy, had great endurance, and was lighter, swifter and had a longer range than the horse used by the U.S.Army. The average adult male was under 14 hands high and weighed some 700 pounds, exhibiting a wide range of solid and mixed colours. Its ancestry can be traced to the Barb horse introduced into Spain during the 8th century Moorish invasion; horses brought to the Americas by the Spanish early in the 16th century came from Cordoba and Andalusia, where the Barb strain survived. Although the date of large scale diffusion into Indian hands is disputed, it is believed that the Ute, Kiowa and Kiowa-Apache were mounted by 1640, and that the Plains peoples to the north had the horse by the early 18th century. Larger horses displaced the pony during the reservation period; by the 1940s it had almost disappeared, and the only Indian-bred horse to survive to modern times is the larger, heavier Appaloosa of the Nez Perce and other Plateau tribes.

Plate L: Headdress

(L1) Arctic: Aleut, c.1850
Long-billed wooden hat (probably spruce), with walrus ivory attachments; probably used as a sun visor when sea hunting.

(L2) Arctic: Kaniag Inuit, c.1850
Kodiak Island hunter's carved wood seal decoy helmet: apart from practical camouflage it may have been invested with symbolic power to attract prey.

(L3) Northwest Coast: Tlingit, c.1900
Decorated with carved and painted totemic designs, this hat has a raven crest topped with two woven rings (reflecting clan status or the number of Potlatches given) to which are attached ermine skins.

(L4) Northwest Coast: Tlingit, c.1900
Woman wearing shaman's headdress with exaggerated simulated bear claws, probably of mountain goat horn, and a beaded cloth tunic.

(L5) Subarctic: Nascapi, c.1891
Woman wearing the style of hat traditional around North West River, Labrador; made in sections of alternating red and blue cloth, it has the upper portion folded over on itself. The hair was wound on a small piece of wood and then bound with cloth or beads.

(L6) Plains: Crow, c.1870
Ceremonial warrior headdress of antelope hide, red stroud cloth, pronghorn antelope horns, hawk, magpie and prairie chicken feathers, beads, bells, ribbon and paint. Sacred war regalia was often decorated with the feathers of birds which scavenged on battlefields.

(L7) Plains: Sioux, c.1900
The symbol of the Native American: the eagle feather crown or war bonnet. Feather crowns are probably ancient in the Americas, associated with chieftainship, war and ritual. The flared crown bonnet probably evolved amongst the Upper Missouri tribes, and was recorded in this form by George Catlin as early as the 1830s. It was particularly associated with the Sioux, Cheyenne and Arapaho, but during early reservation days was adopted by many tribes as an ethnic symbol. The feathers were laced to a hide skullcap (or, later, a traded felt hat with the brim removed).

(L8) Northeastern Woodlands: Mohegan, c.1880
Northeastern Algonkians including the Mohegan and Naragansett all but lost native dress by the 19th century. Male dress for special occasions sometimes included a beaded cloth cape as a symbol of rank. The upright feathered headdress with beaded band may be descended from an earlier form, or copied from the popular Western war bonnet.

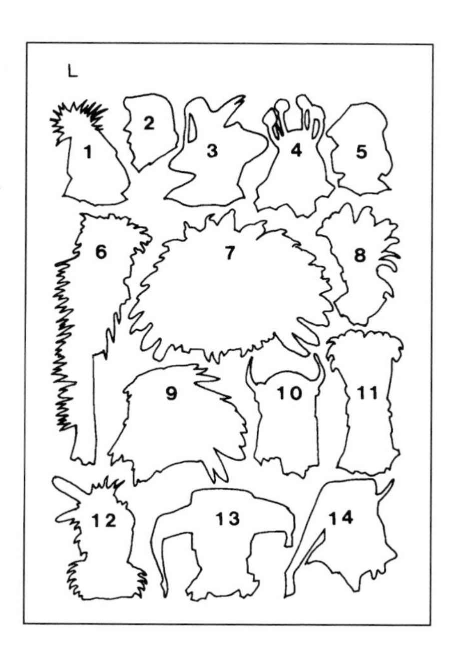

(L9) Plains: Assiniboine, c.1898
The many forms of war bonnet – collections of military symbolism with animal skins, feathers, shells and mirrors added – were once considered sacred. Exact ritual meanings faded with the end of the old warrior days; the bonnet was adopted simply as an ethnic symbol, or by men who had recently been in U.S. military service. The flamboyant eagle bonnets worn for parades by older men among the Assiniboine ("Stonies") at Morley, Alberta province, were once famous.

(L10) Plains: Blackfoot, c.1910
Ceremonial splithorn bonnet constructed on a headpiece of felt or skin covered with weasel (ermine) pelts, as was a cloth trailer usually added behind, with a beaded browband and shaped and polished buffalo horns.

(L11) Plains: Blackfoot, c.1890
Chief wearing older style upright ceremonial bonnet of eagle feathers on a skin or felt base, the browband quilled, beaded, or, as here, studded with brass; there was usually lavish ermine trimming. This ancient style was widely seen on the northern Plains among Upper Missouri tribes, Plains Cree and Blackfoot, among whom both men and women could be entitled to them; characteristic of the Blackfoot is the red-dyed rooster plume at the front. This style was largely replaced by the flared crown bonnet by the early 20th century.

(L12) NE Woodlands & Prairie: Sauk and Fox, c.1867
Warrior wearing a head roach, widely used by Eastern and Midwestern tribes and usually constructed of porcupine and deer hair, with a braided woollen turban, silver earrings and bear claw necklace.

(L13) Plains & Prairie: Pawnee, c.1880
Otter fur turban decorated with multicoloured cut-and-fold ribbonwork; note also silver ball and cone earrings.

(L14) Plains & Prairie: Omaha, c.1870
Chief wearing otter fur turban, the tail decorated with ribbonwork, the other side with ermine and a single horn; and a grizzly bear claw necklace.

Plate M: Headdress

(M1) Northeastern Woodlands: Malecite, c.1860
Woman wearing a peaked cloth hood with the rounded bottom edge characteristic of the Malecite and Penobscot of New Brunswick and Maine. Hoods were no doubt aboriginal, but these late 18th and 19th century Northeastern examples are made from dark trade cloth or velvet, decorated in fine floralistic double-curve and zigzag beaded designs; by this date they were worn only for galas or church festivals.

(M2) Northeastern Woodlands: Micmac, c.1840
Micmac women of Nova Scotia wore similar hoods but squared at the bottom edge. The ancient, probably native double-curve motif is a series of laterally repeated curving designs, probably symbolic (perhaps of canoes); it was used on clothing, pouches, bark containers and canoes by most Northeastern Algonkian peoples, and occurs as far west as the Blackfoot range.

(M3) Plateau: Nez Perce, c.1860
Basketry caps appear among women of the Western peoples from California to Washington State. Those worn by the Nez Perce and some other Plateau peoples were made of cornhusk and other dyed fibres embroidered with coloured grass or wool.

(M4) Southeastern Woodlands: Seminole, c.1930
Some young and middle-aged women still wear this hairstyle, combed over a cardboard frame extending from one side of the head. After about the age of 12 strings of multicoloured glass beads are worn round the neck, with strings added for virtue or as gifts. After middle life they are sometimes removed strand by strand, the last going to the grave with its wearer.

(M5) Southwest: Western Apache, c.1880
Woman's hourglass-shaped leather head ornament covered with cloth, decorated with beadwork and brass tacks, and tied to the hair with ribbons which hang down the back. It is thought to have indicated marriageable age.

(M6) Southwest: Hopi, c.1900
Traditional "butterfly" or "squash blossom" hairstyle symbolizing virginity; the hair is wrapped around two curved sticks into large whorls.

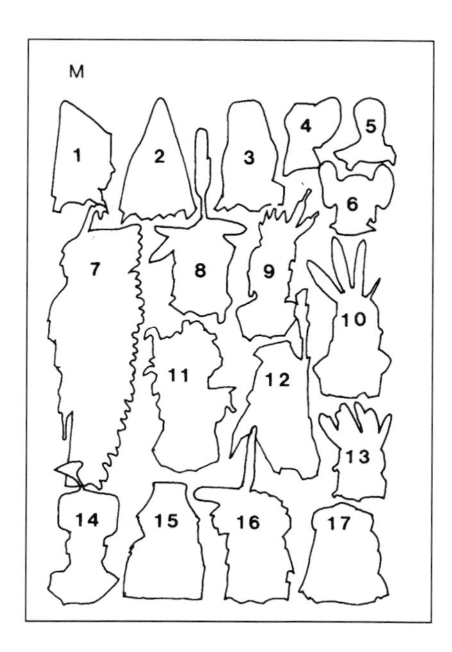

Married women wore their hair tied with a cloth hanging down at the side of the head and over the shoulders. This post-pubescent style is still occasionally seen.

(M7) Plains: Sioux, c.1870
Splithorn society bonnet consisting of cap with shaved horns tipped with dyed horsehair, ermine covering, clusters of feathers, beaded browband and ermine skin drops, the symbolically painted hide trailer with eagle feathers and tin cone "jingles". (These trailers, incorporated into various styles of headdress, were obviously intended to look their best when worn by a mounted warrior.)

(M8) Northeastern Woodlands: Iroquois, c.1900
Gustoweh or "whirling feather" headdress traditional to Iroquois men, and still favoured for ceremonial wear. It was often constructed of hide or cloth over an ash splint framework, with a central eagle feather attached in a tube; occasionally a cluster of smaller split heron, hawk, turkey or owl feathers was also attached. The band was of silver, other metal, or embossed beaded cloth.

(M9) Northeastern Woodlands: Sauk and Fox, mid-18th century
Warrior with head shaved except for a small braid to secure the roach (of porcupine and deer hair, or turkey beards); in early times this was much smaller than the still widely used dancer's roach. The spines of the roach feathers are covered with quill-wrapped sticks or rawhide. He wears sashes of natural fibre interspaced with trade beads or wampum, a trade silver gorget and nose and earrings. Shaven-headed warriors were known as far west as the Pawnee and Eastern Sioux.

(M10) Plains: Lakota, c.1872
Painted eagle feathers fixed upright in the hair, along with an arrow, indicate warrior status; his braids are wrapped with fur, and he wears dentalium and abalone shell earrings. He also wears a "peace medal", as given by various agents and usually bearing Presidents' heads.

(M11) Plains: Blackfoot, c.1900
Sacred "Natoas" (Sun's Turnip) headdress of the holy woman in the Blackfoot Sun Dance ritual, honouring the myths concerning Grandfather Sun, Morningstar, his wife Tailfeather Woman, her son Scarface, Spider and the Forbidden Turnip. The lack of women with knowledge of the ritual led to its decline among the Blackfoot.

(M12) Plains: Crow, c.1880
Noted for their impressive hairstyles, the Crow probably took some forms from their friends the Nez Perce, perhaps including this: an upstanding forelock or pompadour and long back hair stuck together with rows of small spots of pitch. To slim braids at the temples were attached ornaments – coiled brass wire, dentalium shells, hairpipes and trade beads.

(M13) Northeastern Woodlands: Ojibwa (Chippewa), c.1870
Unusual braided hair at the front, with turkey feathers (widely used by all Eastern tribes) fixed upright.

(M14) Southeastern Woodlands: Seminole, c.1880
Turbans were popular with Seminoles and men of other Southeastern tribes during the 19th century; figurines recovered through archaeology may show their use in aboriginal times. The form shown was made by folding and wrapping a commercial woollen shawl; they were sometimes decorated with silver and plumes.

(M15) California: Nisenan, c.1870
Southern Maidu boy wearing "flicker feather" headdress across the forehead, large abalone shell gorget, and bandolier covered with abalone pendants and beads; abalone objects were considered great wealth among the Maidu tribes.

(M16) Southwest: Western Apache, c.1880
Ceremonial war-medecine headdress of clipped turkey feathers and two eagle feathers, imparting protection and swiftness in battle; several Apache war and ceremonial caps were secured by chinstraps.

(M17) Southwest: Western Apache, c.1880
Thick patterned headband, buckskin war amulet decorated with shell braided into the hair, and typical Apache face paint.

Plate N: Women and infants

(N1) Arctic: Inuit, c.1940
Polar Inuit mother at Thule, Greenland, wearing sealskin coat with hood large enough to accomodate infants up to two and three years old.

(N2) Plateau: Kutenai, c.1885
Several eastern Plateau and northern Basin tribes used a cradle based on a long ellipsoidal board, the broad upper part covered with skin or cloth of which the lower part was made into a bag to hold the child. The Kutenai beaded the upper area in geometrical or floralistic patterns. Cradles were usually carried on a chest strap.

(N3) Plateau: Nez Perce, c.1900
Similar cradle form, the upper area beaded with floralistic designs in large symmetrical elements on a coloured background, and here with a beaded cloth bib covering the laced front of the cradle bag. Miniature toy versions were made for girl-children.

(N4) Northwest Coast: Tlingit, c.1890
Bark sling cradle; the button cap is Tlingit in style, the moccasins and bark sling probably of neighbouring Athabascan origin.

(N5) Northwest Coast: Head reshaping, c.1846
Several Northwest Coast tribes, from the Bella Coola in the north to the Alsea in the south, reshaped the heads of babies by use of an additional wooden slat slanting downwards from the top and bound to the head or tied to the cradle base. The Chinook of the Columbia River valley practised the most extreme flattening of the forehead. The so-called Flathead of western Montana did not follow this practice, despite their popular name.

(N6) Northwest Coast: Nootka, c.1850
Ordinary woven basketry cradles were regarded as temporary and expendable. Others, usually of cedar boards, padded with shredded bark and mountain goat wool, were carved and painted with the crest of the child for whom they were intended, and had permanent and sometimes ceremonial value.

(N7) Subarctic: Ahtna
Chair-like birch bark cradle allowing the legs to dangle astride a central flap fastened to the chest by cross ties. The cradle was carried on the mother's back by a robe or blanket and held in position by a wide band around her shoulders or head.

(N8) Subarctic: Kutchin, c.1920
Older infants were sometimes carried by means of a sturdy band looped around the child's buttocks, carried over the mother's shoulders and tied at the front; these belts were heavily beaded, and fringed with wool.

(N9) Basin: Ute, c.1895
The Northern Ute probably adopted the Plateau style cradle (see N2) late in

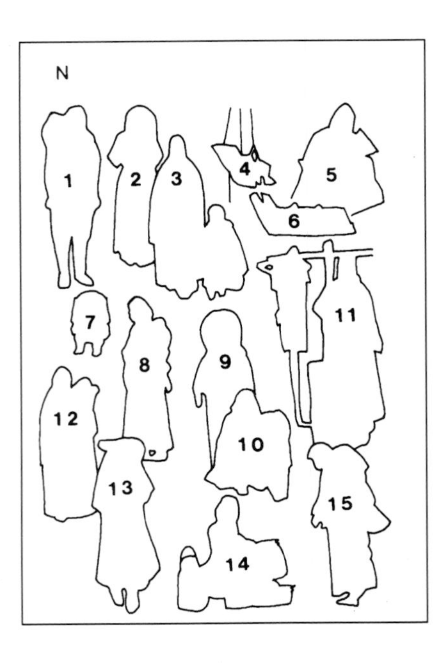

the 19th century, adding an eye shade of willow basketry. There was some concern over possible harmful effects of confining a baby in a cradle for extended periods, but Indians claimed beneficial effects for developing erect posture, apart from ensuring safety during the day. At night a mother would transfer her baby into a soft buckskin bag, or place it in beddings.

(N10) Basin: Shoshone, c.1890
Pine board covered with buckskin, the area above the bag elaborately beaded in geometrical or floralistic designs – these probably being quite a late development. The laced bag front had minor variations for gender, allowing for the insertion of a soft pad between the legs of infant girls, or with holes in the central flap tied over the lacing which allowed infant boys to urinate outside the buckskin pouch.

(N11) Northeastern Woodlands: Iroquois, c.1880
Woman pounding corn with pestle and log mortar, her child hanging safely nearby. The cradle was a board about two feet long, with a projecting bow similar to those described for the Ojibwa (Chippewa) but lacking their distinctive recurve; the bow and top edge of the board were often carved; near the bottom was a foot support. The baby was bound to the board with red or blue cloth decorated with beads or moose hair, and a blanket or netting could be drawn over the bow to protect the face. A burden strap secured the cradle behind the mother's shoulders.

(N12) Subarctic: Slavey, c.1880
Amongst the Northern Athabascans and Métis newborn babies were carried and nursed in cloth bags laced up the front, but lacking the back board of the Cree and Ojibwa. These "moss bags" (from their sphagnum moss internal padding) were sometimes carefully decorated in beaded or silk floralistic designs.

(N13) Northeastern Woodlands: Ojibwa, c.1880
The Ojibwa (Chippewa) used two forms of the same basic cradle type, both based on a cedar board roughly two feet by ten inches, with a hickory hoop or bow fixed and braced at the top to protect the child in case the cradle fell. Among the southern Chippewa (U.S.A.) a short foot brace was attached, and the baby was wrapped to the board with two pieces of cloth. Among the more northern (Canadian) bands and the Cree this was replaced by a U-shaped wooden inner frame, the child being held in a laced bag formed by a rectangular piece of cloth thonged to the sides of the U-frame. In the late 19th century both the wrappers and the bag, usually of dark cloth, were decorated with floralistic beadwork.

(N14) California: Karok, c.1895
Scoop-shaped cradle made of wooden rods sewn together, with a top hanging hoop; the infant was bound in with leather thongs, its feet hanging free. The mother wears the traditional basketry cap of northern California.

(N15) Basin: Paiute, c.1880
The cradle has a flat, wedge-shaped foundation of willow rods with an inverted U-shaped top, covered with bucksin or canvas; a basketry awning protects and shelters the child's head.

Plate O: Women and infants

(O1) Plains: Sioux, c.1885
The cradle was a rectangular bag of hide, backed with rawhide or canvas, with a piece of parfleche inserted under the top and extending to form a square or rectangular back tab beaded with symbolic protective designs. The sides of the bag were often fully beaded in geometrical designs, including box shapes with extending prongs. The Sioux occasionally mounted cradles on frames similar to those of more southerly tribes.

(O2) Plains: Comanche
The Comanche used a rawhide night cradle – simply a rectangle of hide laced tightly around the baby.

(O3) Plains: Kiowa, c.1895
The Kiowa developed the lattice cradle, constructed on a pair of narrow boards with pointed ends extending far above the top of the bag, held in place by crosspieces near its head and foot. The sides of the deep buckskin bag, lined with cloth and reinforced with rawhide, were laced together with deerskin thongs. The bag was beaded with geometrical, or more commonly abstract floralistic designs probably adopted from neighbouring Eastern tribes relocated in Oklahoma; the boards were often decorated with brass studs. The Comanche had similar cradles; use of the boards was also adopted by the Cheyenne and sometimes by the Sioux.

(O4) Plains: Sioux amulets
The Plains peoples customarily enclosed the umbilical cord of a newborn infant in a decorative bag in the shape of a turtle or lizard, which was hung on the cradle as a protective charm.

(O5) Plains: Pawnee, c.1870
The Pawnee shared a similar type of cradle with Prairie Siouan groups such as the Osage, Iowa, Omaha and Ponca. Of the same general form described for the Ojibwa (N13), they had the back board, usually of cottonwood (Pawnee) or cedar (Osage), and the protective upper hoop, but lacked the foot board. Pawnee cradle hoops were partly supported by a thong stay from the carved area, while the Osage had thongs holding the hoop below the carved area. Pawnee carvings derive from ancient symbolism connected with the Morning Star, the Sun, and other natural phenomena.

(O6) Plains: Crow, c.1880
One of the elements of material culture linking the Crow to the Plateau peoples was their cradle construction, which resembled those of the Flathead and Nez Perce except that they replaced the bag with a series of wide straps laced together down the front. Crow cradles were beaded in large geometrical shapes often outlined with white beaded lines.

(O7) Plains: Arapaho, c.1875
Although the Arapaho used cradles similar to the Sioux and Cheyenne, a number of unusual specimens have survived which are attributed to them. A branch of willow, chokecherry or sumac was held in an inverted U-shape by transverse sticks; the cover was a plain piece of buckskin or canvas folded lengthwise and stitched together along one short side. The quilled ornaments usually consisted of a large disc at the top and wrapped ladder-like rawhide bands down the front opening; pendants were either plain or quill-wrapped buckskin strips with small bells or deer claws attached.

(O8) Plains: Cheyenne, c.1885
The Cheyenne often completely covered the bag of their lattice cradles with lazy stitch beadwork in their characteristic stepped, elongated triangles enclosing rectangles, and figures of birds, dragonflies and horses. The colours used were symbolically important, representing life-giving powers.

(O9) Southwest: Pueblo
Throughout the region infants were often carried in a blanket on the mother's back, though several cradle types were also originally used.

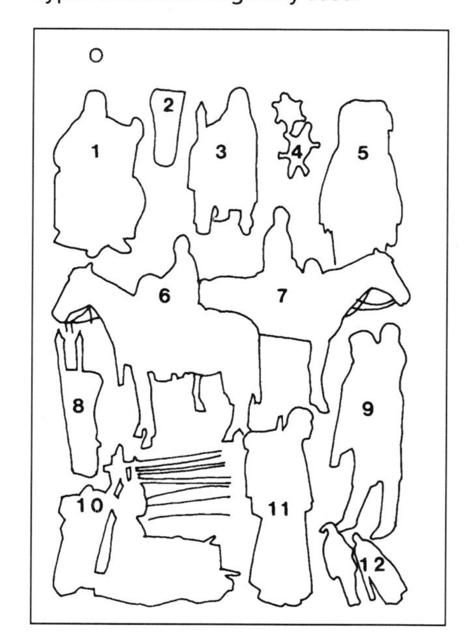

Variants of the basket cradle were found among the Mohave, Pima, Yuma and Hopi; but the Rio Grande Pueblos and Navajo used a board type, the former frequently carving the top in terraces symbolizing clouds, with a flexible wooden hoop canopy.

(O10) Southwest: Navajo, c.1900
Navajo cradles were backed with two boards with pointed or rounded upper ends, a foot rest, and a hoop or canopy of thin, bent wooden splints; all parts were thonged together through holes in the wood. Ornaments and charms were often attached to the bow-shaped canopy. The mother is shown weaving a blanket; the Navajo copied the vertical loom from the Pueblos in c.1700, first weaving cotton, later wool. The earliest Navajo serapes and blankets closely resembled those of the Pueblos; but they gradually developed their own increasingly complex rug designs, associated today with various parts of the Navajo reservation – e.g. Ganado, Two Grey Hills, and Wide Ruins.

(O11) Southwest: Western Apache, c.1890
Some groups used a cradle with a U-shaped or ovoid frame of heavy rods crossed by wooden slats, with a broad bow over the child's head made of narrower yucca slats; the cover was usually deerskin, often coloured yellow. The infant was strapped in with buckskin ties and cushioned with layers of cloth or crushed cedar bark.

(O12) Winnebago dolls
Dolls were made by many tribes; these are from the Wisconsin Winnebago, and are dressed in late 19th century clothes – the male in aprons, the female in a wraparound skirt, all decorated with cut-and-fold ribbon-work.

Plate P: Modern costumes

(P1) Blackfoot dress clothes, mid-20th century
Buckskin shirts and leggings with matching beadwork strips are popular with Blackfoot men for special occasions, particularly among the Canadian branches; the costume is usually of white buckskin, heavily tailored. The bonnet is of eagle feathers tipped with white dics, the frontal cloth bindings wrapped diagonally.

(P2) Oklahoma shawl dancer, c.1989
Pan-Indian intertribal woman's dress: a ribbon blouse and separate skirt in the Woodland tradition, worn with moccasin boots made by a Kiowa lady, and a shawl made by a member of the Comanche Parker family – items acquired by the author in Oklahoma.

(P3) Oklahoma woman's dress, c.1960
The modern buckskin dress developed by the Kiowa, Comanche, Cheyenne and others in Oklahoma and elsewhere was derived from older Southern Cheyenne and Kiowa dresses, and retains several old features: a deep yoke with scalloped edges at the seam with the skirt, horizontal bands of beadwork, and often an associated belt and set of three beaded bags (formerly carrying women's tools). Many ladies wear beaded "princess crowns" and carry shawls or fans for the dance and princess contests.

(P4) Northern Plains Grass Dancer, mid-20th century
So-called Northern Grass Dance costume probably originated in its presently recognizable form among the Plains Ojibwa and Cree of Saskatchewan. The style which became popular on the northern U.S.A. reservations in the 1950s, derived from the spread of the original Grass Dance northwards into Canada in the 1880s, utilized the head roach with beaded headband with a frontal rosette or heart; the harness, rosettes, armbands, collar, tie, belt and cuffs were in geometrical or floralistic beadwork, sometimes matched. These were worn over a shirt and leggings of dark cloth often fringed at the shoulder, aprons, knees and ankles with buckskin, ribbon, or wool. Completely wool-fringed outfits have recently become popular with young men.

(P5) Fancy Dance or Feathers costume, mid-late 20th century
A very popular young men's Pan-Indian costume from Oklahoma, apparently developed in about 1930, giving expression to the Fast War Dance at secular Pow-wows and dances. Although specific parts of the costume can be traced to older native models, the combination of large back and arm bustles with multicoloured fluffy feathers, capes, beaded harness, belt, aprons, and roach or feather headdress was new, and changed from year to year. The costume was adopted in the 1940s-50s by the Sioux and many others, displacing indigenous dance clothes.

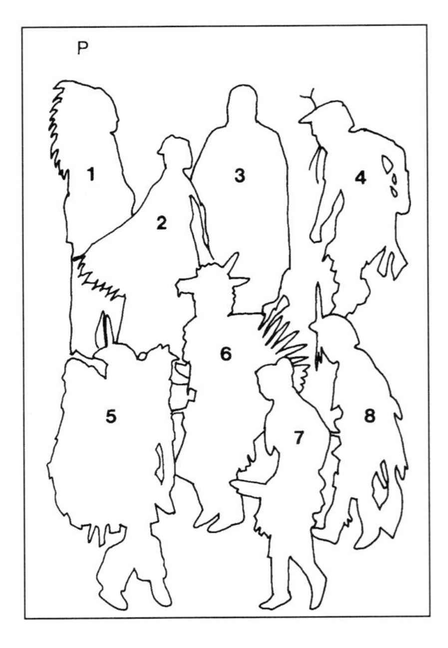

(P6) Sioux "Contemporary Traditional" dance costume, c.1985
In the 1870s the Sioux had distinctive men's dress for the Grass Dance: roach, belts or bustles of scavenger birds' feathers, belt braids of sweetgrass, quilled armbands, cuffs, and otter fur or hairpipe breastplates, later worn over dyed trade underwear for modesty due to missionary influence (cf.D13). It lost popularity to the Fancy Dance and Grass Dance costumes adopted from other tribes during this century; but the early 1970s saw the development of a modern version, "Contemporary Traditional", which has become very popular; recently it is characterized by a feather visor over the eyes. This, along with the Fancy, Straight (Oklahoma) and Northern Grass Dance costumes can all be traced to the spread of the original Grass or Omaha Dance 120 years ago.

(P7) Northern Plains woman's "jingle" dress, c.1985
Originating amongst the Chippewa and Santee Sioux of Minnesota, North Dakota and adjacent Canada late in the 19th century, this spread to many tribes with the development of newer forms of women's dances, and is very popular at modern celebrations. The cloth dress is decorated with rows of long tin cones, giving a loud "jingle" rhythm when dancing.

(P8) Oklahoma Straight Dancer, mid-late 20th century
Costume worn by Osage, Ponca, Oto and Pawnee men who dance in the older style to the songs of the Ponca Heduska and Osage Inlonschka. The costume reinforces family, tribal and ethnic ties, and echoes an older tradition from the days when these Prairie tribes were first settled on reservations in Indian Territory; it descends from the last of their war and clan society rituals. "Straight Dance" refers to the lack of exaggerated dress or movements. The costume consists of a roach with a single feather, scalp feathers, cloth shirt, beaded belt, otter fur trailer, cloth leggings with ribbon-work, scarf and tie slide, and frontally knotted white headband. It is particularly popular at the three annual Osage Pow-wows in northern Oklahoma.

(continued from p. 90)
the Nespelem 45 in 1910, about 150 full blood in 1959, but they have now largely merged with the "Confederated Colville". The 1970 census reported 1,674 Sanpoil, Nespelem, Okanagan and Spokan in the U.S.A.

SINKIUSE or **COLUMBIA** A group of Salishan bands on the east side of the Columbia River from Fort Okanagan to Priest Rapids, Washington state, where one band called Moses-Columbia lived. They were originally estimated to number 1,000; the census of 1910 reported only 52; and the 150 full blood reported in 1959 largely merged with the "Confederated Colville" on the Colville Reservation. In 1970, 33 Columbia and Wenatchee were reported.

WENATCHEE & ENTIAT Two small Salishan groups on the west side of the Columbia River on the Wenatchee and Entiat Rivers around Leavenworth, Washington state. Not all moved to the reservations, but some to the Colville Reservation; these numbered 52 in 1910 and 268 in 1959, both on and off the reservation. They are now part of the "Confederated Colville".

CHELAN A Salish group on the west side of the Columbia, related to the Wenatchee; a few remained until reservation days but appear to have joined the Wenatchee and Columbia on the Colville Reservation.

METHOW A small group on the Methow River in north central Washington. They joined the Columbia or Sinkiuse on the Colville Reservation and lost separate identity.

THOMPSON or **NTLAKYAPMUK** A large interior Salishan tribe living on the Fraser River, British Columbia, from Spuzzum in the south to above Lytton, then along the Thompson River to an area above Spencer Bridge, and east along the Nicola valley. First noted by Simon Fraser in 1809, they subsequently came under the influence of the Northwest and Hudson's Bay traders. Although depleted during the 19th century they continued to occupy village sites which became small reserves. The most important are Spuzzum, Boston Bar, Boothroyd, Kanaka Bar, Lytton, Oregon Jack Creek, Upper and Lower Nicola. The total population numbered 2,742 in 1970.

SHUSWAP An important Salishan tribe north of the Thompson, from the vicinity of Ashcroft north to Williams Lake in the upper valleys of the Fraser River, and along the Thompson River above Kamloops, and also in the valley of the upper Columbia River. Known to the early explorers and later traders and miners, they never removed from their ancient homes, although they were restricted to small reserves usually near old village sites. Their main groups are at Bonaparte, Ashcroft, Dead Man's Creek, Kamloops, Adams Lake, Pavilion, Spallumcheen, Clinton, North Thompson, Canoe Creek, Williams Lake, Alkali Lake, Canim Lake, and High Bar, numbering 3,862 in 1970.

LILLOOET A substantial Salishan people on the Fraser around the town of Lillooet and Anderson Lake, also along the valley of Harrison Lake, Lillooet Lake and River. They show a similar history to their relatives the Shuswap and Thompson, but lost more members in the smallpox epidemic of 1865. Their principal present reserves are at Douglas, Skookum Chuck, Anderson Lake, Lillooet, Fountain, Cayoose Creek, Bridge River and Mount Currie; and they numbered 2,494 in 1970.

KUTENAI or ***KOOTENAY*** A tribe and independent linguistic family of Indians who either migrated or were forced, probably by the Blackfoot, across the Rocky Mountains into what is now southeastern British Columbia. They seem to have split into the upper and lower divisions. The Upper Kutenai pushed south into present Montana on the Tobacco Plains and were influenced by the horse/buffalo Plains Indian culture complex. They used horses for transportation and as a source of wealth, and adopted the Sun Dance and material culture and costume associated with the northern Plains Indians. The Lower Kutenai by comparison were partly sedentary, of the true Plateau culture, subsisting on fish, roots and game, and are famous for a remarkable canoe. In aboriginal times they perhaps numbered 2,000, but only 500 or so by 1855.

Most of the Upper Kutenai, originally from around Jennings and Libby, Montana, under the name Dayton-Elmo band, joined the Flathead and their associates on the Flathead (Jocko) Agency; the Lower Kutenai, with accessions from the Tobacco Plains band, obtained reserves in British Columbia around Creston, Windermere and Cranbrook, and also near Bonners Ferry, Idaho. In 1907, 573 were recorded in Montana and 549 in British Columbia. The Bonners Ferry group returned 106 in 1945, and 115 in 1982. The Kutenai perhaps constitute a quarter of the present, so-called "Confederated Salish-Kootenai", numbering 3,225 in 1985, but many now live off the reservation. In 1970 the Canadian Kutenai at Columbia Lake, Lower Kootenay, St. Mary's and Tobacco Plains numbered 446.

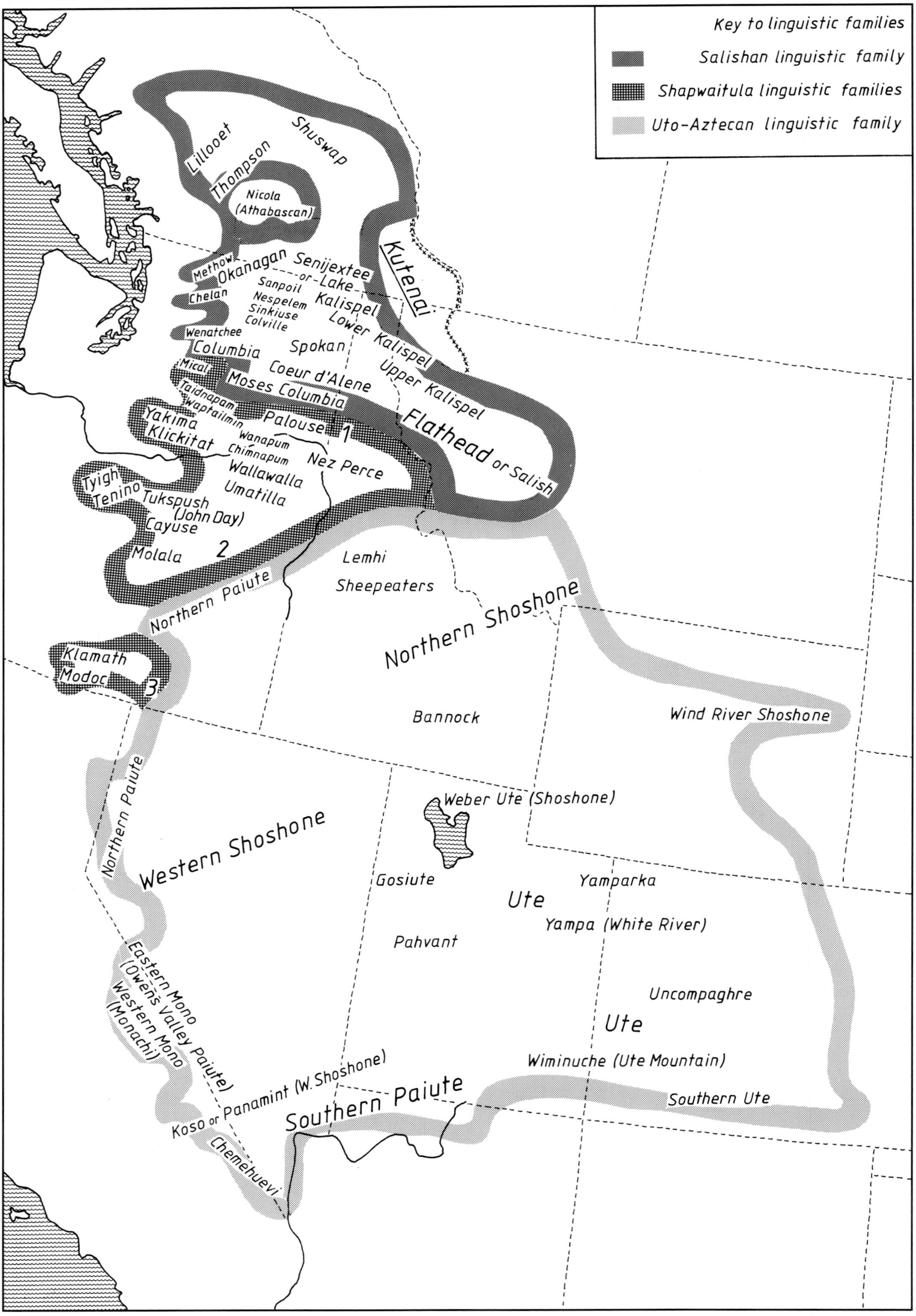

Key to linguistic families

Salishan linguistic family

Shapwaitula linguistic families

Uto-Aztecan linguistic family

Lillooet
Shuswap
Thompson
Nicola (Athabascan)
Kutenai
Methow
Okanagan
Senijextee or Lake
Sanpoil
Nespelem
Sinkiuse
Colville
Chelan
Kalispel
Lower Kalispel
Wenatchee
Columbia
Spokan
Mical
Coeur d'Alene
Upper Kalispel
Moses Columbia
Taidnapam
Waptailmin
Yakima
Klickitat
Palouse
1
Flathead or Salish
Wanapum
Chimnapum
Nez Perce
Wallawalla
Umatilla
Tyigh
Tenino
Tukspush (John Day)
Cayuse
Molala
2
Lemhi
Sheepeaters
Northern Paiute
Northern Shoshone
Klamath
Modoc
3
Bannock
Wind River Shoshone
Northern Paiute
Weber Ute (Shoshone)
Western Shoshone
Gosiute
Yamparka
Ute
Yampa (White River)
Pahvant
Eastern Mono (Owens Valley Paiute)
Western Mono (Monachi)
Uncompaghre
Ute
Wiminuche (Ute Mountain)
Koso or Panamint (W. Shoshone)
Southern Paiute
Southern Ute
Chemehuevi

GREAT BASIN

Language family and tribe	*Meaning*/origin of tribal name, where known
Uto-Aztecan*:	
Western Shoshone	-
Northern Shoshone	-
Bannock	English name
Eastern or Wind River Shoshone	-
Ute	Spanish name
Southern Paiute	Spanish name
Eastern Mono	–
Western Mono	-
Northern Paiute	Spanish name
* see p.137	

The Indians who lived in the vast area of present Nevada, Utah, western parts of Colorado and Wyoming, southern Idaho and adjacent parts of Oregon and California, sharing a similar lifestyle, formed the Great Basin cultural area. The area is bounded by the Snake River in the north almost to the Colorado River in the south. Although the area is not all desert, sparse vegetation, sagebrush and meagre grassland characterize the region. In the east woodland and brush are found in canyons and valleys, and occasional marshy patches dot the area. Animal resources are sparse: squirrels, rabbits and fish were the principal meat with occasional antelope, deer and bison; even gophers and grasshoppers were eaten. The Indian also depended upon piñon nut and acorn harvests from which mush, flour and cakes could be made, augmented by wild plants, seeds, berries and roots. The Indians of the Great Basin were dominated by the food quest in a largely inhospitable and exceedingly demanding climate with extremes of heat and cold.

The area became known to the Spanish in the late 18th century, and to Americans after the explorations of Jedediah Smith (c. 1824-31)and John Fremont; settlement by whites was limited, however, as most immigrant parties crossed the Great Basin en route to California. Consequently the Indians did not suffer removal as elsewhere, but gradually modified to the predominant culture – though at the lowest economic level. Reservations and "colonies" for homeless groups were often established in the late 19th and 20th centuries. The Indians of the area belong mainly to the old Shoshonean linguistic family, specifically to the Numic division, now designated as the Uto-Aztecan family except for the Washoe, whose distant relatives are the Hokans of California.

TRIBES OF THE GREAT BASIN AND PLATEAU, c.1750s-1850
Linguistic and cultural boundaries are necessarily approximate; this sketch map is intended only as a general guide to distribution. Modern state boundaries are shown as broken lines, for orientation only. The numerals in the Shapwaitula linguistic areas indicate (1) Shahaptin, (2) Waiilatpuan, and (3) Lutuami linguistic lamilies. The Kutenai, an independent linguistic group, are so indicated by underlining.

WESTERN SHOSHONE A collective name for a group of scattered bands extending from the arid Death Valley of California through the highlands of central Nevada into northwestern Utah, including the upper reaches of the Owyhee and Humboldt Rivers. They belonged to the Numic division of the Shoshonean or Uto-Aztecan linguistic family. Usually designated in small subgroups such as the "Pine Nut Eaters", two groups are sometimes given separate status: the *Panamint* on the west side of Death Valley, Inyo County, California, and the *Gosiute* of western Utah. The so-called "Weber Ute" of the Great Salt Lake are also classified as Western Shoshone. Shoshone culture was the Great Basin type, with plant procurement a subsistence mainstay, together with harvesting nuts and seeds and some hunting.

White settlers, miners and ranchers followed the earlier explorations of Jedediah Smith and John Fremont. In 1863 a treaty with the United States provided the establishment of reservations, notably Duck Valley on the Nevada-Idaho border, but not until after 1900 did any substantial numbers of Western Shoshone occupy the "colonies" scattered in their old territory. They slipped unnoticed into the white man's mode of living, but at a low economic level. Their population may have been over 3,000 before white contact; in 1937, 1,201 were reported including Gosiute and Panamint; and in 1980, 2,923. The largest groups were at the Duck Valley Reservation, Nevada (900); Skull Valley (60) and Goshute (120), both in Utah; Wells, Elko, South Fork, Carlin, Ely, Ruby Valley, Winnemucca, Battle Mountain, Fallon, Yomba and Duckwater Reservations, all in Nevada, (1,500). The last of the Panamint seem to have merged with the two branches of Mono in Inyo County, California. The Shoshone produced fine coiled basketry. Hand games and Fandangos are still frequently held.

NORTHERN SHOSHONE The Northern Shoshone were bands of Numic-speaking Shoshoneans living in the Snake River valley, Idaho, and as far north as the Salmon River; they are linguistically very close to the Western Shoshone. Their environment was marginally Plateau where it merges into the Great Basin. Their subsistence depended on salmon and other fish, collecting wild roots, yampa, bitterroot and camas, and hunting, which included the bison. Subgroups included the "Salmon-Eaters" and "Mountain Sheep-Eaters" around the Salmon and Lehmi Rivers,"Yamp-Eaters" of the Camas Prairie, and some bands of mixed Shoshone and Paiute on the Oregon border. Historical evidence suggests they they may have been the "Snakes" who once occupied the northern Plains before the Blackfoot expelled them west of the Rockies; nevertheless they developed a veneer of Plains culture, and in the 19th century they also visited the Montana Plains to hunt bison. They participated in the development of trade relations with the Crow. They also adopted the Plains-derived Grass Dance and the Sun Dance, to which they added Christian features; their form of Sun Dance is now shared with the Crow and Wind River Shoshone.

The Shoshone had obtained horses by the late 17th century, which established them as travellers and traders. Whites established trading posts within Bannock and Shoshone territory as early as 1810, and they participated in the annual summer rendezvous with the whites on the Green River, Wyoming. Independent life ended in the 1860s when the Lehmi and Fort Hall Reservations were founded, although Lehmi was closed in 1907 and the population transferred to Fort Hall. There are no reliable population figures for pre-white contact Shoshone. An estimate for 1860 gives 3,000 Shoshone and Bannock; in 1937 3,650 "Northern Shoshone" were reported, and in 1983 about 3,900 were enrolled at Fort Hall Reservation, Idaho. The Shoshone and Bannock still hold annual festivals, Powwows and rodeos, including their Sun Dance at Fort Hall, despite overwhelming modern influences.

BANNOCK A detached branch of the Northern Paiute on the Snake River, Idaho, who became associated with the Northern Shoshone and in time intermixed. In culture they were similar to the Shoshone, and moved with them to the Fort Hall Reservation, Idaho, in 1869. In 1878 an Indian uprising in the area involved some Bannock. In 1910 they numbered 413; in 1937, 342; and in 1945, 337. They are now part of the "Shoshone-Bannock tribe" of Fort Hall, Idaho.

EASTERN or **WIND RIVER SHOSHONE** The ancestors of the Eastern and Northern Shoshone are probably the "Snakes" or "Gens du Serpents" reported by the earliest white traders. Ranging as far north as the Saskatchewan River, they were subsequently expelled from the north by the Blackfoot and ultimately restricted to the Plateau and Basin – except for the Eastern Shoshone, who have occupied western Wyoming periodically since about A.D. 1500, particularly in the watersheds of the Snake, Wind and Sweetwater Rivers. The Comanche split from them in the 18th century. Culturally they were intermediate between Plains, Basin and Plateau, gathering berries and roots, but also skilled buffalo hunters whose women were noted as skilled and rapid butchers. Their material culture resembled that of the true Plains people, their tipis, ritual objects, horse equipment and ceremonialism, including the Sun Dance, reflecting their association with the Plains culture.

They remained generally on good terms with whites during the 19th century through the efforts of Chief Washakie, and the Wind River Reservation was established, which they were forced to share with former enemies, the Northern Arapaho. Religion involved the acquisition of supernatural powers, and tribal welfare derived from the Sun Dance. A modified Sun Dance with some Christian elements is shared with the Northern Shoshone, Ute and Crow and has been an important element in reservation life. Peyote and Pan-Indianism including annual Powwows are also part of continuing Indian life. The Shoshone population may have been 10,000 or more in A.D. 1700. The recent Wind River Shoshone population reports 1,672 (1950) and 2,400 (1981).

UTE A Shoshonean (Uto-Aztecan) people of central western Colorado and central eastern Utah, occupying the drainages and tributaries of the Green River and Colorado River. They are closely connected to the Southern Paiute in language. Their historic culture reflected both Great Basin and Plains traits; eastern and southern bands foraged for bison, but they also collected berries, roots, nuts and seeds. They were divided into a number of subtribes: Capote and Moache in southern Colorado; Wiminuche north of the San Juan River; Uncompahgre in the area of the Gunnison River, Colorado; White River Ute including the Yampa on the White, Yampa and Green Rivers; Uintah in northeastern Utah; Pahvant around Sevier Lake; Timpanogots around Utah Lake, Sanpits around Manti in San Pete valley; and Moanunts or Fish Ute on the upper course of the Sevier River, Utah.

In later years they were concentrated in four bands – Uncompahgre, White River, Uintah and Wiminuche. They were known to the Spanish from the 1600s, and they raided the Hopi, Paiute and Plains tribes. However, from 1750 onwards Apache, Arapaho and Cheyenne exploited Ute hunting grounds in their eastern mountain valleys.

In 1868 a reservation was established in Colorado for Uncompahgre, Moache, Capote, Wiminuche, Yampa and Uintah Utes. In 1880, following the "Meeker Massacre", two reservations were formed in Utah to become the Uintah and Ouray Reservations, and the Uncompahgre and White River Ute moved there in 1880 and 1882. The Wiminuche, Moache and Capote were subsequently located on the Southern Ute Agency along the San Juan River valley of southern Colorado and adjacent New Mexico – now the Ute Mountain and Southern Ute Reservations. The Utes probably numbered 4,500 before the reservation period, but were reduced to 3,391 by 1885. In 1920 there were 449 Uintah, 257 White River, 421 Uncompahgre (Uintah-Ouray Reservation), and 456 on the Ute Mountain and Southern Ute Reservations. In 1980 there were 2,000 Northern Ute, exclusive of 1,000 mixed bloods and 900 Southern Utes. The Bear Dance and Sun Dance were still prominent festivals.

SOUTHERN PAIUTE The term to cover linguistically related Numic Shoshonean bands of southern Utah and Nevada, including parts of Arizona above the Colorado River and extended to include the *Chemehuevi* of San Bernardino County, California. They can be divided for convenience into a number of subgroups – Moapa, Shivwits, Pahranagat, Kaibab, etc. – but there was no tribal organisation; they were divided into bands held together for mutual aid and subsistence collaboration. They were the typical Great Basin people; the quest for food kept them on the movein search of small game, grasshoppers, gophers, fish, nuts, seeds and wild vegetables. Their shelters were simple brush constructions, but they made fine basketry. They seem to have been known to the Spanish from the 16th century, but felt the impact of Euro-American contact in the 19th century when they were gradually settled on reservations. Their present descendants have been connected with the following reservations: Moapa River on the Muddy River, southern Nevada (150); Shivwits, Kanosh, Koosharem, Indian Peaks, Kanarraville, all terminated and restored as the "Paiute Indian tribe of Utah" (200); Kaibab in northern Arizona (150); Las Vegas Colony, Nevada (100); Chemehuevi Reservation, Arizona (500); and Colorado River Reservation, Arizona (350). Only about half live on their reservations and there are longstanding off-reservation communities.

EASTERN MONO or **OWENS VALLEY PAIUTE** A branch of the Uto-Aztecan family closely connected linguistically with the Northern Paiute, who occupied the valley of the Owens River parallel with the southern Sierra Nevada Mountains, Inyo County, California. They are sometimes locally called Paiute; and their descendants are at Benton (with the Paiute), Bishop, Big Pine, Independence, Lone Pine (with Panamint) and throughout Inyo County. They number perhaps 1,800 including the Western Mono (Monache) and Panamint, the three being almost indistinguishable.

WESTERN MONO or **MONACHE** A group of six small Shoshonean (Numic) Uto-Aztecan speaking tribes related to the Eastern Mono and Northern Paiute. Strictly they were more Californian in culture than Great Basin, since they lived beyond the Sierra Nevada Mountains on the upper reaches of the San Joaquin (North Fork), Kings and Kaweah Rivers, California, where they shared a general culture with the neighbouring Yokuts. Their subsistence depended on hunting, fishing and gathering. They probably numbered 4,000 before 1770, reduced to 1,500 by 1910, but both figures combine Western and Eastern Mono. They are now part of the mixed tribal group of the Tule River Reservation and have largely merged with Yokuts at Tule River and in Tulare, Fresno and Madera Counties. At North Fork, Big Sandy and Cold Springs about 150 descendants are still reported separately.

NORTHERN PAIUTE A term which covers Numic-speaking bands of the Uto-Aztecan family and the branch which relates them with the two branches of the Mono of California. They lived in a vast area from Mono Lake, California, in the south through the Walker and Humboldt River drainages, Nevada, north beyond Malheur Lake, Oregon, and west into northeast California. Their habitat was scrub desert and freshwater marshes; they were semi-nomadic gatherers with some hunting and fishing. Their dwellings varied throughout the

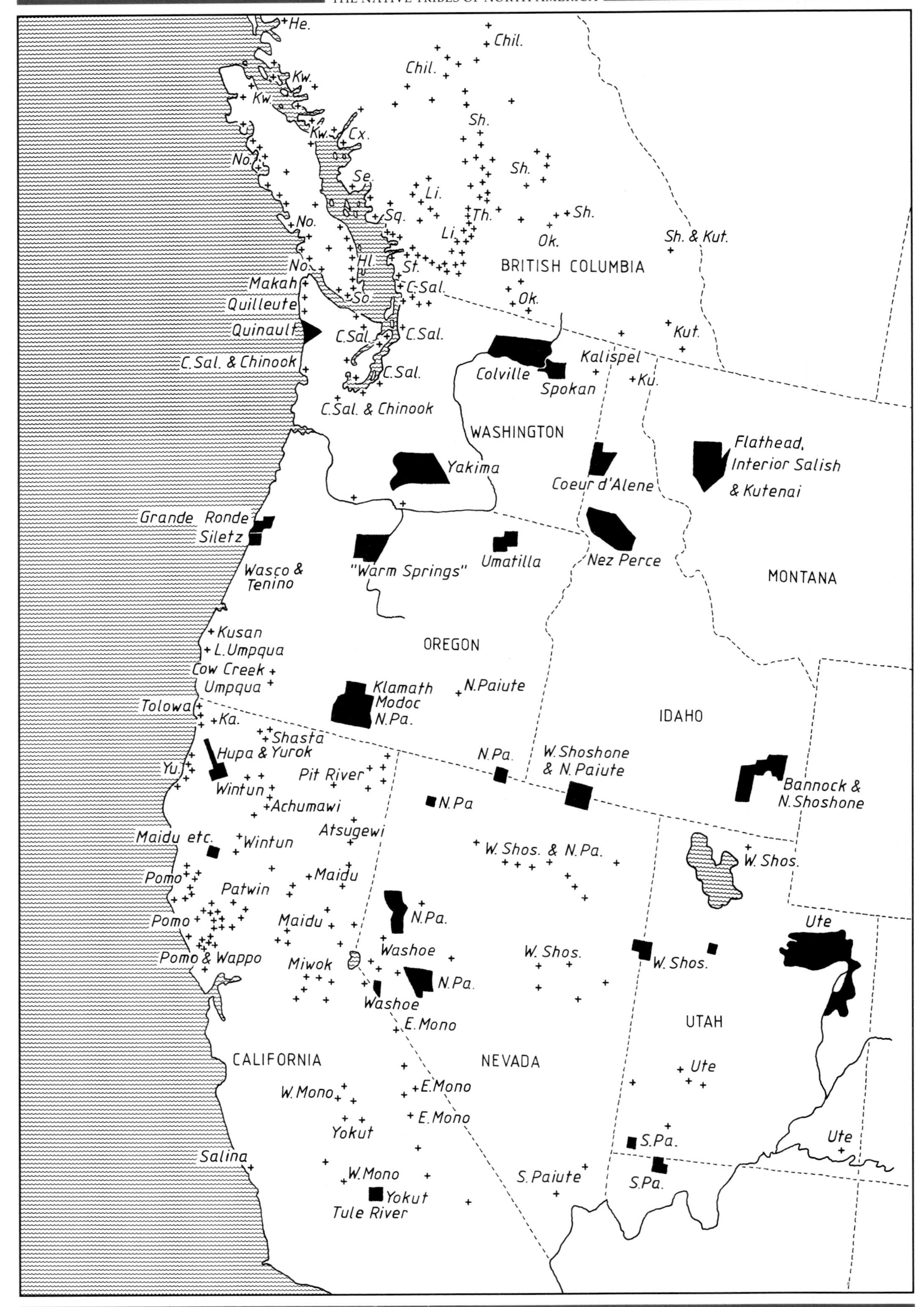
He.
Chil.
Chil.
Kw.
Kw.
Kw.
Cx.
Sh.
No.
Se.
Sh.
Li.
Sq.
Th.
Sh.
No.
Li
Ok.
Sh. & Kut.
No.
Hl.
St.
BRITISH COLUMBIA
Makah
C.Sal.
Quilleute
So.
Ok.
Quinault
C.Sal.
C.Sal.
Kut.
C.Sal. & Chinook
C.Sal.
Kalispel
Colville
Ku.
Spokan
C.Sal. & Chinook
WASHINGTON
Flathead,
Interior Salish
& Kutenai
Yakima
Coeur d'Alene
Grande Ronde
Siletz
Umatilla
Nez Perce
Wasco &
Tenino
"Warm Springs"
MONTANA
Kusan
L.Umpqua
OREGON
Cow Creek
Umpqua
Klamath
Modoc
N.Pa.
N.Paiute
Tolowa
Ka.
IDAHO
Shasta
Hupa & Yurok
N.Pa.
W.Shoshone
& N.Paiute
Yu.
Pit River
Bannock &
N.Shoshone
Wintun
Achumawi
N.Pa
Atsugewi
Maidu etc.
Wintun
W. Shos. & N.Pa.
W. Shos.
Pomo
Maidu
Patwin
N.Pa.
Pomo
Maidu
Ute
Washoe
W. Shos.
W. Shos.
Pomo & Wappo
Miwok
N.Pa.
Washoe
E.Mono
UTAH
CALIFORNIA
NEVADA
Ute
W.Mono
E.Mono
E.Mono
Yokut
Ute
S.Pa.
Salina
W.Mono
S.Paiute
S.Pa.
Yokut
Tule River

GREAT BASIN AND PLATEAU TRIBES, 20th CENTURY

This sketch map necessarily duplicates part of the Northwest Coast area.

Key to abbreviations:

C.Sal	= Coastal Salish	No	= Nootka
Chil	= Chilcotin	Ok	= Okanagan
Cx	= Comox	S.Pa	= Southern Paiute
He	= Heitsuk	Se	= Seechelt
Hl	= Halkomelem	Sh	= Shuswap
Ka	= Karok	So	= Songlish
Kut	= Kutenai	Sq	= Squamish
Kw	= Kwakiutl	St	= Stalo (Cowichan)
Li	= Lillooet		
N. Pa	= Northern Paiute	Th	= Thompson
		Yu	= Yurok

region, including dome-shaped structures covered with brush mats. They seem to have obtained horses in the mid-1700s, which initiated a series of changes introduced by whites, and there were hostile encounters during the mid-1800s. They were ultimately placed on reservations, with total populations given as 3,038 in 1910; 4,420 Northern and Southern Paiute in 1930; 2,590 in 1950; and 5,123 in 1980. The largest reservation populations are at Pyramid Lake, Walker River and Fort McDermitt in Nevada, but others are at Benton and Bridgewater, Mono County, California; Burns, Warm Springs and Klamath Lake, Oregon (mixed with other tribes); Duck Valley, Nevada (with Shoshone); Summit Lake, Winnemucca, Lovelock, Fallon, Reno-Sparks and Yerington, Nevada; Fort Bidwell, XL Ranch, Cederville, Alturas in Modoc County, California (mixed with Pit River); and Susanville, Lassen County, California (mixed with Maidu).

CALIFORNIA

Language family and tribe	*Meaning*/origin of tribal name, where known
Ritwan:	
Yurok	*"downstream"*
Wiyot	district name
Hokan:	
Karok	*"upstream"*
Chimariko	*"person"*
Shasta	-
Achomawi	*"river"*
Atsugewi	-
Yana	*"person"*
Pomo	*"village"*
Esselen	-
Salina	Spanish name
Chumash	-
Washo	*"person"*
Yukian:	
Yuki	*"stranger"*
Wappo	Spanish – *"brave"* or *"fine"*
Penutian:	
Wintun	*"people"*
Maidu	*"person"*
Miwok	*"people"*
Costanoan	Spanish – *"coast people"*
Yokut	*"person"*
Uto-Aztecan:	
Tubatulabal	*"pine nut eaters"*
Tataviam	-
Gabrielino	Spanish – mission name
Luiseño-Juaneño	Spanish – mission names
Kitanemuk	*"house"*
Serrano	Spanish – *"mountaineers"*
Cahuilla	Spanish name
Cupeno	place name
Kawaiisu	*"people"*

The typical cultural characteristics of the Californian area were those found among the tribes who lived along the two main valley systems, those of the Sacramento River and San Joaquin valley including the eastern slopes of the Sierra Nevada north to Mount Shasta and west to beyond Clear Lake. In terms of linguistic diversity the area was one of the most complex in North America. The principal families were Maidu, Wintun, Miwok, Costano and Yokut, now loosely linked to form the Penutian stock; and the Karok, Shasta, Achomawi, Yana, Pomo and others linked into the Hokan super-family.

Food was mainly gathered, including vegetables, acorns, buckeye nuts, seeds and a variety of grasses. They dug roots and bulbs from the ground, and collected kelp and seaweed from the ocean, these often being dried or boiled for soups. They hunted rabbits, quail and gophers, collected grasshoppers and caterpillars, and fished for salmon. Houses were constructed either of coarse grass or bunches of bullrush in dome shapes, or of redwood plank slabs in conical shapes among the coastal people. Clothing was sparse except for elaborate ceremonial dress using abalone shells, many types of feathers, skirts of vegetable fibre or deerskin and some tattooing. Many tribes were excellent basket makers, and the Pomos made reed canoes at Clear Lake.

Religion centered on the worship of ancestral ghosts through the Kuksu cult, a society of spirit or ancestral impersonation involving colourful costume and the initiation of youths by ghosts. Old men with special knowledge often acted as directors, including instruction on morals, hero gods and healing. A variant religion amongst the Patwin was known as the Hesi. These old religions were in part associated with nativistic movements in the second half of the 19th century, incorporating neo-Christian elements; these were the Ghost Dance of 1870, the Earth Lodge cult and the Bole-Maru "Dream Dance". Ceremonies usually took place in large circular semi-underground wooden buildings.

The remaining regions of California reflected other cultural areas. The Mono and Paiute of mountainous eastern parts of the state belong to the Basin. The tribes in the northwestern section are sometimes classed with the Northwest Coast culture because of their wealth accumulation traits, prestige displays and world renewal rituals, such as the White Deerskin ceremonies. Wooden house types, dugout canoes, salmon weirs and twined basketry reflect, if only weakly, the northern culture.

Southern California had cultural affinities with the Southwestern culture, with coiled basketry, large polychrome cave paintings by the Chumash, oceangoing dugout and plank canoes, and communal dwellings, usually round. Toloache or Jimsonweed religion was found in most of the area, with visions obtained from taking the toloache drink. Boys and girls had initiation ceremonials with religious and moral instructions from chiefs.

The reduction of the native population was nowhere greater than in California. In pre-contact times the population was in excess of 300,000, but by 1910 perhaps no more than 25,000 remained, and many of these of mixed white and Indian ancestry. The greatest sufferers were the coastal and central valley tribes – the former as a result of Spanish colonisation, the valley tribes because of the influx of gold-seekers after 1848, when villages were broken up and Indian peoples driven from their land (and often killed) in quasi-military clearance operations by whites. Only where substantial reservations were established did the native population survive in sizable groups. Many were left landless, engulfed by white communities, as a result of which most small groups that remained merged into white culture with resultant intermarriage. Government intervention in the late 19th and early 20th centuries saw the foundation of small reservations around the state called "Rancherias", which managed to give a few hundred people a landbase, but more lived scattered amongst the white population. Descendants survive there, and today California has the largest Indian population of any state, but these are mostly immigrants from other areas of the U.S.A.

RITWAN

A term to include two tribes of northern California, usually considered distinct: the Wiyot and Yurok. These are separate families, perhaps divided 2,000 years ago. An even more remote association with the Algonkian family has been speculatively suggested.

YUROK An important and relatively large and linguistically distinct tribe of northern California, living principally along the lower parts of the Klamath River between its junction with the Trinity River and the coast at Requa. They were part of a culture linking them to the Hupa, Karok, Tolowa and Wiyot. Shamans, sometimes women, obtained power direct from spirits. World renewal ceremonials were important, including the White Deerskin Dance. Houses included the redwood plank type and ceremonial plank sweathouses. Facial tattooing, deerskin clothes, basketry, shell money, slaves and wealth display traits paralleled the Hupa and more remotely the northern tribes. They probably numbered in excess of 3,000 in pre-contact times; but were disrupted after 1827 when the first Hudson's Bay traders invaded their country, and violent clashes with gold-seeking whites occurred after 1850. However, the Yuroks retained some portions of their old land; and there are still sizable groups at Weitchpec, Johnson's (Hoopa-extension), Requa (coast Indian community) and Trinidad. They still number some 3,000 (959 on reserves in 1968), though largely of mixed white-Indian ancestry. There have been recent attempts to revitalize their language and dances. The Shaker Church has its southern limit amongst the Yurok.

WIYOT A small family of Indians on the coast of northwest California between the Mad and Eel River estuaries. They are now thought to be related to the Yurok with whom they shared much of their culture, but much more orientated to a coastal environment. There was heavy emphasis on salmon fishing and on the hunting of deer, elk, and sea mammals. Their ceremonialism was the same as that of the Yurok and Hupa. They suffered a series of atrocities at the hands of whites which reduced their population from 1,000 in 1850 to 131 in 1968, on two small reservations, Blue Lake and Table Bluff (Loleta) in Humboldt County, California.

HOKAN

In 1913 two ethnologists, Dixon and Kroeber, suggested that a number of small Californian families should be considered as one super-family or stock, and suggested the term *Hokan*, derived from the word "two" in some northern California languages, to cover the grouping. The group included the Karok, Chimariko, Shasta, Achomawi, Yana, Pomo, Washo, Esselen, Yuman, Salinan, Seri and Chumash. More recently a link has been suggested with the Lower Rio Grande Coahuiltecans, but the proposal of a link with the Siouan and other families has been abandoned.

KAROK A distinct tribe occupying the middle course of the Klamath River in northern California, starting just north of the Yurok village at Weitchpec

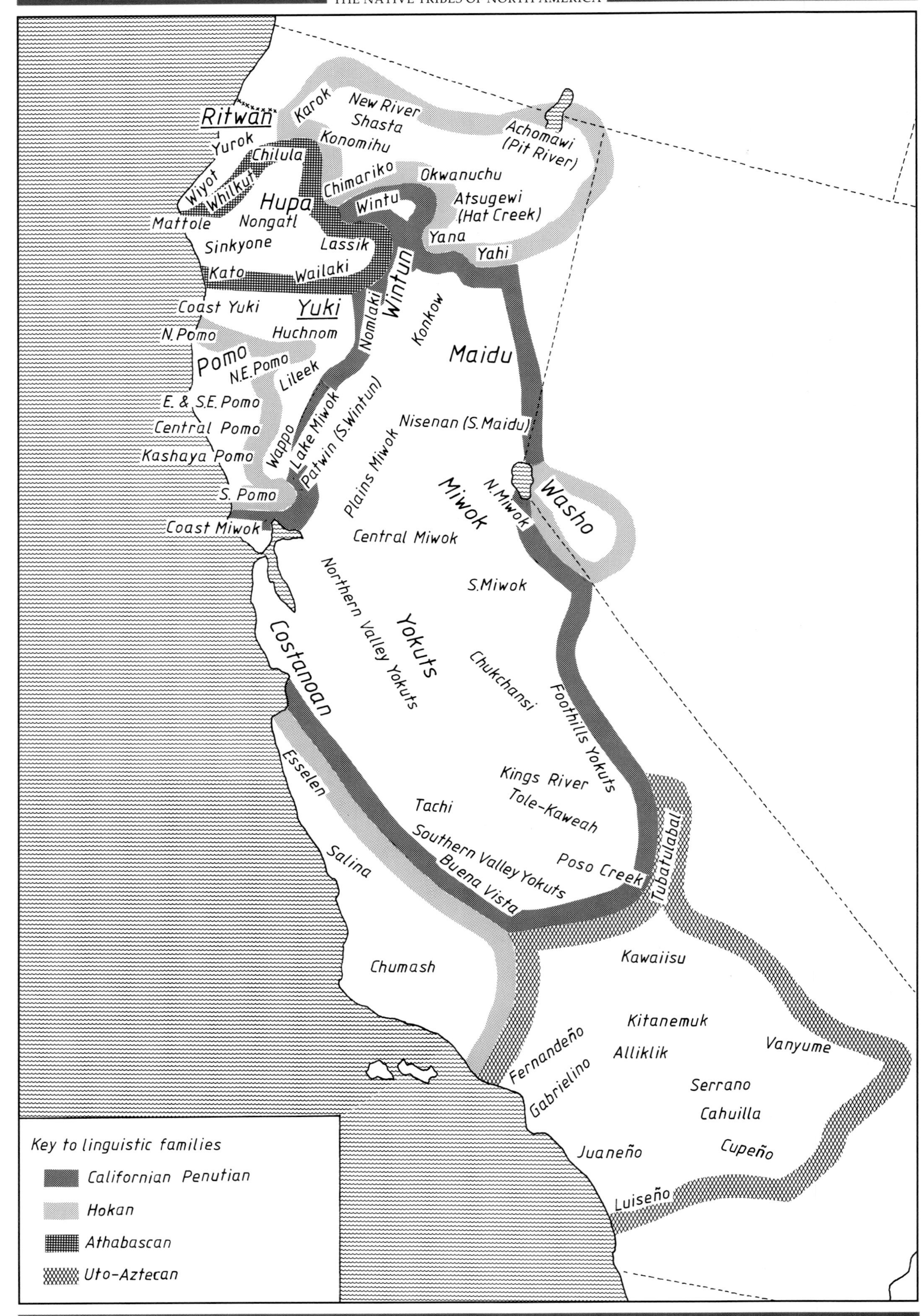
Ritwan
Yurok
Karok
New River Shasta
Konomihu
Achomawi (Pit River)
Chilula
Wiyot
Whilkut
Hupa
Chimariko
Okwanuchu
Wintu
Atsugewi (Hat Creek)
Mattole
Nongatl
Sinkyone
Lassik
Yana
Yahi
Kato
Wailaki
Wintun
Coast Yuki
Yuki
Konkow
N. Pomo
Huchnom
Nomlaki
Maidu
Pomo
N.E. Pomo
Lileek
E. & S.E. Pomo
Patwin (S. Wintun)
Lake Miwok
Central Pomo
Nisenan (S. Maidu)
Wappo
Kashaya Pomo
Plains Miwok
S. Pomo
Miwok
N. Miwok
Washo
Coast Miwok
Central Miwok
S. Miwok
Northern Valley Yokuts
Yokuts
Costanoan
Chukchansi
Foothills Yokuts
Esselen
Kings River
Tole-Kaweah
Tachi
Tubatulabal
Southern Valley Yokuts
Salina
Poso Creek
Buena Vista
Kawaiisu
Chumash
Kitanemuk
Fernandeño
Alliklik
Vanyume
Gabrielino
Serrano
Cahuilla
Juaneño
Cupeño
Luiseño
Key to linguistic families
Californian Penutian
Hokan
Athabascan
Uto-Aztecan

and extending northward to the vicinity of Seiad close to the Oregon border. Their population, over 2,700 in the early 19th century, was densest in three clusters: around Camp Creek at Orleans, Salmon River at Somes Bar and Clear Creek below Happy Creek. Except for a few groups of Hudson's Bay Company traders the Karok knew little of the white man until 1850-57, when a swarm of miners invaded their lands. The Karok displayed a similar culture to that of the Yurok, subsisting on fish, hunting and gathering wild plant foods. Houses were made from split log planks, canoes from hollowed-out redwood. They dressed in deerskins, heavily decorated with nuts and shells for ceremonial use. Their principal rites were those concerned with world renewal, manifest in annual ceremonials similar to those of the Yurok and Hupa.

Despite being overrun by whites the Karok have continued to occupy parts of their old territory, though there has been much intermarriage with whites over the years. They were reported to number 994 in 1905; 775 in 1910; 755 in 1930; and 3,781 in 1972, the last figure including many with little Karok ancestry. However, the World Renewal rites and Brush Dances still survive as an outward expression of continuing Karok identity.

CHIMARIKO A small tribe and linguistic family who occupied a short stretch of perhaps 20 miles of the Trinity River from its junction with the South Fork to Big Bar, in northern California. They seem to have been destroyed by white miners in the 1850s and 1870s. In 1849 they may have numbered 250; only nine survivors were found in 1903, and while a few people of mixed descent may survive, essentially they are extinct.

SHASTA A group of tribes of northern California, culturally partly Californian and partly Plateau. The principal tribe of the group were the Shasta proper who occupied the upper course of the Klamath River, Shasta River and Scott River as far south as Callahan and as far north as Jacksonville, Oregon. There were three small southern groups: the *New River Shasta* of the New and Salmon Rivers; *Konomihu*, also of Salmon River; and the *Okwanuchu* of the upper tributaries of the Sacramento River below Mount Shasta – in total most of present Siskiyon County. The Shasta hunted deer and rabbits, fished salmon, and collected acorns and wild greens. House types were of low-roofed plank construction with side entrance, gathered into villages of five or six dwellings with a sweat house. They also used and obtained in trade buckskin, obsidian, dentalia, haliotis, nuts and woodpecker scalps. The Gold Rush and Rogue River Indian Wars shattered Shasta life and culture, and their population dropped from 3,000 to 100 or so by the 20th century. A few were incorporated on the Grande Ronde and Siletz reservations in Oregon and Round Valley, California, and a few descendants are still reported from Siskiyon County, including about 50 people at Quartz Valley and Ruffeys rancherias; but the aboriginal culture is now practically non-existent.

The Shasta formed a language family sometimes extended to include the Achomawi and Atsugewi.

TRIBES OF THE CALIFORNIAN CULTURAL AREA, c.1780-1840
Linguistic and cultural boundaries are necessarily approximate; this sketch map is intended only as a general guide to distribution. Underlined names indicate small linguistic families distinct from the larger groupings indicated by the shading key.

ACHOMAWI or **ACHUMAWI** One of two tribes who formed the so-called Achomawi or Palaihnihan branch of the Hokan family of languages. They are popularly known as *Pit River* Indians as they occupied the Pit River basin from Big Bend to Goose Lake in north central California. They fished for salmon, bass, catfish and trout, caught wildfowl, and collected vegetable foods and insects. They suffered somewhat less than most native Californians from white invasion, and still numbered about 750 in 1963 – perhaps half their aboriginal population. The present Pit River people live in Shasta, Lassen, Modoc and Siskiyon Counties, at XL Ranch Indian Reservation near Alturas, Likely, Big Bend, Fall River and Hot Springs. Elements are also found on two reservations in Oregon. Like many neighbouring tribes they excelled in basketry.

ATSUGEWI The second tribe of the Palaihnihan branch of the Hokan linguistic stock lived south of their distant relatives, the Achomawi, in two groups: the Atsuge in the lava-strewn valleys north of Mount Lassen, and the Apwaruge in the barren plain to the east around Eagle Lake, Lassen County, California. In common with most northern Californian tribes, fish and acorns were staple foods; although they were out of the salmon area, they were allowed to take a ration from Pit River by the Achomawi. Although they recognized countless native spirits they had few major ceremonials other than puberty rites. Hudson's Bay trappers visited their region in the 1830s, followed in the 1850s by Gold Rush prospectors and settlers, who completely disrupted native life, with murder on both sides leading to virtual annihilation of the tribe. A few Atsugewi survived at Hat Creek, Dixie Valley and Burney, and perhaps 100 or so descendants are still counted.

YANA A small linguistic family on the northeastern tributaries of the Sacramento River between Shasta Lake and Tehama, in three geographical groups plus the *Yahi*, a southern branch. They numbered perhaps 1,500 before a series of bloody massacres by whites (c.1850-1870) reduced their numbers to a mere 100 or so by 1910. Ishi, the last of the Yahi, lived under the protection of the University of California for five years until his death in 1916; he provided a wealth of information on their culture.

POMO An important group of seven related tribes speaking differing dialects forming a family of the Hokan stock centered around Clear Lake and along the coast from Fort Bragg in the north to beyond Stewarts Point in the south in present Mendocino, Lake and Sonoma Counties, California. They were a populous people, numbering over 14,000 in the 18th century. In the mild climate the Pomos used little clothing; in cool weather mantles, capes, robes and skirts of vegetable fibre or skins were worn. They hunted rabbits, deer, sea mammals and bears with bows and arrows, heavy spears, nets and snares. They had ample supplies of fish. The Pomos lived in conical huts of redwood bark or planks, and around Clear Lake houses were built of bunches of bullrush (tule) or coarse-textured grass. They are also known for their excellent quality baskets which survive in abundance in museums. The social core of Pomo life was the family and the small village; and their beliefs were part of a religious complex called the Kuksu, which stressed curing rituals and elaborate forms of dancing and fire-eating to ensure the absence of danger from ghosts.

The Russians established a settlement at Fort Ross in 1811; but the Mexicans made the first serious inroads into Pomo life and culture in the 1820s and 1830s, taking lands and introducing cholera and smallpox. Land loss continued under the Americans, and they ultimately became almost landless in their own country, working on the ranches and farms of white settlers. They did, however, re-establish small settlements in the late 19th century, and a number of small reservations or rancherias have been maintained to the present day.

A revitalization movement, the Bole Maru cult, still survives alongside their own branch of the Methodist Church. The recent population was 2,626 (1970). About 500 live on tribal lands at Manchester, Stewarts Point, Cloverdale, Lytton, Lower Lake, Upper Lake, Sulpher Bank, Hopland, Scotts Valley, Potter Valley, Sherwood, Mark West, Big Valley and other locations, including a few at the larger Round Valley Reservation, where a multi-tribal group of about 500 have long been established.

ESSELEN A tribe and small linguistic family which, based on only fragmentary evidence, has been placed in the so-called Hokan stock. They occupied the coast of mid-California between the Carmel River and Point Lopez below Monterey. First known to the Spanish in 1602, the native Esselen culture vanished with the destruction of the mission San Carlos Borromeo de Monterey in 1770, when they were absorbed by other missions and ultimately lost separate identity. They may have numbered about 500 in the 18th century, but were extinct by 1820.

SALINA or **SALINAN** A group of tribes formerly occupying the coast of central south California and the rugged mountainous interior, from the upper Salinas River near the Soledad Mission almost to San Luis Obispo. There seem to have been two dialects which formed the Salinan language family, now tentatively included in the Hokan stock. They probably numbered over 3,000 before 1771 when the Spanish began missions amongst them, but by the early 19th century rapid acculturation had taken place, and their population was no more than 700 by 1831. This decrease continued after the secularization of the missions in 1834; and only three families were known by the early 20th century near Jolon, descendants from the old San Antonio Mission. In 1928 36 people were reported, and a few descendants are still living, but as a distinct group they have gone. The 1970 census gave 360 Salina and Chumash.

CHUMASH A group of linguistically related people, now included in the Hokan stock, of present Santa Barbara County, California, along the coast from San Luis Obispo to Ventura; they numbered perhaps in excess of 15,000 before the Spanish missions were established in 1772. There seem to have been eight subdivisions of this docile and friendly people. The Spanish were determined to make industrious farmers of the Chumash, but subjected them to a life of toil, mistreatment and destruction of native culture. Following the secularization of the missions in 1834 the Chumash merged or intermarried with Mexicans or were decimated by disease. One small reserve at Santa Ynez was set aside in 1855, and about 50 people of mixed descent were all that were left as a separate Chumash group in 1972.

WASHO A linguistic family and tribe who inhabited the large valleys of the Feather, Yuba and American Rivers of central eastern California and the areas north and south of Lake Tahoe as far as Honey Lake south to Walker River, split equally between present Nevada and California. They have been suggested to belong distantly to the Hokan stock. Culturally they were intermediate between the true Californian and Great Basin cultural types. The many rivers and lakes supplied them with fish; they gathered camas roots, pine nuts and acorns which were cooked into gruel, and also hunted deer and mountain sheep. House types were conical, of bark slabs leaning against a frame of poles, or temporary dome-shaped brush structures. They were very fine basket-makers of both coiled and twined weaves, and several makers became nationally well known. Religion and ceremony were usually associated with the spirits of their subsistence and in connection with communal harvesting. Permanent contact with whites began in about 1840, and the alienation of their resources and lands followed. They numbered about 1,500 in 1850; 725 in 1970; and 695 in 1980. Their main 20th century groups are at Woodfords, Alpine County, California, and Dresslerville, Carson and Reno-Sparks in Nevada. About 100 people still speak the Washo language.

YUKI A group of small tribes in the upper Eel River valley in the Coast Range Mountains of northwest California, and also along the coast between Rockport and Fort Bragg. The Yuki proper lived in the Round Valley area; the *Huchnom* on the south Eel River; and the *Coast Yuki*, perhaps a branch of the Huchnom, in the coastal area described. These tribes, together with the detached southern branch, the Wappo and Lile'ek, form a language family with no known relatives.

Culturally the Yuki led a hunting and gathering existence of typical California pattern and of a fairly simple type, but they had an elaborate ceremonial life. Their existence as an independent people came to an end in 1856 when white farmer settlers destroyed the ecology of their valley homes; many starved, or were massacred by settlers. The establishment of the Round Valley Reservation in 1858 probably saved the handful of survivors. Some estimates put the number of these three groups combined at over 8,000. In 1970 there were 350 Yuki, Wailaki, Nomlaki and Pomo on the Round Valley Reservation or in nearby communities, of whom perhaps 30-35 people were true Yuki by descent, with only a few native speakers left. The last of the Huchnom, known as Redwood Indians, were also merged with others at Round Valley, where a handful of descendants may still be traced; but the Coast Yuki seem to be extinct.

WAPPO The Wappo were related to the Yuki, Huchnom and Coast Yuki, and form the Yukian linguistic family. They lived in the valleys of the Napa and Russian Rivers in Napa and adjacent Sonoma Counties, California, with a detached branch on the south shore of Clear Lake sometimes known as the *Lile'ek*. The culture was a simple central Californian type with subsistence use of plant foods, river life and small game. They excelled in basket making in common with their northern neighbours the Pomo. They were within range of the Spanish settlements and missions, and a number were hispanicized before American settlers moved in. The census of 1910 reported 73 Wappo; and 12 Wappo were reported from the Alexander Valley Reservation in 1951. Perhaps 50 descendants remained by 1970.

PENUTIAN

A language stock of central California composed from five families previously considered distinct: Maidu, Wintun, Costanoan, Miwok and Yokut. The name Penutian is a composite of the stems of the numerical word "two" in Maidu, Wintun and Yokut and "uti" in Costano and Miwok. The stock has also been extended to the Coos, Yakonan and Siuslaw of Oregon, and even to the Chinook and Tsimshian, but the unity is not considered proved by all authorities.

WINTUN The territory of the Wintun consisted substantially of the west side of the Sacramento River valley from the river to the crest of the coastal mountain ranged they consisted of three distinct dialectic divisions. The northern or Wintu division occupied upper sections of the Trinity River and Sacramento River north of Cottonwood Creek to the edge of Shasta County; they were the largest division of the family. The central division, the Wintun proper or *Nomlaki*, occupied the Sacramento valley from Cottonwood Creek south to Grindstone in Glenn County; they numbered some 2,000 at the time of first contact with whites. Finally, the *Patwin* or Southern Wintun lived from just beyond Colusa to San Pablo Bay in Colusa and Yolo Counties. All these divisions were further subdivided into groups who lived either in the hills, plains or river valleys. They were typically Californian in culture; their bark houses were gathered in villages around semi-subterranean earth lodges for ceremonials of the Kuksu type, including the Bole-Maru cultists who performed the "Big Head Dance" – male and female spirit impersonators who wore impressive feather headdresses.

The Patwin suffered first from their exposure to the Mexicans in the late 18th century and subsequently from American contacts from the 1840s onwards. The whole family numbered perhaps 15,000 in the mid-18th century. About 1,000 Wintun have been reported during the present century, but are mixed racially and tribally. The Northern

Wintun are mostly in Tehama, Trinity and Shasta Counties, including Redding (Clear Creek); the Nomlaki are at Paskenta and Grindstone Creek in Glenn County. A few Patwin are at the Colusa Reservation in Colusa County and Rumsey in Yolo County, and others amongst the mixed Round Valley population.

MAIDU A linguistic family of north central California, now usually considered a part of the Penutian stock. They are further dialectically subdivided into three tribes: the *Maidu proper* who occupied the upper reaches of the Feather River south of Eagle Lake around Susanville, Butte Valley and Quincy; the *Konkow* who lived on the east side of the Sacramento River around Chico; and the *Nisenan* or Southern Maidu who occupied the Yuba, Bear and American River valleys around Marysville, Nevada City, Placerville and Auburn. Physiographically they can be divided into groups who formed cultural cleavages into valley, foothills and mountain Maidu. They were participants in the important Kuksu religious cult of the Sacramento Valley, with its wide variety of rituals, impersonations of spirits, distinctive costumes and use of large semi-subterranean dance houses. They used bark or brush lean-to house structures; and had an elaborate system of shell money exchange between mourners and their friends. They also burned property at funeral rites, including some fine baskets made especially to be consumed in this way, all in honour of the dead. Clothing was scant; they often went naked, or wore aprons or breechcloths of buckskin.

The Spanish contact was limited to the Nisenan, but American and Hudson's Bay trappers appeared in the 1820s, and the Gold Rush after 1848 saw the disastrous invasion of their territory by whites. Settlers' livestock upset the ecological balance; Indians killed livestock, and natives were killed themselves in retribution. From a population of 9,000 in 1846 only about 1,100 were reported to survive in 1910 – mostly Maidu in Plumas County, Konkow in Butte County, and Nisenan in Yuba, Placer and El Dorado Counties. In 1970 2,546 Maidu and Miwok were returned, largely of mixed descent. A small number have lived on small reservations and rancherias in these counties, at Susanville, Taylorsville (Maidu), Chico, Mooretown, Enterprise, Berry Creek, Strawberry (Konkow), Nevada City, Colfax, Auburn and Shingle Springs (Nisenan). Despite the economic disadvantages affecting most modern Californian native descendants, there is a heartening renewed interest in their own cultural and traditional values, including the continuation of the Maidu Bear Dance each spring at Janesville.

MIWOK A large group of Indians forming a linguistic family in central California, comprising the main body of the family, the *Eastern Miwok*, in five subdivisions, and two small detached groups, the *Coast Miwok* and *Lake Miwok*. The Coast Miwok were a number of small tribulets in Marin County between Bodega Bay and San Pablo Bay who came under the influence of the Spanish missions, particularly that at San Francisco. They numbered about 2,000 in aboriginal times, but largely disappeared or were absorbed by Spanish colonists, and only a handful of mixed blood survived to the 20th century. The Lake Miwok held a couple of small streams flowing into Clear Lake, and perhaps numbered 500 in pre-contact times; in 1905 41 were reported, and a few still remain at Middletown mixed with Pomo people.

The main body of the family, the Eastern or Valley Miwok, comprised the Bay Miwok between Walnut and Stockton; the Plains Miwok from Rio Vista to Sacramento; the Northern Miwok centering on the Mokelumne River in Calaveras and Amador Counties; the Central Sierra Miwok between Knights Ferry and Murphy's in Stanislaus and Tuolumne Counties; and the Southern Sierra Miwok, on the western edge of the Sierra Nevada and Yosemite National Park. War was usually confined amongst themselves; males were captured, and killed in the dance house. The Bay and Plains Miwok disappeared through the combined effects of the Spanish missions and epidemic diseases, but the interior Miwok and Yokut blocked Mexican settlement. Following California's annexation by the United States and the Gold Rush, remnants eked out a meagre existence on the edges of Sierran towns.

In the early 20th century small reservations or rancherias were established, and some of their descendants still live on these. The Miwok population was given as 670 in 1910, and 763 in 1930; perhaps 1,000 people, some of mixed descent, continue in their old locations today. In 1770 the whole group numbered in excess of 15,000. The few on reserves are found at Shingle Springs, Wilton, Jackson, Sheep Ranch, in El Dorado, Amador, Calaveras, Tuolumne and Mariposa Counties; a few are also reported at Cortina in Patwin country.

COSTANOAN A linguistic term to designate a group of perhaps eight small tribes in 50 villages living south of San Francisco Bay along the coast of California south to Big Sur and inland for about 60 miles, with a population probably exceeding 7,000 in 1750. Originally they lived in domed structures covered with thatched tule or wild grass on a frame of poles. They were first contacted by Spanish explorers in the 17th century, and permanent missions were established in the second half of the

18th century. The changes in lifestyle introduced by the Spanish, together with diseases, reduced their population to 2,000 by 1832, and the Costanoans largely merged with other Indians and Mexicans throughout the 19th century. Perhaps 150 descendants survive today, much mixed with other peoples, but calling themselves "Ohlone". The language is extinct, but early texts and words gathered from survivors show it language to be a separate family within the Penutian stock, forming with the Miwok language a subgroup "Utian".

YOKUT An extensive and large group of 40 or 50 minor tribulets who spoke varying dialects forming a family within the Californian Penutian stock. They were the main people of the San Joaquin valley south to Buena Vista Lake, east to the Sierra Nevada foothills and north to the Stockton area. They are divided geographically and culturally into three groups: the *Northern Valley, Southern Valley*, and *Foothills Yokut*. The Northern Valley group occupied the San Joaquin River valley from Fresco to the Sacramento River, but their aboriginal culture was quickly modified by the Spanish, then after 1822 by Mexicans, and they have few survivors. The Southern Valley Yokut are about 14 groups, of which the Tachi are the most prominent, occupying the southern San Joaquin valley below Fresno in present Kings, Tulare and Kern Counties around Tulare Lake. The Foothills Yokut are about 15 minor groups: starting in the north from Oakhurst are the Northern Hill group in Fresno County (Chukchansi); the Kings River group (Choynimni) in eastern Fresno County; Tole-Kaweah group (Wikchamni & Yawdanchi) in Tulare County; Poso Creek group (Palewyami) in Kern County; and the Buena Vista group in Kings and Kern Counties – the last sometimes included with the Southern Valley section of the family.

For most central Californians wars were usually minor affairs. Food resources were generous enough for villages of 200 or so people. The Yokut were not a political group, their relationship being linguistic; but all their groups made excellent basketry. Shamans who derived their powers from spirit animals had much influence, but the Kuksu cult did not extend as far south as the core of Yokut territory. The Ghost Dance of the 1870s had some converts. The Yokut were encountered by the Spaniards in the late 18th century but the latter's influence was mainly amongst the northern villages. The Mexican period, 1822-1846, saw punitive expeditions into Yokut country, and final cultural collapse followed American settlement in the 1850s. Yokuts survived in small isolated pockets throughout their old territory; but epidemics and absorption into white communities saw their population drop from about 18,000 in 1770 to 533 in 1910, and 791 in 1970. The reservation and rancheria groups are at Picayune (Chukchansi) and Table Mountain (Chukchansi) in Fresno County; Santa Rosa (Tachi) in Kings County; and Tule River (Kings River and Tule-Kaweah), the latter group reported at over 200.

UTO-AZTECAN

A large and widespread languistic super-family of Mexico and the U.S.A., formed by joining the old so-called Nahuatl family (*Aztec*) of central Mexico with their northern related Sonoran language, and hence to the old Shoshonean family of the western U.S.A. The Aztec and their relatives seem to have formed one complete branch; the *Cora, Huichol, Tubar, Mayo, Yaqui,Eudeve, Opata*, and *Tarahumara* another; the *Pima-Pagago* (formerly *"Piman"*) with the *Tepehuan*, yet another. The old Shoshonean family comprises the *Hopi, Takic* (a group of tribal languages in southern California), *Tataviam, Tubatulabal*, and *Numic* (Paiute, Shoshone, Comanche) of California, the Great Basin and the Plains.

TUBATULABAL A name for three small tribes in the upper part of the Kern River valley, California: Bankalachi, Palagewan and Pahkanapil (Tubatulabal proper). They formed linguistically a separate division of the old Shoshonean family now termed Uto-Aztecan. They were first visited by Father Francisco Garcés in 1776. The American invasion after 1850 completely disrupted native life; a massacre by whites in 1863, and epidemics of measles and influenza, saw their population collapse from about 750 in 1850 to about 50 by 1970, with only six native speakers left. Their present descendants are on the Tule River Indian Reservation or in the Kern Valley area of California.

TATAVIAM or **ALLIKLIK** A language, or a remnant of a tribal language, spoken by Indians at the San Fernando Mission, formerly living to the north on Santa Clara River, California, beyond Piru. By 1916 the language was extinct and the descendants of the Indians who spoke it had merged with other Indians, Hispanic or Anglo people.

GABRIELINO The Gabrielinos spoke a language of the Takic section of the Shoshonean family. They occupied an area now covered by the city of Los Angeles in present southern California and adjacent islands. They are so named from the mission of San Gabriel founded in 1771, although Spanish explorers had contacted these people as early as 1520. They shared many of their arts with the Chumash people of the Santa Barbara coast; and had developed a religion with named gods, such as Chingichngish,

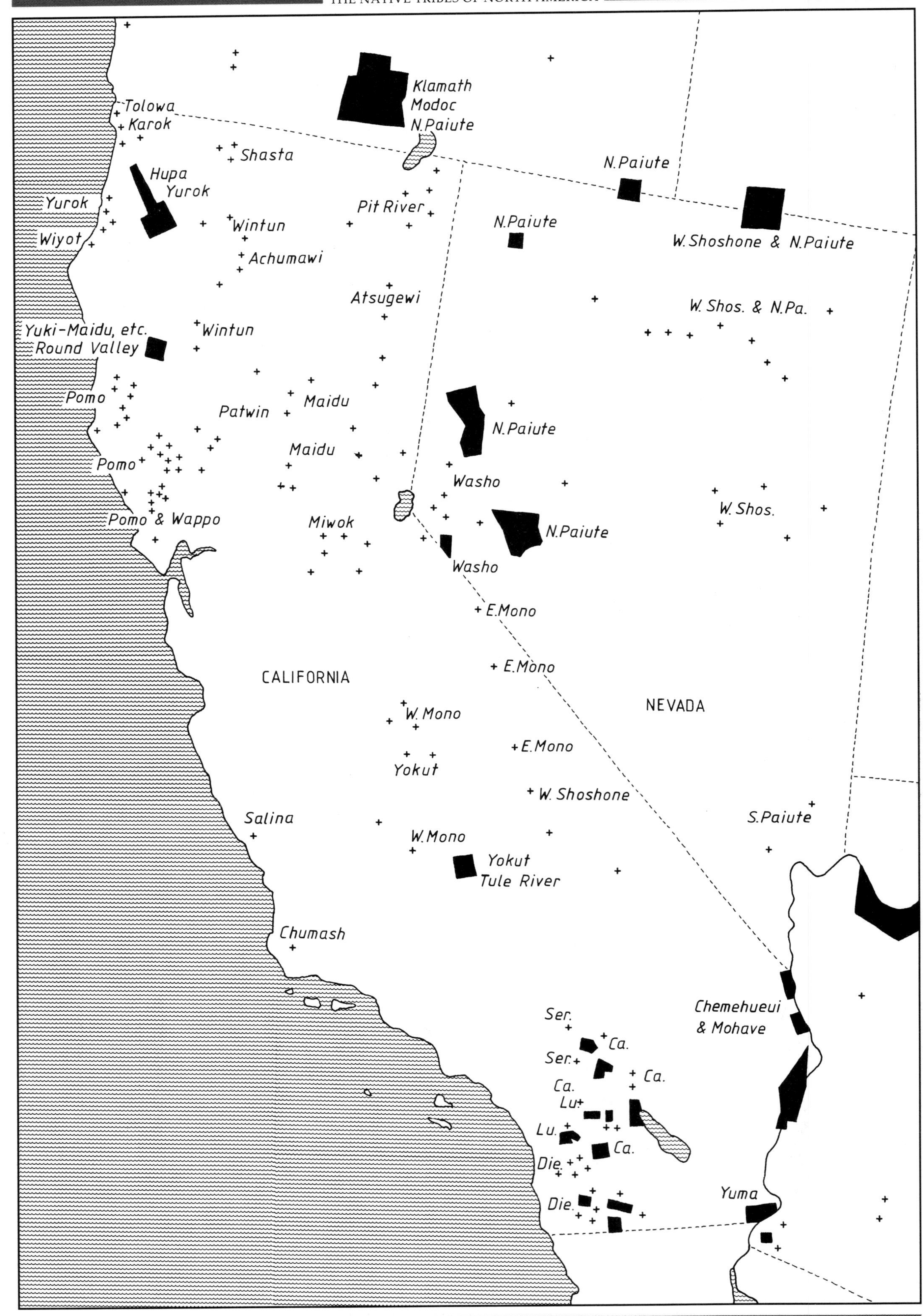

Klamath
Modoc
N.Paiute
Tolowa
Karok
Shasta
Hupa
Yurok
Yurok
Wiyot
Wintun
Achumawi
Pit River
N.Paiute
N.Paiute
W.Shoshone & N.Paiute
Atsugewi
W. Shos. & N.Pa.
Yuki-Maidu, etc.
Round Valley
Wintun
Pomo
Patwin
Maidu
Maidu
N.Paiute
Pomo
Washo
Pomo & Wappo
Miwok
N.Paiute
W. Shos.
Washo
E.Mono
E.Mono
CALIFORNIA
NEVADA
W. Mono
E.Mono
Yokut
W. Shoshone
Salina
S.Paiute
W.Mono
Yokut
Tule River
Chumash
Chemehueui
& Mohave
Ser.
Ca.
Ser.
Ca.
Ca.
Lu.
Lu.
Ca.
Die.
Die.
Yuma

including the erection of temples and the use of vision-producing narcotics, which spread to neighbouring tribes. They were missionized at San Gabriel and San Fernando (Fernandeño) Missions; diminishing in numbers from 5,000 to a few hundred, they became largely hispanicized and merged with larger dominant local races. Although a few people still claim their ancestry they are, to all intents and purposes, extinct. Small Indian groups on the islands of Santa Barbara may have been related; the Nicoleño are sometimes given separate status.

LUISEÑO A Shoshonean (Uto-Aztecan) tribe of the so-called Takic section of the family, closely related to the Gabrielino, Cupeño and Cahuilla, who together form a dialectic subsection; they lived between San Juan Creek and San Luis Rey River in the coastal region of southern California. They lived in small sedentary villages dependent on gathering plant foods, fishing and hunting; houses were conical structures covered with reeds, brush or bark. Their first recorded contact with Europeans occurred in 1796 with the founding of the San Diego Mission, at which time they numbered perhaps 4,000 people; they were later missionized at the San Juan Capistrano (Juaneño) and San Luis Rey Missions. In 1834 the missions were secularized; following revolts against Mexicans and Anglo-Americans the Indians suffered displacement and merger with others into the so-called "Mission Indians". By 1970 about 600 Luiseño descendants were on the La Jolla, Rincon, Pauma, Pechanga, Pala (with others) and Soboba reservations, with others scattered throughout southern California. Attenuated forms of their old religion mixed with Catholicism and colourful fiestas are still a major activity today.

KITANEMUK A small tribe belonging to the Takic division of the Uto-Aztecan family and closely related to the Serrano. They lived on Tejon and El Paso Creeks in the western valleys of the Tehachapi Mountains in present Kern County, California. In general culture they seem to have differed little from either Tubatulabal or Yokut. They appear to have merged with other Indians at San Fernando and San Gabriel Missions, but a few survived separately until the 20th century around Fort Tejon and on the Tule River Reservation, with perhaps 50 descendants; their language is now extinct.

SERRANO A group of Takic speakers who lived east of present-day Los Angeles in the San Bernardino Mountains; a northern group, the *Vanyume* on the Mohave River, are sometimes given separate status. Like their neighbours they were gatherers, hunters and fishers; although the valley floors were largely desert, the upper mountain slopes provided streams and a food supply of nuts, acorns, berries and small game. Family dwellings were usually circular willow structures covered with tule thatching; in addition they had large ceremonial houses where chiefs or religious leaders lived. They are noted for the manufacture of fine coiled baskets. Contact with the Spanish first occurred in about 1771, and they were collected into missions in about 1820. During the American period they have lived together with Cahuilla and Cupeño on the San Manuel, Morongo and possibly Twenty-nine Palms Reservations. They probably numbered 1,500 or more before 1770; perhaps 150 descendants are amongst the present day "Mission Indians" of southern California.

CAHUILLA A substantial Takic-speaking tribe closely related to the Cupeño, Serrano and Kitanemuk, who lived in the mountains, canyons, valleys and deserts north of Salton Sea between the Little San Bernardino and Santa Rosa Mountains of southern California. They lived in rectangular and dome-shaped brush-covered shelters in small villages. Food consisted of small game, acorns, piñon nuts, beans, seeds, and wild fruits, with marginal agriculture providing corn and squash. They had a rich ceremonial life, their rituals reaffirming a relationship to all things, the sacred past, present and nature. The Spanish passed through their country in 1774, and subsequently they were integrated into the mission system. Their population may have been as high as 6,000, but they were reduced to 1,000 by the 1880s. By 1970 they numbered over 1,600, about half on several reservations in southern California: Agua Caliente, Augustine, Cabazon, Cahuilla, Los Coyotes, Morongo, Ramona, Santa Rosa, Soboba and Torres Martinez. There has been considerable intermarriage over the years with the Cupeño, Serrano and Luiseño.

CUPEÑO A small Takic-speaking tribe of the Shoshonean family, now called Uto-Aztecan, who lived east of Lake Henshaw and west of the Santa Rosa Mountains, California. They are very closely related to the Cahuilla but also strongly influenced by

CALIFORNIAN TRIBES, 20th CENTURY

Key to abbreviations of mission groups:

Ser	=	Serraño
Ca	=	Cahuilla
Lu	=	Luiseño
Die	=	Diegueño & Kamia (Ipai-Tipai)

Luiseño religious complexes. They probably numbered 500 when first encountered by the Spanish; subsequently they were missionized and reduced to the social status of near serfs during the Mexican and American periods. They probably number less than 150 people today, but a few are still found on the Pala, Los Coyotes and Morongo Indian Reservations.

KAWAIISU A small Uto-Aztecan tribe belonging to the Numic dialectic group who once lived on the southern foothills of the Sierra Nevada Mountains around present Havilah, California. They were strictly a hunting and gathering people, similar in culture to their neighbours the Tubatulabal and Southern Yokut. Except for puberty rites for boys and girls ceremonials were few, but they had developed shamanism. They were probably contacted by the Spanish, together with other local tribes, in about 1780; and but their culture collapsed following the 1850s when a rush of trappers and farmers invaded their territory. Their original population was about 500, but there are only some 50 descendants today. A few may survive in their old territory and on Tule River Reservation, but they appear to have disintegrated as a group. The Kawaiisu are often classified as a Basin people.

SOUTHWEST

Language family and tribe	*Meaning*/origin of tribal name, where known
Non-Pueblo Dwellers:	
Yuman:	
Havasupai	*"blue water people"*
Walapai	*"pine tree folk"*
Yavapai	*"people of the sun"*
Mohave	*"three mountains"* (possibly)
Maricopa	-
Yuma	Spanish form of native term
Baja California Yumans	-
Cocopa	Spanish form of native term
Diegueño	Spanish mission name
Kamia	-
Uto-Aztecan*:	
Pima	*"no"*
Papago	*"bean people"*
Mexican Border Tribes:	
Seri	Spanish form of native term
Uto-Aztecan*:	
Yaqui & Mayo	-
Tarahumara	-
Tepehuan	-
Lower Pima	-
Eastern Sonoran tribes	-
Northern Chihuahua & Coahuila tribes	-
Coahuiltecan	Mexican place name
Karankawa	-
Tonkawa	*"they all stay together"*
Athabascan :**	
Apache	*"enemy"*
Lipan Apache	*"people"*
Kiowa Apache	-
Chiricahua Apache	*"great mountain"*
Mescalero Apache	Spanish – *"mescal people"*
Jicarilla Apache	Spanish – *"little basket"*
Western Apache	-
Navajo	area name
Pueblo Dwellers:	
Pueblo	Spanish – *"village"*, *"town"*
Keres	coined term
Cochiti	self-designation, i.e. *"person of"*
San Felipe	Spanish name
Santa Ana	Spanish name
Santo Domingo	Spanish name
Zia	*"person of"*
Acoma	*"person of"*
Laguna	Spanish name

Tanoan:

Tribe	Group	*Meaning*/origin of tribal name, where known
Taos	Northern Tiwa	*"in the village"*
Picuris	Northern Tiwa	Spanish form of native term
Sandia	Southern Tiwa	Spanish – *"water melon"*
Isleta	Southern Tiwa	Spanish name
Tigua	Southern Tiwa	-
Piro	Southern Tiwa	-
Nambe	Northern Tewa	*"earth"*
San Ildefonso	Northern Tewa	Spanish name
San Juan	Northern Tewa	Spanish name
Santa Clara	Northern Tewa	Spanish name
Tesuque	Northern Tewa	*"structure at a narrow place"*
Pojoaque	Northern Tewa	*"drink water"*
Hano	Southern Tewa	-
Jemez	Towa	self-designation
Pecos	Towa	self-designation

Zuni	Spanish form of native term
Uto-Aztecan*:	
Hopi	*"peaceful ones"*

* see p.137
** see p.181

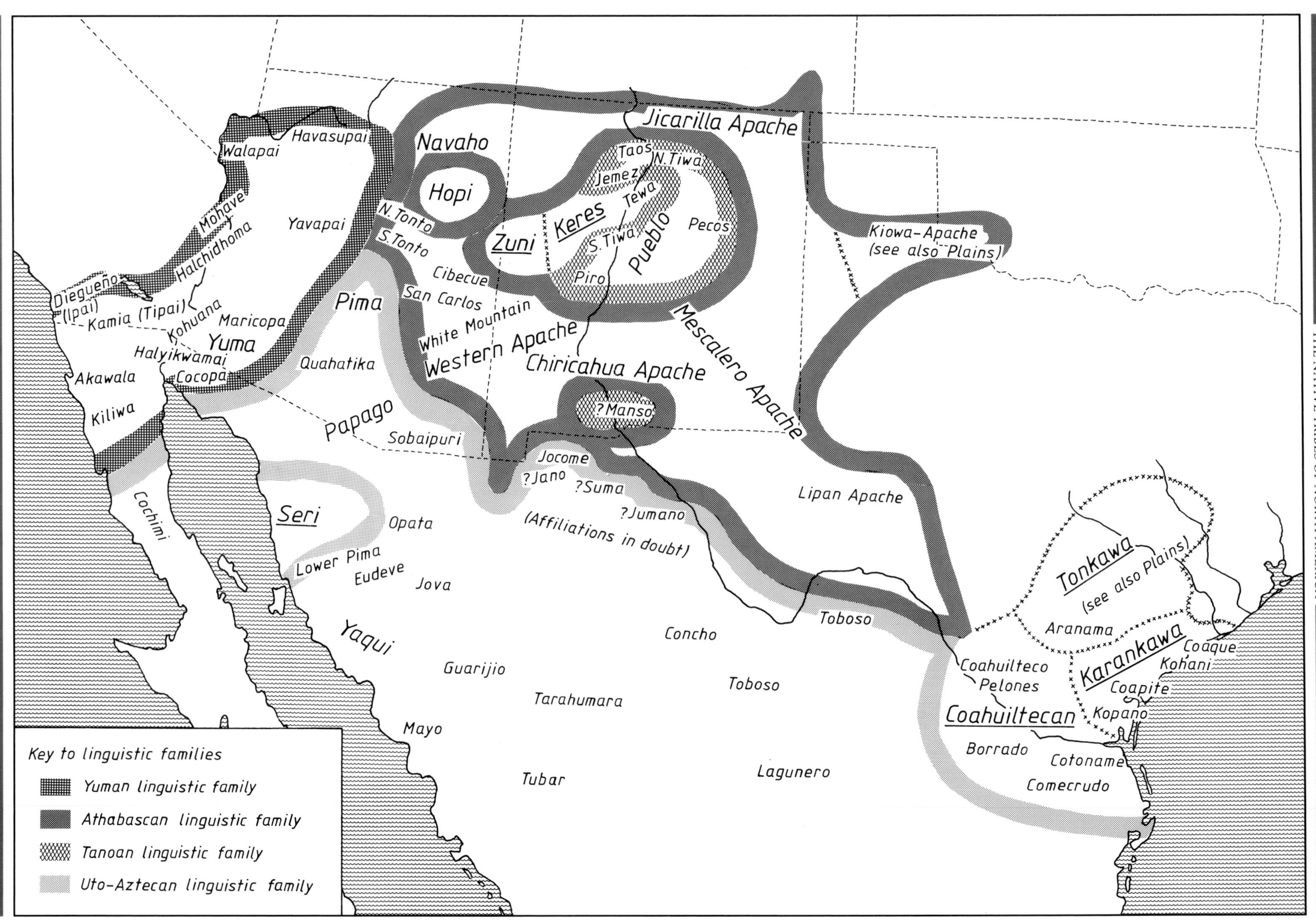
Havasupai
Walapai
Navaho
Hopi
Jicarilla Apache
Taos
N.Tiwa
Jemez
Tewa
Keres
Zuni
S.Tiwa
Pueblo
Pecos
Piro
Mohave
Halchidhoma
Yavapai
N.Tonto
S.Tonto
Cibecue
San Carlos
White Mountain
Western Apache
Chiricahua Apache
Mescalero Apache
Kiowa-Apache
(see also Plains)
Diegueño
(Ipai)
Kamia (Tipai)
Kohuana
Maricopa
Pima
Yuma
Halyikwamai
Cocopa
Quahatika
Akawala
Kiliwa
Papago
Sobaipuri
?Manso
Jocome
?Jano
?Suma
?Jumano
(Affiliations in doubt)
Lipan Apache
Cochimi
Seri
Opata
Lower Pima
Eudeve
Jova
Yaqui
Guarijio
Tarahumara
Mayo
Tubar
Concho
Toboso
Toboso
Lagunero
Tonkawa
(see also Plains)
Aranama
Karankawa
Coaque
Kohani
Coapite
Kopano
Coahuilteco
Pelones
Coahuiltecan
Borrado
Cotoname
Comecrudo
Key to linguistic families
Yuman linguistic family
Athabascan linguistic family
Tanoan linguistic family
Uto-Aztecan linguistic family

The historic southwestern culture derives basically from two sources: one an ancient agricultural tradition, the other a much later northern hunting tradition which the Navajo and Apache, relative newcomers to the area, introduced from about A.D. 1400. Three major prehistoric cultures contributed to the older cultural traditions of the region: Mogollon and Hohokam, which preceded the Pima and Papago, and Anasazi which preceded the Pueblo.

The Mogollon culture, c.500 B.C.- A.D. 1400, acquired agriculture and pottery from Mexico; they were mainly pit-house farmers, and the originators of later developments in the Southwest. This complex originated in Cochise County, Arizona, and spread to neighbouring areas. Hohokam culture, c.300 B.C.- A.D. 1450, developed farther west, centering along the Gila River around present Phoenix, Arizona. It developed irrigation canal systems, fine pottery and stonework. These cultures declined during the early 15th century, and we can assume that the modern Pima and Papago are their descendants.

The Anasazi ("the ancient ones") is a collective term to cover the development of Puebloan culture from about 250 B.C. to A.D. 1700, and incorporates sites within eastern Arizona, western New Mexico and adjacent Colorado. The earliest phases are termed "Basketmaker", 250 B.C.- A.D.700, and "Modified Basketmaker", A.D. 400 – 700. These were followed by three Pueblo periods: the "Development Period"; the "Great Pueblo Period", characterized by large towns with fine masonry apartments, and their abandonment from about A.D.1276 when drought forced the people south to Hopi, Zuni and to the Rio Grande; and finally the "Regressive Pueblo Period",A.D.1300 – 1700, which climaxed with Spanish occupation. Their most famous sites are Mesa Verde, Chaco Canyon, Pueblo Bonito and Kayenta.

The Pueblos possessed elaborate, formal ceremonials based upon a tradition of sacred myths. Most dances are dramatized prayers with participants dressed to impersonate divine spirits, moving in unison exactly rehearsed. Some impersonate Kachinas or animal spirits, who act as intermediaries between man and god. Through such rituals the Pueblo people prayed for rain, crops, sunlight and fertility. All this has survived a Spanish conquest, a Revolution, reconquest and vigorous attempts to Christianize them.

Although many Pueblo villages postdate initial Spanish contact, most seem to have been located close to earlier sites after resubmitting to Spain and accepting a veneer of Catholicism. From the Spaniards they adopted domesticated animals, horses, wheat, fruit trees, sheep and cattle. The use of adobe bricks from moulds to rebuild larger rooms in the Pueblo structures was also of Hispanic origin. From the early 1700s until the American annexation of the Southwest in 1848 the Pueblos and Spanish (or Mexicans, after the 1820s) stood back to back fighting off the Athabascans, who had first appeared in the 15th century. Although warfare between the Navajo and Apache and the Pueblo and Spanish often reached alarming proportions, the former still adopted weaving, pottery, masked dances, and even marginal agriculture from the Pueblos. The Athabascans retained their roving, hunting and raiding northern ways, however; hardy, skilled in combat, incredibly observant and gifted at concealment they were without equals as warriors.

Of all Native American cultures there is no doubt that those of the Southwest are the best preserved, despite the merging of Anglo-American material culture with their own. They still have a timeless quality, with a strong attachment for the still well-supported old religion and ceremonials, from which whites are often excluded. The Navajo are still struggling with dual culturism; but the Apache, despite very harsh treatment during early reservation days, have become successful stockmen, and retain a strong identity as a separate people. Southwestern Indian culture includes the Piman, Yuman, Pueblo, some northern Mexican tribes and some Texas border tribes, plus the southern Athabascans.

TRIBES OF THE SOUTHWEST AND MEXICAN BORDER, c.1600-1860

Linguistic and cultural boundaries are necessarily approximate; this sketch map is intended only as a general guide to distribution. Underlined names indicate small linguistic families distinct from larger groupings indicated by the shading key.

YUMAN

A language family named after the Yuma tribe, located about the middle and lower Colorado River in Arizona, California and adjacent Mexico in a distinctly desert habitat. The Yumans had a relatively simple culture, and were first exposed to Europeans in 1540 when the Spanish explorer Alarcón visited Cocopa country. Some groups were agricultural, representing the northwestern frontier on the continent for the native practice of maize farming. They made basketry and pottery. Linguistic studies have suggested a tentative connection to the Esselen of coastal California and hence to the Hokan stock; but their nearest linguistic relatives were the Cochimi, an extinct group of languages of Baja California, Mexico. The Yumans are located at the junction of three cultural areas – California, Southwest and Baja Californian. The Upland or Arizona plateau branch are the Havasupai, Yavapai and Walapai; the River branch are the Mohave, Yuma or Quechan, Maricopa, Halchidhoma and Kavelchadom; the Delta-California branch comprises the Diegueño, Kamia and Cocopa and finally the Baja California branch, the Kiliwa.

The River Yumans lived in low rectangular earth-covered houses, while the Maricopa adopted the Piman round houses. They practised floodwater agriculture, growing corn, beans and cucurbits. The Upland groups ranged over a wide and arid territory, collected a variety of wild plant foods and had considerable dependence on hunting; they lived in dome-shaped grass-covered shelters. Religion and ceremonialism were not elaborate; beliefs were expressed through shamanism, curing by means of spirits, and dreams. They were often warlike and aggressive, but usually amongst themselves.

HAVASUPAI An Upland Yuman tribe who occupied the plateau area on both sides of the Colorado River, including Cataract Canyon through which flows the Havasu River, a tributary of the Colorado. During the 19th and 20th centuries they consolidated into one group under pressure for land from whites and Navajo, and were ultimately restricted to a reservation of only 500 acres. They were both an agricultural and a hunting and gathering people, living in domed and conical logwood structures covered with thatch or earth. They usually spent their winters on the canyon rim hunting and gathering; summer was spent in the canyon to farm their tiny gardens. They excelled in basketry. Met by Spanish explorers in the 16th century, they changed little until increased contact with whites as late as the 1930s. About 200 people remain at the Supai village, with about 100 elsewhere. Today their income is derived from outside wage work. Their reservation has recently been extended to 160,000 acres.

WALAPAI or **HUALAPAI** A Yuman-speaking tribe of the Upland group, very closely related to the Havasupai and Yavapai and living in the canyons of the Colorado River in Arizona, particularly on the south side of the river from the Coconino Plateau almost to the big bend of the Colorado near present Lake Mead. Their first contact with the Spanish was in 1776. Hostilities between the Walapai and Anglo-Americans in 1866 led to the destruction of their crops and internment on the Colorado River Reservation. They later returned to their old lands and received a reservation there (though representing only a fraction of their old domain) which they continue to occupy. They were originally gatherers and hunters, and more recently stock raisers. The Walapai probably never numbered more than 1,000, and is today about 900, about half of them on their reservation including two extensions at Big Sandy and Valentine.

YAVAPAI This Yuman tribe occupied north central Arizona between the Pinal Mountains in the east as far north as present Flagstaff, then west almost to the Colorado River. They have also been termed "Apache-Mohaves" on the incorrect assumption that they are descended from two tribes; while there has been intermarriage with Apaches they are an independent, separate people. Their habitat was mostly a vast desert with subsistence dependent on plant foods, nuts, acorns, piñon and berries. They also hunted deer, antelope and rabbits. They led a semi-nomadic existence and lived in simple brush shelters and caves. They excelled in coiled basketry. The Yavapai were involved in bloody feuds with Anglo prospectors and miners in the 1860s-70s, and some were interned on the San Carlos Apache Reservation. Ultimately a reservation was established at Fort McDowell east of present Phoenix, Arizona, and smaller reservations at Camp Verde, Middle Verde, Clarkdale, and Yavapai, near Prescott. They probably numbered over 1,500 before 1860; today they have 800 descendants, half at the Fort McDowell Reservation, the rest divided between the other reservations and adjacent towns.

MOHAVE The northernmost Yuman tribe of the Colorado River group, living where the present states of Nevada, California and Arizona adjoin at the Mohave Valley. Although they were known to the Spanish from the 17th century onwards they were too remote from them to be much affected by their missions. However, after the 1820s they came increasingly into conflict with Anglo-Americans, including the U.S. military. Their culture was of the simple desert Yuman type, with plant gathering, some fishing and hunting. They were assigned to the Fort Mojave and Colorado River Indian Reservations close to their original homes. Today they number about 1,500 descendants , perhaps half their population in the 17th century. They enjoy increasing prosperity due to the development of irrigated farmlands and income from land leased to whites.

MARICOPA A Yuman people of the River group, probably occupying lands along the Colorado River in the distant past, but by the time of the Anglo-American presence in the Southwest concentrated along the Gila River. The people now called Maricopa appear to be an amalgam of several older Yuman subgroups: the *Halchidhoma* of the Colorado

River, *Kavelchadom* of the Gila River, and *Kahwan* and *Halyikwamai* close to the Cocopa south of the international border. Some of the modern Maricopa families claim the descent of these incorporated groups. Their present descendants are at Laveen on the Gila River Reservation and at Lehi on the Salt River Reservation, Arizona, with a total number of about 700 people.

YUMA or **QUECHAN** The Yuma are one of the principal tribes of the Yuman linguistic family, who lived at the junction of the Gila and Colorado Rivers in the extreme southwestern corner of Arizona. They were gatherers of wild foods but also planted maize, pumpkins and beans. Their house-types were dome- or rectangular-shaped wooden structures covered with earth or brush. Clothing was of the briefest due to the extreme heat – usually aprons front and rear and, in cooler weather, rabbitskin robes. The Spanish explorer Alarcón passed through their territory en route to meet Coronado in 1540. There followed sporadic subjection to Spanish, Mexican and Anglo-American influences. In 1884 the government established the Fort Yuma Indian Reservation, although some lands were lost during the allotments which followed. Originally numbering perhaps 4,000, they were reduced to 848 by 1937, and now total about 1,500.

BAJA CALIFORNIA YUMANS A number of small groups of Yuman peoples live in Baja California, Mexico. The *Aka'wala* or *Paipai* have descendants around San Miguel; their language seems to be connected with the Upland groups in Arizona. The *Kiliwa* or *Yukiliwa*, also in northern Baja California, are near Santa Catarina and still have a few speakers. The *Cochimi* and other small and almost extinct tribes of southern Baja California are thought now to be sufficiently divergent in language from Yuman to be considered as a separate family.

COCOPA A Yuman tribe who lived at the delta of the Colorado River where it empties into the Gulf of California, now Baja California Norte, Mexico, but also extending into southwestern Arizona. They were a typical River Yuman tribe, but not always on friendly terms with their relatives. They were encountered by the Spanish explorer Alarcón in 1540, and subsequently were slowly modified by Mexican and Anglo-American influences. They probably numbered in excess of 3,000 at one time, but only 1,200 in 1900. Two small reservations have been established near Somerton, Arizona, and had an enrolled population of 500 or so in 1980. A few are still reported from Mexico, around the Hardy River in Baja California and in Sonora, totalling perhaps 300-400.

DIEGUEÑO or **IPAI** A people occupying the border country of southern California in present San Diego County south of the San Luis Rey River – an area of coast, mountain and desert. They form with the neighbouring Kamia (Tipai) and Cocopa a branch of the Yuman linguistic family. They lived principally on wild plant foods, supplemented by hunting and fishing. They became part of the so-called "Mission Indians" of southern California, of both Yuman and Takic origin, who were to a large extent under the influence and control of the Spanish missions from 1769 until secularization during the Mexican period. During the American period they have laboured on ranches, in mines and in towns, with a land base of 13 small reservations which they share with the Kamia. The Diegueño and Kamia together numbered about 1,500 in 1980.

KAMIA or **TIPAI** These Yuman people, now usually considered with the Dieguenо as one tribe "Tipai-Ipai", lived on both sides of the border between California and Baja California, Mexico, their culture being much the same as that of their relatives, and were usually called "Mission Indians". The reservations with Tipai-Ipai resident descendants are at Barona, Campo, Capitan Grande, Cuyapaipe, Inaja-Cosmit, La Posta, Manzanita, Mesa Grande, Pala (with Takic), San Pasqual, Santa Ysabel, Sycuan, Viejas and Jamul; they number about 500. Others are in the general San Diego County area; the Mexican Baja California groups seem to have merged with Hispanic or other natives.

PIMA The Pima or Upper Pima and their close relatives, the Papago, speak a distinct language within the Uto-Aztecan linguistic family. They occupied with the Papago an area of the Sonoran Desert, now part of southern Arizona and northern Sonora, Mexico. The Lower Pima or Pima Bajo referred to elsewhere live far to the south and are also closely related. The extensive range of the Pima and Papago villages was generally south of the Gila River to the Rio Magdalena, Mexico. Before the arrival of the Spanish in the mid-17th century they were part of a desert food-collecting culture grafted on to the successful farming of domesticated plants, corn, beans and squash; this agriculture, of central American origin, was developed by the Hohokam people who were skilful builders of canals to lead river or arroyo water to their fields. Culturally the Pima and Papago are descendants of the Hohokams, who seem to have disappeared in about A.D.1400. Maintaining a sufficient water supply was the major concern of Piman life, so larger communities were found along the San Pedro and Santa Cruz Rivers where a subtribe, the *Sobaipuri*, were located.

The Spaniards brought livestock, wheat and

improved implements for canal and ditch irrigation. They also converted the Pima-Papago population to nominal Catholicism through the establishment of missions. The Americans came after 1854 and, although they exerted control over their territory, there was little settlement pressure and relations were usually satisfactory. While tribal fortunes reached a low point around 1900, on the whole the Pima have adapted to an Indian-Hispanic-Anglo culture adequately. The Pima descendants live on the Gila River, Salt River and Ak-Chin Reservations and in off-reservation communities in Casa Grande, Chandler, Coolidge and Phoenix. During the American period the Pima were those generally settled closer to the Gila River. In 1945 there were 4,702 on the Gila River Reservation and 1,113 at Salt River Reservation; today they number about 8,500. In recent years the Pima have preferred to call themselves *O'otam*.

PAPAGO A division of the Upper Pima Indians of the desert region of southern Arizona and northern Sonora, Mexico. The division between Pima and Papago became widely recognized during the American period after 1854, with the transfer of their territory from Mexico to the U.S.A. The Papagos were delimited to the border area with Mexico, whilst the Pima were adjacent to the Gila River and its tributaries. Food resources were crops of corn, beans and squash which depended on irrigated water, often in limited supply; they also depended on wild foods and hunting. During the Spanish period, 1687-1821, European-derived crops, livestock and improved gardening techniques modified Papago culture. Beginning in 1687 the Papago were Christianized following the foundation of the San Xavier Mission, which became the centre of Papago religious life. Politically each Papago village was autonomous, usually with two locations – one near an arroyo where flash floods provided water for their fields. Papagos were often raided by the Apaches, but they have usually been on friendly terms with the Americans. They seem to have had a belief in a creator "Earthmaker" before their acceptance of Christianity.

Their culture has been one of gradual modification to Hispanic and American gardening and cattle-owning village communities, subsequently extended to wage-earning permanent settlements off the reservations. Reservations were established at San Xavier, Gila Bend, Ak-Chin and Sells in the late 19th and early 20th centuries. They number over 16,000 today, about half on their reservations, the rest at Ajo, Marana, Florence, Tucson, Phoenix and elsewhere. They still hold festivals and dances for harvests and rain, using their own musical instruments, and they still excel in coiled basketry. A few hundred Papago live in Sonora, near Caborca.

MEXICAN BORDER TRIBES:

Brief reference should be made to the Indians of northern Mexico in the states, east to west, of Tamanlipas, Nuevo Leon, Coahuilla, Chihuahua and Sonora. The whole area was colonized by the Spanish in the 16th and 17th centuries and the Indians successfully missionized. By the time of Mexico's independence from Spain the Indians and Mestizos (mixed descent population) had formed the lowest stratum of the social system. In the eastern states tribal independence had collapsed; but in the western states, particularly Sonora, a large Indian population has survived to the present time. Over the years substantial numbers of the Mestizo population have found their way into the U.S.A. Many of the following tribes are part of the general Southwestern culture of the Pima-Papago type, and many are linguistically related to tribes in the U.S.A. as members of the Uto-Aztecan language family. The following tribes are worth noting in this regard:

SERI Of Tiburon Islands and adjacent coastal Sonora, a small tribe with an independent language, perhaps related to the Chontal of Central Mexico and distantly to the Hokan languages of California. About 500 descendants survive.

YAQUI & MAYO Two closely related Uto-Aztecan peoples of central coastal Sonora; the Yaqui number 20,000, the Mayo 30,000, the latter in the Rio Mayo region. About 6,000 Yaqui-Mayo are in Arizona in six communities at Tucson, Tempe, Marana, Scottsdale, Eloy and Pascua. They are noted for their masked dancers and deer dancers with deer antler headdresses.

TARAHUMARA A largely hispanicized Uto-Aztecan people of southwestern Chihuahua; they have numerous descendants, mostly Mestizos, but 50,000 distinctly Indian.

TEPEHUAN A people of the Sierra Madre region of southern Chihuahua, now largely Mestizo. Their language belonged to the Uto-Aztecan family.

LOWER PIMA A Piman enclave in Mexico east of the Yaqui in east central Sonora; a few survive exclusive of Mestizos.

EASTERN SONORAN TRIBES A number of tribes of this region are now culturally extinct, being largely Mestizo. They are the *Opata, Jova, Eudeve, Guarijio* and *Tubar*. All spoke dialects of the Uto-Aztecan language family.

NORTHERN CHIHUAHUA & COAHUILA TRIBES The extinct *Concho* and *Toboso* are thought to have been Uto-Aztecan speakers; but the *Jumano, Suma, Manso, Jano*, and *Jocome* of the Rio Grande region, whose original territory extended into Texas and New Mexico, may well have been Athabascans. They may have been the bands of Apachean people pushing south who are known to have been in contact and conflict with the early Spanish settlers and missionaries, but there is no proof. We know that all these peoples were in revolt at times during the 17th century, were subsequently assimilated into Hispanic society, and are now extinct as separate cultural identities. Possibly the last of them joined the hispanicized Pueblos near El Paso, Ysleta, Senecú and Socorro.

COAHUILTECAN A name given by ethnologists to a large number of relatively unknown minor tribes on both sides of the border in southern Texas: north of the Rio Grande to San Antonio, hence to the Gulf coast and as far west as Eagle Pass, then south into Mexico in northern Nuevo Leon, Coahuilla and Tamaulipas. The truth is that we know almost nothing about them except for the mass of minor tribal, group, band or mission names left from the Spanish colonial period. On the evidence of some linguistic data from Spanish mission records the Coahuiltecan language family was proposed; but it is by no means certain that all the groups of the area were related, and recently the *Comecrudo, Cotoname, Borrado* and *Waikuri* have been given separate status. Speculatively the Coalhuiltecans have been linked to the Karankawan family of the Texas coast, and even more remotely to the Hokan stock, but all is yet unverified.

KARANKAWA A group of small tribes who lived along the Texas coast from present Corpus Christi to Galveston Bay. They have been given independent linguistic status on very limited information. Speculative affiliations have been proposed with the Tonkawa and Coahuilteco but are unverified. From the 16th century onward they were in contact with an assortment of Spanish, French and American castaways, explorers and missionaries. During the American settlement after 1821 the coast tribes subjected the intruders to constant pilfering, and the Karankawas suffered reprisals which finally destroyed them entirely; we hear of a band being exterminated by a group of ranchers in 1858. A few may have crossed into Mexico but all trace of them is now lost. In later years there seem to have been five tribes. Their reputation as cannibals seems unfounded.

TONKAWA A group of small Indian tribes of central Texas who were contacted by the Spanish as early as 1542 on the Trinity River. At one time, before the arrival of the Apache and Comanche, they seem to have been the most important of the peoples of central Texas. They had a distinct language forming a separate family, which on circumstantial evidence has been linked to the Karankawa of the Texas coast. By the mid-18th century, much reduced in number, the Tonkawa seem to have been connected with the San Xavier Missions on the San Gabriel River, Texas. In 1855 the remaining Tonkawas were moved to a reservation on the Brazos River, Young County, Texas; but the hostility of the Texans enforced their removal to Indian Territory (now Oklahoma) in 1857. They suffered a massacre in 1862 when Delaware and Shawnee, with others, killed 137 men, women and children in reprisal for old disputes. The surviving Tonkawas lived for a time at Fort Arbuckle in Chickasaw Nation and later took refuge at Fort Griffin, Texas. They returned to Indian Territory in 1884 when a small reservation was established in present Kay County, Oklahoma. Their total population was perhaps over 1,700 at the time of Spanish contact, but only 350 when first removed to Indian Territory in 1857; just 92 members of the tribe survived when brought from Fort Griffin. A few people have continued to identify themselves as Tonkawa through the present century: 53 in 1910; 46 in 1936; and today, although mixed with Lipan Apaches over the years, a few people around Tonkawa, Kay County, Oklahoma. Although it is difficult to delimit Tonkawan tribes in Spanish colonial times, they seem to have been a warlike people who followed the bison herds for long distances, lived in skin tipis and were fine horsemen.

APACHE The southwestern division of the Athabascan linguistic family comprised seven tribes: the Chiricahua, Jicarilla, Kiowa-Apache, Lipan, Mescalero, Western Apache and Navajo (Navaho). All but the Kiowa-Apache language seem to be closely related branches of a single tongue that were perhaps unseparated before about A.D.1300.

There has been lengthy debate over the route taken by these Athabascans following their separation from their northern relatives of the Mackenzie Drainage of Canada. One theory suggests a migration through the inter-montane region of the American Plateau and Great Basin; a second view suggests a route through the Great Plains, and these Apachean people are credited as the first Great Plains people to be in contact with the earliest Spanish exploration on the Plains in the 16th and 17th centuries. A number of archaeological sites such as Dismal River and others in Nebraska and

Kansas have been presented as Apachean, although some historians consider them more probably Puebloan. In the course of the debate a number of tribal names in old Spanish and French records have been given Apache status, including the *Padouca*, alternatively presented as Comanche, a relatively ancient people of the Plains.

The first hypothesis, however, seems to be generally favoured, with the entry of these Athabascans into the Southwest from about A.D.1400, with an early spatial separation, either before or very shortly after their arrival in the Southwest, first of the Kiowa-Apache and later of the Lipan to the Plains of Oklahoma and Texas. Certainly the Kiowa-Apache represent the greatest problem for the favoured theory, because of their adoption of Plains cultural traits, their long association with the Kiowa, and a tradition – albeit tenuous – of a link to the most southern group of the Northern Athabascans, the Sarsi.

A number of Indian groups of northern Mexico, such as Manso, Suma, Jumano and Janos – names from old Spanish mission records – have also been presented as Apachean, but none survived until reservation days, so their connections are unknown.

LIPAN APACHE An Athabascan tribe of the southwestern Apache group, usually given separate status, who were in the upper Red River area of northwestern Texas as long ago as 1670. At that time they numbered perhaps 3,000 people and already had the advantage of horses and metal weapons. They seem to have pushed eastward several Caddoan peoples who were subsequently armed by the French, which halted and reversed their advance. They seem to have played a large part in destroying Spanish settlements and missions in the San Antonio area; however, the entry of the Comanche into Texas led to diminished numbers and domain.

In later years they occupied an area between the Colorado River (of Texas) and the Pecos River. A few crossed into Mexico. Their language was closest to Jicarilla, and they perhaps split from them in about A.D.1500.

The last of the Lipan were settled in 1905 on the Mescalero Reservation, New Mexico; and there were only two or three old women living in 1981 who knew anything of their ancient language. A few others are said to have been incorporated amongst the Kiowa-Apache and Tonkawa of Oklahoma, but are no longer reported separately. The Lipan, together with the Mescalero and Tonkawa, are thought to have been the originators of the Peyote cult amongst Indians north of the Mexican border.

KIOWA-APACHE The most divergent group of the southwestern Apachean people, who have been associated with the Kiowa of the southern Plains since long before white contact, perhaps for four hundred years. It has been proposed that they may have moved from the north with their allies the Kiowa, and not separated from the main southern group. Superficially at least they are a Plains people, who formed a distinct band within their adopted tribe. In the 1860s they moved to the Fort Sill Reservation, Oklahoma, along with Kiowa and Comanche, with whom they are much mixed. In 1907 they were reported to number 156. The modern Kiowa-Apache live in and about the towns of Anadarko, Fort Cobb and Apache in Oklahoma, and were reported to number about 400 in 1960, including about 40 people who could speak their language. In 1981 they had an enrolment of 833, with only 20 remaining speakers of the language.

CHIRICAHUA APACHE A tribe of the southwestern Apachean group who lived on the west side of the Rio Grande in southwestern New Mexico and adjacent Arizona and Mexico. Although they had almost no tribal cohesion they are sometimes divided into four bands: Chiricahua, Mimbreños, Mogollon and Warm Springs. Their closest linguistic relatives are the Mescalero Apache. Although mission records from the Spanish colonial days do not mention the Chiricahua by this name, they found Indians in their region who were consistently hostile, and many of them were clearly Chiricahua Apaches. By 1853 most of the Chiricahua territory had been transferred from Mexico to the U.S.A., but the hostilities continued between miners, ranchers, settlers and these nomadic Indians. The Government made several attempts to settle at least some on reservations through overtures to leaders Mangas-Coloradas and Cochise, and when these failed some were interned on the San Carlos Reservation. Thus began a long, dramatic and tragic duel between a few hundred Apaches and the troops, scouts and citizens of the U.S.A. and Mexico.

Victorio and most of his followers were killed by Mexican soldiers in 1880, and not until 1886 did Geronimo and his band surrender to General Crook in Sonora, Mexico. The entire Chiricahua people were sent first to Florida and then to Alabama, but in 1894 transferred to Fort Sill, Oklahoma. In 1913, 187 of the remaining Chiricahuas returned to their homelands and settled on the Mescalero Reservation, New Mexico, while 84 chose to remain in Oklahoma. Over the intervening years the Chiricahua people have all but merged with the Mescalero, but perhaps 500 still claimed their descent in 1970. The Oklahoma branch have descendants near Apache and Fletcher towns and number about 150, known as the "Fort Sill Apache".

MESCALERO APACHE A branch of the southwestern Athabascan Apachean peoples who have occupied essentially the same territory of southeastern New Mexico, Texas and the adjacent parts of Chihuahua, Mexico, since the 17th century. Their territory combined high mountain valleys and flats, with cold winters and hot, dry summers. Despite treaties at various times with the Spanish and later Mexican authorities, when Texas and New Mexico were transferred to the U.S.A. the new government recognized no Indian claims to land. A bitter struggle between the Americans and the Mescalero saw many taken prisoner at Bosque Redondo along with the Navajos. In 1872 a reservation was established on the eastern slopes of the White and Sacramento Mountains, New Mexico; and the Mescalero, with additions from the Chiricahua and a few Lipans, have been there ever since.

Like most southwestern Apaches they lived by hunting wild game, antelope, rabbit, and occasionally buffalo, and harvesting wild plants, particularly agave (mescal); prickly pear, wild pea, berries and choke-cherries were also important. The Apaches were expert basket makers; they had buckskin clothing for male and female; their house types were brush wickiups but also, amongst the Mescalero, Lipan and Jicarilla, the tipi of the Plains type. The Apache had no large pantheon of gods but revered two powerful supernaturals,"Child of the Water" and his mother "White Painted Woman"; these culture heroes destroyed monsters with objects and substances which became incorporated into ritual practice. Two important observances are the girls' puberty rites; and masked dancers who impersonate the Mountain Spirits capable of protecting the Apache from hostile forces and epidemic disease, with their distinctive hoods and headdresses. The Mescalero perhaps numbered 2,000 in 1850; in 1888, only 431; 868 in 1945; and 1,300 in 1980, although the last two figures include the mixed Mescalero-Chiricahua population.

JICARILLA APACHE A tribe of the southwestern Athabascans closest to Lipan in language. Their territory was the high country of mesas and basins in the area of northern New Mexico on both sides of the Rio Grande and the upper valleys of the Red River; their hunting territory extended into present Colorado. Their location enabled subsistence to include the hunting of bison as well as antelope and small game, and they also gathered wild berries and fruits. Their early use of the horse and relative proximity to Plains Indians allowed the adoption of cultural traits and material culture from the east and north. Like their kinsmen they raided the Pueblos extensively, and also incorporated both ritual and material culture from that source; they were the Apaches most influenced by Pueblo gardening practices. They probably encountered the Spanish in the 16th century and thereafter waged constant war on them. They were in turn harassed by the Comanche during the 18th century, and hostilities with the Americans continued until 1855.

In 1874 the Jicarilla Reservation was established below Dulce, New Mexico, and has been their home since that time. Their major ceremonials were the Bear Dance, a curing rite; and the Relay Race between two sides, enlisting the aid of culture heroes and deities to ensure food supply. The Jicarilla have retained a surprising amount of traditional religion and beliefs despite modern influences, but do not have the Mountain Spirit rituals of the Western Apache. They numbered 815 in 1900 and have steadily increased since, being reported to number 2,308 in 1980. Stock raising has now given way to wage earning for most Apaches.

WESTERN APACHE A group of Athabascan subtribes speaking similar dialects, in southeastern Arizona from the San Pedro River in the south to the Verde River in the north, and comprising the San Carlos, White Mountain, Cibecue, Southern Tonto and Northern Tonto in that order south to north. The whole group are sometimes known as *Coyoteros*. They have become one of the legendary Indian peoples due to their prowess as warriors, usually fancifully represented in popular books and on film. They probably reached their present location in about A.D.1525, and remained isolated until hostilities with the Spanish intensified after 1765 – although no settlements were established by the Spanish in Western Apache domains. The Apache adoption of the horse and the material culture of equestrian raiders ensured independence until the Americans obtained control of Arizona in 1853. Anglo-American efforts to destroy the Apaches intensified with the concentration of Western Apaches on the San Carlos Reservation, established in 1872 in eastern Arizona south of the Colorado Plateau (San Carlos, Tonto) and the Fort Apache Reservation to the north (White Mountain, Cibecue).

The Western Apache world view was expressed in a cycle of myths that explained the origin of the world and supernatural powers; their major ceremonials were connected with curing or protection against illness, usually performed in special structures. The traditional Apaches have a belief in an impersonal deity, "Life Giver", and culture heroes "Changing Woman" and her son "Slayer of Monsters". The puberty ceremony survives, and Gan or Crown dancers (Mountain Spirit Dances) continue to perform regularly. In 1972 the Western Apache population was 9,622; but the 15,825 reported in 1981 seem too many. The majority are on the San Carlos and Fort Apache Reservations, with a few at Camp Verde, Middle Verde and Clarkdale with the Yavapai. Over the years the Apaches have become fairly successful stockmen and operate tourist facilities, but on the whole social conditions remain below those enjoyed by white Americans.

NAVAJO or **NAVAHO** A tribe forming one of the seven divisions of the southwestern Athabascan Apachean group. They call themselves Diné, and perhaps entered the American Southwest during the 15th century. Linguistically they are closer to the Western Apache than the latter are to Lipan or Kiowa-Apache. Their location was, and still is, the dry desert regions of the northeastern section of Arizona and the northwestern parts of New Mexico, between the San Juan River in the north to the area of the Puerco and San Jose Rivers in the south. The Navajo seem to have been more heavily influenced by Pueblo culture than other Apachean groups, and the adoption of elements of Pueblo population, perhaps before and after the Pueblo revolt against the Spanish in 1680, reinforces a strong Puebloan link. Their pottery and weaving arts are of Pueblo origin.

Although the Navajo were involved in wars against the Spanish and were often successful in driving them away, their culture gradually modified under Spanish influence, including the domestication of sheep and horses; this influence also affected food gathering, agriculture, trade, religion and the arts, which resulted in a hybrid Apachean-Puebloan-Hispanic tradition which survives until the present time. The Navajo origin myth describes ascending from the underworld. The majority of their ceremonials are primarily for curing disease, actual or anticipated; and for the ritualistic restoration of universal harmony once it has been disturbed, usually expressed as the "Blessing Way", through group rituals and singing which give psycho-therapeutic benefit to patients and participants. Other important rituals include the Yeibichei or "Night Chant"; and recently the Peyote cult has become popular with many.

After the U.S.A. obtained control of the Southwest the legendary government scout, Kit Carson, was commissioned to round up the Navajo, and in doing so destroyed their sheep, orchards, food and horses. Some 8,000 Navajo were interned at Bosque Redondo in 1863. They returned some five years later and the Navajo Reservation was established, ultimately covering an area larger than West Virginia or Wales. It straddles four states – Arizona, New Mexico, Utah and Colorado; and during the 20th century three additional communities have been added at Ramah, Valencia County, Canyoncito west of present Albuquerque, and Puertocito northwest of Nagdalena, Socorro County, all in New Mexico. In the years between their captivity and today the Navajo have increased in population from perhaps 10,000 to 166,519 in 1981, being the largest Indian tribe today north of the Rio Grande.

Navajo life today centres on attempts to cope with the many economic and political problems that stem from their cultural isolation, and to ensure that exploitation by various corporations of the mineral resources on their lands will benefit "The People" generally. The Navajos are noted for their fine silverwork, woollen blankets and rugs; and for their continued distinctive dress, particularly of women, derived from 19th century full skirts and long blouses of European fashion.

THE PUEBLOS

The name of the so-called Pueblo Indians of the American Southwest, derived from the Spanish for "village", is a collective term for Indians who lived in permanent stone or adobe structures in compact villages along the Rio Grande in New Mexico, the Zuni of western New Mexico, and the Hopi villages of northern Arizona. The historic Pueblos seem to be descendants of people who built the great architectural wonders at Chaco Canyon, Mesa Verde, Casa Grande and other places spread over five states, which were perhaps at the height of their cultural development during the 13th century. The Pueblos who survived the Spanish conquest are divided into four linguistic families: Tanoan, Keresan, Zuni and Hopi – the latter a divergent branch of the old Shoshonean family, now Uto-Aztecan.

They were sedentary horticulturists with intensive farming, usually in small fields irrigated from streams or storage reservoirs, the chief crops being corn, pumpkins, melons, beans and squash; they also raised a native cotton, a product which was woven into everyday clothing. In addition to agriculture they also hunted deer and antelope, and also bison on the Plains. After contact with the Spanish the Pueblos adopted horses, cattle and sheep, and wheat, grapes, peaches and apples were henceforth extensively grown. They domesticated turkey, which were herded in large flocks, and eagles were kept in captivity for their feathers, prized for ritual use.

The ancient clothing of the Pueblo men consisted of a short tunic of deerhide and leggings reaching the knees, either of skin or of cotton, breechcloth and moccasins. After the introduction of sheep woven woollen garments largely replaced skin, including brightly coloured blankets of native or imported wool, bayeta or yarn. Women's dresses were knee length, in the form of a blanket whose two ends were sewn together over the right shoulder and under the left, belted at the waist. Both men and women often wore their hair fringed at front and sides. They made ornaments of drilled shell and turquoise beads and other stones, and developed a skilful metal-working process derived from the Spaniards.

The Zuni Pueblo seems to have been the first known to the Spanish, in 1539; this inspired the Coronado expedition of 1540. Expecting to find great wealth, and encouraged always by news of what lay beyond, he explored Pueblo country for two years without finding the hoped-for riches. It was not until 1598 that Juan de Oñate set up a permanent colony; and there followed vigorous attempts to missionize, to suppress native religion and to enforce labour and tribute, which eventually led to the Pueblo Revolt of 1680. It was not until 1696 that the Spanish regained control; they were thereafter less harsh in their treatment of the Indians, and the Pueblos continued in their ancient beliefs while adopting a veneer of Catholicism. Few Rio Grande Pueblos maintained their exact original sites after the Revolt, perhaps only Acoma and Isleta. From that time the Pueblos have been notably peaceful towards whites, with a relatively stable culture extracting from the Anglo-American world only that which helps to sustain their own culture in a continuing, pre-ordained, timeless existence.

Their homes were originally without doors, the upper floors being reached by ladders. Corner fire-places and dome-shaped ovens were derived from the Spanish. Floors were paved with stone slabs or plastered like the walls and roofs. The building material used in the western Pueblos is mostly stone held together with adobe mortar, the whole covered with adobe plaster. In the east, since the Spanish conquest, unmoulded adobe brick has been used. The roof beams are usually cottonwood, pine or spruce, with cross poles covered with brush and earth. Recently modern tools and materials have made possible larger rooms with the use of longer timber beams. The Pueblos were excellent basket makers; and their earthenware vessels, ancient and modern, consist of elaborately painted jars, bowls and platters, each Pueblo often developing its own style.

The Pueblos, in common with many Native Americans, have a conception of Nature and God as one; they revered the sky, earth, sun, and the subterranean "Great Ones", recognizing a pantheon of supernatural spirits usually living under the world or in the sky and at the four cardinal points. These forces of nature, both cosmic – sun, moon, earth, wind and fire – and animal spirits such as water-serpents and spiders, or the dead, all exhibit anthropomorphic characteristics. These are friendly or hostile, requiring respect and veneration by secret societies and fraternities such as Kachina or Kiva societies, who dress in impersonation of the supernaturals in ritual dances to bring rain or good health. Such rituals usually take place in specially constructed semi-subterranean chambers known as Kivas, or on village plazas. These ceremonies were arranged in calendrical cycles. The Kachina cult impersonations of supernaturals, mostly cosmic forms, are associated with the Western Pueblos of the Hopi and Zuni, whilst animal impersonations are more common amongst the Rio Grande Pueblos – a reflection of their traditional reliance on hunting as well as farming. These animal-propitiating ceremonies share the stage with Church Saints' Days where Catholicism has been more influential. Other societies were the Clowns (Koshares) who, in addition to fun-making, were sacred. Membership in these esoteric societies was by initiation at adolescence. The Spanish introduced the official position of "Governor" at each Pueblo as part of their colonial administration, a political appointment sometimes passed on by descent, which continues today.

In 1885 the Indians of the 19 Pueblos of New Mexico, including Zuni, were reported as numbering 7,762, a drop from about 10,000 after the Pueblo Revolt of 1690. By 1946 this number had risen to about 14,500. In 1970 the total population, including Zuni and Hopi, was reported as 30,971.

KERES or KERESAN

An independent linguistic family of Pueblo Indians of the Rio Grande, New Mexico, comprising the Pueblos of Cochiti, San Felipe, Santa Ana, Santo Domingo, Zia, constituting the eastern or Queres group, and Acoma and Laguna, who form the western or Kawaiko group. They trace their origins to the underworld whence they had emerged from an opening, and took up residence on the Rio de los Frijoles. They later abandoned the Rio and moved south, where Coronado visited them in 1540. They took part in the Pueblo Revolt of 1680, and were subsequently missionized, at least superficially, although they have remained a conservative people until the present time. In 1930 they numbered 4,134 in total, and in 1945 6,036.

COCHITI PUEBLO This Pueblo village is in Sandoval County on the west bank of the Rio Grande and is the northernmost of the Keresan-speaking villages. This small Pueblo witnessed all of the Spanish expeditions into New Mexico and took an active part in the Revolt of 1680. A large number a people no longer live on the reserve, although they return for the feast of San Buenaventura in July, when the Corn Dance is performed. They are noted

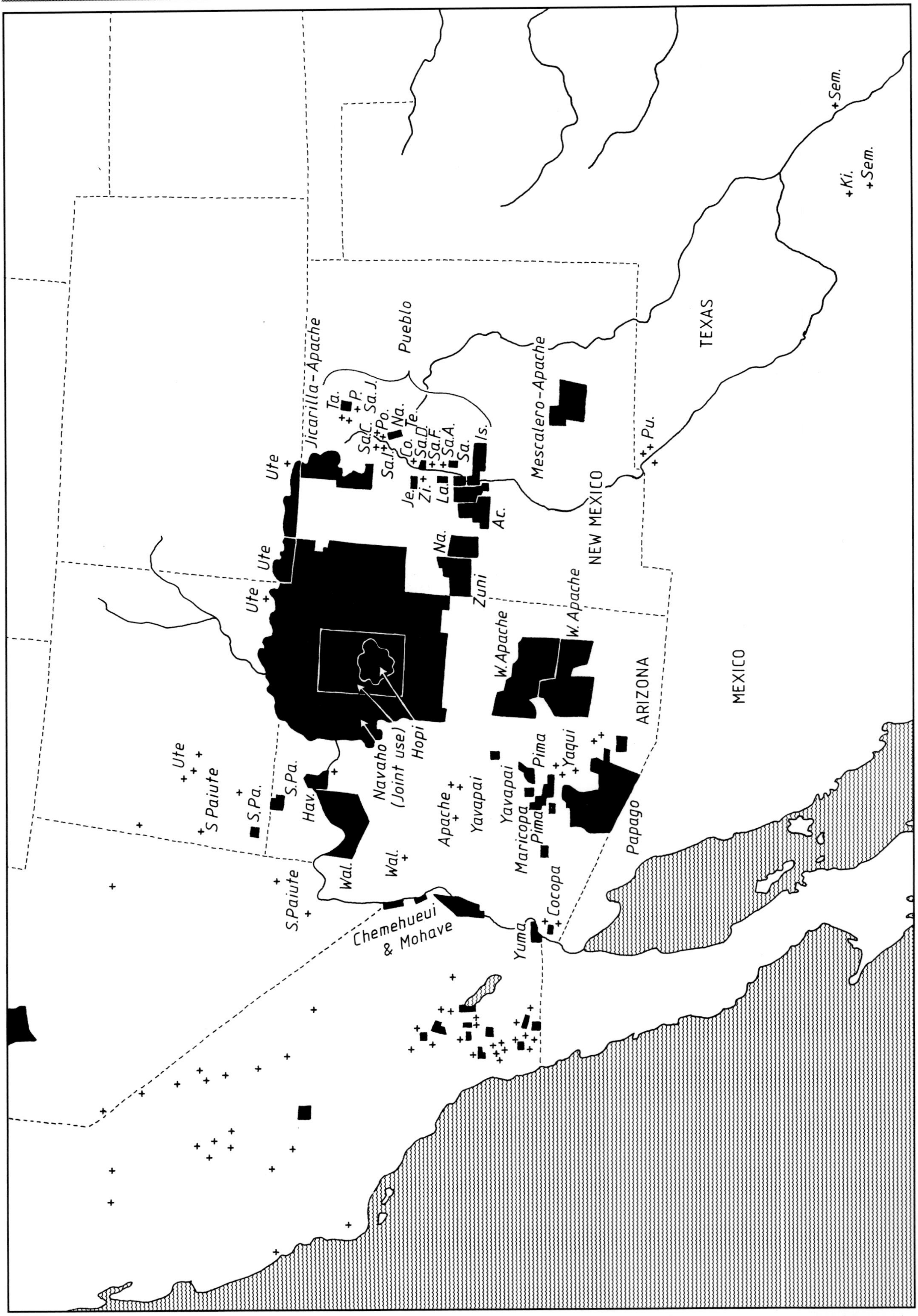
TEXAS
NEW MEXICO
ARIZONA
MEXICO
Pueblo
Jicarilla-Apache
Mescalero-Apache
Ta.
P.
Sa.J.
Sa.C.
Po.
Na.
Sa.I.
Co.
Te.
Sa.D.
Sa.F.
Sa.A.
Sa.
Is.
Je.
Zi.
La.
Ac.
Na.
Zuni
Ute
Ute
Ute
Ute
W. Apache
W. Apache
Navaho
(Joint use)
Hopi
S.Pa.
S.Pa.
S Paiute
S.Paiute
Hav.
Wal.
Wal.
Apache
Yavapai
Yavapai
Pima
Yaqui
Maricopa
Pima
Papago
Cocopa
Yuma
Chemehueui
& Mohave
Pu.
Sem.
Ki.
Sem.

for creamy-yellow pottery with black designs and also for making cottonwood drums. They numbered 465 in 1956, and 799 in 1968, but only 376 in the Cochiti Pueblo itself.

SAN FELIPE PUEBLO The central village of the five eastern Keresan Pueblos on the west bank of the Rio Grande ten miles north of Bernalillo. They hold a special relationship to Cochiti and were perhaps once a single people, but there were villages in this area when Coronado passed through in 1540. Although few arts and crafts are now pursued, the secret societies function and ceremonials are still held. In 1956 they numbered 941, and in 1970 1,811, a large number living away from the Pueblo.

SANTA ANA PUEBLO A small but conservative Keresan-speaking Pueblo on the Jemez River eight miles from its junction with the Rio Grande, plus the village of Ranchitos. In 1956 they numbered 353, and in 1977 498. Pottery making was revived in 1973.

SANTO DOMINGO PUEBLO A Pueblo located on the east bank of the Rio Grande seven miles south of Cochiti, and the largest of the eastern Keresan Pueblos. Their ancestors probably occupied the Pajarito Plateau at one time. They have managed to maintain a core of basic Indian religion and beliefs; a cacique selects tribal, civil and religious officers for their dramatic ceremonials held in August. Pottery of varying quality has been made, and large amounts of jewellery. In 1956 they numbered 1,455, and 2,511 by 1970.

ZIA PUEBLO (SIA) A Keresan-speaking Pueblo on the Jemez River about 30 miles north of Albuquerque, New Mexico. Presumably they are descendants of an older, larger Pueblo, `Old Zia'. Although they have been nominally Catholic since 1692, a few societies are extant. They have gained a livelihood in the recent past from grazing sheep and goats on surrounding lands. They are noted for making fine pottery with white or yellow-buff backgrounds and varied naturalistic designs of deer, birds and leaves. In 1956 the Pueblo had a population of 327, rising to 555 in 1972.

ACOMA PUEBLO The westernmost Keresan Pueblo and one of the most impressive, situated on a mesa almost 400 feet high some 50 miles west of Albuquerque, New Mexico – sometimes known as the "Sky City". A number of satellite communities have been established over the years at Acomita, Santa Maria de Acoma and McCarthys. Traditionally they share a basic culture with other Puebloan groups, particularly the Keresans, in social structure, religious and political systems. The Acoma Pueblo vies with Hopi for the title of the oldest continuously inhabited village in the U.S.A. Acoma pottery has hard, thin walls with white to yellow-brown slip and is decorated with geometric motifs and parrot-like birds in overall designs. In 1956 the tribe numbered 1,888, rising to 2,512 in 1966.

LAGUNA PUEBLO One of two western Keresan-speaking Pueblos and the largest of all Rio Grande Pueblos, who now occupy six villages at Paguate, Mesita, Encinal, Paraje, Seama and Casa Blanca, plus the Laguna Pueblo 40 miles west of Albuquerque, New Mexico. The Pueblo was established in 1699. Their close location to Spanish and Anglo communities during the 19th century resulted in some acculturation, but religious and secular officers (that of "governor" imposed by the Spanish in 1620) still follow the Keresan pattern despite internal factionalism. They numbered 3,475 in 1956 and about 5,800 in 1975, of whom some 2,500 live away from the reserve in towns and cities throughout New Mexico and the United States. Rich uranium deposits have been found on Laguna lands.

SOUTHWESTERN TRIBES, 20th CENTURY

Key to abbreviations:

Hav	= Havasupai	Po	=	Pojoaque	
Na	= Navaho	Sa	=	Sandia	
Wal	= Walapai	SaA	=	Santa Ana	
Pueblos:		SaC	=	Santa Clara	
Ac	= Acoma	SaD	=	Santo Domingo	
Co	= Cochiti	SaF	=	San Felipe	
Is	= Isleta	SaI	=	San Ildefonso	
Je	= Jemez	SaJ	=	San Juan	
La	= Laguna	Ta	=	Taos	
Na	= Nambe	Te	=	Tesuque	
P	= Picuris	Zi	=	Zia	

TANOAN

A major linguistic grouping of Pueblo Indians apparently distantly related to the Kiowa language to form the Kiowa-Tanoan stock. An even more distant relationship has been suggested with Uto-Aztecan and Zuni. The Tanoan family is divided into Tiwa, Tewa and Towa as follows: Northern Tiwa (Taos and Picuris); Southern Tiwa (Sandia, Isleta, Tigua and Piro); Northern Tewa (Nambe, San Ildefonso, San Juan, Santa Clara, Tesuque, Pojoaque); Southern Tewa (Tano, now Hopi-Tewa); and Towa (Jemez and Pecos). In 1937 the Tiwa numbered 2,122; the Tewa 1,708, excluding Tano; and the Towa 648 (Jemez). The Pecos merged with the Jemez and the Piro, who with refugees from

Isleta moved to the El Paso area after the Pueblo Revolt of 1680 and joined with others to form three hispanicized Pueblos, of which only Tigua is still extant. Some authorities have placed the old Manso of Mesilla valley in southern New Mexico into the Tanoan family, but more probably they were Athabascans and long hispanicized.

TAOS PUEBLO The northernmost Pueblo located ten miles east of the Rio Grande and 70 miles north of Santa Fé, New Mexico. Their language is Northern Tiwa, a dialect of Tanoan. Traditionally one of the more prosperous communities, surrounded by fertile agricultural land, this impressive multi-storey Pueblo is about 600 years old. It is geographically close to the Plains Indians, from whom the tribe adopted elements of material culture – and recently the Peyote religion, which has caused much factionalism. In 1956 they numbered 1,137, and 1,463 in 1970. In 1847 there was a revolt against the Americans which resulted in the destruction of the old mission at the Pueblo.

PICURIS PUEBLO A small Tiwa-speaking Pueblo town 20 miles south of Taos, New Mexico, numbering 158 in 1956 and 172 in 1972. Good micaceous pottery has been traditionally made at Picuris. The Pueblo has been in the same vicinity as the present buildings since at least 1591. They are closely related to Taos.

SANDIA PUEBLO One of the three Southern Tiwa dialects of the Tanoan family is spoken by the people of this Pueblo located 14 miles north of Albuquerque, New Mexico. Although the site is a post-contact village there are a number of prehistoric sites in the vicinity. The Pueblo was burned by the Spanish after the Pueblo Revolt of 1680. Religion remains a means of retaining their identity in a location close to Anglo-Hispanic communities. They have retained the Corn, Eagle, Buffalo and other dances, plus their cacique and governor, a position instigated originally by the Spanish. Their population was 74 in 1900, and 265 in 1971.

ISLETA PUEBLO The second of the three Southern Tiwa dialects of the Tanoan family is spoken by the inhabitants of this Pueblo situated on the west bank of the Rio Grande 13 miles south of Albuquerque, with an outlying settlement, Chiskal. The Spanish destruction of religious chambers, masks and paraphernalia led to the Revolt of 1680, which drove out the Spanish settlers for several years. Farming has remained important until recent years, and they have produced a commercial style of pottery. In 1956 they numbered 1,759, and in 1974 2,710.

TIGUA PUEBLO A hispanicized Pueblo located south of El Paso, Texas, near the Mexican border at Ysleta del Sur, a village founded for refugees from the Tiwa villages (particularly from Isleta) following the Revolt of 1680. They have about 350 descendants including another community, Tortugas, in Las Cruces, New Mexico.

PIRO Another hispanicized group of Tiwa refugees from the upper Rio Grande who established villages just inside Chihuahua, Mexico, at Senecú and Socorro. Both groups have long ceased to exist as separate Indian communities, and probably merged with various other Indian remnants, Manso and Tigua, in the area. The ancient Piro probably numbered 6,000 before being exposed to Apache attacks in the early 17th century.

NAMBE PUEBLO A small Pueblo, and now largely hispanicized, 15 miles north of Santa Fé, New Mexico, formerly speaking a Northern Tewa dialect of the Tanoan family. The present village is probably post-contact but there are ruins of an earlier Pueblo close by. The population was 184 in 1956, and 356 in 1972. Women from this village once produced a good grade of micaceous cooking ware and wove belts of cotton.

SAN ILDEFONSO PUEBLO This Pueblo is situated on the Rio Grande 20 miles northeast of Santa Fé. They speak a Northern Tewa language of the Tanoan family, and claim descent from people who moved out of the valleys and cliff homes on the Pajarito plateau. This Pueblo was involved in the Revolt of 1680, and was one of the last to accept Catholicism in the 19th century. Since then they have often been factionalised. Maria and Julian Martinez, both famous potters, came from this Pueblo, producing a dull black paint on polished black ware. The Buffalo-deer Dance and the Plains orientated Comanche Dance are still performed on San Ildefonso's Day. They numbered 138 in 1900, and 413 in 1973.

SAN JUAN PUEBLO The largest and northernmost of the six Tewa-speaking Tanoan Pueblos, located five miles north of Española on the east bank of the Rio Grande. It was in this vicinity that the Spanish founded their first provincial capital in New Mexico before moving to Santa Fé in 1610. They suffered considerable persecution by the Spanish civil and ecclesiastical authorities until they arose in revolt in 1680. San Juan pottery is polished red and black ware with some incised and carved types. In 1956 they numbered 934, and 1,721 in 1977.

SANTA CLARA PUEBLO A Northern Tewa-speaking Pueblo town of the Tanoan family located on the west bank of the Rio Grande in Rio Arriba County. They traditionally lay claim to the cliff dwellings of Puye. The present day Pueblo occupies almost the same site as viewed by the 16th century Spanish. They are often regarded as one of the wealthiest Pueblos, with a resource-rich land base. The Santa Clara Indians make polished black and red pottery with modern variations. Their population was 669 in 1956 and 1,204 in 1974.

TESUQUE PUEBLO The southernmost of the six extant Rio Grande Tewa Pueblos, just ten miles north of Santa Fé, New Mexico. Despite their close proximity to Spanish and late Anglo-American influences they have retained many ceremonials which have ancient quality. Tesuque women formerly made grey-cream pottery. In 1956 they numbered 185, and 281 in 1973.

POJOAQUE PUEBLO A small Pueblo, now largely hispanicized, located 16 miles north of Santa Fé, New Mexico. Although archaeological investigations on the Pojoaque Reservation suggest a large population with extensive farming in protohistoric times, by 1712 they numbered only 79. In 1970 there were 46 residents. Their former language was a Northern Tewa dialect of the Tanoan family. Religious ceremonials are no longer held.

HANO & POLACCA Two small Puebloan villages on the easternmost mesa of the Hopi Reservation in northeastern Arizona, descendants of a Rio Grande Tewa people known as *Tano*. They emigrated to the Hopi First Mesa in about A.D.1700 and have largely intermarried with their hosts over the years. Hano is now known as *Tewa-Village* and still looks like an old Hopi style Pueblo; they are a fully integrated Hopi people sharing their culture and ceremony. In 1972 there were 218 at Tewa-Village and 782 at Polacca, a more recent settlement.

JEMEZ PUEBLO The people of this Pueblo speak Towa, a dialect of Tanoan. The Pueblo is located on the Jemez River 30 miles northwest of Bernalillo, in an area where several villages were reported by the 16th century Spanish explorers. They were participants in the Pueblo Revolt of 1680 and suffered the traumas and punitive expeditions that followed. Although native arts have weakened over the years, their political and religious organizations still function under a cacique and his staff, who appoint the officers of societies, the moieties and clans. Like most Pueblo cultures of the 20th century, theirs has been a mixture of native, Spanish and Anglo influences. In 1956 they numbered 1,137, and 1,939 in 1970.

PECOS PUEBLO Formerly a Pueblo located about 18 miles southwest of Santa Fé, New Mexico. In the early 18th century they were subjected to attacks by Comanches and Apaches, and further weakened by smallpox epidemics which reduced their population from about 1,000 to 189 in 1792; in 1838 the last of them, just 17 in number, finally moved to Jemez Pueblo. They spoke a Towa dialect of Tanoan.

ZUNI PUEBLO A tribe, a Pueblo and a linguistic family whose villages and present reservation are in McKinley County in the western part of New Mexico. Hawikah, one of their towns, was first seen by the Spanish in 1539; and the following year Francisco Vàsquez de Coronado captured the town during his expedition to find the "Seven Cities of Cibola", perhaps the seven villages of the Zuni. The Spanish were only partly successful in their attempts to missionize the Zuni, and in 1820 further attempts were abandoned, partly due to increasing raids by Navajo and Apache. The heritage of Spanish contact was the adoption of some crops, horses, burros, and a system of secular government. Three summer farming villages – Ojo Caliente, Pescado and Nutria – were established around Halona, the remaining central Zuni Pueblo, and Tekapo, a fourth village, was established about 1912.

The population has grown from about 1,500 at the beginning of the American period in 1848 to 3,439 in 1956, and 7,306 in 1970. The Zunis have been noted for their pottery, chalky-white slip with large brown-black designs, often large rosettes, deer, frogs and dragonflies, but the art has diminished in recent times. The Zunis produce a great deal of turquoise and silver jewellery. Their social and religious organizations were composed of four interlocking systems of clans, the Kiva-Kachina society, the curing societies and the priesthoods. The Shalako, a splendid portrayal of religious pageantry, is held in late November.

HOPI PUEBLOS The Hopis speak a language of the Shoshonean family, now called Uto-Aztecan; and have lived in the same area of northeastern Arizona for over 1,600 years. Their present Pueblos are located on three mesas west of Kearns Canyon, the main administrative centre for the Hopis. On the First Mesa are the Tewa towns of Hano and Polacca, who joined the Hopi in the 18th century, Shitchumovi (Sichómovi), and Walpi; on the Second Mesa are Shipanlovi, Mishongnovi and Shungopavy (Shungópovi); and on the Third are Bakabi, Hotevilla, Oraibi (the oldest inhabited village in the U.S.A.), Upper and Lower Moenkopi, and Kyakotsmovi (Kiakóchomovi) or New Oraibi. Hopi country is the southern escarpment of Black Mesa, a highland area about 60 miles wide; and their present reservation, a square within the Navajo Reservation, is a continuing source of disagreement between the tribes concerning ownership.

The basis of Hopi life in a harsh, dry environment has been the cultivation of corn, beans, squash and melons, to which they added European fruits. Spanish activity in the area was never extensive, although they were known from 1540 to the invaders, who made various attempts to establish missions; but all churches were destroyed in 1680 and further attempts abandoned after 1780, the Hopis being left in isolation to follow the indigenous culture lost to so many tribes. Their American experience began in 1848 when the U.S.A. obtained the Southwest from Mexico. This initiated a series of factional splits, particularly at Oraibi, between conservative and liberal forces. Hopi social structure contains a number of interlocking social and religious organizations, the latter exhibited in an annual cycle of masked Kachina or unmasked ceremonials in Kivas or on plazas. The Hopis' pottery is characteristically mottled yellow-orange with asymmetric curvilinear black designs. They are the only major basketmaking Pueblo tribe in recent times, mainly using flat coiled technique with abstract birds, whirlwinds and Kachina designs. In 1970 7,236 Hopis were reported, a large increase in recent years. The Hopis are renowned for their Snake Dance held to bring rain for crops.

NORTHWEST COAST

Language family and tribe	*Meaning*/origin of tribal name, where known	**Language family** and tribe	*Meaning*/origin of tribal name, where known
Tlingit	*"people"*	Tillamook	place name
Haida	*"people"*	Siletz	-
Tsimshian	*"inside of the Skeena River"*	**Chimakum:**	
Wakashan:		Chimakum	-
Nootka	*"circling about"*	Quileute	village name
Makah	*"cape people"*	Hoh	-
Ozette	-	**Chinookian:**	
Kwakiutl	*"beach on the north side of the river"*	Chinook	village name
Salishan:		Clatsop	*"dried salmon"*
Bella Coola	English name	Cathlamet	village name
Comox	*"house"*	Skilloot	-
Seechelt	place name	Cathlapotle	*"people of the Lewis River"*
Puntlatch	-	Multnomah	*"those towards the water"*
Squamish	*"people"*	Watlala	-
Nanaimo	*"bunch people"*	Clowwewalla	-
Cowichan	*"warm the back"*	Clackamas	-
Songish	name of local group	Chilluckittequaw	-
Stalo	*"upriver"*	Wishram	-
Semiahmoo	-	Wasco	*"cup (or small bowl) of horn"*
Nooksack	*"place of broken roots"*	**Coos**	-
Lummi	-	**Yakonan**	*"people of bay (or river)"*
Samish	-	**Kalapuyan**	-
Upper & Lower Skagit	-	**Takelma**	*"those dwelling along the river"*
Swinomish	place name	**West Coast Athabascans:**	
Snohomish	place name	Coquille	*"people who live on the stream"*
Snoqualmie & Skykomish	-	Umpqua	*"grass people"*
Suquamish	place name	Tututni	-
Duwamish	place name	Chastacosta	-
Twana	*"a portage"*	Taltushtuntude	-
Clallam	*"strong people"*	Dakubetede	-
Muckleshoot	-	Chetco	*"close to the mouth of the stream"*
Puyallup	place name	Tolowa	-
Nisqually	place name	Hupa	place name
Squaxon	-	Chilula & Whilkut	*"people of the Bald Hills"*
Cowlitz	*"people of the river"*	Mattole	place name
Upper Chehalis, Lower Chehalis	village name (or *"sand"*)	Nongatl	-
Queets	-	Sinkone	-
Quinault	village name	Lassik	chief's name
		Wailaki	*"north language"*
		Kato	*"lake"*

The Indians of the Northwest Coast occupied a relatively narrow strip between the interior mountains and the Pacific Ocean, being relatively isolated from the rest of the continent. It was and is a heavily forested land, mild and wet, covering the area of the Pacific coast from Yakutat Bay, Alaska, to northern California. The mountainous coast is deeply indented by sounds and fjords encompassing many islands. The coastal peoples were set apart by their industries, arts, beliefs and customs from interior tribes. Notwithstanding the uniformity of their culture, closer study discloses many independent tribal characteristics and divergent development.

The peaks of Northwest Coast culture were formed by the Haida-Tsimshian-Tlingit of the far north and the Kwakiutl of British Columbia with the Nootka of Vancouver Island, both characterized by a highly developed red cedar wood carving art of totem poles, house fronts, masks and other ceremonial items, distinctive totemic painting and superb basketry. In the southern area through present Washington and Oregon this distinctive culture weakened, although the Coast Salish produced some carving and fine basketry, and the Chinook held occasional Potlatch ceremonies like those of the north. The Potlatch was basically a wealth display and distribution festival held by prominent men, which became exaggerated due to the activities of the Hudson's Bay Company who infiltrated the coastal areas during the early 19th century.

The art of carving and erecting large memorial columns (totem poles) is probably not ancient on the north Pacific coast. Early explorers do not seem to have remarked on them, so we may speculate that it was the acquisition of metal tools from traders which gave the Indians the means of developing techniques to express their wood carving art in its most exaggerated forms. Before these totems had reached their imposing proportions carving seems to have been used for grave posts, house fronts, masks, and stone objects of considerable antiquity. We can also speculate that carved poles were fashionable, with ambitious chiefs announcing their wealth and identity by the commemoration of ancestors whose spirits could be beautifully represented in animal, bird or mythological forms – e.g. Eagle, Raven, Owl, Bear, Beaver, Wolf, Frog, Shark, Whale, Halibut and Salmon – on impressive poles.

Along the coast of Washington and Oregon the zoomorphic carving and painting of the northern tribes diminished. The Chinooks were great traders of dried salmon, dentalium shells, and sometimes slaves from California in return for material culture from the northern tribes. Houses were more crudely made and for single families. In southern Oregon and northwestern California head deformation, as practised in the north on young children, was unknown; redwood replaced cedar as the primary wood; and deer skin robes and skirts replaced the woven cedar bark robes of the north. Shamanistic secret societies, such as the Cannibal Dancers of the Kwakiutl, were unknown in the south. The southern tribes made fine basketry or imported it from the Californian tribes further south.

Northwest Coast culture collapsed largely through the conversion of the tribes to Christianity, the influence of the Gold Rush in Alaska and the Yukon, and the invasion of the Oregon and Washington River valleys by settlers during the 19th century. Their population was drastically reduced in some areas, and the whole culture fell into decay, while governmental pressure forced potlatching to be abandoned amongst the Kwakiutl, with the confiscation of many ceremonial objects.

TLINGIT The Tlingit were a group of Northwest Coast Indians along the south coast of Alaska between the present northern part of British Columbia and the ocean. Although primarily a fisher folk they were favourably situated to become highly successful traders, acting as middlemen between the interior Alaskan tribes and white traders. They were fine woodcarvers, rank high as basket makers, and are renowned for their "Chilkat blankets" of mountain goat wool and cedar bark. The basic political group was the village, divided into two phratries, Wolf and Raven totems. They lived in large community houses like most west coast people, and were dependent on the sea for food. Recent linguistic studies suggest that the Tlingit are related to the Athabascan and Haida, together termed "Na-Dene".

The principal Tlingit subtribes were, north to south (but excluding the so-called "Inland Tlingit", an Athabascan people), as follows: Yakutat (Yakutat Bay), Gohaho (mouth of Alsek River), Chilkat (Lynn Canal), Huna (Goss Sound), Auk (Stephens Passage), Taku (Taku River and Inlet), Hutsnuwn or Killisnoo (Admiralty Island), Sitka (Baranof and Chichagof Islands), Sumdum (Port Houghton), Kuiu (Kuiu Island), Kake (Kupreanof Island), Stikine (Stikine River), Henya (west coast Prince of Wales Island), Hehl (on Behm Canal), Sanya (Cape Fox), and Tongass (Portland Canal).

They numbered some 10,000 in 1740; 6,763 in 1880; and 3,895 in 1950, but had recovered to about 7,000 by 1970. Their main locations today are Yakutat, Klukwan, Juneau, Mount Edgecumbe, Sitka, Kake, Wrangell, Ketchikan and Klawak.

HAIDA These people were the original inhabitants of the Queen Charlotte Islands, Canada, and part of Prince of Wales Island in Alaska. They had the most

(continued on p. 168)

(see page 167 for captions to figures 19 to 41)

19

20

21

22

23

24

25

26

27

28

29

30

31

32

33

34

35

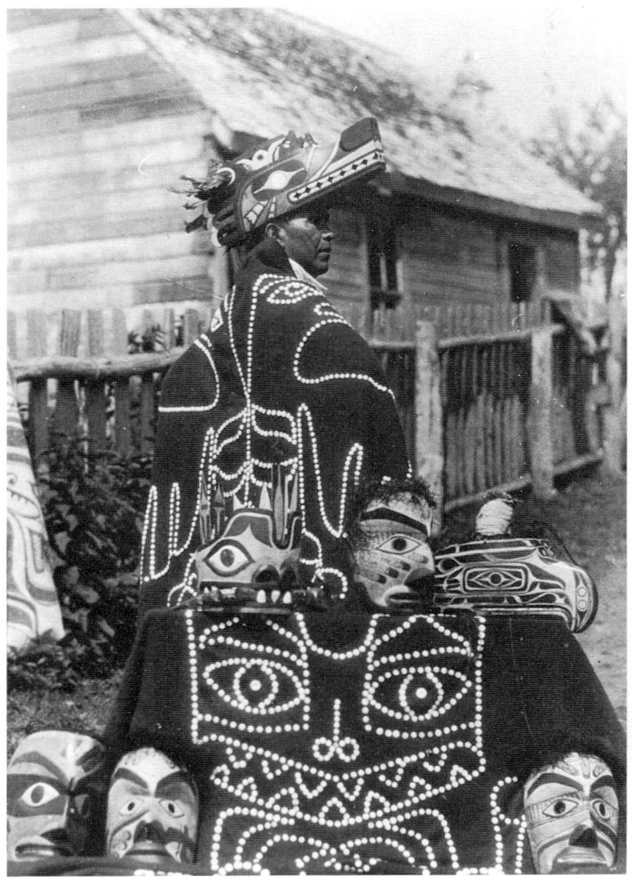

36

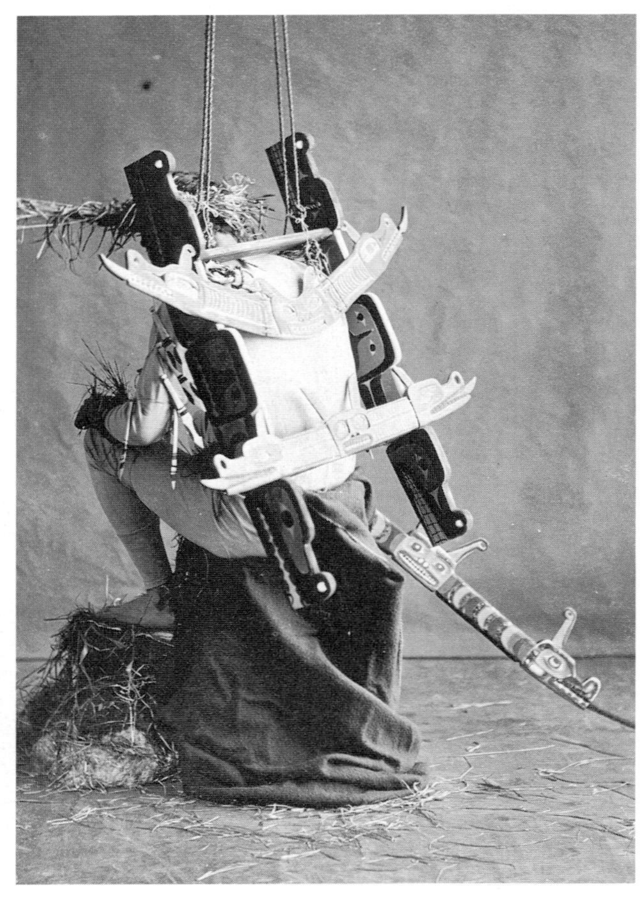

37

38

39

40

41

PHOTOGRAPH CAPTIONS

Pages 159 to 166

(19) Pretty Young Man (Blackfoot name Ma-Ko-Yo-Mah-Kan ?) photographed c.1910 with a tipi painted with Elk designs. See commentary to colour plate GI for discussion of motifs. (Harry Pollard Collection, Provincial Museum & Archives of Alberta)

(20) Deer Ham, an Iowa Indian, photographed in Washington D.C. c.1870, probably by A.Zeno Shindler.

(21) Pawnee Tribal Council, Oklahoma, 1939. For the photograph they wear a mixture of materials of their own and other tribes; the settlement of over 50 tribes in Indian Territory led to the merging of many styles of dress and art from several different areas.

(22) Shavings, a Crow chief photographed in Montana in 1880. He wears a typically resplendent Crow shirt, panel leggings, and moccasins with animal tails hanging from the heels – probably signifying warrior status. (Montana Historical Society, courtesy Ian West)

(23) Pretty Eagle, a member of the Crow delegation to Washington D.C., 1880, photographed by C.M.Bell. His hairstyle and shirt decoration are typical of his people. (Pitt Rivers Museum, Oxford)

(24) Group of Crow warriors in Montana, 1887, including Pretty Eagle (front left) and Plenty Coups (front, third left). The photograph shows a wide variety of clothing, including capotes and a buffalo coat. (Montana Historical Society, courtesy Ian West)

(25) Bannock mother and child, 1910, showing typical Basin/Plateau cradleboard. Although the mother is largely obscured, note dress decorated with cowrie shells, and beaded and brass-studded belt. (Courtesy Richard Hook)

(26) The Kiowa warrior Tape-Day-Ah ("Standing Sweat House"), c.1875; he was reputed to have been a member of every Kiowa war party between 1870 and 1874. Note the southern style of tailored, fringed shirt, decorated fur turban, and bowcase and quiver made from mountain lion skin. (Soule Photos, courtesy Ian West)

(27) Ute warrior wearing shirt and leggings typically decorated with broad beadwork strips and many bells; note characteristic beaded strips around ankles of leggings, and broad bandolier strap over left shoulder. (Courtesy Richard Hook)

(28) Navajo mother and child, Window Rock Reservation, Arizona. Note the characteristic cradleboard with sunshade; and the mother's typical Navajo costume and silver jewellery. (Courtesy Ian West)

(29) Three Yuma women, c.1900; decorative facial tattooing is visible centre and right. (Courtesy Ian West)

(30) Jicarilla Apache group, 1904. Although the costumes of this tribe were Plains-influenced there were many purely Jicarilla traits: e.g. the women's broad, tacked leather belts, woollen hair ties, and the style of dress yoke shown at right.

(31) Pueblo Buffalo Dance, 1990; the men wear buffalo headdresses and kilts decorated with the serpent symbol, the unmarried girls sun-disc bustles. (Courtesy Ray Whiteway-Roberts)

(32) Pueblo Corn or Tablita Dance, 1990; enacting long-surviving rituals, the dancers carry evergreen branches and the men gourd rattles, while the women wear elaborate tablita headdresses. (Courtesy Ray Whiteway-Roberts)

(33) Thompson River Salish woman; of particular interest is the beaded and studded headband worn over the burden strap which supports her basket. (Courtesy Ian West)

(34) Tsimshian memorial ("totem") poles, c.1910, at Kitwanga on the Skeena River, British Columbia – home of the Gitskan tribe, an important Northwest Coast people who excelled at wood carving.

(35) Makah man, Neah Bay, Washington State, c.1910, wearing wolf mask and blanket decorated with buttons in totemic designs. Displayed in the foreground are other carved and painted masks typical of Northwest Coast tribes. The Makahs still inhabit the northwest tip of the Olympic Peninsula, Washington.

(36) Kwakiutl war dancer with hoisting frame, photographed in 1904 by Charles H.Carpenter. Charlas Nowell, who posed for this picture, was one of the last Kwakiutl dancers to be suspended by his pierced skin. The artifacts are now in the Field Museum, Chicago. (Cambridge University Museum of Archaeology & Anthropology)

(37) Bella Coola Indians, brought to Germany by the Norwegian ship's captain Adrian Jacobsen, performing a dance from the winter ceremonial cycle in Berlin, c.1885. (Cambridge University Museum of Archaeology & Anthropology)

(38) The Vancouver Island Nootka weavers Annie Williams and Emma George, photographed at the 1904 St.Louis Exposition where they demonstratd their expertise in basketry.

(39) A selection of modern dancers photographed at the famous annual Crow Fair, Montana; this group includes modern traditional costumes, a fancy dancer, a young girl shawl dancer, and in the background a "jingle" dress dancer – see commentary, colour plate P. (Courtesy Ray Whiteway-Roberts)

(40) Crow lady wearing traditional cloth dress of two contrasting colours, with imitation elk teeth, while participating in the parade at the 1987 Crow Fair, Montana. (Photograph Jonathan Smith)

(41) Stoney (Assiniboine) Indians from Morley, Alberta, photographed at Banff Indian Days, c.1950; second right is George Maclean (Walking Buffalo), who toured the world for the Moral Rearmament movement. (Photograph Nicolas Morant)

(continued from p.158)

spectacular culture of the Northwest Coast tribes. They lived in large community houses of heavy hand-hewn timber, decorated inside and out with carved and painted figures of massive proportions. Their totem poles were the finest and tallest; and they are equally noted for their carvings in black argillite, a soft stone found in the Queen Charlotte Islands. Spanish explorers were probably the first Europeans to reach the islands in the 18th century, followed by numerous traders and finally by the establishment of a Hudson's Bay post at Masset. Originally the Haida numbered 8,000, but by 1895 had been reduced by smallpox, consumption, and liquor to only 593 in two remaining villages, Masset and Skidegate, Queen Charlotte Islands, with about the same number (known as Kaigani) at Kassan and Hydaburg on Prince of Wales Island, Alaska. In 1960 there were 391 in Alaska and in 1970 1,367 in Canada, mostly at Masset and Skidegate. The Haida language formed a separate speech family, but a distant connection with the Athabascan and Tlingit has been suggested as a stock called "Na-Dene".

TSIMSHIAN This family is a combination of three closely related tribes of northern British Columbia: the *Tsimshian proper* on the lower Skeena River and Annette Island, Alaska; the *Niska* on the Nass River and neighbouring coast; and the *Gitskan* or *Kitkskan* on the upper Skeena River. They may be distantly related to the Chinook and hence to the speculative stock, the Penutians. As fishermen they took salmon, codfish and halibut and at the same time hunted seals, sea lions and whales. The interior bands hunted bear and deer and collected berries. Villages consisted of large wooden houses of cedar planks, arranged in a row facing the sea or river; in front canoes and boats were placed on runways or on the beach. Four phratries – Raven, Wolf, Eagle and Grizzly Bear – were distributed amongst the three tribes. They were part of the strong art and carving tradition of the coastal people, and shared with the Tlingit and Haida the northern centre of this remarkable culture.

The coastal Tsimshian were probably visited by Spanish, English and American navigators, and later the Hudson's Bay Company established posts in the early 19th century. Their country was also overrun by miners during the Klondike Gold Rush. The Tsimshians have reserves in their old territory at Metlakanhtla (Alaska), Port Simpson, Metlakatla, Kitselas (Tsimshian proper), Gitlakdamix, Canyon, Greenville, Kincolith (Niska), Kispaiox, Hazelton, Kitancool, Kitwanga and Kitsegukla (Kitksan). In 1780 the whole group numbered 5,500; in 1908 there were 1,840 Tsimshian, in 1906 814 Niska, and in 1902 1,120 Kitksan. In 1970 the same groups numbered 2,863, 2,364 and 2,503 respectively in British Columbia; and in 1950 there were 797 at Metlakanhtla, Alaska.

WAKASHAN

A language family of Indian tribes formed by two separate groups: the Nootka of the west coast of Vancouver Island, and the Kwakiutl of the northern coast of the Island and large parts of the adjacent coastal mainland of British Columbia. The Wakashan group has been suggested to be remotely connected to the Salishan and Chimakum into a larger linguistic grouping known as "Mosan".

NOOTKA or **NUTKA** An important native people of the western shore of Vancouver Island, from Cape Cook on the north to beyond Barkley Sound. Although they were known to European maritime explorers from 1592 on, Captain Cook gave the first accounts of these Indians in 1778. The settlement of Victoria and the missionary work of the Roman Catholic Church gradually modified the traditional Nootka culture. The Nootka were both a sea and river people; they fished for halibut and cod, gathered kelp, and hunted whales, seals and sea otters. They also gathered berries, fruits and roots. They were an integral part of Northwest Coast culture; while their carving and painting were generally not as elaborate as those of the northern tribes, they excelled in basketry. They are believed to have numbered 6,000 in 1780; slowly reduced to 2,159 by 1907; but recovered to 3,409 by 1970, and 4,720 in 1984. They have continued to occupy 18 small village reserves on Vancouver Island, the main ones at Kyoquot, Ahousaht, Clayoquot, Hesquiaht, Nootka, Ohiet, Port Alberni (Sheshaht) and Ucluelet.

MAKAH A branch of the Nootka located on Cape Flattery, Washington. Spanish, British and American trading vessels contacted the Makahs towards the end of the 18th century. Their economy was based upon the sea, and they hunted whales and seals. The Makah were involved with a treaty in 1855 which established their reservation on the tip of Cape Flattery within their former homeland. They probably numbered 2,000 in 1805, but declined due

TRIBES OF THE NORTHWEST COAST, c.1780-1850

The geographical nature of this area dictates that it be illustrated in two vertical halves, northern on the left, southern on the right. Linguistic and cultural boundaries are necessarily approximate; these sketch maps are intended only as a general guides to distribution. Underlined names indicate small linguistic families distinct from larger groupings indicated by the shading key.

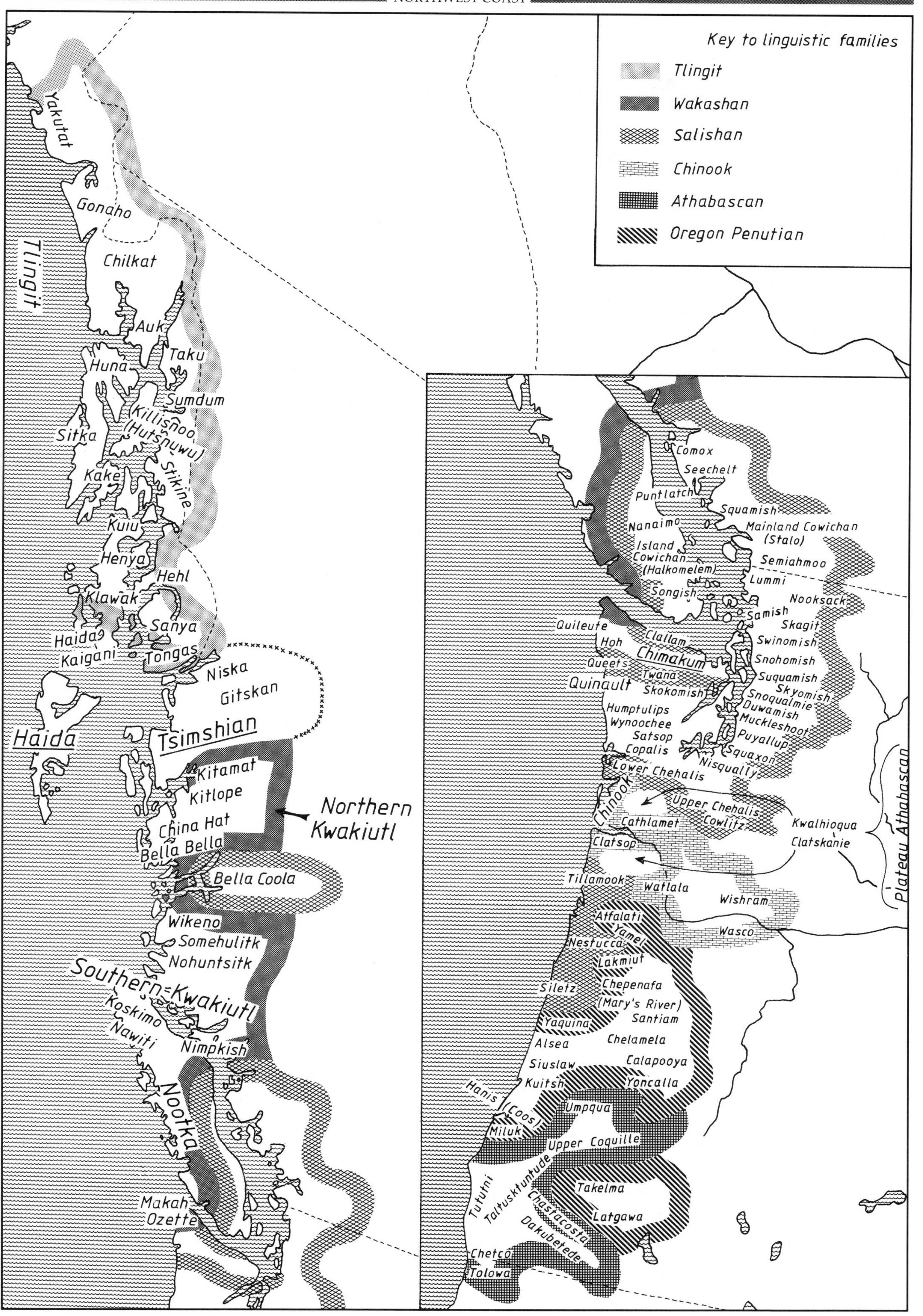
Key to linguistic families
Tlingit
Wakashan
Salishan
Chinook
Athabascan
Oregon Penutian
Yakutat
Gonaho
Chilkat
Tlingit
Auk
Taku
Huna
Sumdum
Killisnoo (Hutsnuwu)
Sitka
Kake
Stikine
Kuiu
Henya
Hehl
Klawak
Sanya
Haida
Kaigani
Tongas
Niska
Gitskan
Haida
Tsimshian
Kitamat
Kitlope
Northern Kwakiutl
China Hat
Bella Bella
Bella Coola
Wikeno
Somehulitk
Nohuntsitk
Southern Kwakiutl
Koskimo
Nawiti
Nimpkish
Nootka
Makah
Ozette
Comox
Seechelt
Puntlatch
Squamish
Nanaimo
Mainland Cowichan (Stalo)
Island Cowichan (Halkomelem)
Semiahmoo
Lummi
Songish
Nooksack
Samish
Skagit
Quileute
Clallam
Swinomish
Hoh
Chimakum
Snohomish
Queets
Twana
Suquamish
Quinault
Skokomish
Skyomish
Snoqualmie
Duwamish
Humptulips
Muckleshoot
Wynoochee
Satsop
Puyallup
Copalis
Squaxon
Nisqually
Lower Chehalis
Chinook
Upper Chehalis
Cathlamet
Cowlitz
Kwalhioqua
Clatskanie
Plateau Athabascan
Clatsop
Tillamook
Watlala
Wishram
Atfalati
Yamel
Nestucca
Wasco
Lakmiut
Chepenafa
Siletz
(Mary's River)
Yaquina
Santiam
Alsea
Chelamela
Siuslaw
Calapooya
Kuitsh
Yoncalla
Hanis
(Coos)
Umpqua
Miluk
Upper Coquille
Tututni
Taltuskuntude
Takelma
Chastacosta
Latgawa
Dakubetede
Chetco
Tolowa

to smallpox to about 500 in 1850; they numbered 435 in 1905, and 919 in 1985. The modern Makah have a museum, and hold native language classes; "Makah Days", annual gatherings for salmon barbecues, canoe races and Indian dances, are held each August.

OZETTE Probably a subgroup of the Makah, occupying a village at the mouth of the Ozette River, Washington, south of their kinsmen. Sites around the village seem to have been occupied for several hundred years. In 1872 some 200 people lived there and at a small reservation established at Cape Alava in 1893. However, in the years since then the Ozettes have drifted away to other reservations, and by 1937 only one person remained. Recent archaeological excavations at the old village site have revealed the importance of whaling and other maritime pursuits. Various fine examples of material culture have also been recovered from the site.

KWAKIUTL The second division of the Waskashan family, who occupied the whole coast of British Columbia, except for the Bella Coola, from Douglas Channel to Cape Mudge. They effectively formed a number of village tribulets which can be arranged dialectically as follows: starting in the north, the *Haisla* division were the Kitamaat on Douglas Channel and the Kitlope on Gardner Canal; the *Heitsuk* division were the Bella Bella on Dean Channel and Milbanke Sound, China Hat or Haihais on Mussel Inlet, Somehulitk and Nohuntsitk on Wikeno Lake, and Wikeno or Oweekano on Rivers Inlet; the Southern Kwakiutl were the *Kwakiutl* proper of Smith Inlet, Kingcombe Inlet, Gilford and Turnour Islands, Knight Inlet on the mainland, Hope Island (Nawiti), Alert Bay (Nimpkish), Klaskino Inlet (Koskimo), Quatsino and Fort Rupert (Kwawkewltk) on Vancouver Island.

They were known to English and American coastal marine explorers during the late 18th century, but it was the establishment of the Hudson's Bay posts in the mid-19th century which profoundly modified Kwakiutl culture, particularly amongst the northern groups. In 1780 the northern branches numbered 2,700 and the southern tribes 4,500; but by 1906 they numbered only 852 and 1,257 respectively. In 1970 the Haisla and Heitsuk numbered 848 (Kitamaat) and 1,245 (Bella Bella, Oweekano etc.) respectively; and the Southern Kwakiutl 2,715 (Alert Bay, Fort Rupert etc.). They are particularly noted for their superb woodcarving and painting art, for totem poles, house gable fronts and columns, mortuary posts and masks. They also participated in the wealth display and distribution complex known as the Potlatch ceremony, which was accompanied by feasting, hospitality, and the bestowal of gifts in honour of important headmen, but which also led to family feuding. In recent years Alert Bay has seen a revival of Kwakiutl art and culture.

SALISHAN

The coastal division of the Salishan family occupied the coastal area of British Columbia from the Strait of Georgia south through the Puget Sound area of Washington State, along the coast as far south as the Siletz River, Oregon, except around the mouth of the Columbia River (occupied by the Chinook). There was one detached northern branch, the Bella Coola of Burke Channel, British Columbia. The Coast Salish practised the wealth and gift distribution ceremony known as Potlatch, particularly in the north where they were influenced by the Kwakiutl culture. They generally lived in cedar plank houses facing rivers or the sea; and, where in contact with the Kwakiutl, have a tradition of complex wood-carving art which weakened to the south into simpler art forms. Two dominant subsistence and material resources among the Salish were salmon and red cedar, and they excelled in basketry and textiles. They were essentially a river and bay people in a heavy forest area with a moist, mild climate.

BELLA COOLA A Salish people living on the north and south Bentinck Arm of the Burke Channel, British Columbia, surrounded by northern branches of the Kwakiutl and sharing with them the typical Northwest Coast cultural traits. They have continued to occupy the village of Bella Coola, and were reported to number 311 in 1902, 334 in 1949, and 597 in 1970. They are not to be confused with the Bella Bella, a local Kwakiutl branch.

COMOX A Salish people at the northern end of the Strait of Georgia on both sides of Discovery Passage and centering on Cape Mudge. Culturally they were heavily influenced by the Southern Kwakiutl. Their descendants are still connected with their former villages at Klahoose, Homalco and Sliammon on the Islands and British Columbia mainland, plus the Courtenay band on Vancouver Island. The tribe were reported to number 828 in 1970. The Seechelt and Pentlatch were very closely related to the Comox, and they are now called collectively "Northern Coast Salish".

SEECHELT A Salish people on the southern arms of Jervis Inlet, British Columbia, numbering 236 in 1902 at their village. The same village was returned at 471 in 1970.

PUNTLATCH or **PENTLATCH** A small group on

Vancouver Island near Qualicum, sometimes classed as Comox or Cowichan. There were 42 people under the name Qualicum in 1970.

SQUAMISH A Salish people at the northern end of Howe Sound and Burrard Inlet, mainland British Columbia, originally in many villages but restricted to six villages in 1909. In 1970, 1,143 were reported from Burrard Inlet and 1,089 from Squamish.

NANAIMO & SNONOWAS Two small Salish groups who belong with the Cowichan group with whom they are often considered as one, living on Vancouver Island near present Nanaimo. In 1907 the Nanaimo were given as 161; in 1970, 525. The Snonowas are now listed under the name Nanoose, given as 46 in 1907 and 86 in 1970.

COWICHAN, ISLAND, or HALKOMELEM The Cowichan occupied the southeastern coast of Vancouver Island between the Comox to the north and the Songish to the south, including a number of islands. The term is also sometimes extended to the mainland Stalo or Fraser River Cowichan. Their native life was disrupted in the early 19th century when Hudson's Bay traders came to the area, leading to the foundation of Victoria. There are six major Vancouver Cowichan groups – Chemainus, Cowichan, Halalt, Lyacksun, Malahat and Penelakut – and their descendants numbered 2,184 in 1970.

SONGISH or **SANETCH** or **STRAITS** A group of Salish people on the southern coast of Vancouver Island including adjacent islands. The founding of Victoria in the 1840s brought to an end independent native life. A number of Songish reserves still exist – Tseycum, Beeche Bay, Panquachin, Tsawout, Esquimalt, Tsartlip, Sooke and Songhees – in their old territory, and they numbered about 1,130 in 1970. The Songish, Cowichan, Squamish, Semiahmoo, Lummi, Clallam and Nooksack are now sometimes collectively termed "Central Coast Salish".

STALO or **STAWLO** or **FRASER RIVER COWICHAN (MAINLAND HALKOMELEM)** The mainland Cowichan occupied the lower Fraser River valley from Yale to where Vancouver City now stands. In 1809 Simon Fraser passed through their country, and their subsequent history was linked to the Hudson's Bay Company. By the end of the 19th century approximately 30 small villages became Indian reserves and continue to the present day; the largest are Katzie, Chehalis, Cheam, Skwah, Soowahlie, Tzeachten, Seabird Island and Musqueam. In 1970 they numbered 2,650 or so, and a total of 6,031 when including their Vancouver Island relatives (Island Halkomelem).

SEMIAHMOO A small, apparently separate Salish band at the boundary between British Columbia and Washington State, where 24 were reported at a small reserve bearing their name in 1970. They were probably closely related to the Songish and Lummi.

NOOKSACK Small Salish tribe on the Nooksack River, northern Washington State. After the Point Elliott Treaty of 1855 they were to move to the Lummi Reservation, but few did; they have maintained themselves around Everson, Nooksack and Deming, Whatcom County, on fragmented allotments of 3,000 acres, with a population of 505 in 1970.

LUMMI Related to the Songish of southern Vancouver Island, they lived around Lummi and Bellingham Bays, Washington. Signatories to the Point Elliott Treaty, 1855, they relinquished a large area and moved to the Lummi Reservation, where they are still reported to number over 600. A small group, Swallah, on the San Juan Islands were probably very closely related to or part of the Lummi.

SAMISH A small group inhabiting various islands south of Bellingham Bay, Guemes Island area, Washington. A few joined the Lummi, but most maintained themselves off reservations around the Anacortes district. One modern group, known as San Juan Indians, are probably descendants at least in part of this tribe. They have some 500 descendants. They are related to the various groups now called "Central Coast Salish".

UPPER & LOWER SKAGIT A group of Indians on the Skagit River in Whatcom and Skagit Counties, Washington. Influenced by the Hudson's Bay traders from 1827 onward, they were included in the Point Elliott Treaty of 1855. The Lower Skagit of Whidbey Island, Puget Sound and the mouth of the Skagit River have a few descendants in the Bow and Edison area but have largely disappeared. The Upper Skagit descendants live in numerous scattered public domain allotments in Skagit County near Sedro Woolley, and other places and number 300 or so. Another modern group in the area, the Sauk-Suiattle, are also descendants of the Skagit River Indians and number about 260; a few members of this group joined the Lummi and Swinomish. The small Kikiallus band of Mount Vernon and the Stillaguamish at Arlington and on the river of the same name can be included in this group.

SWINOMISH This tribe occupied the mouth of the Skagit River and Whidbey Island, being closely related to the Skagit. They were a sea oriented people, living on fish and other marine life. After the Point Elliott Treaty of 1855 most Swinomish people moved to the Swinomish Reservation. In 1985 the "Swinomish" numbered 624, but a number of Skagit, Samish, Snohomish, Suquamish and Duwamish have joined the Swinomish over the years. The early population of these Salish coastal tribes cannot be accurately estimated as serious epidemics reduced many in the early years of the 19th century. The Swinomish, Skagit, Stillaguamish and Snohomish are now collectively called "Northern Lushootseed".

SNOHOMISH This tribe lived at the mouth of the Snohomish River near Marysville and southern Whidbey Island, Washington. They were among the various tribes trading at Fort Nisqually from 1833 on. After the Point Elliott Treaty of 1855 they moved to the Snohomish Reservation, now called the Tulalip Reservation, where they formed a large part of the multi-tribal grouping there, numbering 1,099 in 1985 under the name "Tulalip".

SNOQUALMIE & SKYKOMISH Two closely related groups of the Snoqualmie and Tolt River basins. As signatories to the Point Elliott Treaty some were included with the Snohomish at Tulalip, but most remained off reservations in their old territory; they number about 500 descendants today.

SUQUAMISH Occupied an area between Hood Canal and Puget Sound. Suquamish subsistence depended upon the harvest of fish, shellfish, roots and berries. The Port Madison Reservation was established for the Suquamish after the Point Elliott Treaty of 1855; somed 200 tribal members still lived on the reservation in 1985, but many more live in surrounding areas.

DUWAMISH Lived on the east side of Puget Sound near the site of the present city of Seattle; Chief Seattle was a member of this tribal group. A few members of this group moved to Port Madison, Muckleshoot and other reservations, and a number survived in public domain. They have about 300 descendants, although many have merged with the Suquamish. The Sammamish were a Duwamish subtribe.

TWANA or **SKOKOMISH** A large body of Salish on the Hood Canal, Washington. They had wide trading ties, and a complex ceremonial and social structure including the use of slaves. They signed the Point-No-Point Treaty of 1855 and moved to the Skokomish Reservation at the head of Hood Canal. Their population was 507 in 1984; this also included the last of the Chimakum people and a few Clallam.

CLALLAM The most numerous, warlike and powerful tribe of the Coast Salish people in present Washington State. Their population before the epidemics of the early 19th century was between 2,000 and 3,000. As traders they linked with their relatives on Vancouver Island and Twana, and even with Indians beyond the Cascade Mountains. Their location was present Clallam County below the Strait of Juan de Fuca between Port Discovery Canal and the Hoh River. They were under the influence of the Hudson's Bay Company until the Point-No-Point Treaty of 1855, when a few moved to the Skokomish Reservation, but most remained in Clallam County. Three reservation communities have been purchased over the years – Lower Elwha near Port Angeles, Jamestown and Port Gamble – with a total enrolled population of 1,200, but they have more descendants in the greater west coast area.

MUCKLESHOOT A Salish tribe on the White River a few miles inland from Puget Sound near present Kent and Auburn, where a reservation is located which bears their name. They were probably an amalgam of several minor groups grouped together after the Medecine Creek Treaty of 1854. The Muckleshoots numbered 194 in 1937, and 425 in 1984.

PUYALLUP A Salish group related to the Nisqually who lived at the mouth of the Puyallup River and the southern end of Vashon Island near the present city of Tacoma, Washington. After the Medicine Creek Treaty the Puyallup were principally located on the reservation which bears their name a few miles from Tacoma. They were reported to number 322 in 1937, and 1,286 in 1984; but they have had other groups join them over the years – Cowlitz, Nisqually, Squaxon etc. – and by no means all live on the reservation.

NISQUALLY A large body of Indians in 40 villages on the Nisqually River, Thurston County, Washington, near present Olympia. They were included in the Medicine Creek Treaty of 1854 and most located at the Nisqually Reservation. The Steilacooms were a band probably related to the Nisqually or Puyallup, but never moved to either Nisqually or Puyallup reservations. The population of the Nisqually Reservation was 62 in 1937, and 182 in 1984 – a vast decline from their original population. The non-reservation Steilacooms claim several hundred descendants, mostly around the Tacoma area. The Nisqually, Squaxon, Steilacoom, Puyallup, Suquamish and Snoqualmie are now collectively called "Southern Lushootseed".

SQUAXON or **SQUAXIN** Related to the Nisqually, the Squaxon and closely connected Sahehwamish lived on the innermost inlets of Puget Sound between Hood Canal, Budd Inlet and Nisqually River. After the Medicine Creek Treaty a small reservation was established on Squaxon Island; but only a portion of these groups have lived there, given at 29 in 1949 and 302 in 1984. The so-called Shaker Church, a mixture of Christian and native beliefs, had its origins amongst the Squaxons and still has a following. Together with their linguistic relatives in the "Lushootseed" group and Twana they form the Southern Coast group of the Salishan family.

COWLITZ Several Salish groups on the middle and lower course of the Cowlitz River, Lewis County, Washington. They appear to have mixed with the Kwalhioquas and branches of the neighbouring Chehalis groups, but probably numbered in excess of 1,000 in the early 19th century. They also had contacts with the interior tribes, particularly the Klickitats. Much reduced by epidemics in the 1850s, the Cowlitz merged with the Chehalis, Chinook and Klickitats, with descendants now counted at Puyallup, Quinault and Yakima Reservations, although a number have maintained themselves in their ancestral homelands. They number 300 or so, but many others claim their descent.

UPPER CHEHALIS or **KWAIAILK** A number of Salish groups on the Upper Chehalis River, Washington, around present Oakville and Tenino in Grays Harbor, Lewis and Thurston Counties. A combined group of Kwaiailks, Lower Chehalis and Chinook have occupied a small reservation at Oakville since 1864, with a population given as 382 in 1984.

LOWER CHEHALIS An important Salish group on the lower course of the Chehalis River, Washington, at the entrance to Grays Harbor. A few combined with the Upper Chehalis on the Chehalis Reservation; others merged with the Satsops, Humptulips and others on Quinault Reservation; a few may have incorporated with the Chinook on the Shoalwater Indian Reservation, Tokeland; but they do not exist today as an independent tribe. In the same general area are other minor tribes who seem to have been either divisions of the Chehalis groups or Quinault, but have been given independent status by various writers – the *Copalis* north of Grays Harbor; the *Humptulips* and *Whiskah* on the north shore of Grays Harbor; the *Wynoochee* on the Wynoochee River; and the *Satsop* on the Satsop River – though these no longer exist as separate peoples. The Chehalis groups with the Cowlitz and Quinault form the Southwestern Coast Salish.

QUEETS or **QUAITSO** A Salish people on the Queets River, Jefferson County, Washington. They moved to the Quinault Reservation following the Quinault River Treaty in 1855, and are no longer reported separately from the other Indians on that reservation, although they probably have some 100 descendants.

QUINAULT The largest and most important Salish people on the Pacific shore of Washington State, living mainly in the valley of the Quinault River and near Taholah, the site of their principal village. They remained fairly isolated until the Quinault River Treaty of 1855 and the establishment of their reservation. They probably numbered over 1,000 at the time of Lewis and Clark's arrival in 1805. Diminished to a reported 196 in 1907 (probably a partial count), they numbered 1,293 in 1945 and 1,623 in 1984, with accessions from other tribes over the years. The tribe still holds canoe races, salmon barbecues and dances at Taholah at various times each year.

TILLAMOOK The Coast Salish domain was broken by the Chinook on the lower Columbia River, but they reappear south of that great river in present northwestern Oregon. The Tillamook and closely related bands, *Nehalem* and *Nestucca*, lived around the Nehalem and Salmon Rivers in present Tillamook County, Oregon, and were the largest Coast Salish group south of the Columbia. Lewis and Clark estimated the group at 2,200 in 1805, but they had declined to 200 by 1900. A few Nestuccas appear to have been reported amongst the Grand Ronde Indians. The census of 1970 gave 139 for the whole group.

SILETZ The southernmost Salish tribe on the river which bears their name, in Lincoln County, Oregon. Remnants were included on the Siletz Reservation as part of the much larger "Confederated Siletz" and are no longer reported separately.

CHIMAKUM

A small linguistic family formed by the grouping of three tribes: the Chimakum proper, Quileute and Hoh. The Chimakum proper may have been a Quileute subgroup who lived around the southern shores of the Strait of Juan de Fuca, Washington State. They signed the Point-No-Point Treaty of 1855, but numbered less than 100 at that time. They joined the Twana at the Skokomish Reservation, where only three remained separate in 1890, and a few others merged with the Clallam.

QUILEUTE or **QUILLAYUTE** The principal tribe of the Chimakum family, at the mouth of the Quillayute River in Washington. The Pacific Ocean was their main source of subsistence, and they were proficient seal and whale hunters. They traded with American and Russian seafarers from 1792 on. Refusing to move to the large Quinault Reservation, they were assigned their own reservation at La Push, Washington, in 1889. They numbered 383 in 1985.

HOH This tribe may have been originally a division of the Quileute people on the Hoh River, Washington. A small reservation was established for the tribe in 1893 at the mouth of the Hoh River, where a few people have lived ever since, with a population of 91 in 1985.

CHINOOKIAN

A small family of Indians inhabiting the lower Columbia River in Washington and Oregon as far up that river as The Dalles. The Chinooks were primarily a bay and river people, dependent on fishing (salmon) as well as game. They lacked the developed woodcarving art of the west coast tribes of British Columbia and northern Washington, although often classified in the same cultural area. They have been classified as the Upper and Lower Chinook, referring to their location on the Columbia River. They were first noticed generally by Lewis and Clark in 1805, and afterwards were greatly diminished in numbers by diseases brought by white traders. The majority of the individual tribes forming this family became extinct as separate identities before 1900; but a few hundred have fused with other tribes on the Warm Springs, Yakima, Chehalis, Quinault and Grande Ronde Reservations in Washington and Oregon; the largest single element by 1950 were the Wasco at Warm Springs, Oregon. A few have maintained themselves off reservations.

Before their decline in population the Chinookian tribes became the greatest traders on the Columbia River, a great water highway stretching from the area of the coastal tribes into the immense interior. Their geographical position at the mouth of that river up to The Dalles gave them the opportunity to become middlemen in the development of trade relationships between the coast and the interior. The development of the Chinook Jargon, an Indian trade language based originally on Chinook words but later incorporating an increasing vocabulary of European origin, bears witness to the importance of the Chinook tribes in pre-1840 trade relations. Contacts and trade took place largely on the Columbia River at Celilo or The Dalles, when material culture from the northern edge of the Plains mingled with and was exchanged for material from as far as Alaska. From there the Nez Perce were the main outlet to the northern Plains via their associations with the Crow and to a lesser extent the Flathead.

THE "LOWER CHINOOK":

CHINOOK PROPER or **LOWER CHINOOK** A Chinookian tribe inhabiting the mouth of the Columbia River, giving their name to include tribes to the interior of similar language under the name Chinookian stock. Their territory extended to Shoalwater Bay in the north, and the tribe numbered 800 in 1800. They gained considerable fame through their trading with British and American companies, and the Chinook Jargon, a trade language of the northwest originally based on the Chinook language, existed until 1900. From Lewis and Clark, Nov. 1805: "This Chinook nation is about 400 souls, inhabit the country on the small river which runs into bay below us and on the Ponds to the North West of us, live principally on fish and roots, they are well armed with fusees and sometimes kill Elk, Deer, and fowl."

Their few remnants mixed with the Chehalis or remained in public domain, and had almost disappeared as a separate people by 1945 when 120 "Upper Chinook" remained on the Quinault Reservation, Washington; although of mixed origin they included descendants of the Chinook proper. A few more have been associated with Shoalwater Bay and Chehalis reserves, and some have never been on reservations. In 1970 609 "Chinook" were reported, excluding Wasco, apparently accounting for the whole family. Two smaller groups, the Wahkiakum and Willapa Indians, probably belong to this group.

CLATSOP An important coastal Chinookian tribe of the Cape Adams area, Clatsop County, Oregon. From Lewis and Clark, who estimated their population at 300, in 1806: "The Clatsaps, Chinnooks, Killamucks etc. are very loquacious and inquisitive; they possess good memories and have repeated to us the name and capacities of the vessels etc. of the many traders and others who have visited the mouth of the river (Columbia); they are generally low in stature, proportionably small, reather lighter complected and much more illy formed than the Indians on the Missouri and those of our frontier; they were generally cheerfull but never gay. With us their conversation generally turns upon subjects of trade, smoking, eating and women. In common with other savage nations they make their women perform every species of domestic drudgery; their women are also compelled to gather roots and assist them in taking fish which articles form much the greater part of their subsistence; notwithstanding the servile manner in which they treat their women they pay much more respect to their judgement and opinions in many respects than most Indian nations."

With the mixed remnants of the other ruined neighbouring tribes they moved to the Grande Ronde Reservation, Oregon. In 1910 they were reported as numbering 26 persons. The Clatsop are not now separately entered amongst the general Indian population of the Grande Ronde Agency, the population of which was about 700 in 1955, although most have lost their identity as Indians. In 1956 the Reservation and Indian people of Grande Ronde were no longer recognised, and the Reservation as such was terminated. However, they have recently been reactivated and have filed land claims against the U.S. Government.

CATHLAMET A tribe forming a dialect division of the Chinookian stock near the mouth of the Columbia River in Oregon and Washington, to a point up that river near the present city of Rainier on the south bank. In 1806 Lewis and Clark estimated them at 300: "The Killaniucks, Clatsops, Chinooks, Cathlahmahs and Wac-ki-a-cums resemble each other as well as in their person and dress as in their habits and manners their complexion is not remarkable, being the usual copper brown of the most tribes in North America." About 50 or 60 were reported in 1849. A remnant of the Cathlamet may have moved to the Yakima Reservation with the Wishram, or to the Quinault Reservation with the mixed Chinook-Chehalis, but as distinct groups they no longer exist.

THE "UPPER CHINOOK":

SKILLOOT A small Chinookian tribe at the junction of the Cowlitz River and the Columbia River in Washington State; their principal subdivision was the Cooniac. Dialectically they were said to be close to the Clackamas. At the time of Lewis and Clark (1806) they were living on both sides of the Columbia opposite the mouth of the Cowlitz and perhaps numbered 1,000, although often reported considerably higher. In 1850 they numbered about 200, and continued to diminish until they lost separate identity; a few may have accompanied relatives to reservations but they are not returned as separate. A number of non-reservation descendants claim their ancestry.

CATHLAPOTLE A tribe or group of Chinookian Indians on the Lewis River in Clarke County, Washington, about 150 miles from the mouth of the Columbia River. A few may have lasted until reservation days but they are now extinct as an independent group.

MULTNOMAH or **WAPPATO** A Chinookian tribe of the Sauvie Islands at the mouth of the Willamette River, Oregon. Remnants joined with related groups and lost separate identity; they were closely related to the Clackamas. Several bands can be attributed to this tribe.

WATLALA (CASCADE INDIANS) A Chinookian tribe at the Cascades of the Columbia River and the Willamette River in Oregon. Remnants joined the Wishram and Wasco and lost separate identity. Related to the Clackamas.

CLOWWEWALLA A Chinookian tribe of the Clackamas dialect, formerly living in Oregon on the Willamette River, a tributary of the Columbia. They have for many years been extinct as a separate people. The Cushooks, Chahcowahs, Willamette-Tumwater and others where divisions of this tribe. The last of this people were said to be on the Grande Ronde Reservation.

CLACKAMAS A tribal division of the Chinook stock giving their name to a dialect group. They apparently moved to the Grande Ronde Reservation, Oregon, and remained separate until recently, being reported under this name in 1945-89. This may, however, be a combination of various Chinook remnants.

CHILLUCKITTEQUAW A Chinookian tribe of Hood River on the south side of the Columbia, and on the north side of the Columbia in Klickitat and Skamania Counties, Washington, along the White Salmon River. A few remained separate as late as 1895, mixed with a few Tenino (Waiam) at Celilo Falls and Warm Springs.

WISHRAM Probably the largest of the Chinookian tribes, living farther up the Columbia River than any of their kinsmen. They lived principally in the present Klickitat County, Washington, and were closely related to the Wasco on the opposite (south) side of the Columbia. In 1800 they numbered about 1,000. In 1855 the remnants of the Wishram with a few other Chinook families where assigned to the Yakima Reservation. About 250 were incorporated with other tribes on that reservation, and the 274 "Upper Chinook" reported in 1910 may have been these Indians. They are not reported separately from the other Indians of the Yakima nation today, although a marked strain of their blood may survive.

WASCO A Chinookian tribe of the inland branch, their closest relatives being the Wishram, living near the present The Dalles in Wasco County, Oregon, on the Columbia River. They were joined by the remnants of the Watlala and others and removed to the Warm Springs Reservation, where a portion still remain as a separate people. In 1910 they returned a number of 242 persons; 227 in 1937; and 260 in 1945. They are the only independently reported Chinook group today. The Dalles Indians, Wasco and Wascopan were divisions of this tribe.

COOS or ***KUSAN*** A small language family formed by two tribes in a narrow strip of the Oregon coast between the Coos and Coquille Rivers. The northern division were the *Hanis* or Coos proper, who lived around the bay and river which bears their name; the southern division were the *Miluk* on the Lower Coquille near its estuary. The combined population of the two groups has been estimated at 2,000 in 1780. They obtained subsistence from the sea, gathered clams, and from the land obtained camas roots and berries; they also had dugout canoes. Some members of both groups were ultimately placed at the Siletz Reservation on the southern "Yachats" portion of the agency. In 1910, 93 were reported under the name Kus; in 1937, only 55; and 228 "Kusa" in 1945. Today two reorganized groups, descendants of several tribes but including Coos people who lost ancient lands around Coos Bay and on the old Yachats (Alsea) Reservation, Siletz agency, are petitioning the U.S. Government for financial recompense. The total number of people with Coos ancestry is about 300, considerably mixed with other tribal groups and whites. The Coos have been linked linguistically to the Siuslaw and Lower Umpqua and with the other Alseans as the Oregon branch of the Penutian stock.

YAKONAN or ***ALSEAN*** A group of Indians on the Oregon coast forming a small linguistic family. From north to south these were the *Yaquina* on the Yaquina River near present Newport, Oregon; *Alsea* on the Alsea River; *Siuslaw* on the Siuslaw River near Florence, Oregon; and *Kuitsh* or *Lower Umpqua* on the lower Umpqua River near Reedsport, Oregon. The Siuslaw were the most linguistically divergent. They were coastal and riverine people, wealthy in dentalia shells; they hunted seals, and held slaves. Because of their coastal location they came into contact with white trading vessels in the late 18th century; in 1780 they perhaps numbered 5,000. The usual reductions followed, hastened by the activities of the Hudson's Bay Company, the influx of white miners, and the Rogue Wars of the 1850s. Remnants were moved to the Siletz Reservation on that part known as the Southern or Alsea Reservation. In 1910 a census reported only 29 Alsea, 19 Yaquina and seven Siuslaw; and in 1930, nine Kuitsh. They are all now part of the so-called "Confederated Siletz Indians of Oregon".

KALAPUYAN A group of eight tribes speaking three languages, formerly inhabiting the valley of the Willamette River, Oregon. They were probably related to the Takelma and more distantly to the Coos and Yakonan into a stock called Oregon-Penutian. The *Atfalati* lived around Forest Grove, northwestern Oregon, and the *Yamel* above present McMinnville, Oregon, these forming one dialect division of the family. Continuing south were the *Luckiamute* on the river which bears their name; the *Santiam* around present Lebanon, Oregon; *Chepenafa* or *Mary's River* near Corvallis, Oregon; *Chelamela* on Long Tom Creek west of Eugene, Oregon; and *Calapooya* near Eugene, Oregon, all of whom spoke the central Kalapuyan dialect. Finally, above Oakland, Oregon, were the *Yoncalla*, who spoke the southern dialect.

The Kalapuyans as a whole suffered greatly from the smallpox epidemics of 1782 and 1783. After coming into contact with white fur traders they ultimately abandoned their native economy, and were unable to resist white encroachments into the Willamette valley. Following treaties in 1851 and 1855 the remnants of all the Kalapuyan tribes moved to the Grand Ronde Reservation, Oregon, where their descendants are now organized as the "Confederated Tribes of the Grand Ronde Community of Oregon", although the reservation lost its recognition by the Bureau of Indian Affairs in 1956. The census of 1910 reported 44 Atfalati, five Calapooya, eight Luckiamute, 24 Chepenafa, nine Santiam, five Yamel and 11 Yoncalla; in 1930 the whole group was reported at 45 persons. At least 24 different tribes were included in the Siletz-Grand Ronde complex, making it almost impossible for any one small group to preserve its identity. In 1955, 700 people were reported descended from the original tribes of Grand Ronde Reservation shortly before termination, when the Federal Government suspended its responsibility for any services and removed restrictions on their property. These services were partly restored in the 1970s.

NORTHWESTERN TRIBES, 20th CENTURY

Key to abbreviations:

Ca	=	Carrier	No	=	Nootka
Chil	=	Chilcotin	Ok	=	Okanagan
C.Sal	=	Coast Salish	Se	=	Seechelt
Cx	=	Comox	Sh	=	Shuswap
Gi	=	Gitskan	Sk	=	Sekani
Hal	=	Haisla	Sl	=	Slavey
He	=	Heitsuk	So	=	Songish
Hl	=	Halkomelem	Sq	=	Squamish
Idt	=	Inland Tlingit	St	=	Stalo (Cowichan)
Ka	=	Kaska	Tg	=	Tagish
Kut	=	Kutenai	Th	=	Thompson
Kw	=	Kwakiutl	Tl	=	Tlingit
Li	=	Lillooet	Ts	=	Tsimshian

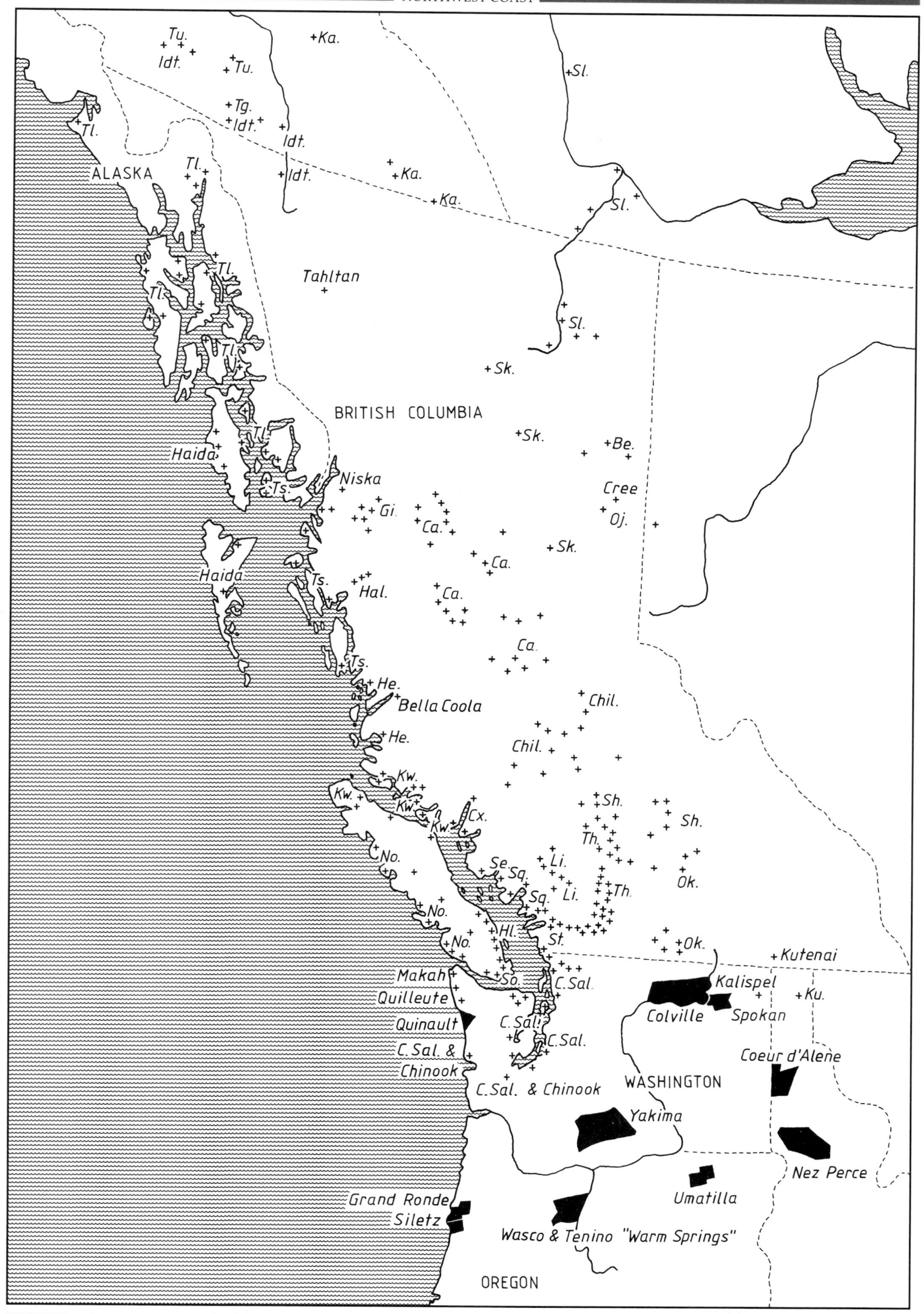
ALASKA
BRITISH COLUMBIA
WASHINGTON
OREGON
Tu.
Idt.
Ka.
Sl.
Tg.
Tl.
Tahltan
Sk.
Be.
Haida
Niska
Cree
Oj.
Gi.
Ca.
Ts.
Hal.
He.
Bella Coola
Chil.
Kw.
Cx.
Sh.
Th.
No.
Se.
Sq.
Li.
Ok.
Hl.
St.
Kutenai
Makah
So.
C.Sal.
Kalispel
Ku.
Quilleute
Colville
Spokan
Quinault
C.Sal. &
Chinook
Coeur d'Alene
C.Sal. & Chinook
Yakima
Nez Perce
Grand Ronde
Siletz
Umatilla
Wasco & Tenino "Warm Springs"

TAKELMA A small linguistic family comprising two separate tribes: the *Takelma* on the east side of the Klamath and Coast Mountains in the middle Rogue River area around Grants Pass, Oregon; and the *Latgawa* in the upper Rogue River area around Jacksonville, Oregon. Their houses were small brush shelters in summer and constructed of split sugar pine boards for winter. They decorated their costumes with dentalia shells, and tattooing was common. They also had cultural traits from California, and they prized obsidian and Shasta basket hats. They resented intrusions on their lands and were involved in the so-called "Rogue Wars" of the 1850s, after which the U.S. Army decided to send the remaining Takelma and Latgawa to the Grand Ronde Reservation many miles to the north, where they arrived both overland and by sea. The Takelma probably numbered in excess of 1,000 in 1800 but later figures incorporate them in a mixed group known as "Upper Rogue River". Two groups of "Rogue River" were returned from Grand Ronde in 1937, numbering 58 and 46.

WEST COAST ATHABASCANS

We do not know for certain when the Athabascan tribes arrived in the area, but it was probably along the coast, perhaps 1,000 years ago. They seem to have left three small tribes in their wake: the *Nicola* amongst the Thompson River Indians of British Columbia; the *Kwalhioqua* in the Willapa Hills of southwestern Washington; and the *Clatskanie*, probably Kwalhioqua who crossed into Oregon before 1775 and occupied an area about 70 miles inland from the mouth of the Columbia River. These tribes are extinct. However, the large territory held by the major communities of the Pacific coast Athabascans extended not quite continuously from the Umpqua River in Oregon to the head of the Eel River in California. The Californian tribes numbered about 7,000 and the Oregon groups about the same in aboriginal times.

COQUILLE Sometimes known as Upper Coquille, or Mishikhwutmetumme; an Athabascan tribe on the east fork of the Coquille River, Oregon, west of Myrtle Creek. They lived in lean-to houses of cedar planks and subsisted on acorns, deer, and fish including salmon. Some were forced onto the Siletz Reservation, where 15 "Upper Coquille" were reported in 1910. A mixed blood faction known as the "Coquille tribe" are a few dozen people of Coos-Coquille extraction living in their old location who are today seeking settlement of their land claims. The "Confederated Tribes of Siletz" numbered about 900 shortly before termination of reservation status in 1956; the Coquille were one of many ancestries who form the group.

UMPQUA Often known as "Upper Umpqua", they lived mostly on the south fork of the Umpqua River, Oregon, near present Roseburg, where they were met by Astorian fur traders in the early 19th century. They numbered some 400 in the mid-19th century; forced north to the Grand Ronde Reservation, they reported 84 in 1902. One band, the Cow Creek Indians, survived in their old homes, and a few descendants still live around Riddle south of Myrtle Creek, Oregon, numbering 221 in 1985. These were part of a reported 700 people in southwestern Oregon in 1956, descendants of Athabascans, Coos, Siuslaw and others living in some 37 different locations but chiefly around the Roseburg and Coos Bay areas. The same general group were reported as numbering 730 in the 1970 census.

TUTUTNI An Athabascan tribe of the Illinois and lower Rogue Rivers in southwestern Oregon who also occupied the coast south to the Chetco River; they are commonly called "Coast Rogues". They were contacted by the British explorer George Vancouver in 1792. Although subsequent contact with other vessels and inland fur traders brought epidemics they still numbered around 1,300 in 1850. They suffered the same fate as many other southwestern Oregon groups, being shipped to the Siletz-Grand Ronde complex in 1857. By 1910 only 383 survived; in 1930 just 41 were reported under this name; a few others under the names "Maguenodon" and "Joshua", numbering 39 and 45 respectively in 1945, seem to be of Tututni origin. They are now part of the "Confederated Siletz". A group known as the *Naltunnhtunne* may have been very closely related to, or a subgroup of, the Tututni.

CHASTACOSTA A small Athabascan tribe on the lower course of the Illinois River near its junction with the Rogue River. They joined the general Indian resistance to white settlement in their lands but were moved north to the Siletz Agency where a few remain. They were given as 153 in 1858, 30 in 1937, and 20 in 1945.

TALTUSHTUNTUDE A small Athabascan tribe from the upper middle course of the Rogue River, Oregon, on Galice Creek, who were subsequently moved to the Siletz Reservation. A group called "Galice Creek" numbered 42 in 1937, and ten in 1945.

DAKUBETEDE Small Athabascan tribe from Applegate Creek, a tributary of the upper Rogue River, Oregon; probably now extinct.

CHETCO An Athabascan people of the mouth of the Chetco River near present Brookings, Oregon. They lived in wooden plank houses and were closely allied to the Tolowa to the south. They aided other "Coast Rogue" Indians in the general resistance of 1853-1856, and were moved north to the Siletz Reservation, where they numbered only nine in 1910.

TOLOWA or **SMITH RIVER** An Athabascan tribe who occupied the Smith River drainage and some of the nearby coast in the extreme northeastern corner of California. Linguistically they were closer to the Rogue River tribes to the north than to their relatives to the south. They resided in permanent villages along the coast in winter, and in late summer they moved inland for salmon and acorns. Their house types were low peaked redwood plank dwellings with gable end entrances. Tolowa society was dominated by acquisition of wealth, usually dentalium shells, obsidian blades and woodpecker scalps. Ceremonialism associated with the taking of the first salmon and sea lion suggests that they belonged with the northern Californian "World Renewal" complex of the Karok, Yurok and Hupa type. The overland explorations of Jedediah Smith were their first contacts with whites, and intensive white settlement of this region came after 1850. They probably numbered more than 1,000 in pre-contact times; but the census of 1910 gave only 121 Tolowa, a result of diseases and numerous attacks by whites on their settlements. Two small reserves (called "rancherias" in California), at Crescent City and Smith River, Del Norte County, California have been home for some Tolowa descendants, reported as numbering 37 and 113 respectively in 1945.

HUPA or **HOOPA** Probably the largest and most important Athabascan tribe in California, living principally on the Trinity River above its junction with the Klamath. Salmon and acorns provided the bulk of their diet. They were participants in the elaborate northwestern California rituals called "World Renewal" or "Big Time", involving complex ceremonial such as the White Deerskin and Jumping Dances. Wealth display linked them culturally northward rather than to central California. They lived in small villages of rectangular plank houses, wore buckskin aprons and skirts, and excelled in basketry. Extensive contacts with whites came after 1850, but the establishment of the Hupa Reservation in their homeland helped maintain their numbers. They probably numbered more than 1,000 in 1851; 420 were reported in 1906, and 992 in 1962. Over the years they have settled into a rural American lifestyle, self-supporting and economically perhaps the most advanced among the surviving Indians of California. They still hold the White Deerskin Dance.

CHILULA & WHILKUT Two small Athabascan tribes who were almost indistinguishable from each other, and from the Hupa. The Chilula lived on Redwood Creek west of the Hupa, and the Whilkut on the upper course of Redwood Creek and part of the Mad River to the southwest. The last of the Chilula moved to the Hupa Reservation and are no longer reported separately. The Whilkut suffered heavily at the hands of whites. A few "Redwood Indians" seem to have been incorporated on the Round Valley Reservation, although a few continued to live in their old homes and have mostly intermarried with whites; consequently neither element still exists as a distinct group.

MATTOLE A small Athabascan tribe on the Bear and Mattole Rivers, northwestern California, and a strip of adjacent coast about 45 miles long. They perhaps numbered 1,000 in pre-contact times; the census of 1910 reported only 34; and 30 "Bear River Indians" were living at the Rohnerville Reservation, Humboldt County, California, in 1970.

NONGATL A minor Athabascan group on the middle Eel River, upper Mad River and Van Duzen River east of Ruth Lake. A few may have survived until reservation days at Hupa or Blue Lake.

SINKONE An Athabascan group living mostly on the south fork of the Eel River, northwest California, to Shelter Cove on the coast. They are probably no longer separate.

LASSIK These Indians occupied the drainage of the main Eel River and headwaters of the Mad River in northwest California. They are no longer distinct as a separate group.

WAILAKI Occupying the Eel River, south of the Lassik, to Big Bend Creek, they were probably intermediate culturally between the central Californian Wintu and their own relatives to the north. The last of these people seem to have been located on the Round Valley Reservation and are no longer a separate group.

KATO or **CAHTO** The Kato were the southernmost Athabascan tribe of California in present Mendocino County, the area of the upper drainage of the south fork of the Eel River. Originally numbering some 500, they had been reduced to about 60 by 1910, residing on the Round Valley Reservation and the small rancheria at Laytonville. In 1972 they numbered 95. All traces of their former culture have apparently gone.

SUBARCTIC

Language family and tribe	*Meaning*/origin of tribal name, where known
Athabascan (Northern Athabascan):	
Ingalik	Eskimo name
Kolchan	-
Tanaina	*"people"*
Koyukon	*"people of the river"*
Tanana	*"Tanana River people"*
Ahtena	*"ice people"*
Han	*"those who dwell along the river"*
Eyak (possibly separate family)	-
Kutchin	*"those who dwell on the flats"*
Tutchone	*"crow people"*
Tagish	place name
Inland Tlingit	*"people"*
Tahltan	place name
Tsetsaut	*"those of the interior"*
Kaska	-
Sekani	*"dwellers on the rocks"*
Beaver	English name
Carrier	English name
Chilcotin	*"people of the river"*
Nicola	English name
Slavey	English name
Mountain	English name
Hare	English name
Bear Lake	English name
Dogrib	English name
Yellowknife	English name
Chipewyan	*"pointed skins"*
Algonkian*:	
Northern Ojibwa	
Cree	French version of own name
West Main Cree	
Western Woods Cree	
Tête de Boule (Attikamek)	French – *"round heads"* (*"white fish"*)
Montagnais-Nascapi	French – *"mountaineers"*
Beothuk	*"human body"*

* see p.21

A cultural area of North America comprising the whole of present Quebec, Newfoundland, the northern parts of Ontario, Manitoba, Saskatchewan, Alberta, the northern interior of British Columbia, the Yukon, the drainage of the Mackenzie River about Great Slave and Great Bear Lakes, and the interior of Alaska. The Indians, except for the Beothuk, are drawn exclusively from the Algonkian family in the east and the Athabascan family in the northwest. Within this vast area culture remained quite constant, though flexible, within strictly hunting and fishing parameters. The climate is harsh, with long, severely cold winters and short, warm summers. Temperatures below – 40°F are common, but often reach 80°F in summer, accompanied by a dense insect life which plagues man and animal alike.

Much of the area is Arctic lowlands with abundant coniferous spruce, tamarack, willow and alder. The topography of the whole area ranges from forest to lake, swamp, prairie, tundra, mountain and sea.

Animals of economic significance to the Indians include moose, caribou, bear, fox, wolf, otter and beaver, and fish include whitefish, grayling, trout and pike. A significant number of Athabascan groups were found in the great mountain chain of the Yukon territory and British Columbia, in the lush river valleys of spruce, fir, cedar and hemlock forests. Only at Cook Inlet, Alaska, were the Indians partly dependent upon the sea for food. Salmon was important to some Alaskan groups. Fishing became more important at the close of the fur trade era.

Religion focused on the relationship between the animal spirits and man, and the impersonal spirits of animated natural elements such as fire, wind and water. Shamans were important in helping to prevent disease and to enlist the power of animals. Communal ceremonies were few, except where sometimes influenced from other cultures such as Eskimo or Northwest Coast; the Ingalik, Tanaina and other western Athabascans had a rich ceremonial life in part derived from coastal cultures.

Northern life became influenced by the network of fur trading ports from the late 18th century on. European goods gradually transformed clothing, housing and settlement patterns, and missionary influence modified religion, which also produced a few semi-Christian nativistic cults similar to those found elsewhere in North America. Artistic traditions were also modified as floralistic beadwork on cloth largely replaced porcupine quillwork and painting in the decoration of native costume.

ATHABASCAN, ATHAPASCAN or ATHAPASKAN

One of the most widely spread linguistic families of North American Indians. The family has been tentatively allied to the Haida and Tlingit into a larger generic group. They are believed to be the last Indian group, exclusive of the Eskimo, to enter North America from Asia via the Bering land bridge, perhaps c.5,000 B.C., and have for the most part occupied – in scattered groups – vast areas of Subarctic Alaska and northwest Canada beyond Hudson Bay. Perhaps 1,600 years ago some Athabascans emigrated to the Pacific coast in southwestern Oregon and northern California; and about a thousand years later a significant group entered the American Southwest to become the Navajo and Apache.

NORTHERN ATHABASCAN sometimes called DENE

Terms to cover the northern groups of Athabascan speakers, in all about 30 languages, who occupied in relatively small bands an area embracing the Canadian and Alaskan Subarctic from the west coast of Hudson Bay to the interior of Alaska, including the northern parts of Manitoba, Saskatchewan, Alberta, Yukon and British Columbia, much of the drainages of the Peace, Liard, Pelly, Peel, Mackenzie, Porcupine, Yukon, Tanana and Copper Rivers. In this vast area their culture was relatively uniform, being wholly without agriculture and primarily dependent on moose, caribou or deer hunting. Houses were constructed of bark or skins, modified into the log houses of fur trade influence during the late 19th century. Before trade goods became available clothing was of dressed skins cut to fit the whole body. Vessels, toboggans and canoes utilized wood, bark, sinew and skins. The fur trade gradually modified Northern Athabascan culture; guns, knives and steel traps were adopted in pursuit of furbearing animals. Despite their meagre resources and harsh environment these peoples excelled in decorative porcupine quillwork and later in beadwork on clothing.

INGALIK A group of Athabascans living in the basins of the Yukon and Kuskokwim Rivers, north and east of Holy Cross; the most westerly group in Alaska. A northern division on the Innoko River, the *Holikachuk*, are sometimes now considered as a separate group. Their ceremonial life seems to have been influenced by the Eskimo from whom they borrowed heavily, and their Potlatches suggest Northwest Coast influences. The Russians established trade with the Ingalik during the early 19th century and modified their culture and religion as a consequence. A population for the group has been estimated at 1,500 at contact, reduced to about 500 during thee late 19th century. In 1974 530 were estimated at Holy Cross, Anvik and Shageluk with some Eskimo and white admixture added over the years. The Holikachuk descendants are at Grayling and number perhaps less than 100.

KOLCHAN A group of Athabascan bands on the upper Kuskokwim River in Alaska, sometimes considered a branch of the Ingalik but related more closely to the Tanana, with whom they are much mixed. Their life and culture was similar to that of the Ingalik and Tanana. They have about 150 descendants at McGrath, Nikalai and Takotna.

TANAINA The Athabascan groups in the vicinity of Cook Inlet, Kenai Peninsula, and the areas north and west in Alaska – not to be confused with the Tanana. Their culture was somewhat intermediate between the coastal Tlingit and the interior Athabascans, being much more dependent in early times on salmon, but they also hunted moose and caribou. Contact with Russians in the late 18th century established their association with the fur trade and the Orthodox Church. Much reduced by severe epidemics during the 19th century, their population decreased from 4,000 to 1,500. In 1974 about 530 persons of largely Tanaina descent lived at Nondalton, Pedro Bay, Tyonek, Lime Village and Eklutna.

KOYUKON Athabascan bands in three groups occupying the middle area of the Yukon River,

Alaska, plus parts of the Koyukuk and Tanana Rivers. An older name for at least part of these people was Koyukokhotana. Direct contact began in 1858 when the trading post at Nulato was established by the Russian-American Company. The Koyukon viewed the supernatural world through the animal spirits, and held elaborate mortuary ceremonials and memorial Potlatches. They have been slowly modified over the years by Roman Catholic and Episcopalian missionaries. Their clothing featured the double-V caribou hide tunics and trouser-moccasins. Their vast habitat was a mixture of forest, mountain and lowland flats. Their population was perhaps 2,000 in pre-white contact times; today about that number are reported at the villages of Kaltag, Nulato, Koyukuk, Galena, Ruby, Hughes, Allakaket, Stevens and Rampart, mostly Koyukon with other Athabascan and Eskimo admixture.

TANANA A convenient name to cover several Athabascan Indian groups along the Tanana River, Alaska, in three divisions: the *Lower Tanana* near present Fairbanks, the *Tanacross* around the town of the same name, and the *Upper Tanana* or *Nabesna*. Contact with whites came first to the Lower Tanana; closest to the Yukon River trading posts in the early 19th century, they were gradually modified in culture due to the fur trade, missionary influence and mining activities. They were dependent upon caribou and other big game and fishing. Their material culture included canoes, skin boats, toboggans, sleds, fish weirs, caribou skin clothing, dyed porcupine quills and beadwork on decorated festive costume. The Tanana groups perhaps numbered 700 in 1880, but there had already been a reduction due to introduced diseases which continued well into the early 20th century. Today about 600 descendants are at Minto, Nenana, Tanacross, Tetlin and Northway.

AHTENA A group of Athabascans of the Copper River basin region of Alaska, often divided into lower and upper divisions, but who were never a tribal political unit. Russians attempted to ascend the Copper River in 1796 and during most of the early 19th century; the tribe were hostile to foreigners, including the coastal Eskimo. The Ahtena were linked to a trade network with other natives involving animal hides, native copper and later European trade goods. Except for the changes brought by trade goods and guns obtained from whites there were few permanent contacts with Europeans until about 1900. They still hold Potlatch ceremonials given by wealthy chiefs to honour both the living and the dead. They numbered perhaps in excess of 500 at the time of Russian contact, but were reduced to some 300 by about 1900. They seem to have recovered their numbers, but not all the 500 or so Indians in the old Ahtena area are true Ahtena. Most of their descendants are at Cantwell, Chistochina, Cakona, Gulkana, Cooper Center and Chitina in Alaska.

HAN A small Athabascan group on the Yukon River close to the present boundary between the Yukon Territory and U.S. Alaska in a heavily forested region. In similar fashion to other Northern Athabascans the Han wore clothing of caribou skins with leggings and moccasins made in one piece. They used bark and skin canoes, snowshoes, and toboggans and depended on fish and meat for food. They were one of the last Athabascan groups to be contacted by whites, from Fort Yukon; but missionary influence followed, and the Gold Rush effectively destroyed much of the traditional Han culture. Their few descendants remained at Eagle and Moosehide, later Dawson, where about 300 are still reported.

EYAK A small group of Athabascans who lived on the southern coast of Alaska between Prince William Sound and the Tlingit of Yakutat Bay, close to the mouth of the Copper River. A few descendants remain at Eyak (Cordova). Some studies have suggested that these people and their culture may have been a mixture of Tlingit, Athabascan, Eskimo and even Asiatic origins, and suggest that they should be treated as a separate family. Five speakers were left in the 1960s in the villages of Yakutat and Cordova, the youngest a woman of 42.

KUTCHIN One of the most important branches of the Athabascan family, scattered in nine or ten groups over a wide area extending from the middle Yukon River region in Alaska, including the upper Koyukuk River tributaries, eastward along the Porcupine River, and thence into the area which drains into the Mackenzie River Basin, including the Peel River and Arctic Red River areas. Their habitat varies from the broad lowlands of the middle Yukon and Mackenzie Rivers to the cordillera and boreal forests, all characterized by long, severe winters and short, warm summers. The easternmost bands – those of the Mackenzie drainage – have usually been referred to as "Loucheux". The hunting of caribou for food, clothing and tools provided most basic raw materials, but freshwater fish and fowl were also important. Caribou hide clothing for males and females was characterized by fitted garments, hoods and combined trouser-moccasins decorated with porcupine quillwork and painting. During the late 19th century traders introduced beads and European clothing. House types were both surface and semi-subterranean log and brush structures.

The earliest known encounter between the Kutchin and Europeans was with the Mackenzie party in 1789. In 1806 Fort Good Hope was established, and in 1847 Fort Yukon was founded in the territory of the western Kutchin bands. Gradually modified in culture throughout the 19th and 20th centuries, they numbered perhaps 5,000 in pre-European contact times but declined to below 1,000 in 1860. In 1968 2,150 Kutchin were reported at Arctic Village, Venetie, Fort Yukon, Circle and Chalkyitsik in Alaska and Old Crow (Yukon), Fort McPherson, Arctic Red River, Aklavik and Inuvit (Northwest Territories) in Canada.

TUTCHONE Athabascans of present southern Yukon Territory east of the Saint Elias Mountains, through a vast plateau dissected by the Teslin and Pelly Rivers forming the tributaries of the upper Yukon River: a mixture of tundra, boreal forest and meadowlands supported moose, caribou and mountain sheep which, together with salmon, provided their main food and clothing source. They seem to have been the intermediate traders between the Tlingit and the interior Upper Tanana and Han. During the 19th century their own efforts to secure a direct trade with the coastal tribes seem to have been blocked. The Klondike Gold Rush and the building of the Alaska Highway effectively changed native northern life. The total number of people covered by the term "Tutchone" was perhaps less than 1,000 in 1880, and about the same number of descendants are still reported from Ross River, Pelly Crossing, Carmacks, Whitehorse, Champagne, Aishihik and Kluane, all in Yukon Territory, but including some Tagish and others.

TAGISH A small but important Athabascan group about Tagish Lake at the headwaters of the Yukon River in southern Yukon Territory, Canada. Two mountain passes connected the Tagish with the Tlingit of the Northwest Coast, and the interaction between the groups led to the adoption of many coastal traits by the Tagish. The first direct contacts with whites were in the 1880s, but the Klondike Gold Rush of 1898 brought major changes. Their general culture was similar to that of other cordilleran Athabascans, perhaps with greater dependence on fishing. The coastal public display of status and wealth distribution ceremony known as "Potlatch" is still an important native function. About 200 people of Tagish descent live at Carcross and Whitehorse in the Yukon today; some are probably part of the Inland Tlingit.

INLAND TLINGIT A group of Indians about Teslin village in southern Yukon and Atlin in northern British Columbia. Despite their name some students believe them to be an Athabascan people originally called Taku who adopted Tlingit as their language owing to extensive trade and intermarriage with the coastal Tlingit; others claim they were Tlingit who moved into the Taku Basin from the coast. Their material culture, including their dress, was a colourful mixture of coastal and interior traits including the varied use of west coast totemic decoration. They also held traditional style Potlatches until recently. In 1978 250 were at Teslin and 161 at Atlin.

TAHLTAN The Tahltan were Athabascan bands centered on the upper basin of the Stikine River in the northwestern interior of British Columbia, Canada, particularly around Telegraph Creek. The Tahltan, together with the Kaska, Tagish and Taku, were once referred to as *Nahani*. Their habitat included parklands and heavy forests, with moose and caribou providing meat and hides for clothing. They had extensive contacts with the coastal Tlingit and indirectly with the white fur trade, but direct European contact became established after 1874. The Tahltan used pitched and lean-to wooden shelters and smokehouses. The Tahltan probably numbered 1,000 in pre-European contact times, but declined to less than 300 by 1900. They are still principally located on a reserve near Telegraph Creek, and numbered 702 in 1969, including a few at Kinaskan Lake. Hunting, trapping and fishing remained basic to Tahltan subsistence until the mid-20th century.

TSETSAUT A small Athabascan group from the interior cordillera of northern British Columbia who seem to have moved to the upper Nass River and thence to the Portland Canal. In 1885 a remnant of 12 men and their families moved to the Anglican mission at Kincolith where they merged with the Niska. They subsequently became extinct as a separate people.

KASKA These people occupied a stretch of the Liard River where present Yukon Territory and British Columbia adjoin at Watson Lake, and also along the Dease River tributary. They are very closely related to the Tahltan and Tagish Athabascans and were once collectively called Nahani. They shared some cultural traits with their relatives and thence with Northwest Coastal culture, but also with more distant relatives of the Mackenzie drainage area. Continuous contact with whites began in the 1820s with the establishment of a Hudson's Bay post on the Liard, followed by increasing intrusion by miners and freelance traders and trappers. In 1969 there were 533 Kaska in the Liard River Band near Lower Post and Watson Lake, excluding a few who have joined other groups over the years.

SEKANI The country of the Sekani was the valleys of the Finlay and Parsnip branches of the Peace River in north central British Columbia. Their language suggests a close relationship with the Beaver Indians and Sarsi and they may originally have been all one people. Their land was a vast area of high plateau, mountains, numerous rivers, lakes and streams, often covered with dense forest. As the Peace River is part of the interior Mackenzie drainage there was little dependence on salmon, but they hunted moose, caribou, mountain sheep and, in the eastern part of their domain, bison and wapiti. White traders had an early impact on Sekani culture, and Simon Fraser established two North West Company posts in their territory in the early 19th century. In recent times they have been associated with trading posts at Fort Ware, Fort Grahame and Fort Mcleod. They suffered greatly from an influx of white miners from 1861 onwards. Their population may have been 800 in early times, but only 160 were reported in 1923; 290 in 1934; 336 in 1949; and 523 in 1973. Not all were true Sekani, many being of mixed descent and a number now being considered Métis. Their present population is principally located at Finlay River (Ware) and McLeod Lake, British Columbia.

BEAVER These people lived in the prairies and woods on both sides of the Peace River, northwest of Lesser Slave Lake. They were among the first Northern Athabascans to experience European contact in 1792. They were gradually pushed westward by the Cree, who were armed with guns. During the 19th century they were bound to the trading pasts at Forts Dunvegan, Vermillion and St.John. Their present descendants are at the Boyer River reserves near Fort Vermillion, Horse Lake and Clear Hills, all in Alberta, but are heavily mixed with Cree; they number about 400. Perhaps the same number are in British Columbia at Fort St. John, Halfway River and West Moberly Lake. They probably numbered about 1,000 in aboriginal times, though scattered over a vast area. They are closely related to the Sekani and Sarsi.

CARRIER A group of Athabascan bands inhabiting the upper branches of the Fraser River in north central British Columbia, particularly in the areas around Babine, Stuart and François Lakes. Their first contact with Europeans came with the Alexander Mackenzie expedition in 1793; subsequently, following Simon Fraser's visit in 1805, trading posts were established in their territory. They lived in semi-sedentary villages, leaving at regular seasons for fishing and hunting. They borrowed many customs from the coastal Tsimshians in the Hazelton area and there has also been considerable intermarriage. The impact of fur traders, missionaries and miners had begun to erode their Potlatch-rank complex by the end of the 19th century. They were heavily dependent upon fishing, collecting roots and berries, and hunting beaver, goat, moose and caribou for subsistence. Their structures included wooden gabled houses of the coastal type, semi-subterranean earth-covered lodges and brush shelters. They numbered about 8,000 in 1793. The Carriers who lived about Babine Lake were sometimes referred to as *Babine* by traders, from the French word meaning labret, lip ornaments. Their present-day descendants are at Moricetown, Burns Lake, Omineca, Lake Babine, Fraser Lake, Stony Creek, Stuart-Trembleur Lake, Takla Lake, Nazko, Ulkatcho, Kluskus and Quesnal, scattered through about 100 small reserves with a population exceeding 5,000.

CHILCOTIN A branch of the Athabascans living on the Chilcotin River, a western branch of the Fraser system in central British Columbia. They are closely related to the Carrier tribes to the north and together are sometimes called *Takulli*. Their material culture was fairly simple, including wooden rectangular and gabled houses, snowshoes for winter travel, spruce bark and dugout canoes, fur blankets and robes, buckskin moccasins, aprons and kilts. They hunted elk, deer, caribou, mountain goat, and more recently moose. Fishing was also important. They had coiled basketry with imbricated designs, but few other plastic or graphic arts. In the late 18th century indirect contacts were made with the European-stimulated fur trade, and Fort Alexandria was established in Carrier country. By the late 19th century they were in six bands: Toosey at Riske Creek below Williams Lake; Stone and Anaham, south and north of the Chilcotin River; Alexis Creek at Redstone on the upper Chilcotin; Alexandria above Williams Lake; and Nemaiah Valley at Chilko Lake. Their present descendants number about 1,800 people, perhaps twice the ancient population. Their traditional resources are now largely depleted.

NICOLA A designation of a small group of Athabascan-speaking Indians in the Nicola and Similkameen valleys, British Columbia, possibly of Chilcotin origin, though culturally they belong with the Thompson Indians with whom they have now apparently merged. The language has been extinct since about 1910.

SLAVEY or **SLAVE** A group of Athabascans who lived along southwestern tributaries of the

Mackenzie River, the Hay, Liard and Nelson systems where the present boundaries of Alberta, British Columbia and Northwest Territories adjoin; they also occupied the Mackenzie valley itself from Great Slave Lake to Great Bear River. The Slavey people and their relatives to the north and east lived in a region of relatively poor resources, and subsistence was won from one of the harshest regions of North America. While the lakes and waterways were rich in fish and berries, helping to supplement a diet of moose and caribou, starvation was a constant threat. They had snowshoes, bark canoes and conical skin- or bark-covered structures resembling the Plains tipi; a low wooden shelter of logs, chinked and covered with earth or moss, was also used. Meagre and scattered resources precluded permanent settlements until early 20th century influences reduced their semi-nomadic way of life. Their clothes were made from moosehide; they excelled in the ornamentation of clothes with porcupine quillwork, and later with glass beads obtained from European traders. The Slavey seem to have been pushed north by invading Crees, and their name may derive from their status as Cree captives.

Initial European contact came with the Alexander Mackenzie expedition in 1789; subsequently the Hudson's Bay Company founded a number of trading posts in their territory, and Slavey life and culture were gradually modified. For many generations Slavey descendants have been concentrated in a number of areas influenced by specific trading posts, and some 4,000 people are today distributed as follows: Hay River, Fort Providence (Great Slave Lake), Fort Liard, Fort Simpson, Fort Wrigley and Fort Norman, all in the Northwest Territories; Fort Nelson in British Columbia; and on several reserves in the Upper Hay River region near Lake Assumption, Alberta. The present number is twice their original population, although a proportion are Métis.

MOUNTAIN & GOAT INDIANS Terms applied to some Athabascan bands on the eastern slopes of the Mackenzie Mountains between Forts Liard and Good Hope, sometimes reported as members of other groups such as Kaska, Dogrib or Slavey. However, on historical, environmental and linguistic grounds they are now considered independent. Their largest group seems to be those at Fort Norman, but they are not reported separately from the Slavey by the Canadian Indian Affairs Branch.

HARE These people lived in the forested areas west of Great Bear Lake, Northwest Territories, Canada, including part of the lower Mackenzie River valley. Although they are not a tribe in the usual sense, communal feasting, dancing and gambling have created a strong sense of identity among them. They seem to be linguistically related to the Slavey, Mountain and Bear Lake Indians. Living in one of the coldest and harshest environments, starvation was a persistent feature of their existence. Their culture was generally similar to that of the Slavey, Dogrib and Kutchin, with subsistence dependent on the supply of caribou, moose and fish. Hare skins were used for some clothing, hence their group name, but tunics and later jackets were usually of moose or caribou hide. They have long been associated with Fort Good Hope on the Mackenzie River, where their descendants still number about 500 people.

BEAR LAKE INDIANS Athabascan people of Great Bear Lake, previously considered as mixed Hare, Slavey or Dogrib, but now separately recognized although essentially a mixed people. About 600 people, mostly at Fort Franklin on Great Bear Lake, consider themselves to be Bear Lake Indians, although reported as "Hare" by the Canadian Indian Affairs Branch.

DOGRIB The Athabascan people living between Great Slave Lake and Great Bear Lake. Their general culture echoed that of other Northern Athabascans, characterized by scarce resources, particularly in the intensly cold winters. Fish, caribou, moose and hare were subsistence food. Clothing consisted of caribou hide coats and dresses, usually tailored, unlike the V-front garments of the Kutchin. Footwear included moccasins of the ankle wrap type and moccasin boots. They have been known to Europeans from the mid-18th century, and their culture was partly modified from that period by guns, knives and other goods introduced by traders. Until about 1950 they spent most of their time in the bush, with seasonal activities of a traditional pattern, in particular hunting fur-bearing animals to be exchanged at trading posts. Most modern Dogrib descendants are in the Fort Rae district (or Rae settlement) at Yellowknife, Detah, and also mixed with others at Snowdrift and Fort Franklin. They number about 1,700 including Métis, which exceeds their aboriginal numbers. Their name is thought to be of Cree origin, meaning dog side.

YELLOWKNIFE So named from copper found in their territory, this Athabascan group – who appear to be closely related to, if not strictly part of, the Chipewyan Indians – lived east of the Dogrib Indians, who were often openly hostile to them. In the early 19th century they were described as suffering periods of starvation and disease. They seem to have been absorbed by the Dogribs at Yellowknife or by the Chipewyans at Snowdrift and Fort Resolution. The Yellowknife Indians reported by the various Canadian censuses in recent years usually refer to the "Dogrib people at Yellowknife" in the District of Mackenzie.

CHIPEWYAN One of the largest Northern Athabascan groups, they should not be confused with the Chippewa. They inhabited a vast forest-tundra area of present northern Manitoba, Saskatchewan and the Northwest Territories District of Mackenzie south and east of Great Slave Lake. They have had the longest and most continuous contact of all Northern Athabascans with Europeans, beginning in about 1682 with the establishment of York Factory by the Hudson's Bay Company. Subsequently they became middlemen in extensive trade with more remote tribes. Their ancient domain has been modified over the years by their involvement in the Canadian fur trade, resulting in a number of bands moving south from their forest-tundra domain to true boreal forest. They were often on unfriendly terms with the Crees, who encroached on their territory, and were seriously affected by European-introduced diseases. The northern bands depended upon the Barren Ground caribou in a region affected by long, severe winters.

Their traditional beliefs were based on the concept of power given in dreams by spirit animals; this power controlled game, and could be used for curing. Their dress was originally of caribou hides, but European clothes were adopted in the 19th century. Shelters were often conical tipis of caribou skins. During the late 19th century the Chipewyans gradually affiliated into groups associated with various trading posts. In aboriginal times they are thought to have numbered over 8,000, today about 5,000.

Their principal bands today are at Fort Churchill, Brochet and Northland (Manitoba); Lac La Hache (northeastern Saskatchewan); Fond Du Lac and Stony Rapids east of Lake Athabasca, and several minor groups collectively known as Portage La Loche, English River, Peter Pond Lake (all in northern Saskatchewan). In Alberta they are at Janvier, Gregoire Lake, Fort McMurray, Fort Mackay, Fort Chipewyan, Fort Fitzgerald and Fort Smith; and in the Northwest Territories at Salt River, Resolution and Snowdrift. In all areas there has been intermarriage with the Crees. Despite their harsh environment Chipewyan women have produced very fine quillwork, beadwork and silk embroidery over the years, and their work is well represented in museum collections.

NORTHERN OJIBWA & SAULTEAUX Although originally an Eastern woodland people the Ojibwa, like their northern cousins the Crees, were from early contact days induced north and west by the fur trade activities of the Hudson's Bay Company; and from the 1670s onwards the Northern Ojibwa have occupied the interior of Ontario and the so-called Saulteaux – the areas about Lake Winnepeg and Lake of the Woods in present Manitoba and western Ontario. They became dependent upon European trade goods which they secured in return for furs, at first from posts on James and Hudson Bays and later from interior posts. Their material culture became a mix of native and European elements; they retained native snares, birch bark canoes, toboggans and birch bark, spruce or hide dwellings; but they also adopted guns, commercial traps, canvas tents, log cabins and lately even outboard motors. Native dress also changed to European style, though moccasins were still used until recently. Their Woodland traditions reveal themselves in the Midewiwin (Grand Medicine Society), vision quest, and certain forms of decorative art. They also seem to have had belief in Kitchi-Manitou, a paramount beneficent force, a power in all natural things, and the comic culture hero they call Nanabush. Many Saulteaux communities are now Christian, often Pentecostal.

Many have moved to urban Winnipeg, and they have suffered more than most through disruptive Euro-Canadian influences. Their early population is difficult or impossible to separate from other Ojibwa, but their descendants were reported to number about 30,000 in 1978. The Northern Ojibwa numbered 10,555 at Big Trout Lake, Caribou Lake, Fort Hope, Deer Lake, Osnaburgh and other places in north central Ontario, plus Garden Hill, St.Theresa Point and other locations in northeastern Manitoba. The so-called Saulteaux have 30 reserves about Lake Winnipeg, Lake of the Woods and Lac Seul; the largest groups are Roseau River (sometimes given as Plains Ojibwa), Berens River, Fort Alexander, Peguis, Little Grand Rapids, Fairford and Lake St.Martin in Manitoba; and Pikangikum, Islington, Grassy Narrows, Rat Portage, Whitefish Bay, La Seul and other places in southwestern Ontario, numbering 18,869. In some locations Ojibwa speakers are called "Cree".

CREE The Kristineaux or Cree Indians were one of the largest and most important native tribes of the North American continent. They were an Algonkian people related to the Montagnais, Menomini, Sauk, Fox, Kickapoo and Shawnee. The term "Kristineaux" from Kenistenoag or KnistEn'o is the French version of their native name, the form "Cree" being contracted from Kristineaux during the fur trade period. The designation has no literal translation; and neither does the Plains-Cree term for themselves, "Nehuawak" or "Nehiyawak".

The Crees' importance was due mainly to the position they held in the Canadian fur trade, and the influence that position gave them with other tribes. During the rearrangement of the Cree bands in western Canada while engaged in the activities of the Hudson's Bay Company, the Cree were scarcely a tribe in the popular sense but rather a collection of bands, groups, even families, scattered through an immense area. At the height of Cree power no tribe in North America ever occupied such a large area. Whilst the Cree were scattered so widely there were only minor dialectical differences between most of the bands; however, due to long separation there were slight differences between the languages of the Plains and Woods Cree. In short, before their historic westward expansion they were a typical eastern Subarctic tribe of the Algonkian linguistic stock. They can be generally subdivided into the *West Main Cree*, *Woods Cree* and *Plains Cree*. However, there were probably Cree in the west before the advance of the fur trade, and an old group known as the *Rocky Cree* may have been in Saskatchewan before European contact. Missionaries organised a form of written syllabary of the Cree language which is still widely used.

WEST MAIN CREE This is the modern term to cover the Cree bands formerly occupying the low-lying west coast of James Bay in northern Ontario, and formerly more commonly known as (or at least as part of) the *Swampy Cree* or *Maskegon*; and more specifically the Barren Ground, Fort Albany, Monsoni and Kesagami Cree. Beginning in the late 17th century these coastal Cree had adapted to the fur trade and missionary teachings with a gradual modification in their native culture. Contacts with Europeans go back to 1668 and 1671 when trading posts were established in reach of the Swampy Cree. Besides being skilful hunters, they also fished; both meat and fish were heat-dried to be preserved as winter food, often mixed with berries and grease. The Swampy Cree shared with the Northern Ojibwa and Saulteaux most religious beliefs, including the "shaking tent" rite in which power was acquired from non-human helpers. Their descendants are at Moose Factory, Fort Albany, Attawapiskat, Winisk, Severn, York Factory, Fox Lake, Shamattawa and Churchill, and numbered 6,345 in 1978.

WESTERN WOODS CREE The Woods Cree are usually designated the western extension of the Swampy Cree in Manitoba, Saskatchewan and Alberta, Canada, during the later decades of the 18th century and early 19th century. These Cree retained their basic boreal forest culture, though modified by their dependence upon the fur trade. They followed the European traders and explorers deep into the north country, forcing the Chipewyans north and the Beaver to the Rocky Mountains. Their material culture was largely replaced by European goods at an early period, but they retained snowshoes, toboggans, skin lodges and bark canoes, plus some elements of aboriginal dress such as moccasins. They seem to have excelled in decorative porcupine quillwork, painting, silkwork and beadwork. They believed in a Great Spirit and feared the Windigos (ice giants) who caused cannibalism. The Hudson's Bay Company was the economic authority of the whole region until the introduction of modern Canadian influences such as housing programmes, health centres, and the developing micro-urban community. Their language, however, is still widely used.

The population of the ancestors of Swampy and Woods Crees may have been 20,000 in the 18th century; they numbered 35,550 in 1978, exclusive of Métis, in eight bands in Ontario (Constance Lake, Timagami, Matachewan and others); 15 bands in Manitoba (Cross Lake, Fisher River, Gods Lake, Mathias Colomb, Nelson House, Norway House, Oxford House, The Pas, and others); nine bands in Saskatchewan (Lac la Ronge, Montreal Lake and Peter Ballantyne being the largest); and 13 bands in Northern Alberta (Driftpile, Little Red River, Wabasca, Whitefish Lake, Sturgeon Lake, Fort Vermillion and several others). In a number of locations they are much mixed with Northern Ojibwa and Saulteaux. For many years Cree and Cree Métis women have made moccasins, pouches, mittens and jackets decorated with rich floralistic patterns in beads and silk for sale or trade at the trading posts. Such items have found their way into many museums in the U.S.A., Canada and Europe.

TETE DE BOULE or **ATTIKAMEK** A branch of the Cree who still inhabit the upper St.Maurice River region in Quebec, Canada, and were perhaps contacted by Europeans as early as 1630. The general culture was similar to the Montagnais-Nascapi to the north and the Algonkin to the south. Although heavily influenced by the French-controlled fur trade of the area, and subjected to Iroquois penetration, they continued to live independently until the introduction of Euro-Canadian industrialisation in recent times. Their native dress seems to have disappeared at an early time, but they excelled in birch bark work and made excellent canoes. They presently have 3,000 descendants at Obedjiwan, Weymontachie and Manouan in central Quebec; most still speak their native language, and they are politically organized with their Montagnais neighbours.

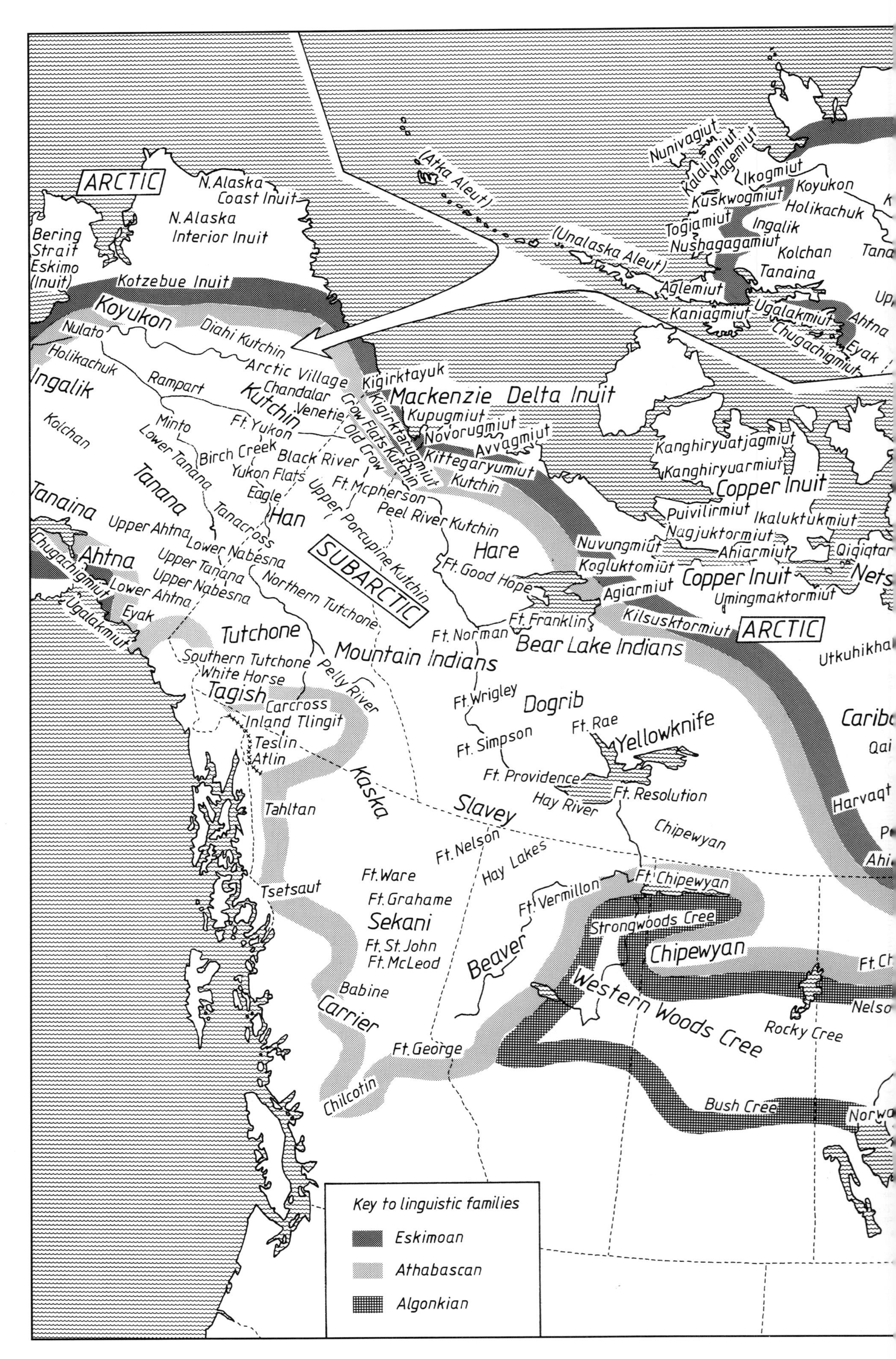

ARCTIC
N. Alaska Coast Inuit
N. Alaska Interior Inuit
Bering Strait Eskimo (Inuit)
Kotzebue Inuit
Koyukon
Nulato
Diahi Kutchin
Holikachuk
Ingalik
Rampart
Arctic Village
Chandalar
Kutchin
Venetie
Kigirktayuk
Kigirktarugmiut
Crow Flats Kutchin
Old Crow
Mackenzie Delta Inuit
Kupugmiut
Novorugmiut
Avvagmiut
Kittegaryumiut
Kutchin
Minto
Kolchan
Lower Tanana
Ft. Yukon
Birch Creek
Black River
Yukon Flats
Ft. Mcpherson
Peel River Kutchin
Tanana
Eagle
Han
Upper Porcupine Kutchin
Tanaina
Upper Ahtna
Tanacross
Lower Nabesna
Ahtna
Upper Tanana
Upper Nabesna
Chugachigmiut
Lower Ahtna
Eyak
Ugalakmiut
Northern Tutchone
SUBARCTIC
Hare
Ft. Good Hope
Tutchone
Southern Tutchone
White Horse
Pelly River
Mountain Indians
Ft. Norman
Ft. Franklin
Bear Lake Indians
Tagish
Carcross
Inland Tlingit
Teslin
Atlin
Ft. Wrigley
Dogrib
Ft. Rae
Yellowknife
Ft. Simpson
Ft. Providence
Kaska
Tahltan
Slavey
Hay River
Ft. Resolution
Chipewyan
Ft. Nelson
Hay Lakes
Ft. Ware
Ft. Grahame
Sekani
Ft. St. John
Ft. McLeod
Tsetsaut
Ft. Vermillon
Ft. Chipewyan
Strongwoods Cree
Chipewyan
Beaver
Western Woods Cree
Babine
Carrier
Ft. George
Chilcotin
Rocky Cree
Bush Cree
(Atka Aleut)
(Unalaska Aleut)
Nunivagiut
Kalaligmiut
Magemiut
Ikogmiut
Kuskwogmiut
Koyukon
Holikachuk
Togiagmiut
Ingalik
Nushagagamiut
Kolchan
Tanaina
Aglemiut
Kaniagmiut
Ugalakmiut
Ahtna
Chugachigmiut
Eyak
Kanghiryuatjagmiut
Kanghiryuarmiut
Copper Inuit
Puivilirmiut
Ikaluktukmiut
Nagjuktormiut
Nuvungmiut
Ahiarmiut
Qiqiqtar
Kogluktomiut
Agiarmiut
Copper Inuit
Umingmaktormiut
Kilsusktormiut
ARCTIC
Utkuhikha
Caribo
Qai
Harvaqt
Ahi
Ft. Ch
Nelso
Norwa
Key to linguistic families
Eskimoan
Athabascan
Algonkian

TRIBES OF SUBARCTIC AND ARCTIC, c.1790-1890

Linguistic and cultural boundaries are necessarily approximate; this sketch map is intended only as a general guide to distribution.

MONTAGNAIS-NASCAPI The Algonkians of Quebec and Labrador from the St.Lawrence north to James Bay. The Labrador and northern Quebec bands are sometimes given separate status as Nascapi (Naskapi). They belong to the Cree dialectic branch of the family, and the bands on the east coast of James Bay are now locally called *East Main Cree.* They were skilful hunters using snares, traps and bows, and when near the sea killed seals with harpoons. They fished with lines and bone hooks, and used wooden spears with bone points and light birchbark canoes. They were without agriculture, although they collected wild berries and roots, and hunted moose, caribou and deer. Clothing was made from caribou or moose hides and included coats, leggings, mittens and fur robes with hoods attached. They had toboggans, portable conical lodges and wigwams. They ritualized their supernatural powers around good health and hunting, and a belief in the trickster-transformer figure. The Montagnais, a term used for most of the southern bands, were met by Champlain in the early 17th century ; missionary and fur trade influences followed, but until fairly recently the northern bands have been quite remote from white culture. Today television, snowmobiles, prefabricated homes and white-run schools are found in most communities.

In 1650 they perhaps numbered 5,500, gradually diminishing to 2,183 in 1906, but were numbered as 11,697 in 1971. Their main southern (St.Lawrence) bands are at Bersimis, Romaine, St. Augustin, Mingan, Sept-Iles, Escoumains and Natashquan; their interior bands at North West River (Labrador), Lake St.John, Mistassini, Nemaska, Waswanipi and Chimo; and their James Bay bands are at Fort George, Eastmain, Rupert House, Paint Hills and Great Whale River – these latter groups usually being referred to as "East Main Cree". They were noted for the very fine linear and curving painted designs on their ceremonial dress, examples of which survive in museum collections in Europe and North America.

BEOTHUK The original inhabitants of the island of Newfoundland, perhaps met by Europeans as early as 1497, and subsequently known to explorers and fishermen. They were known for their use of red ochre, hence "Red Indians". Over the years they were in constant dispute with invading French, English and Micmac, and were often murdered on the slightest provocation. By the 18th century they were restricted to Red Indian Lake and Exploits River; they perhaps numbered 450 in 1768, 72 in 1811, and only 14 in 1823. Shanawdithit or Nancy April, the last of her people, died in 1829. From the limited data available the Beothuk language appears to be an isolated family, though perhaps very distantly related to Algonkian. They were a river and bay people, living in wigwams and using a very distinctively-shaped bark canoe.

ARCTIC

Language family and tribe	*Meaning*/origin of tribal name, where known
Eskimoan or Eskimaleut:	
Aleut	*"island"* (possibly)
Inuit or Eskimo	*"people"*, or *"raw meat eaters"*

The Arctic cultural area, exclusively the home of the Eskimo – now usually called Inuit – and the Aleut, extends in a 5,000-mile sweep from Siberia to Greenland, including most of the islands and coastal areas of Alaska, Canada including Labrador, and Greenland. Their land is almost treeless, and bounded by tundra to the south. It is a region where the climate is so cold and the coasts lashed by storms of such magnitude that it seems beyond the margins within which human beings can survive, let alone flourish.

The Eskimos' ancestors seem to have been the last major influx of people from Siberia across the Bering Straits, perhaps between 5000 and 6000 B.C., with the Aleuts probably splitting from the main body fairly early on. These proto-Eskimo people probably reached modern Greenland in about 2000 B.C.; archaeologists have discovered there the remains of settlements which they term the Dorset culture. Further west along the coast of the Beaufort Sea the remains of another early culture have been found, which has been termed Thule. It is believed that the Thule people or their descendants rapidly swept eastward from about A.D.800; they settled along the ice-free shores of Greenland and absorbed the Dorset people. At about the same period they abandoned most of the northernmost islands in the Arctic, perhaps due to climatic changes.

The Eskimo for the most part relied for their subsistence on the sea, where the food chain ensured a large population of seals, whales and walruses. In summer, when the usually featureless landscape briefly became warm and sustained exuberant flora and fauna, they turned inland to hunt caribou, returning to the coast in autumn and winter to fish and hunt sea mammals through blowholes in the ice or along deep fissures. They survived mostly on fat and meat, much of which was eaten raw, which gave them all the vitamin C required for health. Their tools, spears, harpoons, sleds, kayak frames and even bows often had to be pieced together in composite constructions from driftwood and antler since they had only limited access to trees (although in Alaska they fashioned wooden masks that remind us of Northwest Coast culture, and there were other cultural exchanges with the Subarctic Athabascans).

The tribes most markedly divergent from what we think of as typically Eskimo were the Chugachigniut or Chugach on Prince William Sound, Alaska, and the Kaniagmiut of Kodiak Island. Both mummified their noble dead, built house types of wooden slabs which resembled those of the Tlingit, and developed whale-hunting techniques strangely similar to those of the Nootka far to the south. Their housing varied from the iglu (igloo) of ice blocks amongst some Canadian Eskimo to sod, wood and whalebone semi-subterranean huts at winter village sites, and seal or caribou skin lodges in summer. They were and are superb sea and ice navigators, travelling by kayak or dog-drawn sleds. Their world swarmed with supernatural beings, usually interpreted by shamans. They practised infanticide and left old people to die alone in times of great hardship, but exaggerated stories mask their unique ability to survive in their harsh, cold and dark environment. Beyond the family social organisation was largely lacking.

In this respect they were unlike the Aleuts, who had a structured society of chiefs, commoners and slaves. The Aleuts were influenced by Europeans from the mid-18th century when Russian mariner explorers settled on their islands and began the sea-otter fur trade in which the Aleuts participated; conversion to the Russian Orthodox Church followed. They were makers of fine waterproof clothing and, unlike the Eskimo, excelled in basketry. They also used a two-man kayak or *baidarka*.

The Aleuts apart, the Eskimo fall into two linguistic divisions: the first consists of the Siberian Yupik, the Pacific Eskimo (Chugachigmiut) and Alaskan Eskimo (Kuskwogmiut etc.); the other comprises all the remaining tribes to the east. The Siberian Eskimo may be a resettlement from Alaska or the remains of the original people from whom all the Eskimo originally split, or a mixture of both. The Greenland Eskimo have had a long association with at first the Norsemen and later Danes, with considerable mixture amongst the East Greenland Eskimo. European influences came later to the Canadian Eskimo tribes, but by the early 20th century twill tents, white-made whale boats, guns, and sewing machines were widely used – as was a form of syllabary similar to the Cree system, introduced by missionaries.

It is difficult to estimate their population before the introduction of European diseases – perhaps 60,000, reduced to half that number by 1900; but a recent estimate, including those in Greenland, would indicate a recovery to a figure in excess of their original population.

ESKIMOAN or ESKIMOALEUT

The linguistic family of the northern edge of the New World, extending into Greenland in the east, along the Canadian and Alaskan coastline and into Siberia. The family combines the Eskimo, now often termed Inuit, and the divergent Aleut of the Aleutian Island chain. Their racial separation from the Indian is emphasized by a combination of linguistic, cultural and racial divergence, which taken together suggest a separate people. They are distinctly Mongol, of short, stocky build – perhaps a relatively late arrival from Asia. The culture area known as "Arctic" is that of the Eskimo and Aleut together.

ALEUT The original inhabitants of the long Aleutian Island chain and the Alaska Peninsula, in two general divisions. The *Atka* division held several of the outer islands as far as Attu Island and including parts of Agattu Island, Unalga Island in the Andreanof group, and Atka Island. The *Unalaska* division held the inner islands from Unalaska Island in the Fox group, Unimak Island, the Shumagin and Pribilof Islands, and the western Alaskan Peninsula, almost to Pilot Point. They became known in the 1740s to the Russians, who cruelly mistreated and exploited them. Within a few decades their numbers were reduced from 16,000 to little more than 2,000. In their rain-soaked islands they developed waterproof clothing made from translucent seal skin, often with caribou hair seam decoration of extraordinary delicacy. During the early 19th century the remaining Aleuts were converted by the Russian Orthodox Church and generally assumed some of the culture brought by Europeans, and there was considerable intermarriage. In 1867 they were, with Alaska, transferred to the control of the United States. In 1910 they were reported to number only 1,451, many of mixed descent. Today small communities are still found, notably at Atka, on St.Pauls and St.George Islands, Unalaska, Akutan, King Cove, Belkofski, Sand Point, Port Noller, and in a few other locations outside their former area, perhaps numbering 2,500 in total.

ESKIMO or **INUIT** Whilst the Eskimo constitute one complete linguistic family with the Aleut, they are usually considered independently from the native inhabitants of the rest of the continent, chiefly on physical grounds. The earliest archaeological sites in the Arctic have been dated to between 2500 and 2000 B.C., and are designated as Independence I, Pre-Dorset, Dorset and Thule cultures, the latter dated to approximately the 13th century, and all the direct ancestors of the Eskimoan people. They seem to have spread east and south to the Gulf of St.Lawrence, around the entire northern and northeastern coast of Canada, plus some parts of Greenland; along the coast of Hudson Bay, Baffin Land and other northern islands; the coast of Alaska including Kodiak Island, and to the detached Chugach on Prince William Sound.

Despite a number of separate tribes and a linear range of occupation of over 3,000 miles, the Eskimo language varies sufficiently only to be classified into two divisions: the Pacific or Alaskan division, and the Canadian or Northern group. The distribution of the Eskimo was as follows:

The **Labrador Eskimo** included those groups which extended from the Strait of Belle Isle along the coast of Labrador, Ungava Bay, Hudson Strait and the east side of Hudson Bay as far south as Fort George. The most important groups were the *Tahagmiut* or *Tarramiut* of northern Quebec, *Itivimiut* of the east coast of Hudson Bay, and *Kigiktagmiut* or *Qikirmiut* of Belcher Islands. Their present communities are at Rigolet, Hopedale, Nain, Makkovik, Port Burwell, Port Chimo, Tasiujaq, Aupaluk, Koartac, Wakeham, Saglonc, Ivujivik, Akulivik, Povungnituk, Port Harrison, Sanikiluaq and Poste-de-la-Baleine.

The **Baffin Island Eskimo** are the inhabitants of the eastern half of the Island who include the *Nugumiut* of Frobisher Bay, *Akuliarmiut* below Amsdjuak Lake, *Padlimiut* on Home Bay, *Qaumauangmiut* on the Meta Incognita Peninsula, *Akudnirmiut* of Buchan Gulf, and *Sikosuilarmiut* of the Foxe Peninsula. Their present settlements are at Cape Dorset, Lake Harbour, Frobisher Bay, Broughton Island, Clyde River and Pangnirtung.

The **Iglulik Eskimo** held the western part of Baffin Island, and the Melville Peninsula south beyond Wager Bay almost to Chesterfield Inlet. They include the *Tununirmiut* of Eclipse Sound, *Tununerushirmiut* of Admiralty Inlet, *Aivillirmiut* or *Aivilingmiut* on the Ross Welcome Sound and Melville Peninsula, and *Sagdlirmiut* or *Sadlermiut* on Southampton Island. Their present communities are at Arctic Bay, Pond Inlet on Baffin Island, Igloolik,

Hall Beach, Repulse Bay and Coral Harbour.

The **Netsilik Eskimo** held the area west and south of the Gulf of Boothia. They include the *Arveotormiut* or *Arviqtuurmiut* of Somerset Island, *Netsilingmiut* on the Boothia Peninsula, *Utkuhikhalingmiut* or *Ukkusiksaligmiut* on Back River, and *Iluilermiut* on Adelaide Peninsula and King William Island. Their settlements today are at Grise Fiord, Resolute, Spence Bay, Pelly Bay and Gjoa Haven.

The **Caribou Eskimo** included a number of groups on Chesterfield Inlet, Baker Lake and Thelon River almost to Churchill in northern Manitoba. Their present settlements are at Chesterfield Inlet, Baker Lake, Rankin Inlet, Whale Cove and Eskimo Point.

The **Copper Eskimo** held the southern part of Banks Island, Victoria Island on both sides of Coronation Gulf, Bathhurst Inlet and Queen Maud Gulf, including amongst others the *Kanghiryuarmiut* on Banks Island, *Kogloktogmiut* or *Kogluktomiut* on the lower part of the Coppermine River. Their descendants are at Sachs Harbour, Norman, Cambridge Bay, Coppermine, Bathhurst Inlet and Umingmaktok.

The **Mackenzie Eskimo** were a number of groups around the delta of the Mackenzie River and Cape Bathhurst. Their present groups are at Tuktoyaktuk, Paulatuk, Aklavik and Inuvik, the latter two settlements shared with the Athabascan Kutchin.

The **Greenland Eskimo** were a number of groups chiefly on the western coast, including a northern section above Cape York on the Hayes Peninsula known as *Polar Eskimo*, and an eastern group around Angmagssalik on the east coast.

The **Alaskan Eskimo** can be divided as follows. The *North Alaskan Eskimo* extended from Point Barrow to Point Hope; south of them were the *Northern Interior Eskimo* on the Coville River south to the Continental Divide; the *Kotzebue Eskimo* chiefly on Kotzebue Sound and Kobuk River; and the *Bering Strait Eskimo* located on Norton Sound. There were a number of Eskimo groups on the southern part of Norton Sound and the mouth of the Yukon River; the *Kuskwogmiut* on the Kuskokwim River; *Nunivagmiut* on Nunivak Island; *Yuit* on St.Lawrence Island; *Togiagmiut* on Togiak Bay and River; *Aglemiut* on the upper Alaska Peninsula; *Kaniag* on Kodiak Island; *Chugach* on Prince William Sound; *Ugalakmiut* of Kayak Island; and finally the *Yuit* of Cape Chukotsky, Siberia.

The Alaskan Eskimo groups today are North Alaskan Eskimo at Barrow and Point Hope, in about six groups numbering some 3,000; Northern Interior Eskimo at Anaktuvuk Pass, numbering about 200; about 12 communities of Kotzebue Eskimo, the largest being Kotzebue, Noatak, Selawik and Noorvik, and totalling about 4,000; and Bering Strait Eskimo in about 30 small settlements, the largest at Nome, Shishmaref, Wales, Teller, White Mountain, St.Michael, Mountain, Koyuk, Unalakleet and Shaktolik, numbering in all some 5,000. The Yukon River Delta area has about 20 groups including those south to Toksook Bay, the main ones being at Kotlik, Alakanuk, Scammon Bay, Hooper Bay, Cheyak, Tanunak, Kipnuk, and totalling about 4,000. The Kuskokwim River groups are at Kwigillingok, Eek and Kwethluk, plus Togiamiut at Togia, Clarks Point and Dillingham, numbering together about 5,000; on Nunivak Island are about 300 at Nash Harbour and Mekoryok; on St.Lawrence Island about 1,000 people live at Gambell and Savoonga; on the upper Alaska Peninsula are about six communities including Chignik, Pilot Point, Egegik and others, totalling perhaps 1,000. The Kodiak Island Eskimo have about ten groups, the largest at Kodiak, totalling about 1,500; and the Prince William Sound Eskimo at Port Graham and Seward, much mixed with Athabascans, number perhaps 300. These figures give a total Eskimo population for Alaska of perhaps 25,000.

Of the **Canadian Eskimo**, those grouped as Labrador Eskimo number about 4,000; the Baffin Island Eskimo, with groups at Pangnivtung, Frobisher Bay and Lake Harbour, about 2,500. The Iglulik Eskimo include about 1,000 in the Pond Inlet area, 500 in the Chesterfield area, and 200 on Southampton Island. The Netsilik number perhaps 1,000 in the Spence Bay district; the Caribou Eskimo of the Chesterfield, Baker Lake and Eskimo Point areas total some 2,000; the Copper Eskimo of the Cambridge Bay and Coppermine areas, 1,500; and the Mackenzie Eskimo, about the same number in the Aklavik district. The total numbers for Canada are thus over 14,000. The population of the Greenland Eskimo was about 13,500 in 1922.

The above is by no means a complete list; but a total recent population of over 60,000, including the Siberian Eskimo, seems probably correct, and compares fairly closely with their original numbers.

* * *

The Eskimo was, and in many locations still is, a hunter – with a few exceptions, such as the Caribou Eskimo, a shore-dwelling sea hunter – and wholly carnivorous. They were skilled in the making of the equipment necessary to win all the food they required from the sea and its margins, in a climate and a terrain which seem beyond the limits at which man could survive. Their seal skin or caribou hide clothes, with the hair left on, were skilfully prepared and stitched to provide astonishing insulation against the cold; a person so dressed could sleep in the open at –30°C. Their fitted tunic, called *parka* in the west or *anorak* in the east, was worn with trousers

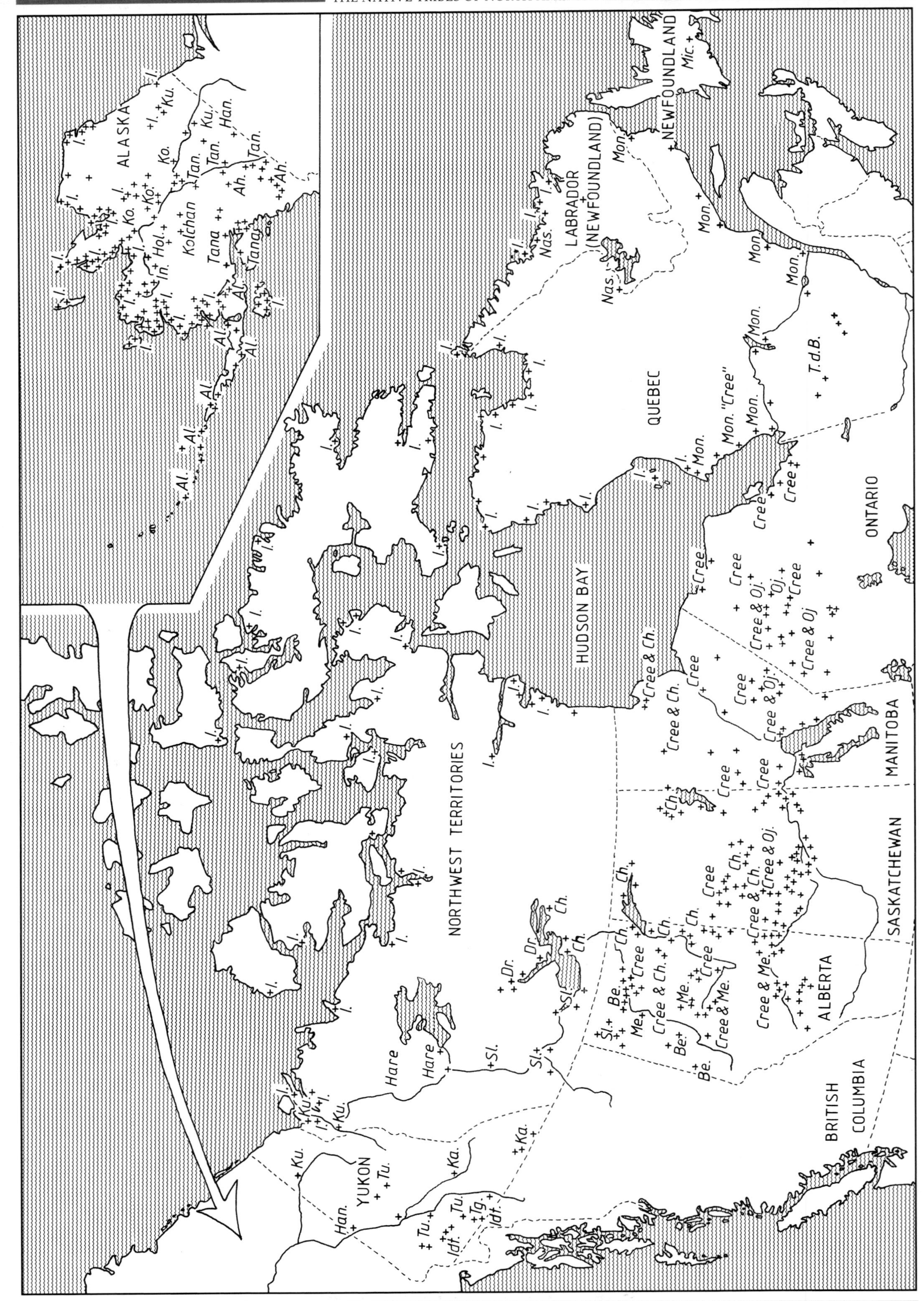
ALASKA
NEWFOUNDLAND
LABRADOR (NEWFOUNDLAND)
QUEBEC
ONTARIO
HUDSON BAY
MANITOBA
SASKATCHEWAN
ALBERTA
BRITISH COLUMBIA
NORTHWEST TERRITORIES
YUKON
Kolchan
Tana
Hare
Cree
Cree & Ch.
Cree & Oj.
Cree & Me.
Mon. "Cree"
T.d.B.

of polar bear or mole skin and seal skin boots. In extreme cold two layers of clothing were worn for added insulation. Numerous regional styles of tunic displayed variations in cut and decoration characterized by hoods and long tails front and back, sometimes reaching to the ankles.

The igloo was a dwelling known only to the Central Eskimo groups of northern Canada, built of compacted snow blocks accurately spiralled to form a domed structure; heat and light were generated by oil lamps, which kept the temperature inside just below freezing point. Most Eskimos, however, built the *karmat* – a hut of stone, whalebone and/or sod; but modern prefabricated bungalows with electric cookers and oil-fired furnaces are now known to all parts of the north. Two forms of water transport were known – the *kayak* in the east and *umiak* in the west. They also used a true sled with runners, drawn by dog teams, on ice or frozen mud. Their principal food supply during the dark winter was seal, during the summer caribou; other sources of food were walrus, whale, musk-ox and wild fowl.

SUBARCTIC AND ARCTIC TRIBES, 20th CENTURY

Key to abbreviations:

Ah	=	Ahtna
Al	=	Aleut
Be	=	Beaver
Ch	=	Chipewyan
'Cree'	=	Locally called Cree
Dr	=	Dogrib
Hol	=	Holikachuk
I	=	Inuit (Eskimo)
Idt	=	Inland Tlingit
In	=	Ingalik
Ka	=	Kaska
Ko	=	Koyukon
Ku	=	Kutchin
Me	=	Métis
Mon	=	Montagnais
Nas	=	Nascapi
Oj	=	Ojibwa
Sl	=	Slavey
Ta	=	Tanana
Tan	=	Tanaina
TdB	=	Tête de Boule
Tg	=	Tagish
Tu	=	Tutchone

Two major rituals were celebrated annually: one to release the sea animals, and the other to welcome the return of the sun, the herald of winter's end. In both celebrations costumed figures, often masked and simultaneously male and female, suggest the renewal of creation. Shamans used symbolically decorated costume. Female tattooing earned the subject rewards in the afterlife for her endurance of pain for the sake of beauty. Female parkas had extended hoods to allow the carrying of babies; and the tailoring and manufacture of the parka established a metaphysical identification with the animals on which these peoples relied for their existence. Their oral history and cosmology comprise a series of opposites – male/female, land/sea, man/animal, winter/summer, dark/light – simultaneously separate and joined; when ritualized, the engendered tensions were released.

In recent times the Eskimo have negotiated a series of policies and agreements with central governments, which they usually distrust. The aims of the community and of centralized power are often opposed; but these native peoples know that they are custodians of a land of precious resources, a prize greater than the institutions of commercial and industrial development that threaten its – and their – future.

THE INDIAN TODAY

The present Native American population is found in every state and every major urban area of the U.S.A., and is particularly significant in states in which reservations were established during the 19th century, for example Oklahoma, New Mexico and South Dakota. During the recent past many Indians have migrated to California and New York, with large concentrations in various cities. Conversely, a few states have almost no Indian population and no sizeable Indian communities or Government Reservations founded for native people; typical of these are Kentucky and Tennessee.

In Canada every province has a sizeable Indian population, since historically the native peoples were not pressured to move (or at least, not great distances) from their traditional homes. The reserves are more evenly distributed, if smaller, than in the U.S.A. On the whole Canadian Indians seem to have fared somewhat better than many in the United States, and traditionally have had a more positive attitude to government and the white culture. The belief that this is so, while probably not wholly true, is widely held by Indians and whites.

On the face of it the reservation system (or band reserve system in Canada) seems to have been a positive move to secure and preserve at least a fraction of Indian land in perpetuity. It should be remembered, however, that the infamous Dawes or Allotment Act of the 1880s disposed of areas of land unallocated to Indian families on many reservations – a process unchecked until the Indian Reorganization Act of 1934, by which time many reservations were simply jurisdictional areas rather than continuously Indian-owned areas of real estate. Today we find some reservations in the least accessible parts of the country, often long distances from urban centres of employment, with poor economic opportunities and a diminished land base: a classic environment for social deprivation.

In Canada and the U.S.A. alike no single generalized description can accurately portray Indian economic, cultural or social status relative to dominant white culture or to older traditional Indian values. So broad is the variation in the lifestyles of Native Americans that a number of very different descriptions could truthfully be applied to the social and economic conditions prevalent on particular reservations and in particular communities. The loss of a land base was accompanied by other pressures militating against the continuity of distinctively native culture, religion, kinship, dress and ceremony. Among these were the suppression of native speech, and the boarding school system which took youths to off-reservation establishments where they were subjected to excessively harsh discipline. Despite the generally more enlightened philosophy and improved teaching techniques of more recent times, Indian scholastic achievements are often disappointing.

There was further U.S. Government pressure during the 1950s for the termination of federal services to a number of Indian reservations where the people had made an almost complete transfer to Euro-American culture; at a stroke the Klamath (Oregon), Menomini (Wisconsin) and a number of other smaller groups were no longer federally recognized as Indians. During the 1970s federal domination of U.S. Indian Service programmes served to retard rather than enhance the progress of Native American people. Gradually the Government has come to encourage tribal officials to plan and administer their own programmes for themselves; but many groups have yet to solve the difficulties posed by history, isolation, disruption, poor Bureau of Indian Affairs administration, which leave Native Americans as the poorest ethnic group in North America.

There are, however, some reasons for cautious optimism. What remains of Indian lands are today often described by native people as "sacred", and jealously guarded. Some land has been successfully reclaimed, and substantial sums of money have been obtained from federal and state sources in recompense for land loss in times past. (Some of these claims, by groups whose ethnic heritage is a mixture of Indian, African-American and Euro-American, appear to be encouraged by the possibility of such rewards.) Present Indian leaders claim that their ancestors' view of land tenure was so different from that of whites that Indians did not understand fully the implications of the treaties which they signed with government agents.

Many Indians and people of Indian descent have successfully accomodated Euro-American culture, some for many generations, and have always viewed the dominant culture as a goal. Native American people are found in all the professions, and in social, industrial and commercial concerns; they count a U.S. Vice President, a World War II general, a premiere ballerina, movie stars, two Olympic gold medal winners, the president of an oil company, historians, anthropologists and artists amongst their children. Many present day tribal communities boast up-to-date administrative offices complete with computer facilities, libraries and museums, and run programmes to preserve tribal histories and languages. Many of these advances have been achieved by tribes who, through various changes in their fortunes, fell heirs to mineral or oil deposits, such as the Oklahoma Osage; or by tribes with a long association of social and commercial contact with Euro-American culture.

Considering their disadvantages, the Native American communities remain a vibrant section of the American and Canadian population; and since the general re-evaluation of social attitudes born of the 1960s Indians can claim, with some justification, a special place as conservationists and protectors of natural resources, with a clearer perception of man's meaningful existence and with a strong spiritual attachment to their fellow beings and their natural surroundings. Presumably because so many of the older Indian traditions reported by the earliest ethnographers in the 19th century now seem to have been lost (with the exception of those of some Southwestern groups), it would appear that some ideas have been reciprocally adopted from the general American sub-culture prevailing in the 1960s. Not all the rhetoric now employed to promote "Indian culture" seems to agree with the finer points of known cultural or historical detail; but it is sufficient to note that many Indians believe these things implicitly.

They also feel that somehow their culture, and specifically their material culture, was stolen by whites. It is certainly the case that deserted and archaeological sites have been desecrated by white curio-hunters, and that economically deprived native people sold their heirlooms at a fraction of their true value. Nevertheless, we should recognize that very little material culture would have been salvaged had not European and American collectors, antiquarians, explorers and latterly art dealers promoted interest and research into indigenous cultures and their arts, notwithstanding their sometimes dubious motives and methods.

But Indian culture does survive, both old and new. Amongst the older nativistic traditions (sometimes rejuvenated) are the Longhouse religion of the Iroquois, the Green Corn ceremony of the Seminole and Creek, the Sun Dance of the Plains and Plateau, and the timeless calendrical ceremonies of the Pueblos. The newer Indian culture is that termed "Pan-Indianism" by anthropologists. It is expressed outwardly in social and political contexts, but perhaps most visibly by the ubiquitous "Powwow", which merges traditions of song and dance from various Indian cultures, heavily modified and largely bereft of old religious traits. Each year many groups present their own Powwows, organized by elected officers, inviting Indians from far and wide to attend, providing feasts and cash prizes for the best dancing and costume, and promoting tribal and Indian ethnic unity and cohesion. The choreography is largely derived from the dramatic warrior society dances of the eastern Plains people, notably Omaha and Ponca adopted by the Sioux (amongst whom it was known as the Omaha dance and Omaha society), and by Oklahoma Indians who also adopted the dance to the exclusion of their own clan ceremonies. The dance, which at times took on quasi-religious overtones, has a history of diffusion for well over one hundred years. Known variously as War Dance, Omaha Dance or Grass Dance, it involves ever-changing regalia referred to as fancy dance, war dance, straight dance or grass dance clothes, traditional or contemporary, dependent upon the Indian fashion of the day. Women have developed their own dances to accompany the men: Round Dances and Owl Dances of partly white origin, the Stomp Dance originally from the southeast, and the Eagle Dance from the southwest, all contribute to the contemporary scene. The Powwow has been adopted by tribes well outside the Plains area; the Iroquois, for example, use the Powwow dances as an adjunct to their own social dances.

* * *

Readers should also recognize that the racial separation of white and Indian was never as clear as popular history would have us believe. For many generations from the 17th century onward French trappers and traders mixed with the Crees and Ojibwas, leaving a marked strain of their blood, which resulted in the emergence of the Métis. This people, who in the early 19th century settled around the Red River near present Winnepeg, Manitoba, have been described as a cultural bridge between whites and the Native Canadians. Following the Riel Rebellion of 1885 they largely dispersed west to Alberta and Saskatchewan.

In the eastern United States a number of other mixed blood groups claim Indian ancestry. Although detailed histories of these groups are often lacking, there are general similarities. They have been, until recently, isolated rural people of mixed Indian, Euro-American and African-American background. The tribal origins are often blurred, perhaps because of a multi-remnant background; in colonial times refugees of various marginal peoples banded together until the present day tri-racial groups emerged.

The largest such group in the U.S.A. are the so-called *Lumbee* of Robeson County, North Carolina, numbering 27,520 in 1970. Physically they appear distinctly Indian, but they lack all knowledge of an Indian language or customs save for adopted Pan-Indian traits. So far they have been unable to persuade the Government that their genealogy is complete enough for them to be recognized as an Indian people. In this regard we should also note other post-colonial Indian mixed blood groups or claimants to such ancestry, briefly: the *Pools* around Towanda, Pennsylvania; *Keating Mountain Cherokee* of Pennsylvania; *Jackson-Whites* of Ramapo Valley, New Jersey; *Sandhill Indians* of Monmouth County, New Jersey; *Pineys* of Burlington County, New Jersey; *Moors* of Cumberland County, New Jersey, and Kent County, Delaware; *Wesorts & Portobocco* of Maryland; *Guineas* of West Virginia; *Browns* of Rockbridge County, Virginia; *Issues* of Amherst County, Virginia; *Cubans* of Person County, North Carolina; *Haliwa* of Halifax and Warren Counties, North Carolina; *Waccamaw* of Columbus County, North Carolina; *Cheraw* of Rockingham County, North Carolina; *Melungeons* of Magoffen County, Kentucky; *Coe Clan* of Cumberland County, Kentucky; *Blues* of Marlboro County, South Carolina; *Summerville Indians* in several counties, South Carolina; *Carmel Indians* and others in Hardin, Drake and Vinton Counties, Ohio; *Altamaha* of Burke County, Georgia; *Creoles* in Florida and Alabama; and *Cane River* and *Sabine-Red Bone* Indians of Louisiana.

These groups add several thousand to the increasing number of people who are still proudly Native Americans but who present a bewilderingly complex range of ethnic, cultural and social traits drawn from many sources. What such groups have in common is that they usually subsist at the lowest economic levels; often live in inadequate, crowded and unsafe homes; endure limited employment opportunities; and are beset by various problems which once seemed endemic, but which are now moving slowly toward the hope of solution, principally through their own efforts.

Glossary

Allotment Legal process, c.1880s-1930s, by which land on Indian reservations not allocated to Indian families was made available to whites.

Anthropology The study of man.

Anthropomorphic In the shape of or having the characteristics of man, god or animal.

Appliqué Decorative technique involving sewing down quills (usually porcupine) and seed beads onto hide or cloth often using two threads, resulting in a flat mosaic surface.

Apron Male apparel, front and back, which replaced the breechcloth for festive costume during the 19th and 20th centuries.

Argillite A steatite found on the Queen Charlotte Islands, British Columbia, used by the Haida people to fashion pipes and small totem poles.

Babiche Leather thongs, usually for making snowshoes and hunting bags, in northern Canada.

Bandolier bag A prestige bag with a shoulder strap, usually with heavy (often floralistic) beadwork, worn by men and sometimes women at tribal dances. Common amongst the Ojibwa and other Woodland tribes.

Beads European glass beads seem to have been traded in native America from the earliest days of contact, replacing native shell, bone or stone beads. The early trade beads were mostly of the large necklace type, followed later by many types of small "seed" beads. On the Plains the traders introduced a larger "pony" bead during the early 19th century. Most of the seed beads came from Italy, later Bohemia, in many colours opaque, transparent and translucent, and many sizes.

Boots Hide moccasins and combined leggings or boots worn by Eskimo, Southern Plains and Southwestern tribes.

Buckskin Hide leather from animals of the deer family, wapiti, moose or elk used for clothing. Less commonly used for dress were buffalo , mountain sheep, mountain goat and caribou.

Canoes Two main types were the birch bark- covered frame used in the Northeast and Subarctic and the dugout (hollowed) log form of the Southeast. Characteristic variations are illustrated in the colour plates.

Catlinite A slate or steatite, usually red, named after the artist/explorer George Catlin, who visited the site of the mine at present Pipestone, Minnesota. Made into pipes for ceremonial smoking.

Clan Families descended from a common ancestor.

Coiling A method of making pottery in the American Southwest, in which the walls of a vessel are built up by adding successive rope-like coils of clay.

Complex Social or religious traits and beliefs, often consisting of several parts and ideas but usually related, giving a strong sense of ethnic and emotional cohesion.

Confederacy A group of tribes or villages bound together politically or for defence (e.g.Iroquois, Creek).

Coup From the French,"a blow": to approach an enemy or animal close enough to touch by hand or "coup stick" was considered to be an honourable feat amongst Plains Indians.

Curvilinear Patterns made up of or bounded by curved lines.

Double-curve Two opposed incurves, usually in quills or beads, attached to each other at the ends, used to decorate articles of ceremonial clothing amongst the Northeastern tribes.

Drum or Dream Dance A variation of the Plains Grass Dance adopted by the Santee Sioux, Southern Ojibwa (Chippewa) and Menomini during the 19th century. Amongst these groups the movement had religious features which advocated friendship, even with whites.

Ethnic Designation of divisions of humankind.

Ethnology A branch of anthropology which deals with comparative cultures, distribution of peoples, characteristics and folklore of races.

Generic Describing the origin of a group with common characteristics, animal, human or material.

Gens A clan united by descent through the male line from a common ancestor.

Geometric Patterns characterized by lines, angles, triangles, squares and rectangles or a composition of these elements, used to decorate clothing in quillwork or beadwork.

German silver A nonferrous alloy of copper, nickel and zinc, known also as nickel silver; traded to Woodland and Plains tribes, who became expert metalworkers.

Giveaway The Indian custom of presenting gifts as a way of honouring guests or recipients at a celebration or Powwow.

Hairpipes Tubular bone beads made by whites and traded to the Indians, often made up into vertical and horizontal rows called breastplates.

Housepost Part of the structure of a Northwest Coast house to support the roof, often carved with family or ancestral emblems.

Incising A method of scraping decorative or symbolic designs on a rawhide or bark surface.

Kachinas Supernatural beings impersonated by costumed Pueblo Indians in religious ceremonial. Dressed kachina dolls instruct children to recognize the different spirits.

Kiva The structure, often subterranean, which serves as a ceremonial chamber for Pueblo Indians in the Southwest. Each village usually has several kivas.

Lazy stitch A Plains Indian technique of sewing beads to hide or cloth, giving a final ridged or arch effect in lanes about eight or ten beads wide.

Leggings Male or female, covering ankle and leg to the knee or thigh (male), usually buckskin or cloth.

Longhouse The religion of conservative Iroquois, whose rituals still take place in special buildings (rural grange type) also called longhouses. These buildings represent the old bark longhouse, and a micro-form of Iroquoia itself.

Medicine bundle A group of various objects, sometimes animal, bird or mineral, etc., contained in a wrapping of buckskin or cloth, which give access to considerable spiritual power when opened with the appropriate ritual. Mostly found amongst the eastern and Plains tribes.

Moccasins Buckskin footwear, either hard-soled (Plains) or soft-soled (Woodland and Subarctic).

Moiety A ceremonial division of a village or tribe.

Pan-Indian Describes the modern mixed intertribal dances, costumes, Powwows and socializing leading to the reinforcement of ethnic and nationalist ties.

Parfleche A rawhide envelope or box made to contain clothes or meat, often decorated with painted geometrical designs.

Peyote The Native American church, a part-native and part-Christian religion originating in Mexico but developed amongst the Southern Plains tribes in Oklahoma, which has spread to many native communities.

Potlatch A wealth distribution ceremony amongst Northwest Coast Indians.

Powwow Modern celebration, often intertribal and secular, held on most reservations throughout the year.

Prehistoric For American Indian archaeology this refers to Indian life and its remains dated before A.D.1492.

Pueblo An Indian village in New Mexico or Arizona.

Rancherias Small reservations in California.

Rawhide Usually hard, de-haired hide or skin used for parfleche cases, moccasin soles, shields, drum- heads, etc.

Reservation Government-created lands to which Indians were assigned, removed or restricted during the 19th and 20th centuries. In Canada they are called reserves.

Ribbonwork Cut and folded ribbons of silk (later of man-made fabrics) applied to broadcloth in geometrical or curvilinear patterns. Common amongst the Woodland and Prairie tribes.

Roach A headdress of deer hair. Very popular for male war-dance costume, this originated among the eastern tribes and later spread among the Plains Indians along with the popular Omaha or Grass Dance, the forerunner of the modern war and straight dances.

Rosette Disc or circular area of decoration using quills or beads, such as found on Plains men's shirts.

Silver Sterling and coin silver, an impure silver used in Southwestern jewellery, originally using melted-down U.S. and Mexican coins.

Sinew The tendon fibre from animals, used by Indians and Eskimos as thread for sewing purposes.

Smoked tanning A buckskin tanning process to maintain the leather in a supple condition.

Snowshoe A wooden frame covered with babiche, worn on the feet to prevent the wearer from sinking into soft snow.

Stitches Various stitches are used to sew beads to hide or cloth, usually called appliqué, lazy, spot or crow stitch.

Stroud A coarse trade cloth imported from England.

Sun Dance The annual world renewal religious ceremonial complex of the Plains Indians, whose sacred rituals took place in specially constructed "lodges" of poles and brush, the roof of rafters supported on the focal point for the dancers – the "centre pole". For fuller discussion, see introduction to "Plains and Prairie" section.

Sweat lodge A low, temporary, oval-shaped structure covered with skins or blankets in which men sat in steam produced by splashing water on heated stones as a method of ritual purification.

Syllabics A form of European-inspired writing consisting of syllabic characters used by the Cherokees in the 19th century and in other forms by the Crees and Eskimos.

Termination Withdrawal of U.S. Government recognition of the protected status of, and services due to, an Indian reservation.

Thread Fine flax, cotton, silk or modern fibres used to sew seams, beads or quills.

Tipi The conical lodge of the true High Plains nomads, constructed of bison (buffalo) hide erected on a framework of "lodge" poles. Since the destruction of the bison herds the covers have been made of canvas; they are usually erected during Powwows or for Peyote meetings.

Totem pole A memorial post or pole set up in front of a house, usually carved in a series of emblematic or crest symbols of family lineage, mythical or historical events, amongst Northwest Coast Indians.

Tribe A group of bands, sometimes (but not necessarily) linked together genetically, politically, geographically, by religion or by a common origin myth; but a common language is the main criterion. Several tribes were so scattered that they did not form a "tribe" in any popularly recognizable sense. Some "tribal" groups are only so in terms of ethnographical studies, the word being a convenient tool to describe collectively fragmented groups or collections of small groups of peoples who themselves recognized no such association.

Turquoise Semi-precious stone used in Southwestern jewellery.

War bonnet The headdress worn by Plains Indian men, of a circle of eagle feathers on a crown, which became popular among many tribal groups in the 20th century as a symbol of Indian identity.

War dance Popular name for the secular male dances which developed in Oklahoma and other places after the spread of the Grass Dance from the eastern Plains/Prairie tribes in the 19th century, amongst whom it was connected with war societies. Many tribes had complex war and victory celebrations.

Weft and warp The horizontal and vertical threads of a loom for weaving quillwork and beadwork.

Wigwam Oval or conical lodges of the northeastern Algonkians, constructed of birch bark or rush mats fixed to a frame of saplings.

Selected Bibliography

ANDREWS, Ralph W. — *Indian Primitive*
(Superior Publishing Co., 1960)

BANCROFT-HUNT, Norman & NORMAN, Werner — *The Indians of the Great Plains*
(Orbis Publishing, London, 1981)

BLISH, Helen H. — *A Pictographic History of the Oglala Sioux*
(University of Nebraska Press, Lincoln, 1967)

BRASSER, Ted J. — *"Bo'jou, Neejee!" : Profiles of Canadian Indian Art*
(National Museum of Man, Ottawa/ The National Museums of Canada, 1976)

BRODY, Hugh — *Maps and Dreams*
(Jill Norman and Hobhouse Ltd., London, 1981)

" " — *Living Arctic*
(Faber & Faber Ltd., London,1987)

COE, Ralph T. — *Sacred Circles : Two Thousand Years of North American Indian Art*
(Arts Council of Great Britain, 1976)

" " — *Lost and Found Traditions: Native American Art 1965-1985*
(University of Washington Press in assoc. with The American Federation of Arts, 1986)

CONN, Richard — *Robes of White Shell and Sunrise: Personal Decorative Arts of the Native American*
(Denver Art Museum, Denver, Colorado, 1974)

" " — *Native American Art in the Denver Art Museum*
(Denver Art Museum, 1979)

" " — *Circles of the World: Traditional Art of the Plains Indians*
(Denver Art Museum, 1982)

" " — *A Persistent Vision: Art of the Reservation Days:* The L.D. & Ruth Bax Collection of the Denver Art Museum (Denver Art Museum, 1986)

COREY, Peter L. (Ed.) — *Faces, Voices and Dreams:* A Celebration of the Centennial of The Sheldon Jackson Museum, Sitka, Alaska, 1888-1988
(The Division of Alaska State Museum & Friends of the Alaska State Museum, 1987)

DANZIGER, Edmund J.,Jr. — *The Chippewas of Lake Superior*
(University of Oklahoma Press, Norman & London, 1979)

DIXON, Dr. Joseph K., — *The Vanishing Race: The Last Great Indian Council*
(Doubleday, Page & Co., Garden City, New York, 1914)

DOCKSTADER, Frederick J. — *Indian Art In America: The Arts and Crafts of the North American Indian*
(Promontory Press, New York)

DUNCAN, Kate C. — *Some Warmer Tone: Alaska Athabaskan Bead Embroidery*
Alaska Historical Commission Studies in History No. 131
(University of Alaska Museum, Fairbanks, 1984)

" " — *Northern Athapaskan Art: A Beadwork Tradition*
(University of Washington Press, Seattle & London, with assistance of J.Paul Getty Trust, 1989)

EMMONS, George T., (Ed., with Frederica de Laguna & Jean Low) — *The Tlingit Indians*
(University of Washington Press, Seattle & London/ American Museum of Natural History, New York, 1991)

EWERS, John C. — *Murals In the Round: Painted Tipis of the Kiowa and Kiowa-Apache Indians*
(Smithsonian Institution Press, Washington D.C., for Renwick Gallery of the National Collection of Fine Arts, 1978)

" " — *Plains Indian Sculpture: A Traditional Art from America's Heartland*
(Smithsonian Institution Press, Washington D.C., 1986)

EWERS, John C. — *Blackfeet Crafts:* Indian Handicraft Series, Education Div., U.S. Bureau of Indian Affairs (Haskell Institute, Lawrence, Kansas, 1944)

FARR, William E. — *The Reservation Blackfeet, 1882-1945: A Photographic History of Cultural Survival* (University of Washington Press, Seattle & London, 1984)

FEDER, Norman — *American Indian Art* (Harry N. Abrams, New York, 1965)

FERG, Alan (Ed.) — *Western Apache Material Culture: The Goodwin and Guenther Collections* (University of Arizona Press for Arizona State Museum, 1987)

FLEMING, Paula R. & LUSKEY, Judith — *The North American Indians in Early Photographs* (Dorset Press, New York,1988)

FLETCHER, Alice C. & La FLESCHE, Francis — *The Omaha Tribe, Vols. I & II* (University of Nebraska Press, Lincoln & London, 1972)

GIDLEY, M. — *With One Sky Above Us: Life on an Indian Reservation at the Turn of the Century* (Windward/Webb & Bower, 1979)

GIDMARK, David — *The Algonquin Birchbark Canoe* Shire Ethnography Series (Shire Publications Ltd., Aylesbury, Bucks.,UK, 1988)

GILBERT, William H.,Jr. — *Surviving Indian Groups of the Eastern United States* (Smithsonian Institution, Washington. D.C.; Annual Report, 1948)

GILMAN, Carolyn & SCHNEIDER, Mary Jane — *The Way To Independence: Memories of a Hidatsa Indian Family 1840-1920* (Minnesota Historical Society Press, St.Paul, 1987)

GILPIN, Laura — *The Enduring Navaho* (University of Texas Press, Austin, 1968)

GULICK, Bill — *Chief Joseph Country: Land of the Nez Perce* (The Caxton Printers, Ltd., Caldwell, Idaho, 1981)

HABERLAND, Wolfgang — *Ich, Dakota: Pine Ridge Reservation, 1909* (Dietrich Reimer Verlag, Berlin, 1986)

HAIL, Barbara A. — *Hau, Kola!* The Plains Indian Collection of the Haffenreffer Museum of Anthropology: Vol.III, Studies in Anthropology and Material Culture (Haffenreffer Museum of Anthropology, Brown University, 1980)

" " (Essay) & SCHWARZ, Gregory C. (Catalogue) — *Patterns of Life, Patterns of Art:* The Rahr Collection of Native American Art (Hood Museum of Art, Dartmouth College, with University Press of New England, Hanover & London,1987)

" " & DUNCAN, Kate C. — *Out of the North:* The Subarctic Collection of the Haffenreffer Museum of Anthropology (Haffenreffer Museum of Anthropology, Brown University, 1989)

HANSON, James A. — *Metal Weapons, Tools, and Ornaments of the Teton Dakota Indians* (University of Nebraska Press, Lincoln, 1975)

HARRISON, Julia D. — *Métis: People between Two Worlds* (The Glenbow-Alberta Institute in assoc. with Douglas & McIntyre, Vancouver/Toronto, 1985)

HARTLEY, William & Ellen — *Osceola: The Unconquered Indian* (Hawthorn Books Inc., New York, 1973)

HASSRICK, Royal B. — *The George Catlin Book of American Indians* (Watson-Guptill Publications, New York, 1977)

HAWTHORN, Audrey — *Kwakiutl Art* (University of Washington Press, Seattle & London, 1967)

HESKI, Thomas M. — *"Icastinyanka Cikala Hanzi", The Little Shadow Catcher: D.F. Barry, Celebrated Photographer of Famous Indians* (Superior Publishing Company, Seattle, 1978)

HODGE, Frederic (Ed.) — *Handbook of American Indians North of Mexico,* 2 Vols., Bureau of American Ethnology Bulletin 30 (Smithsonian Institution, Washington D.C., 1907-1910)

HODGE, William H. — *The First Americans Then And Now* (Holt, Rinehart & Winston, 1981)

HOOK, Jason — *The American Plains Indians,* Men-at-Arms Series 163 (Osprey Publishing, London, 1985)

HOOK, Jason — *The Apaches*, Men-at-Arms Series 186 (Osprey Publishing, London, 1987)

HORSE CAPTURE, George P. & POHRT, Richard A. — *Salish Indian Art from the J.R.Simplot Collection* (Buffalo Bill Historical Centre, 1986)

HOWARD, James H. — *The Plains-Ojibwa or Bungi:* Reprints In Anthropology Vol.7 (J & L Reprint Company, Lincoln, Nebraska, 1977)

HOWARD, James H. — *The Dakota or Sioux Indians* Reprints In Anthropology Vol.20 (J & L Reprint Company, Lincoln, Nebraska, 1980)

" " — *The Canadian Sioux* (University of Nebraska Press, Lincoln & London, 1984)

HUNGRY WOLF, Adolf — *The Blood People, A Division of the Blackfoot Confederacy: An Illustrated Interpretation of the Old Ways* (Harper & Row, New York, Hagerstown, San Francisco, London, 1977)

ISAAC, Barbara (Ed.) & BROWN, Ian W. — *The Hall of the North American Indian: Change and Continuity* (Peabody Museum Press, Cambridge, Massachusetts, 1990)

JOHNSON, Michael G. — *American Woodland Indians,* Men-at-Arms Series 228 (Osprey Publishing, London, 1990)

JONAITIS, Aldona — *From the Land of the Totem Poles:* The Northwest Coast Indian Art Collection at the American Museum of Natural History (American Museum of Natural History, New York/ British Museum Publications, London, 1988)

JOSEPHY, Alvin M. Jr. (Ed.) & BRANDON, William — *The American Heritage Book of Indians* (American Heritage Publishing Co.,1961)

KAPLAN, Susan A. & BARSNESS, Kristin J. — *Raven's Journey: The World of Alaska's Native People* (University of Pennsylvania Museum, 1986)

KEYWORTH, C.L. — *California Indians,* The First Americans Series (Facts on File, New York & Oxford, 1991)

KING, J.C.H. — *Thunderbird and Lightning: Indian Life in Northeastern North America 1600-1900* (British Museum Publications Ltd., London, 1982)

KOPPER, Philip — *The Smithsonian Book of North American Indians Before the Coming of the Europeans* (Smithsonian Books, Washington D.C., 1986)

LENZ, Mary Jane — *The Stuff of Dreams: Native American Dolls* (Museum of the American Indian, New York, in assoc. with National Endowment for the Humanities, 1986)

LYFORD, Carrie A. — *The Crafts of the Ojibwa:* Indian Handicrafts Series, U.S.Bureau of Indian Affairs (Phoenix, Arizona, 1943)

MACNAIR, Peter L., HOOVER, Alan L., & NEARY, Kevin — *The Legacy: Tradition and Innovation in Northwest Coast Indian Art* (Douglas & McIntyre, Vancouver/Toronto; University of Washington Press, Seattle; with The British Columbia Provincial Museum, 1984)

MAILS, Thomas E. — *The Mystic Warriors of the Plains* (Doubleday & Co. Inc., Garden City, New York, 1972)

" " — *Plains Indians: Dog Soldiers, Bear Men and Buffalo Women* (Prentice-Hall Inc., 1973)

" " — *The People Called Apache* (The Ridge Press Inc./ Rutledge Books Division & Prentice-Hall Inc., 1974)

MARKOE, Glen E. (Ed.), DeMALLIE, Raymond J. & HASSRICK, Royal B. — *Vestiges of a Proud Nation:* The Ogden B. Read Northern Plains Indian Collection (Robert Hull Fleming Museum, Burlington, Vermont, 1986)

MOMADAY, N. Scott (Intro) — *With Eagle Glance: American Indian Photographic Images, 1868 to 1931* (Museum of the American Indian, New York, 1982)

MOONEY,James — *The Aboriginal Population of America North of Mexico* (Smithsonian Misc. Coll., Vol.80, No.7, 1928)

MORGAN, Lewis H. & LLOYD, H.M. (Ed.) — *League of the Ho-De-No-Sau-Nee or Iroquois,* 2nd Edition, 2 Vols. (Dodd, Mead, New York, 1901)

NABOKOV, Peter & EASTON, Robert — *Native American Architecture* (Oxford University Press, Oxford & New York, 1989)

PENNEY, David W. (Ed.) — *Great Lakes Indian Art*
(Wayne State University Press & Detroit Institute of Arts, 1989)

POWELL, John Wesley — *Indian Linguistic Families of America North of Mexico: 7th Annual Report of the Bureau of American Ethnology*
(Smithsonian Institution, Washington D.C., 1881)

POWELL, Fr.Peter J. — *People of the Sacred Mountain, Vols. I & II*
(Harper & Row)

" " (Ed.) with Ann S.Merritt — *To Honor the Crow People:* Crow Indian Art from the Goelet & Edith Gallatin Collection of American Indian Art
(Foundation for the Preservation of American Indian Art and Culture, Inc., Chicago, 1988)

ROBERTS, Kenneth G. & SHACKLETON, Philip — *The Canoe: A History of the Craft from Panama to the Arctic*
(Macmillan of Canada, Toronto, 1983)

ROOSEVELT, Anna C. & SMITH, James G.E. (Eds.) — *The Ancestors: Native Artisans of the Americas*
(Museum of the American Indian, New York, 1979)

RUBY, Robert H. & BROWN, John A. — *A Guide to the Indian Tribes of the Pacific Northwest*
(University of Oklahoma Press, Norman, 1986)

SCHERER, Joanna C. with WALKER, Jean B. — *Indians : The Great Photographs That Reveal North American Indian Life, 1847-1929, From The Unique Collection of the Smithsonian Institution*
(Ridge Press Inc. & Crown Publishers Inc., 1973)

SCHMITT, Martin F. & BROWN, Dee — *Fighting Indians of the West*
(Charles Scribner's Sons, New York & London, 1948)

SCRIVER, Bob — *The Blackfeet: Artists of the Northern Plains*
(The Lowell Press, Inc., Kansas City, 1990)

SPECK, Frank G. — *The Nanticoke Community of Delaware*
(Museum of the American Indian, Heye Foundation; cont. from Vol.II, No. 4; New York, 1915)

" " — *Decorative Art of Indian Tribes of Connecticut*
(Canada Dept. of Mines, Memoir 75; Government Printing Bureau, Ottawa, 1915)

STURTEVANT, William C. (General Editor): — *Handbook of North American Indians*
(Smithsonian Institution, Washington, D.C.):
Vol.15, Northeast
(Ed.Bruce G.Trigger; 1978)
Vol.8, California
(Ed.Robert F. Heizer; 1978)
Vol.9, Southwest
(Ed. Alfonso Ortiz; 1979)
Vol.6, Subarctic
(Ed.June Helm; 1981)
Vol.10, Southwest (2nd vol.)
(Ed.Alfonso Ortiz; 1983)
Vol.5, Arctic
(Ed.David Damas; 1984)
Vol.11, Great Basin
(Ed.Warren L.D'Azevedo; 1986)
Vol.4, History of Indian-White Relations
(Ed.Wilcomb E.Washburn; 1988)
Vol.7, Northwest Coast
(Ed.Wayne Suttles; 1990)

SWANTON, John R. — *Indian Tribes of the Lower Mississippi Valley and adjacent Coast of the Gulf of Mexico:*
Bureau of American Ethnology, Bulletin 43
(Smithsonian Institution, Washington D.C., 1911)

" " — *Early History of the Creek Indians and Their Neighbors:*
Bureau of American Ethnology, Bulletin 73
(Smithsonian Institution, Washington D.C., 1922)

" " — *The Indians of the Southeastern United States:*
Bureau of American Ethnology, Bulletin 137
(Smithsonian Institution, Washington D.C., 1946)

" " — *The Indian Tribes of North America:*
Bureau of American Ethnology, Bulletin 145
(Smithsonian Institution, Washington D.C., 1952)

THOMAS, Davis & RONNEFELDT (Eds.) — *People of the First Man: Life Among the Plains Indians in Their Final Days of Glory: The First-hand Account of Prince Maximilian's Expedition up the Missouri River, 1833-34: Watercolours by Karl Bodmer* (Promontory Press, 1982)

THOMPSON, Judy — *The North American Indian Collection: A Catalogue* (Historical Museum, Berne, Switzerland, 1977)

" " — *Pride of the Indian Wardrobe: Northern Athapaskan Footwear* (Published for the Bata Shoe Museum by the University of Toronto Press, 1990)

THWAITES, Reuben G. (Ed.) — *Original Journals of the Lewis and Clark Expedition 1804-1806,* 8 vols. (Dodd & Mead, New York, 1904-05)

TURNER, Geoffrey E.S. — *Indians of North America* (Blandford Press Ltd., Poole, Dorset, 1979)

UNDERHILL, Ruth M. — *Red Man's America* (University of Chicago Press, Chicago, 1953)

VIDLER, Virginia — *American Indian Antiq·es Arts and Artifacts of the Northeast* (A.S.Barnes & Co., So··h Brunswick & New York/ Thomas Yoseloff Ltd., London, 1976)

VIOLA, Herman J. — *The Indian Legacy of Charles Bird King* (Smithsonian Institution Press/ Doubleday & Co., 1976)

WALTERS, Anna Lee — *The Spirit of Native America: Beauty and Mysticism in American Indian Art* (McQuiston & Partners/ Chronicle Books, San Francisco, 1989)

WALTON, Ann T., EWERS, John C., & HASSRICK, Royal B. — *After the Buffalo Were Gone:* The Louis Warren Hill,Sr., Collection of Indian Art (NW Area Foundation/Indian Arts & Crafts Board, Dept. of Interior, Washington D.C.`/Science Museum of Minnesota, St.Paul; 1985)

WILDSCHUT, William & EWERS, John C. — *Crow Indian Beadwork: A Descriptive and Historical Study* (Contributions, Vol.XVI; Museum of the American Indian Heye Foundation, New York, 1959)

WISSLER, Clark — *The American Indian* (Oxford University Press, New York, 1938)

WOOLEY, David (Ed.) — *Eye of the Angel: Selections from the Derby Collection* (White Star Press, Northampton, Maine, 1990)

WRIGHT, Muriel H. — *A Guide to the Indian Tribes of Oklahoma* (University of Oklahoma Press, Norman, 1951)

WYATT, Victoria — *Images from the Inside Passage: An Alaskan Portrait by Winter & Pond* (University of Washington Press, Seattle & London, in assoc. with Alaska State Library, Juneau; 1989)

No named authors:

Akicita: Early Plains and Woodlands Indian Art from the collection of Alexander Acevedo (The Southwest Museum, Los Angeles, 1983)

The North American Indian Collection of the Lowe Art Museum (Lowe Art Museum, University of Miami, 1988)

The Spirit Sings: Artistic Traditions of Canada's First Peoples (McClelland & Stewart, Toronto/ Glenbow Museum, 1987)

INDEX

This index is limited to the names of tribes and sub-tribes, and linguistic groups. Page numbers of main entries in each relevant case are printed in bold.

A

B

C

Q

R

S